The Principle of Harmony with Nature as a Legal Foundation

Raquel Domingues do Amaral

The Principle of Harmony with Nature as a Legal Foundation

A Proposal for the Ethical and Legal Consideration of Non-Human Living Beings and Ecosystems

Springer

Raquel Domingues do Amaral
Appeals Panel of the Federal Special Courts of Mato Grosso do Sul
Federeal Justice of Brazil
Campo Grande, Brazil

ISBN 978-3-032-05474-6 ISBN 978-3-032-05475-3 (eBook)
https://doi.org/10.1007/978-3-032-05475-3

The original submitted manuscript has been translated into English. The translation was done using artificial intelligence. A subsequent revision was performed by the author(s) to further refine the work and to ensure that the translation is appropriate concerning content and scientific correctness. It may, however, read stylistically different from a conventional translation.

This Springer imprint is published by the registered company Springer Nature Switzerland AG.
The registered company address is: Gewerbestrasse 11, 6330 Cham, Switzerland

I dedicate all the hours of this research to my parents, Sebastião and Terezinha; my children, Octavio Augusto, Henrique, and Beatriz Marie; my partner, Marcelo; the eternal Pope Francis; and Professor Cirne-Lima (in memoriam); my black cat, Cat; to Pachamama, with all her human and non-human children; and to all the people who died during the COVID-19 pandemic

Preface

The planet Earth shows unequivocal symptoms of illness. The biosphere behaves like an infected organism, and the signs of this severe infection can be measured by the accumulation of carbon in the atmosphere and oceans due to increasing deforestation, wildfires, eutrophication of lakes, rivers and seas, desertification, accelerated extinction of species, climate imbalance manifested in floods and long periods of drought, and, finally, the most severe zoonotic pandemic that has claimed thousands of human lives.

Ecological science points out, with empirical and objective data, a sharp illness of the Earth that affects all living beings and constitutes a challenge for the continuity of the human species.

Since the Rio de Janeiro Conference in 1992, scientists have been calling for a change in humanity's attitude to reverse the deteriorating state of the biosphere. In 2012, the United Nations launched the 2030 Agenda, establishing 17 Sustainable Development Goals, a document that makes a universal call to action to end poverty, protect the planet, and ensure that all people experience peace and prosperity. A systematic analysis of these 17 goals shows that they will only be achieved if there is engagement from all states and, above political will, a change in the way we understand the relationship between human beings and the natural world.

In 2009, intergovernmental negotiations were initiated to promote a harmonious relationship with nature. On December 21, 2009, the first UN General Assembly Resolution on Harmony with Nature, Resolution 64/196, was issued, requesting the Secretary-General to issue a first report on harmony with nature. The document was inspired by the experiences of the Constitutions of Bolivia and Ecuador, which recognized the Rights of Mother Earth, so that on April 22, 2009, the UN, through Resolution 63/278, instituted International Mother Earth Day.

This institution of International Mother Earth Day can no longer be appreciated merely as a commemorative day of exaltation to nature, as it is a choice of the member states, which recognized the Earth and its ecosystems as a common home to all beings, including humans. In Resolution 63/278, the need to promote harmony with nature was established to achieve a balance between economic, social, and environmental needs for the present and future generations.

The UN General Assembly recognized that the depletion of natural resources and rapid environmental degradation are the result of unsustainable patterns of consumption and production, which compromise the continuity of the human species. Thus, it proposed the adoption of a behavioral paradigm to the member states, based on the idea of a harmonious relationship with the biosphere. This new relationship is defined in the various resolutions adopted since 2009, which directly address harmony with nature from various aspects and, mainly, from the perspective of recognizing intrinsic value in non-human living beings and holistic organic entities.

However, it is observed that the recognition of intrinsic value and rights to nature is still an unknown theme for legal systems of most states that are part of the UN, due to the strong anthropocentric paradigm on which social institutions, the economy, and the law itself rest. Therefore, it is necessary to establish the meaning of harmony with nature in the statement of Resolution 64/196 and, especially, to recognize its normative dimension.

The restoration of human harmony with non-human living beings and ecosystems is essential to contain the anthropogenic crisis that threatens to lead the biosphere to entropic death, which, in its normative recognition, has become a demand of public conscience common to the various peoples of the Earth, as can be inferred from the interactive dialogs held within the United Nations.

The great natural law of harmony with nature needs to be recognized by legal systems around the world for humans to change their relationship with nature. Only from the moment when the intrinsic value and subjectivity of nature are recognized, both ethically and legally, will there be the necessary changes in consciousness and behavior for the continuation of life in Earth's biosphere.

Motivated by these reflections and by the COVID-19 health crisis, my desire to research and write about the normativity of the principle of harmony with nature in my research for the doctoral thesis in state law was born, carried out between the years 2018 and 2021, as part of a project at the Federal University of Mato Grosso do Sul and the University of São Paulo.

Faced with the terrifying picture of the zoonotic pandemic, I began to wonder what would be the real cause of this severe anthropogenic ecological crisis that affects planet Earth—impacting the climate, the soil, biodiversity, and human health. Where would the end of Ariadne's line be, the one that can remove the biosphere from the labyrinth of the anthropogenic crisis? Would it be just an economic or social problem, or is its root deeper, in the way humanity conceives and relates to nature?

The compulsory pandemic confinement was announced as imprisonment, but, after a few days, for me, it was a strange redemption; it opened a parenthesis in the great acceleration, and my garden became the microcosm that reconnected me with the cosmos. An ontological bridge between books and life was established in those days. Under a clearer and more unclouded sky, after years, I returned to contemplate the dynamics of life in the incessant work of bees, small birds, worms, and a variety of insects working for life, as if they were all coordinated by the same driving principle. A vital principle that also pulsed in me, in those who fought against death, intubated in hospital beds or deprived of oxygen in their own homes, waiting for an ambulance.

In the communion of this impulse for life in all living beings, in people who struggled to escape from SARS-CoV-2, in the virus itself that proliferated with avidity, in the sky that became bluer and clearer with each day of confinement, revealing the summit of the mountains, I glimpsed Ariadne's thread—the need for harmony among all. However, would this be the same harmony with nature that Resolution 64/196 of the UN speaks of? The great challenge was to capture the harmony of my garden for the signs of this text, to explain and fill with life the harmony in the UN Resolutions.

Within the walls of my wild garden, the biosphere pulsed vigorously, like a holographic enclave of life, in a city desperate for the sirens of ambulances announcing death. The sapiens were besieged in my neighborhood and all over the globe, not by the bizarre and monstrous aliens of Hollywood, but by SARS-CoV-2. Meanwhile, the bees continued to dive into the flowers, the field thrush chirped, the jaboticabas were sweeter than ever, and the cats and dogs played. We were the only vulnerable target of the great pandemic attack.

This vulnerability revealed the biological dimension of humanity and its connection with all spheres of life, including the virosphere, which announced that sapiens were not the center but a link in the web of life. The circumstance whispered that the change should be in the anthropocentric paradigm itself, which once separated culture from nature and restricted the recognition of intrinsic value, dignity, and subjectivity only to human beings, while attributing to non-human living beings and ecosystems an instrumental value of mere resources and merchandise.

The change should start in the human relationship with nature, and from then, the research began to make sense. Perhaps, under other circumstances, I would not have reached the end of Ariadne's line. Then came a second doubt: the ethical account of harmony with nature, present in the declarations and ethical principles that guide the United Nations—especially the Harmony with Nature reports established by Resolution 64/196, Principle 1 of the Rio Declaration (1992), and the Earth Charter—could it be considered a general principle of international and internal environmental law?

After this question, more disturbing ones arose: What would be the legal nature of this harmony between all human and non-human living beings, as stated in the context of the Harmony with Nature reports by representatives of states, scholars, and peoples of various origins and traditions? Would it be a political guideline? An ethical principle? Is it possible to recognize in harmony with nature the necessary characteristics to consider it a legal principle?

Once harmony with nature is recognized as a legal principle of international environmental law, would this principle also be codified in Brazilian domestic law? What is its constitutional normative basis?

What would be the concrete and immediate consequences for the legal system of recognizing harmony with nature as a legal principle? What are the functions of this principle, and what is its impact on human relations with nature?

Does the recognition of harmony with nature as a legal principle have the power to change the way humans relate to nature, imposing ethical duties and legal obligations on humanity in its relationship with the natural world? Would the recognition of intrinsic value, dignity, and subjectivity for the plant world, the animal world, and ecosystems weaken or strengthen the human rights that have been achieved?

This work was advanced by these reflections and questions, and I ran through the timelines in search of answers. Finally, the keys to open the letters placed in time capsules by Heraclitus, Plato, Spinoza, Henri Bergson, Heidegger, and Hans Jonas came into my hands. Professor Carlos Roberto Velho Cirne Lima generously handed me the keys to the philosophy of life in his beautiful texts. For thirty days, I read and reread his work; he was my great guide in constructing the principle of harmony with nature. He was the master who established the bridge between the sense of harmony in the signs of the texts of the UN Resolutions and the sense of radiant life in the garden or agonizing in hospitals. Then, I researched his address to request an audience. That's when I discovered that he had left this earthly dimension sixty days after I became acquainted with his work, on July 1, 2020. However, philosophers are immortal, and even on another plane, his work was fundamental to this endeavor, as will be seen in the course of reading the chapters dedicated to Ontology and Ethics.

Throughout the chapters, we intend to demonstrate that harmony with nature, mentioned in the statement of Resolution 64/196 of the UN, emerges, first, as the recognition of a principle inherent in the natural laws that govern the Earth's biosphere and, for this reason, it has been reproduced over the centuries by human language in ethical narratives rooted in the ancestral culture of Western and Eastern peoples and, above all, in the way of life of the original peoples.

The research also aims to show that harmony with nature is a legal principle of international environmental law, which is based on the common morality of peoples, as a demand of public conscience that emerges from the historicity of the struggle for the recognition of the rights of non-human living beings and holistic organic entities since classical antiquity.

We will show that at the normative core of the principle of harmony with nature is the principle of ecological balance, whose main function is to weigh and balance two magnitudes: social well-being, resulting from the principle of human dignity, when in conflict with ecological integrity. From the tension of these two values, the great synthesis—the principle of sustainability—emerges.

The principle of harmony with nature has an integrative function, which emerges as a source of law to enable the recognition of biological dignity; that is, the biodignity of living beings and holistic organic entities, from which it is intended to unfold the concept of biological legal personality and, consequently, recognize the existence of biological persons: plant, animal, and systemic.

The ultimate goal of this research is to present the principle of harmony with nature as a legal source legitimizing biological legal personality, based on the concept of biodignity, biological legal personality, and, consequently, propose the recognition of the biological person, with its unfolding into biological persons: (i) plant; (ii) animal; and (iii) systemic.

The approach to the normativity of the principle of harmony with nature is structured in five phases: (1) An analysis of the presence of harmony with nature in the natural laws of the Earth system will be conducted; (2) subsequently, harmony with nature will be demonstrated through the general theory of legal principles; (3) the concept of general principles of law in the context of international law will be revisited to verify the hypothesis of the emergence of harmony with nature as a general principle of law; (4) then, harmony with nature will be examined within the conceptual context of principles in the sphere of international environmental law; and (5) finally, the normative structure of the principle of harmony with nature will be analyzed.

In conclusion, the aim is to demonstrate the compatibility of the legal principle of harmony with the human rights already achieved, considering its positive impact on reducing the entropic acceleration of the biosphere in the Anthropocene, as it constitutes a new ethos and legal paradigm for human relations with non-human living beings and holistic organic entities, as members of a single, plural, and interconnected community in the web of life.

Campo Grande
March 17, 2025

Raquel Domingues do Amaral

Acknowledgments I thank the creator and Saint Augustine, my spiritual and philosophical guide; Pope Francis and Professor Carlos Roberto V. Cirne Lima (in memoriam); my parents, Sebastião and Terezinha, my first teachers; Marcelo das Neves Martins, my kind partner; my lovely sons and my daughter, Octavio Augusto do Amaral Santos, Henrique Domingues do Amaral Corniglion, and Beatriz Marie Domingues do Amaral Corniglion; the loving team Ursula Filártigas Henning, Alcilene Cristino Bremm, Marcos Spengler, Rosane Pinheiro, Miriam Barbosa, and Juliana Venâncio; my heart friends, Catarina Guató, Abadia Macedo, and Maria Durvalina; Professors Dr. Livia Gaigher Bosio Campello, Dr. Ynes da Silva Félix, Dr. Luciana Davi de Oliveira, and Dr. Cláudia Vansessa Bergamini; Professors Dr. Vladmir Oliveira da Silveira, João Salm, and Antônio Hilário A. Urquiza; and federal judges Dr. Marisa Ferreira dos Santos and Professor Dr. Consuelo Yoshida. I also thank my friends Micael Carlos Andrejzwsk, Jean Marcos Ferreira, Ronaldo José da Silva, Professor Dr. André Ferreira de Oliveira, João Felipe Menezes Lopes, Ricardo Damasceno de Almeida, Professor André Luis S. Fonseca, Jaqueline Karina R. de Lima, and Professor Dr. Aurélio Tomaz da Silva Briltes. I give special thanks to Minister Herman Benjamin, who paved the way for ecological ethics in the Brazilian Judiciary.

Contents

Chapter 1
The Environmental Crisis: Symptoms of the Anthropocene

In February 2000, at a meeting in Cuernavaca, Mexico, Nobel laureate atmospheric chemist Paul Crutzen, after hearing several scientists describe the dramatic climate changes on the planet, intervened, suggesting that we were no longer in the Holocene, a geological era that began 11,700 years ago and, for his colleagues at that meeting, extended to the present day. Crutzen suggested to his colleagues that, due to the impact of human activities on Earth, we had already entered another era, which could be named by combining the Greek words *anthropos* and *cene,* the suffix used by geology to identify geological epochs, that is, Anthropocene.[1]

After this historic meeting, Crutzen and biologist Eugene Stoermer published an article on the Anthropocene, in which they described the impact of human activity on the planet, acting as a geological force. They argued that this human interference of stratigraphic proportions is based on the following evidence: (a) an increase in the release of sulfur dioxide into the atmosphere, approximately 160 Tg/year, a quantity twice as large as natural emissions; (b) synthetic fixation of nitrogen in the soil due to the use of fertilizers in agriculture; (c) an increase in the release of nitric oxide (NO) into the atmosphere due to the burning of fossil fuels, with the corresponding increase in the volume of photochemical ozone; (d) an increase in the emission of greenhouse gases (GHGs), with a 30% rise in the emission of carbon dioxide CO_2 and more than a 100% increase in methane (CH_4); (e) destruction of coastal wetlands by humans, with a loss of 50% of the world's mangroves; and (f) modification of the geochemical cycles of water.

Crutzen and Stoermer took into account the impact of human activities on a global scale, both on land and in the atmosphere, to recognize that humans have become a central force in geological and ecological changes, and thus

[1] Davison (2019).

R. D. d. Amaral, *The Principle of Harmony with Nature as a Legal Foundation*,
https://doi.org/10.1007/978-3-032-05475-3_1

presented to the scientific community the word "Anthropocene" to designate this new geological era, whose driving force is the human being.[2]

They proposed the last part of the eighteenth century as the starting point of the Anthropocene, based on data recovered from studies of ice core samples, which show a growth in the atmosphere of various domestic gases, particularly CO_2 and CH_4, and also taking into account the invention of the steam engine by James Watt. Finally, they conclude that unless there are catastrophes, such as a pandemic, the impact of an asteroid, or a nuclear war, humanity will continue to be a geological force for millennia.[3]

After Crutzen and Stoermer published this article, the topic gained traction in the scientific world, but geologists still needed to be convinced. Geology, guided by strict scientific criteria—more precisely stratigraphic—defines the chronological order of epochs in the history of the planet on a timescale called the International Chronostratigraphic Chart. This timescale is the basis of geology, and altering it is a very rigorous scientific procedure, which is conducted by an official body, the International Commission on Stratigraphy (ICS). In 2006, at a meeting of the Geological Society of London, a stratigraphy scholar named Jan Zalasiewicz proposed the analysis of the concept of the Anthropocene by the ICS, which is dedicated to the study of rock layers to define the timescale of the geological history of the planet, which is 4.6 billion years old. The Geological Society of London agreed to Jan Zalasiewicz's proposal, and he was appointed to lead a team of geologists to investigate the proposal of the Anthropocene as a geological epoch. However, Zalasiewicz, in forming his team, did not limit himself to inviting stratigraphic scientists and, in addition to traditional geologists, brought to his study group scientists who study broader processes, such as the carbon cycle, as well as an archeologist and an environmental historian.[4]

To prove the feasibility of adopting the Anthropocene proposed by Crutzen, the group of scholars needed to demonstrate that the Holocene, a geological epoch characterized by climatic stability, constancy of carbon dioxide levels, and sea level, had come to an end after nearly 12 millennia. They then began their research by analyzing the atmosphere. During the Holocene period, the amount of CO_2 in the air, measured in parts per million (ppm), ranged between 260 and 280, but data from 2005 showed an increase to 379 ppm and subsequently to 405 ppm. According to the group's research, the last time carbon dioxide levels were this high was three million years ago, during the so-called Pliocene. Following their studies, the group began to examine plants and animals, as mass extinction is a hallmark of geological time change. These changes bring discomfort to animal species and require them to adapt to new environments, meaning some species cannot survive. Thus, Anthony Barnosky, a member of the Anthropocene study group led by Zalasiewicz, warns in his research that a mass extinction is underway. Another hallmark of the Anthropocene is the so-called technofossils; that is, in

[2] Crutzen and Stoermer (2000), p. 17.

[3] Crutzen and Stoermer (2000), p. 17.

[4] Davison (2019).

making our utensils, we have left fragments buried in sediments, which will form part of the rocks of the future.[5]

In 2016, Zalasiewicz and the 23 members of the working group wrote a paper stating that the Anthropocene was "functional and stratigraphically distinct" from the Holocene.[6] In this paper, Zalasiewicz and his research colleagues assert that humans are indeed altering the planet, including in these alterations impacts on "long-term global geological processes." They clarify that the requirements for the formal recognition of a new geological epoch depend on demonstrating that humans are altering the Earth system in such a way as to imprint what they call a "stratigraphic signature in sediments and ice," differentiating the rock layers and the ice layers of the poles with distinct marks from those that characterized the Holocene.

In their research to verify whether there was indeed a "stratigraphic signature" diffused and persistent on Earth by humans, capable of justifying the stratigraphic definition of the "Anthropocene," the team pointed out "anthropogenic stratigraphic signals," which result from three interconnected factors: (a) acceleration of technological development; (b) rapid growth of the human population; and (c) increase in resource consumption.

The combination of these factors led to a considerable increase in the use of metals and minerals, fossil fuels, agricultural fertilizers, and the acceleration in the modification of marine, terrestrial, and coastal ecosystems to serve human use. The direct consequence of this was the loss of natural biomes, which gave way to agriculture, cities, roads, and other buildings. There was also a growing replacement of wild animals and plants by domesticated species to meet human demand for food. They report that anatomically modern *Homo sapiens* emerged approximately 200,000 years ago, so that at the beginning of the Holocene, in 12,000 BC, humans had already colonized all continents, with the exception of Antarctica and the South Pacific islands, and at that time, the population was 2 million inhabitants spread around the globe.

Throughout the Holocene period, humans had an increasing influence as the population gradually grew. Eight thousand years ago, the human population on Earth was already 18 million, and it was during this period that agricultural practices began, along with deforestation and the increasing emission of CO_2 into the atmosphere through burning. However, it was in 1800 that the human population on Earth reached the one billion mark. From then on, there was a gradual growth in the human population, with the period from 1750 to 1940 being slower but becoming exponential from 1950 to 2010. This inflection point in 1950 coincides with the so-called period of the "great acceleration."[7]

Zalasiewicz and his team detail the anthropogenic signals capable of justifying the formal admission of the Anthropocene based on stratigraphic criteria: (1) presence of

---

[5] Davison (2019).

[6] Waters et al. (2016).

[7] Waters et al. (2016).

the so-called technofossils on Earth, in the rock layers—that is, materials manufactured by humans, such as ceramics, glass, bricks, copper alloys, concrete, elemental aluminum, and organic polymers (plastics). (2) Presence of plastics in rivers, lakes, and in shallow and deep-sea sediments. (3) Combustion of fossil fuels with the release of black carbon particles, inorganic ash spheres, and black carbon spherical particles, which leave a permanent marker in sediments and glacial ice. (4) Modification of sedimentary processes across over 50% of the Earth's surface soil for human use, generating "anthropogenically modified" materials, which are deposited in artificial landfills or in soils prepared for cultivation but end up spreading through the oceans, causing eutrophication of coastal waters and coral bleaching. (5) Deforestation of primary forests, leading to soil erosion. (6) Sediment retention in dams and mining expansion, with the distribution of industrial metals such as cadmium, chromium, copper, mercury, nickel, lead, and zinc. Accumulation of platinum, rhodium, and palladium waste in soils adjacent to highways. (7) Presence of radiogenic elements and radionuclides in sediments and ice resulting from the precipitation of nuclear tests. At this point, they ponder the feasibility of establishing the initial marker for the Anthropocene—that is, a "standard and global stratigraphic age"—on the date of the detonation of the Trinity atomic device in Alamogordo, New Mexico, on July 16, 1945. (8) They cite as a major anthropogenic mark the evolution of the carbon cycle recorded in glacial ice cores, whose concentration jumped from 120 ppm in 1850 to 400 ppm today. (9) They also point to the increasing emission of methane, which has been recorded in ice cores, with the concentration varying from 590 to 760 parts per billion (ppb) until 1700. In 2004, studies carried out in Antarctic ice cores observed an increase in this concentration to 900 ppb, the highest concentration recorded in the last 800,000 years. (10) Global warming, with a global average temperature increase of 0.6–0.9°C between 1896 and 2005. (11) Significant increase in the global average sea level, by 3.2 ± 0.4 mm per year, from 1993 to 2010. (12) They also cite recent biotic changes. They highlight that, even though the Earth still has most of the species present at the beginning of the Holocene, current trends of habitat loss due to forest fires and overexploitation could lead the Earth to the sixth mass extinction—that is, the extinction of 75% of species. They point to a serious alteration of the set of species worldwide and attribute this reduction in fauna and flora diversity to transglobal invasions of geologically unprecedented species.[8]

Based on these stratigraphic signatures, the research group led by Zalasiewicz proposes the admission of a new geological epoch, as these anthropogenic marks are completely different from the stratigraphic marks that characterize the Holocene. However, it is up to the ICS to accept the formalization of the Anthropocene as a geological epoch.

In a recent consultation (April 2020) on the website of the ICS, we found that there has not yet been an analysis or deliberation on Zalasiewicz's proposal.

[8] Waters et al. (2016).

The fact is that "every cubic meter of water, every hectare of land now has the human mark," as Hamilton rightly observes, because in the reflection on the Anthropocene, one cannot fail to consider the volitional element of the human being. That is, the anthropogenic impacts on the planet are a manifestation of human power over nature, and it is not a depersonalized force but, above all, an act of will and, therefore, imponderable. Hamilton ponders that the rhythm of the market metabolism is faster than the rhythm of the Earth system, but, in the Anthropocene, the human species deliberately entangled its future with the geological future of the Earth. There is an intersection of the Earth system with the social system of humans, so the Anthropocene cannot be examined only from the stratigraphic geological point of view; there must be an interdisciplinary focus on social sciences, geology, and Earth system sciences.[9]

In this line, a broader definition of the Anthropocene has been consolidated, based on the contributions of Earth system scientists, a scientific field that brings together climatology, global ecology, geochemistry, atmospheric chemistry, and oceanography. The approach of Zalasiewicz's study group goes beyond purely stratigraphic data and considers, as an anthropogenic signature, all the elements already detailed in the previous paragraphs. However, there is still a third definition of the Anthropocene that establishes the concept from the "cumulative impact of civilization."[10] In this perspective, the Anthropocene represents a threshold of change in the way human beings relate to the natural world.

For a broader understanding of the topic, it is worth reflecting on the analysis of Christophe Bonneuil, who examines the Anthropocene within four major narratives, which aim to explain this epoch: the naturalist narrative, the post-nature narrative, the eco-catastrophic narrative, and the eco-Marxist narrative.

The naturalist narrative is predominant and includes names of great scientists such as the already mentioned Paul Crutzen, Will Steffen, John McNeill, and Dipesh Chakrabarty. This naturalist narrative recognizes the human species in an undifferentiated way "as the causal force" that changes the Earth. For this current, a species evolved from the level of "hunters collectors to act as a global geological force."[11] As Bonneuil highlights, the *anthropos* of the Anthropocene is, for this current, a species that mastered fire and tools and thus began to enjoy a rich protein diet that expanded its brain mass, allowing it to develop language, self-awareness, and intelligence. Thus, with a cognitive advantage over other species, it began to use fossil fuels for its evolutionary enterprise, impacting the atmosphere, oceans, and climate. The use of fossil fuels exponentially increased its power, culminating in the so-called great acceleration from 1945, making it an unconscious "telluric force."

Bonneuil criticizes the naturalist current, considering that it completely ignores the volitional factor and treats the *anthropos* of the Anthropocene in a generic and

[9] Hamilton (2015), p. 62.

[10] Hamilton (2015), p. 71.

[11] Bonneuil (2015), p. 38.

undifferentiated way—the human species, a biological category—completely disregarding the notion of specific social groups, that is, the cultural aspects that influenced the Anthropocene. Bonneuil asserts that this narrative focuses on the "human species" and "obscures the asymmetries among human beings about nature—unequal access to environmental goods and exposure to environmental harms," pointing out that nature was transformed along with a certain type of social order marked by social, racial, gender, and also unequal geopolitical relations. Thus, socioecological asymmetries cannot be ignored, as they also cause ecologically unsustainable developments. The naturalist perspective is mistaken for disregarding the volitional, social, and cultural elements and blaming the human species generically for the environmental crisis; however, as Bonneuil maintains, the "great acceleration" was the result of the choice of policies by countries and institutions, practiced within a colonialist policy of human exploitation by humans.

Indeed, Bonneuil is correct when he emphasizes that "a serious analysis of the causal chain that led to the current climate rupture cannot separate the curve of greenhouse gas emissions from the historical creation of a certain type of social order."[12] Bonneuil's opinion is corroborated by the following excerpt from the "Environmental Overview 2020" report, prepared by the countries that make up the Organization for Economic Cooperation and Development (OECD) group:

The carbon footprint of OECD countries, relative to carbon emitted anywhere in the world to meet domestic final demand, is generally higher than domestic emissions (+18%). This is because OECD countries have increasingly outsourced the production of consumer goods to other countries [. . .] The *per capita* amount is highly related to material living standards.[13]

As can be seen, the richest countries have been emitting carbon for a longer time, and even now, when they seek to follow emission reduction protocols, they are outsourcing the industrial production of consumer goods to the so-called peripheral countries. This strategy only transfers carbon production to other countries, which shows that the causal chain of climate rupture cannot be analyzed in a purely naturalistic way and dissociated from the prevailing geopolitical and cultural order on the planet. Thousands of human beings in peripheral countries did not participate in the decision-making that led the Earth to the Anthropocene.

The post-nature narrative, in turn, defends the possibility of a "good Anthropocene"[14] in a world without nature. For this line of thought, nature is always a cultural and technological construction. They are also called eco-pragmatists who, despite not contesting the ecological ruptures of the Anthropocene, believe that humans took control of the planet thousands of years

---

[12] Bonneuil (2015), p. 40.

[13] In the original: "*The carbon footprint of OECD countries that accounts for all carbon emitted anywhere in the world to satisfy domestic final demand is generally higher than domestic emissions (+18%). This is because OECD countries have increasingly outsourced the production of consumer goods to other countries. [. . .] The per capita footprint is highly correlated with material living standards*" OECD (2020), pp. 20–21.

[14] Bonneuil (2015), p. 40.

ago and will continue to control nature. As Bonneuil points out, they "radicalize the Baconian project to increasingly artificialize the Earth."[15]

The ecocatastrophic narrative, which preaches the collapse of industrial civilization with the end of humans devoured by the Earth itself, prefers the myth of Medea to Gaia. That is, it places the Earth not as the loving mother who forgives everything and regenerates, but as the mother who will devour her offspring in the face of the despair of imminent systemic collapse.[16] For this current, the Anthropocene represents the exhaustion of natural resources. It works with the concepts of cyclical development of ecosystems: growth, collapse, and reorganization. It advocates resilience to withstand these processes without losing the main resources and functions. Examples of projects based on the ecocatastrophic narrative are permaculture (permanent culture), transition cities, and *degrowth*[17] (economic deceleration). This current prioritizes palliative measures for the catastrophe and works locally, within communities.

Finally, the eco-Marxist narrative views the Anthropocene as a result of the second contradiction of capitalism—that is, its inability to sustain nature. For this school of thought, the Anthropocene is the story of capitalism's unsustainable metabolism within the Earth system. In this vein, capitalist expansion and the mechanisms of imperialist domination are considered the primary causes of the Anthropocene.

This work considers that, to understand the serious moment of ecological crisis that marks the so-called Anthropocene, it is necessary to listen to and reflect on all narratives to construct the texture of the grand narrative that is the harmony among all beings. However, to weave a new narrative based on harmony, it is necessary to understand the delicate interrelation of all living and amorphous beings that make up the Earth system. For this reason, the next topics will examine the most critical points of the great ecological crisis that is sickening the Earth system, through the analysis of statistical data and forecasts from research in various scientific areas.

[15] Bonneuil (2015), p. 48.

[16] Bonneuil (2015), p. 49.

[17] By "degrowth," we understand a form of society and economy that aims at the well-being of all and sustains the natural basis of life. To achieve degrowth, we need a fundamental transformation of our lives and an extensive cultural change. The current economic and social paradigm is "faster, higher, more." It is built and encourages competition among all human beings. This causes acceleration, stress, and exclusion. Our economy destroys the natural basis of life. We are convinced that the common values of a degrading society should be care, solidarity, and cooperation. Humanity needs to understand itself as part of the planetary ecological system. Only in this way can a self-determined life in dignity for all be possible. Degrowth. https://www.degrowth.info/en/what-is-degrowth/.

1.1 The Big Question of the Anthropocene: Is CO_2 Increasing Because the Atmosphere Is Getting Warmer, or Is the Atmosphere Getting Warmer Because CO_2 is Increasing?

The study of the problems that deregulate the Earth system in the Anthropocene begins with the analysis of scientific investigations on the evolution of carbon dioxide emissions and their influence on climate warming, given the close link between CO_2 emissions and the planet's temperature. Richard Alley, a researcher of paleoclimatic records, dynamics, and sedimentary deposits of large glaciers, in an interview given at the National Climate Seminar, explains that the relationship between carbon dioxide emissions and temperature can be observed in the last century, the last 100,000 years, the last 100 million years, or even the last billion years.[18] Professor Alley clarifies that, by analyzing the cores of glaciers, it is possible to verify that throughout the Earth's climatic history, every time CO_2 emissions doubled, there was an increase of about 3°C in the temperature of the atmosphere, with a margin of error of 1°C.

Khoiyangban and Gupta[19] describe the atmosphere as a protective layer composed of gases that envelop the Earth, protecting it from the hostilities of outer space, given that it absorbs the sun's electromagnetic radiation and maintains the Earth's thermal balance. This is because, in addition to absorbing solar radiation, it also prevents the loss of heat from the planet's surface. The atmosphere is mainly composed of nitrogen and oxygen gases and, in smaller quantities, argon and carbon dioxide.

When we talk about global warming, we refer to the increase in the average temperature of the atmosphere and the oceans, which occurs due to the transmission of the sun's short-wave radiation and the absorption of the Earth's long-wave radiation. This process has been exacerbated by the accumulation of certain gases, such as carbon dioxide (CO_2), methane (CH_4), nitrous oxide (N_2O), and chlorofluorocarbons (CFCs)—gases known as GHGs—as they hinder the Earth's radiation from escaping and increase heat. The term "greenhouse effect" was proposed by Joseph Fourier in 1824 and investigated quantitatively by Svante Arrhenius in 1896. According to the Intergovernmental Panel on Climate Change, "the average global temperature at the end of the twentieth century was recorded as being higher by 0.40–0.76°C than at the end of the nineteenth century, with about two-thirds of the increase occurring only in the last three decades,"[20] an increase that is associated with the emissions of GHGs.

The brake on climate change involves stabilizing the radiation balance, that is, achieving a balance between the absorption and emission of radiation. Khoiyangban and Gupta explain that the amount of solar radiation received should

[18] Alley (2012).

[19] Khoiyangban and Gupta (2012), p. 381.

[20] Khoiyangban and Gupta (2012), p. 381.

be, on average, equal to the sum of the outgoing reflected solar radiation and the outgoing infrared radiation emitted by the climate system or, in other words, the Earth should radiate into space the same amount of energy it receives. The change in this equation is called radiative forcing. Currently, GHGs form a partial layer that retains part of this radiation, making the planet warmer.[21]

Among all the GHGs, the most important is CO_2, as it is responsible for 60% of the total greenhouse effect. The main anthropogenic source of carbon dioxide is the industrial sector, which produces it through the combustion of fossil fuels; the manufacturing of goods such as glass, cement, and ceramics; chemicals such as ammonia, nitric acid, carbides, titanium oxide, methanol, and ethylene; the production of metals such as iron, steel, iron alloys, aluminum, lead, zinc, and copper; the textile, food, and beverage industry; and the pulp, lubricants, and paraffin industry.

Carbon dioxide is also released by terrestrial biota, emissions from the soil itself, and forest fires. Changes in land use from 1850 to 1990 accounted for half of the global increase in carbon dioxide. This resulted not only in an imbalance in the Earth's heat equation but also in a depletion of soil fertility.

Kurz, when specifically addressing CO_2 emissions to facilitate the understanding of the scale of carbon dioxide production, took as a sample one million cubic meters of dry wood that was recovered after a major storm in Sweden. He explains that this amount of wood contains a quarter of a million tons of carbon and clarifies that the carbon annually released by the burning of fuels totals eight billion tons—that is, 32,000 times the amount of carbon contained in the pile of one million cubic meters of wood taken as a sample. This is equivalent to half of the trees in the forests of Canada.[22]

Kurz adopts for the measurement of CO_2 released into the atmosphere the Keeling Curve, a methodology developed by Charles Keeling in 1958 to measure the concentration of CO_2 in the Northern Hemisphere caused by a volcano in Hawaii. He warns that in 2011, an atmospheric concentration of CO_2 of 391 ppm was exceeded, which is 40% above the concentration levels of CO_2 in the pre-industrial era, which was 280 ppm. He clarifies that this measure of the concentration of CO_2 in the pre-industrial era was obtained by analyses of ice cores. Alley corroborates these data by analyzing bubbles found in the ice core. Over the last 800,000 years, bubbles have been trapped in the ice core in Antarctica, Greenland, and other places; these recently captured bubbles reproduce the percentages of CO_2 that were released into the atmosphere for millennia. With this method, a fairly accurate estimate of the levels of CO_2 in the atmosphere can be obtained. In addition to the ice cores, Alley explains that the presence of a larger amount of CO_2 in the atmosphere has increased the acidification of the oceans, and this change in the pH of the seawater is recorded in the chemical composition and isotopes of some shells.[23]

---

[21] Khoiyangban and Gupta (2012), p. 380.

[22] Kurz (2011), pp. 21–24.

[23] Alley (2012), p. 5.

He emphasizes that the evolution of the increase in CO_2 release into the atmosphere is worrying, as in 1990, 3.2 billion tons were released per year, and in 2011, this amount jumped to 8 billion tons. He stresses that from 2000 to 2009, the increase in CO_2 released into the atmosphere was 4.1 billion tons of carbon per year.

Kurz explains that for each ton of CO_2 emitted, biological systems, oceans, and forests absorb half a ton. The problem is that it is not known whether this 50% reduction will continue to exist in a scenario of climate change. He also emphasizes that there is no scientific certainty about this and considers two possible scenarios: (a) in an optimistic horizon, the warming of the planet could accelerate the growth of forests and thus there would be greater absorption of CO_2; or (b) in a more realistic horizon, warming would increase decomposition—that is, the melting of permanent subsurface ice—with the release of carbon from peat, the decomposition of the tundra system, and the increase in forest fires, all of this rapidly increasing the release of more CO_2 without a corresponding absorption.

In addition to the emissions caused by human actions in the burning of fossil fuels, ecosystems themselves naturally release a large amount of CO_2 into the atmosphere. Thus, even if anthropogenic emissions were reduced, the concentration of CO_2 would still persist. If climate changes advance, human efforts to reduce CO_2 emissions will be futile, considering that global warming will lead terrestrial ecosystems to release large amounts of CO_2 into the atmosphere. The circumpolar tundra system, which contains three times more carbon and peat in its soil than the atmosphere, will overload the atmosphere with CO_2 the more it suffers the impact of CO_2.[24]

Kurz warns that 50% of CO_2 is absorbed by nature itself, 27% is absorbed by forests, and that limiting climate change is the first step to balancing CO_2 emissions. However, this does not seem so simple, given the question posed by Alley: "To what extent is CO_2 increasing because the atmosphere is getting warmer and to what extent is the atmosphere getting warmer because CO_2 is increasing?"[25] The author explains that CO_2 is a temperature amplifier but clarifies that the issue cannot be simplified, as in the long term—millions of years—the warmer atmospheric temperature tends to reduce CO_2 levels. However, in the short term, over decades and even centuries, the effect is the opposite: The more the atmosphere's temperature increases, the more CO_2 is released into the atmosphere. In shorter periods—decades and even centuries—nature cannot absorb the CO_2, and this generates more heat, releasing even more CO_2 and creating a vicious circle.

Alley clarifies this relationship between the increase in CO_2 and the increase in temperature as follows: Faced with a larger amount of CO_2 in the atmosphere, nature begins to work, producing various chemical reactions in an attempt to remove the excess CO_2; this exhaustive work is ineffective in the span of decades and further raises the temperature. With the rise in temperature, there will be

[24] Kurz (2011), pp. 21–24.

[25] Alley (2012), p. 6.

melting of ice from the tundra system, wildfires, and more CO_2 will be emitted into the atmosphere.

It is thus almost impossible to interrupt the cycle of CO_2 emissions by nature itself, but it is possible to reduce artificially caused emissions by human action, an urgent measure for the survival and prosperity of humanity, as the deleterious effects of uncontrolled emissions are already present, altering the healthiness of the planet.

The OECD countries' report, Environment at a Glance 2020, published in February 2020, highlights the continued growth of GHG emissions worldwide, despite relative stability in OECD member countries. Historically, OECD countries were the largest emitters of CO_2 and other GHGs, but since 1990, they have started to emit at a slower pace than other countries. The rate of CO_2 emissions in developing countries has increased due to industrialization, which demands large amounts of fossil energy. The report points out that CO_2 resulting from the combustion of fossil fuels and biomass, along with industrial processes, accounts for more than 70% of global GHG emissions, which, when combined with CH_4 and N_2O, totals 98% of emissions.

OECD countries continue to depend on fossil fuels for 80% of their energy supply, mainly oil and gas. The OECD report points out that, globally, CO_2 emissions from energy use have increased by 60% since 1990, 41% since 2000, and, after three years of stability, they increased again in 2017, reaching a record of 32 billion tons.[26]

The report also points out that, currently, OECD countries are responsible for about 35% of global CO_2 emissions resulting from energy consumption. However, a reduction is observed, as in 1990, they emitted 50% of all global CO_2, and in 2005, 47%. Despite this reduction, if the amount of emissions per inhabitant is considered, OECD countries emit 9 annual tons per capita, while countries from other regions emit, on average, 4 annual tons per capita. This amount of annual per capita CO_2 emissions in OECD countries has remained stable since 1990.[27]

Regarding the emissions of GHG group gases, OECD countries reached their peak in 2007 and have been gradually falling since then, decreasing by 9%, according to the report. One of the reasons for this slowdown was the economic crisis of 2008. However, this reduction is not sufficient, considering the high speed of climate changes. The aforementioned report points out the peak of GHG levels in the atmosphere in 2018: 147% CO_2, 259% CH_4 (methane), and 123% N_2O (nitrous oxide)—the highest levels since the pre-industrial era. These alarming rates cause long-term climate changes and directly impact the environment, with rising sea levels, ocean acidification, and climate imbalance, along with an increase in natural disasters around the globe. Climate-related disasters have caused direct economic losses, and around 77% of the losses from disasters in general are related to climate tragedy, which, monetized from 1998 to 2017,

[26] OECD (2020), pp. 20–21.

[27] OECD (2020), p. 11.

represents losses of the order of 3 trillion dollars and, most seriously, losses that are borne proportionally by developing and vulnerable countries.[28]

In addition to carbon dioxide, methane, and nitrous oxide, several other gases have a direct impact on climate change: CFCs, hydrofluorocarbons, perfluorocarbons, and sulfur hexafluoride. The nefarious and direct effects of fine particulate black carbon ($PM_{2.5}$), which result from the incomplete combustion of fossil fuels, such as diesel oil, kerosene, biomass, and biofuels, whose sources are motor vehicles, homes, businesses, agricultural burning, and forest fires, cannot be underestimated. The pollution with black carbon has been quite worrying in the Arctic region, considering that it has influenced the amount of radiation in the Arctic and caused warming of the region at a rate equivalent to twice the global average rate, with the consequent melting of ice.[29]

We cannot also disregard the pollutants that indirectly contribute to the greenhouse effect: non-methane volatile organic compounds, nitrogen oxide, and carbon monoxide. The reactions of these pollutants form tropospheric ozone (O_3), which is one of the greenhouse gases.[30]

The OECD report points out that all these pollutants are contributing to the increase in global warming, which accelerated from 2018, even in member countries. In this line, tackling climate change is part of the objectives outlined in the 2030 Agenda for Sustainable Development under Goal 13: "Take urgent action to combat climate change and its impacts."[31]

1.2 The Mark of Biotic Changes in the Anthropocene: Biodiversity at Risk

One of the most important phenomena in the balance of ecosystems is symbiosis or mutualism between life forms. Most of these mutualisms occur between ectothermic organisms, that is, those that cannot regulate their own body temperature, so they are immediately affected by climate changes. Mutualism occurs with the mixture of species of different origins and phylogenetic physiologies that interact under a set of conditions. The warming of the planet has altered the distribution of several species involved in mutualism, with devastating results. Corals, for example, due to the warming of the waters, are losing their symbionts and becoming bleached.[32]

Brittany L. Sulaini, when addressing coral bleaching, reports that these sessile aquatic animals have helped build the ocean ecosystem for over two hundred million

[28] OECD (2020), pp. 20–21.

[29] OECD (2020), p. 23.

[30] OECD (2020), p. 11.

[31] Platforma Agenda (2030). http://www.agenda2030.org.br/osods/.

[32] Six (2011), p. 10.

years, in an important symbiotic relationship with algae, which live within the coral polyps, producing their food through photosynthesis and sharing it with the corals. This symbiotic relationship works very well and is beneficial for both organisms, as the reefs are located in shallow and transparent waters with high solar incidence, allowing the algae to produce enough food to sustain themselves and the corals as well. However, there has been an interruption of this symbiotic relationship, with the expulsion of the algae from the coral polyps, which, as a consequence, lose their color and become white. The mass bleaching of corals is leading to their death.

The interruption of the symbiosis between corals and algae is attributed to the increase in the temperature of the ocean waters. Sulainis reports that approximately 25% of the carbon dioxide produced by human activity is absorbed by the oceans, which causes acidification of the water. With the rise in temperature, this not only expels the algae from the polyps, interrupting the mutualism, but also impacts the development of corals in their larval stage. She warns that corals have not shown the ability to adapt to climate change, which could lead to their extinction.[33]

Another significant report on the unpredictable impact of climate change on the biosphere comes from Six's research on the action of beetles on the pine trees of the United States' mountains. The increase in temperature facilitated the proliferation of beetles in the large mountain pines. Previously, these beetles could not reach these trees, as the cooler temperatures at higher altitudes did not allow their spread. With the rise in temperature in recent years, the beetles have taken over the large mountain pines, and just in Yellowstone, since the first reports in 2000, pines covering millions of hectares have been lost. These thousands of trees were attacked by ambrosia bark beetles, native species of the region that were not harmful, but with the increase in temperature and greater aridity, they experienced a population increase and became harmful to the large mountain trees.[34]

In dealing with pollinating insects in North America, the National Research Council analyzed the relevance of the symbiotic relationship between the population of pollinating insects and the flora of the United States, Mexico, and Canada.[35] It reports that about three-quarters of more than 240,000 plant species on the planet depend on natural pollinators, such as insects, bats, birds, and other animals, emphasizing that pollinators are at the base of a productive chain that sustains humans, as most of the fruits, vegetables, and seeds that provide us with fibers, drugs, and fuels are pollinated by animals. The report particularly highlights the role of bees in the pollination of forages and hays that serve as food for livestock, which provide the protein base of human food. Among the various groups of pollinators, the report points to the decline of the bee *Apis mellifera*, responsible for the production of 90 commercial crops. This decline has been caused by mites resistant to the use of pesticides, by the invasion of Africanized bees, and by the

[33] Sulainis (n.d.), pp. 25–29.

[34] Six (2011), pp. 11–12.

[35] National Research Council (2007).

decay of domesticated and managed bees in commercial agriculture. The study also points to the decrease of other species of wild pollinators, such as bees, bats, and butterflies threatened with extinction. Among the causes of the decline of these native pollinators are the degradation and loss of *habitats*, as well as the changes in phenological synchrony and in the distribution of pollinators and plants resulting from global climate changes, which prevent interactions between flowers and pollinators. It cites as an example the case of the interruption of the migratory routes of hummingbirds, bats, and butterflies.[36]

The consequence of this decline in native pollinators is the extinction of plant populations. There are approximately 250,000 cataloged angiosperms on the planet, which produce flowers, edible fruits, and seeds, and are the food base for most terrestrial and aquatic animal species. In addition to providing nutrients for most organisms, they also enable multidimensional structures for the human species, which extract from angiosperms their food, fibers, drugs, and fuels. Most of these plants need pollen transfer for their fertilization, with three-quarters of the planet's angiosperms depending on the action of 200,000 animal pollinators.[37] It was precisely through this symbiosis that angiosperms achieved ecological dominance approximately one hundred million years ago. This mutual association with animal pollinators ensured a movement of gametes that allowed them greater genetic diversity and resistance. It was the genetic variability through recombination associated with crossing that enabled resistance to herbivorous pathogens throughout evolution.[38]

This interaction between plant and pollinator, which involves approximately 400,000 living beings, is mutually beneficial, as the animal pollinators are compensated for their hard work of delivering pollen with the rich nutrients of the plants that keep them alive and strong. Pollen is food for bees, butterflies, flies, birds, and bats. Some plants, in addition to providing pollen to their pollinators, also offer them resins, oils, and fragrances that contribute to the formation of these animals' pheromones, thus ensuring their mating and genetic perpetuation.[39]

It is clear that this is a delicate network of mutualism that has been maintained for millions of years but is now compromised by the decline of pollinators. The impairment of the mutualistic relationship existing between plant species and bees is called colony collapse disorder. Since 2009, the bee population (*Apis mellifera*) has been constantly decreasing. For several researchers, this decline in the bee population may be attributed to the misuse of pesticides, or even certain types of microbes, such as fungi, bacteria, and viruses, which can alter bees at a cellular level, changing their DNA and RNA chains and affecting their cognitive function.[40] Environmental factors such as habitat loss and climate change are also cited

---

[36] National Research Council (2007), p. 22.

[37] National Research Council (2007).

[38] National Research Council (2007), p. 22.

[39] National Research Council (2007), p. 29.

[40] Wood (n.d.).

as causes for the decline in bee populations. The so-called colony collapse disorder is highly significant, given that bees are responsible for increasing the yield of 96% of crops that require animal pollination and 75% of crops pollinated by insects.[41]

In the event that we can no longer rely on bees for the pollination of wild plants and cultivated crops, the food industry will have to resort to artificial means, which would increase the cost of food, leading to serious global food insecurity. The United States Department of Agriculture (USDA) published in 2007 the results of a study on colony collapse disorder, which clarified that beekeeping performs pollination for over 90 commercial crops grown in the United States, adding 15 billion dollars annually to the value of crops produced in that country. This study presents data published in 2007 by the Pollinators Committee of the National Research Council of the American National Academy of Sciences, reporting the serious difficulties faced by beekeeping in recent decades. In the winter of 2006–2007, there was a loss of 30–90% of bees. It was noted that 50% of this loss was not related to the already-known attacks of mites and parasites. The cause of death was not identified, and thus, they named the phenomenon colony collapse disorder.[42]

The report from the committee, created by the USDA to address the issue, points out that the sequencing of the bee genome shows they are weak in detoxifying enzymes, which makes them vulnerable to pesticide poisoning. In addition, they have a weak immune system, so they need social interaction to protect their colonies from diseases.[43]

Research from the USDA shows that a new class of insecticides, known as neonicotinoids and used in the cultivation system to combat pests, have been poisoning bees. One of the derivatives of this pesticide, imidacloprid, was banned in France for affecting the short-term memory of bees and impairing their navigation back to the hives.[44]

Colony collapse disorder, within the context of the current ecological crisis, is of great relevance, as it may represent not only a threat to the weakening of flora, with the extinction of angiosperm populations, but also puts at risk the very food security of the human species. The global value of pollination done by insects in one year was calculated at 153 billion euros in 2005. Without bees to perform the service of pollinating wild and cultivated plants in agriculture, the global food industry would have to use artificial means of pollination, which would greatly increase the cost of food, leading to a wave of global shortages and hunger.[45]

The OECD, when dealing with biodiversity, points out that the main factors causing the loss of biodiversity on the planet are the use and change of land cover, degradation, and overdevelopment of infrastructure. It reports a 15% increase in infrastructure development in the OECD area since 2000, which represents a built

---

[41] Wood (n.d.), p. 174.

[42] CCD Steering Committee (2007), p. 6.

[43] CCD Steering Committee (2007), p. 7.

[44] CCD Steering Committee (2007), p. 16.

[45] Wood (n.d.).

area of 290 km^2 per inhabitant in OECD countries, three times the world average. Globally, the area modified by infrastructure since 1990 is equivalent to the territory of the United Kingdom (244 thousand km^2).

Across the planet, 27% of lands that had semi-natural vegetation cover have been lost to other types of vegetation since 1992, representing an area of 2.3 million km^2, with OECD and G20 countries responsible for half of this loss, which has occurred mainly in Brazil, China, Russia, the United States, and Indonesia.[46]

The OECD also addresses the loss of marine biodiversity, pointing to enormous pressure from illegal fishing, irregular coastal development, high pollution levels, ocean acidification, maritime transport, and pollution caused by marine fuels.[47]

One of the greatest threats to marine biodiversity is plastic waste and microplastics released into the oceans. It is estimated that over 800 coastal marine species are affected by plastic ingestion, entanglement, and ghost fishing. The nongovernmental organization *World Animal Protection* reports that:

> nets, lines, and fishing gear, when lost or discarded at sea, are now one of the greatest threats to marine life. Each year, the volume of fishing materials dumped into the oceans reaches 640,000 tons. These materials injure, mutilate, and even kill hundreds of thousands of animals per day, a phenomenon known as ghost fishing.[48]

According to the OECD, between the years 2012 and 2016, there was a 26% increase in the number of aquatic mammal and seabird species affected by the ingestion of marine litter, which includes organic mantles resulting from the decay of vegetation.[49]

The drastic decrease in marine biodiversity is a major threat to human subsistence on the planet, considering that 20% of the animal protein consumed worldwide comes from fish. Moreover, we cannot forget the economic benefits resulting from tourism in coastal cities around the world.[50]

Finally, biodiversity, or biological diversity, according to the Convention on Biological Diversity, can be understood as "the variability of living organisms from all sources, including, among others terrestrial, marine and other aquatic ecosystems and the ecological complexes of which they are part; this includes diversity within species, between species, and of ecosystems."[51] The preservation of biodiversity is fundamental for sustainable development, as it is biological diversity that has provided the human economy with biological resources, which encompass

---

[46] OECD (2020), pp. 20–21.

[47] OECD (2020), p. 50.

[48] World Animal Protection. https://www.worldanimalprotection.org.br/pesca-fantasma. Accessed 20 Apr 2020.

[49] OECD (2020), pp. 20–21.

[50] OECD (2020), p. 50.

[51] Convenção sobre Diversidade Biológica. Article 2. http://www.planalto.gov.br/ccivil_03/decreto/1998/anexos/and2519-98.pdf.

"genetic resources, organisms or parts of them, populations or any other biotic component of ecosystems with use or potential value for humanity."[52]

The protection of biodiversity is urgent, as it is essential for humanity, which vitally needs biological resources; hence, it was safeguarded in Goals 14 and 15 of the 2030 Agenda for Sustainable Development:

> Goal 14. Conserve and promote sustainably use of the oceans, seas and marine resources for sustainable development;
> Goal 15. Protect, restore and promote sustainable use of terrestrial ecosystems, sustainably manage forests, combat desertification, halt and reverse land degradation and halt biodiversity loss.[53]

1.3 The Anthropogenic Mark of Eutrophication

Eutrophication is compromising the health of lakes and watersheds worldwide. Song Toan Pham Phu warns about the risks of eutrophication caused by the presence of nitrogen and phosphorus from industrial waste in lakes and rivers of developing countries around the world. He clarifies that eutrophication is a natural phenomenon that has been happening for thousands of years; however, its speed and intensity have increased in recent decades due to human activity. The accumulation of nitrogen and phosphorus in lakes and rivers triggers the uncontrolled growth of algae, which deteriorates water quality, creating hypoxic zones with the loss of fish and stationary living beings that inhabit lakes and seas. The author explains that the biochemical basis of the eutrophication process lies in the photochemical reaction that increases the biomass of phytoplankton, whose decomposition causes the destruction of aquatic ecosystems.[54] This occurs because the dying algae are decomposed by bacteria, a process that consumes the oxygen dissolved in the water, necessary for the life of fish and other living beings, and thus the water becomes hypoxic, creating a dead zone.[55]

Lisa Borre argues that the proliferation of harmful algae is a global problem, considering that climate change has made lakes warmer, triggering the increase of cyanobacteria. She cites, as an example, Lake Winnipeg in Canada, which was declared the most threatened lake in the world in 2012 because of the proliferation of toxic algae. Similarly, Lake Zurich in Switzerland and Lake Taihu in China are compromised by the rampant increase of cyanobacteria.

---

[52] Convenção sobre Diversidade Biológica. Article 2. http://www.planalto.gov.br/ccivil_03/decreto/1998/anexos/and2519-98.pdf.

[53] Agenda 2030 Platform. Available at http://www.agenda2030.org.br/os_ods/.

[54] Pham Phu (2014), p. 178.

[55] United States Geological Survey (USGS). Available at https://www.usgs.gov/mission-areas/water-resources/science/nutrients-and-eutrophication?qt-science_center_objects=0#qt-science_center_objects.

She reports that a study promoted by the National Science Foundation of the United States in 2011, on the phenomenon of eutrophication in The Great Lakes, concluded that the main cause of massive algal proliferation is:

> [...] the confluence of long-term trends in nutrient management practices on farms and a changing climate, including more frequent extreme precipitation events [...]. This means that, unless something is done to reduce nutrient inputs from agriculture and other obvious sources or to halt the ongoing climate changes, the proliferation of harmful algae will likely become more common in the future.[56]

Eutrophication is usually caused by cyanobacteria, which are the only known freshwater algae currently capable of producing toxins potent enough to harm human health on a global scale. They can also cause economic damage, including loss of tourism revenue, decreased property values, and increased costs of treating drinking water.

In the United States, the proliferation of toxic cyanobacterial algae in water has been linked to diseases and deaths in humans and animals in at least 43 states. In August 2016, approximately 19 states received guidance from the country's public health system regarding cyanobacterial harmful algal blooms.[57]

Another example of the deleterious effects of eutrophication caused by high loads of nitrogen and phosphorus in rivers is the excessive volume of these nutrients in the Mississippi–Atchafalaya Basin, which causes a hypoxic zone in the Gulf of Mexico—an area where oxygen levels drop to very low levels, reaching less than 2 ml per liter of water. This low-oxygen condition causes fish to abandon the area and poses a high risk to the life of stationary organisms living in the deep waters of the Gulf. According to research from the Louisiana University Marine Consortium, the flow of the Mississippi and Atchafalaya rivers in May 2020 was 30% above the average for the period from 1980 to 2018.[58] This increased flow carried 136,000 metric tons of nitrate to the Gulf in May 2020, which was 2% above the average for the period from 1980 to 2018.

The environmental problems caused by the eutrophication of lakes are also among the most concerning in China. Rapid economic growth, large-scale urbanization in recent decades, and increasing demand for meat production have led to a large release of nitrogen- and phosphorus-rich nutrients into Chinese rivers, which carry these nutrients to the lakes. Lake Taihu, one of the three largest lakes in China, is located in a highly industrialized region and has been suffering from an acute and growing process of eutrophication since 1987. In 2007, the proliferation of toxic algae in Lake Taihu reached intolerable levels, leading to the interruption of the drinking water supply to the population of Wuxi. Many attempts to clean Lake Taihu have been made, including mechanical removal of algae,

---

[56] Borre (2013).

[57] United States Geological Survey (USGS). https://www.usgs.gov/mission-areas/water-resources/science/nutrients-and-eutrophication?qt-science_center_objects=0#qt-science_center_objects.

[58] United States Geological Survey (USGS). https://nrtwq.usgs.gov/mississippi_loads/#/GULF_PRELIM.

washing with Yangtze water, and wetland restoration, but nothing has been effective.[59] Mengru Wang et al. point out that the cause of eutrophication is the constant river transport of nitrogen and phosphorus to the lake. These nutrients originate from synthetic and organic fertilizers and sewage waste. In 2012 alone, 61,000 tons of nitrogen were dumped into Lake Taihu. The authors argue that only external control, such as reducing the use of fertilizers in the region and improving sewage treatment, could effectively reduce eutrophication in Lake Taihu.

1.4 The Anthropogenic Mark of Desertification and Its Impact on People's Food Security

Lívia Campello asserts that the phenomenon of desertification cannot be reduced to just a meteorological or environmental problem, as it is "a disruption of the balance between the environment and the human exploitation system, caused by a climatic, socioeconomic, and environmental crisis that, in turn, triggers a new degradation process, making it difficult or impossible to conserve the soil, essential for sustainable development."[60]

In this regard, Haktanir, Karaca, and Omar studied the desertification of an area of 1,423,232 km^2, located between Asia, Europe, and Africa, in the territories of Turkey, Lebanon, Syria, and Iraq. They report that the planet loses an area of more than six million hectares annually due to desertification processes. This is a serious problem for the planet's food security, considering that, according to the authors, the minimum arable area needed to feed a person is 70 m^2. Thus, considering the average increase in the human population, even without the loss of arable land due to desertification, the planet would already be experiencing an increase in the risk of food insecurity in the coming decades.[61]

Haktanir, Karaca, and Omar point out several aggravating factors of desertification in the Tigris and Euphrates Basin region, including the climatic limitations resulting from global warming, extensive clearing of natural vegetation, loss of biodiversity, excessive pastures, expansion of agriculture over natural habitats, inadequate irrigation techniques, soil salinization, water and wind erosion, all compounded by the population increase in Iraq, Syria, and Turkey, whose demographic growth could reach 50% by 2025. They highlight that global warming has heightened tension in this area, leading to increased evaporation. This situation is particularly serious in the Mesopotamia Basin, as the region receives only 150 to 300 mm of annual rainfall and suffers severe moisture loss, with evaporation rates ranging from 1500 to 2500 mm per year. In addition to water scarcity, sandstorms exacerbate soil erosion. In Turkey, 73% of cultivated lands are prone to erosion.

[59] Wang et al. (2019), p. 866.

[60] Campello (2006), p. 22.

[61] Haktanir et al. (2004), p. 140.

Another critical issue is soil salinization, with 61% of agricultural lands in Iraq threatened by salinity. In Turkey, approximately 109,124 km^2 are already deserts, and about 374,441 km^2 are at risk of desertification. These areas are likely to become uninhabitable, as sandstorms not only cause respiratory diseases but also render economic activities, particularly agriculture, unfeasible by impairing the physiological functions of plants during pollination and inflorescence. The cost of soil degradation in Syria already accounts for 12% of the country's value.[62]

Levi J. Cramer emphasizes that, among the reasons for the conflict in Syria, in addition to popular dissatisfaction with the Bashar al-Assad regime, the negative impacts of climate change on the planet, which have severely punished that region with huge losses in food production,[63] should also be considered.

Cramer reports that, between 1961 and 1990, there was a drop in precipitation of 11% in winter and 8% in spring, and, according to forecasts, it is estimated that this decrease in rainfall will worsen by approximately 22% between 2070 and 2099, with an average annual temperature increase of 4°C. In some regions of Syria, the situation is very serious, with a decrease of 50% in rainfall in the period from 2007 to 2008, which has severely compromised food production in the region.

This decrease in rainfall caused long droughts, contributed to the increase in desertification areas, and, in return, there was a population increase of 50%. This led to greater pressure for agricultural production. Land cultivation, lacking techniques, has increased water erosion, which also contributes to desertification.

The scarcity in agricultural production in Syria raised food prices and caused widespread hunger. The drought affected 1.3 million people, and 160 villages were abandoned. These hungry and outraged people, who migrated to larger cities, mainly to Damascus, were co-opted by the rebels; their dissatisfaction and suffering were another factor against the Assad regime, and they swelled the ranks of the rebel movement.

Joel Jay Kassiola and Sujian Guo, when addressing the environmental crisis in China,[64] dedicate a chapter of their work to the issue of desertification in dry lands. The authors emphasize that the degradation of rural lands in the dry areas of eastern China is a significant problem for the planet, as the dust blown from the degraded dry areas affects not only China but also several countries in East Asia and the western side of North America.

These dry rural areas in Northern China receive less than 380 mm of precipitation annually, are characterized by sparse vegetation, formed by pastures, dry shrubs, and deserts, and extend over one-third of the Chinese territory. This means that in China, there are 3.32 million km^2 of dry lands, of which 2.64 million km^2, or 79% of these lands, are affected by desertification. The area of soil degradation due to desertification has already encompassed 27.5% of the Chinese territory, threatening the livelihood of 400 million people.

---

[62] Haktanir et al. (2004), p. 140.

[63] Cramer (n.d.).

[64] Kassiola and Guo (2010).

Kassiola and Guo report that, since 1949, the annual area of desertification has been increasing from 1650 km^2, between 1950 and 1970 to 2100 km^2 in the 1980s, 2460 km^2 in the 1990s, and, at the turn of the twenty-first century, annual desertification rose to 3463 km^2.

Due to this scenario of desertification, thousands of people were deprived of their livelihoods, forcing an exodus from the affected regions. More than 700,000 people from the desertified regions of China were relocated to other areas.

For Kassiola and Guo, the predominant cause of the desertification process in China's dry lands is excessive human activity, inappropriate soil cultivation, overgrazing, uncontrolled firewood collection, misuse of water, and increasing industrialization. Only 5.5% of desertification results from wind erosion of dune sands.

1.5 The Anthropogenic Mark on South America's "Green Ocean"

In 2014, Antônio Donato Nobre produced a report on the role of the Amazon Rainforest in the Earth's climate system, highlighting the serious, harmful effects of deforestation, as well as the measures that could be adopted to prevent the climate collapse resulting from uncontrolled deforestation.

In this work, Nobre points out that the Amazon Rainforest has stood firm for tens of millions of years, overcoming natural events such as volcanism, glaciations, meteors, and geophysical cataclysms that shook the planet. However, in the last 50 years, like the Greek warrior Achilles, it has had its vulnerable point discovered and hit, and is already staggering, weakened:

> The enemy's arrow is the chainsaw, the chain, the fire, the smoke, the soot, and other human-origin factors, which arose from the wrong, uncontrolled, and terrible use of the inventions of the Anthropocene, the new era in which humanity has become a geological force capable of changing the face of the planet.[65]

The author explains how the Amazon Rainforest is important for the climatic and pluviometric stability not only of Brazil but also of other South American countries. Nobre reveals in the report that, in research conducted with Adriana Cuartas[66] in 2007, using forest evaporation data collected at the LBA project's flux towers, they arrived at an estimate of the amount of water that flows daily from the soil to the atmosphere through the trees. The calculation they made for the total amount of water transported by the xylems in the tree trunks from the soil to the troposphere, in an area of 5.5 million km^2, which corresponds to the forest that covers the Amazon Basin, totals an incredible 20 billion tons per day. This amount of water would be 25 billion tons if the forest still existed in its pristine state of

[65] Nobre (2014), p. 25.

[66] Nobre (2014), p. 13.

1500. The author compares this volume of water with the flow of 17 billion tons gushed daily by the Amazon River into the Atlantic to highlight the magnitude of the work that trees provide to the Earth system. A single tree can pump more than a thousand liters per day.

Nobre explains that the deep roots of the trees draw water from the soil and pump it up 40 and even 60 m in pipelines in the xylems of the trunks. Upon reaching the leaves, this water passes through laminar structures, which function as chemical solar panels that absorb the energy of the sun and the touch of the winds, and then vaporize the water into the atmosphere. In this process of transferring water from the soil to the atmosphere by transpiration, there is an absorption of heat on the surface, so that plants interfere with rains, winds, and climate.

According to Nobre, pumping this colossal amount of water into the atmosphere is just the first part of the work necessary to produce rain, considering that the nucleation of clouds over the forest is still necessary to generate rain. He explains that clouds are clusters of small droplets that condense from vapor, and that for this condensation to occur, besides low temperatures, a solid or liquid surface is still needed to act as a "seed," where the vapor molecules will be deposited. This role is played by atmospheric aerosols: dust particles, pollen grains, salt, and soot. It happens that in the troposphere above the Amazon Rainforest, the concentration of these aerosols is very low. So, there was a certain mystery around how the nucleation of the abundant amount of rain in the region happened.

He reports that in research on gas exchange carried out within the LBA project, scientists from INPA, USP, Holland, Germany, and Italy discovered the gases that are expelled by the aromas of the forest: biogenic volatile organic compounds, the BVOCs. These volatile compounds are sprayed by the leaves and spread through the atmosphere above the forest, where they mix with the humid atmosphere and, under solar radiation, oxidize and precipitate, constituting a very fine dust that serves as the necessary surface for the formation of the condensation nuclei of the generous rains that fall on the forest:

> Poetically speaking, this is the pixie dust that magically appears in the air, loaded with vapor, and triggers the heavy rains from the low clouds, the sprinklers of the Garden of Eden. While the BVOCs are in the form of gas, dissolved in the air, the rain does not wash them away. Only when they oxidize and precipitate as aerosols forming the rains, are they washed away. But there are always more BVOCs waiting to form more pixie dust for the next rain.[67]

This process of transpiration and condensation, mediated by trees, changes the pressure of the atmosphere and draws moisture from the Atlantic Ocean to the interior of the continent. The high condensation of vapor in the atmosphere above the forest causes a reduction in atmospheric pressure, which acts as a vacuum for the winds of the ocean trade current—winds that are loaded with moisture and bring more rain to the Amazon. If the forest continues to be deforested, there will be a reduction in evaporation on the continent, so that evaporation in the Atlantic

---

[67] Nobre (2014), p. 15.

Ocean will be greater, which will cause a reversal of the flow. The moist winds will leave the land for the sea, a process that will be deleterious not only for the Amazon region, which will enter a cycle of droughts with the risk of desertification, but also for South America.

Even during the last great drought in the Amazon in 2005, the forest maintained the active rhythm of tree transpiration, as observed by Nobre: "During the peak of the 2005 drought, the hardest hit parts of the Amazon were the ones that 'greened' the most, that is, in the area where it rained less (as recorded by the TRMM satellite) more new leaves sprouted in the tree canopies (as seen by the MODIS sensor on the Earth satellite)."[68]

This resistance of the trees during the 2005 drought occurred because they accessed, with their deep roots, the groundwater and managed to pump, through the xylems of their trunks, the water that maintained transpiration on the surface, along with the condensation of clouds. Thus, even during the period of drought, the forest functioned as a "biotic pump," sucking in the moist air from the neighboring ocean.

In discussing the relevance of the Amazon Forest for the climatic stability of South America, Nobre emphasizes that 70% of the continent's GDP is in the quadrilateral delimited by Cuiabá to the north, São Paulo to the east, Buenos Aires to the south, and the Andes Mountains to the west. He cites the study by José Marengo[69] and his collaborators on the circulation of the trade winds, which are sucked into the Amazon, loaded with moisture from the equatorial Atlantic, and circulate over the Amazon Forest to the Andes Mountains. These moist air currents encounter the 6 km-high barrier formed by the Andes, making a turn in Acre and bringing a large amount of moist air to the richest quadrilateral in South America during the summer. Nobre points out in his report "that the Amazon is indeed the headwaters of the air springs of most of the rain in South America."[70]

Thus, according to the theory of the biotic pump, considering that the precipitation in the Amazon is due to the transpiration capacity of the trees, the elimination of this exuberant and millennial vegetation could lead to the total cessation of the "biotic pumping," which means to say that the moist equatorial air would no longer be pulled from the ocean to the continent. On the contrary, there would be a reversal in the direction of the flow, because when the condensation becomes greater in the ocean, there will be suction of the moist air from the continent, creating a zone of aridity in the Amazon region and a great impact on the level of rainfall, which could even cease completely.[71]

According to data from the PRODES project of INPE, the total accumulated deforestation (clear-cut) in 2019 reached 796,000 km^2, which is 19.9%.[72] However,

[68] Nobre (2014), p. 17.

[69] Nobre (2014), p. 18.

[70] Nobre (2014), p. 19.

[71] Nobre (2014), pp. 21–22.

[72] National Institute for Space Research. http://www.obt.inpe.br/OBT/assuntos/programas/amazonia/prodes/pdfs/2020_03_SistMonitINPE_English.pdf. Accessed 25 May 2025.

to analyze the devastation of the Amazon Forest with greater realism, it is important to take into account that the PRODES system only records clear-cut deforestation, without indicating other aspects of degradation. Nobre cites a report that documented research conducted within INPE in 2008,[73] whose objective was the complementarity of the operational systems PRODES and DETER. This study highlights the difference between deforestation, clear-cut, and areas in the process of deforestation due to progressive forest degradation. It also explains that the PRODES system has only measured annual clear-cut rates since 1988. Clear-cut is understood as "the process in which the forest cover is completely removed in a short interval of time." DETER also detects areas in the process of deforestation due to progressive forest degradation and explains that "this process in the Amazon usually involves selective logging and frequent burning, leading to the gradual loss of the forest system and its ecological functions. This process has not been fully mapped by PRODES, but only in its final stage, when the complete removal of the forest occurs."[74]

Thus, these data, collected in the PRODES project of INPE, which point out the total accumulated deforestation (clear-cut) in 2019 at the level of 796,000 km^2, that is, 19.9%, refer only to clear-cutting and do not reflect the actual degradation.[75]

Deforestation through forest degradation is progressive, slower, and harder to detect by satellite. It occurs as follows: First, the most valuable timber is removed, then the wood intended for construction, and finally, the lighter trees are harvested for the production of plywood and boards. This process can take several years, as the exploitation is done in phases by different companies specialized in each phase. In the end, the undergrowth is removed, and a few more robust trees are left, such as chestnut and palm trees with no commercial value. This remnant makes it difficult to detect deforestation by satellite; however, in these areas, approximately "50% of the canopy (tallest trees)"[76] has already been eliminated. At this stage, grass is already being sown, and after a year, cattle are already placed in the forest. In the second year, the grass is burned, and the second cleaning occurs, leaving only about 10–20% of the canopy. A large number of dead trees remain standing. In the third year, another burning is done, which definitively destroys the part of the forest that was trying to resist. This entire degradation process takes approximately three years and is not detected by the PRODES system.

Nobre emphasizes that a pioneering study on degradation found in the state of Mato Grosso, from 2007 to 2010, "only" 7856 km^2 with clear-cutting, but another 32,926 km^2 of degraded forests, and also that in this:

> [. . .] same period, INPE mapped 64,205 km^2 of degraded forest versus 39,026 km^2 of clear-cutting for the Brazilian Amazon. Using the ratio between these areas, one can extrapolate the area of degraded forest for the entire Brazilian Amazon. In the estimate,

---

[73] National Institute for Space Research (2008).

[74] National Institute for Space Research (2008), pp. 15–16.

[75] National Institute for Space Research (2008).

[76] National Institute for Space Research (2008), p. 39.

> by 2013 the total degraded area may have reached 1,255,100 km^2. Adding to the measured area of clear-cutting, the cumulative impact on the biome by human occupation may have reached 2,018,079 km^2.[77]

This acute removal of the forest, whether by clear-cutting or by continuous degradation, deeply compromises the functioning of the "biotic pump," reducing its ability to import humid air to the region. In addition, smoke and soot harm cloud nucleation, as they only create polluted and sterile clouds that do not generate rain.[78]

He warns that we are close to the point of no return, that is, the chain reaction where the forest system, in absolute and uncontrolled imbalance, will seek another state of equilibrium: the savanna and desertification. Nobre refers to a study in which the hypothesis of the savannization of the Amazon was considered[79] and further asserts that:

> According to this study, there would be two possible states of equilibrium for vegetation in the Amazon. One corresponding to the current distribution of vegetation, where the tropical forest covers most of the basin, and another with the tropical forest in the East of the Amazon being replaced by savanna. With progressive drying, the introduction of fire, and large-scale modification of the forest, the savanna would be favored by the new climatic equilibrium, to the detriment of the forest. In the second state of equilibrium, even remaining areas of non-deforested forests would disappear as such, turning into savannas.[80]

However, there is still a more terrifying hypothesis: with the complete debilitation of the "biotic pump," there could be a 100% reduction in rainfall in the Amazon, leading to desertification and the elimination of any human activity in the region. This chaotic scenario would influence areas beyond the Amazon region.

And outside the Amazon? Since most of the water that irrigates the productive granary in the quadrilateral of South America comes from the Amazon forests, the future climate of the continent could dry up considerably, ultimately resembling the present-day climate of Australia: a vast interior desert, surrounded on one side by fringes of humid areas near the sea.[81]

As can be seen, the savannization or desertification of the Amazon will compromise climate stability in much of Brazil. Nobre points out that the rain falling in the Southeast, South, and Central-West of Brazil, in Paraguay, and in Argentina is formed by the Amazonian "biotic pump." Thus, the loss of this biotic treasure that brings humid currents to the interior of the continent will also bring economic and social ruin to a large part of South America.

This process of disintegration of natural ecosystems on cataclysmic scales reaches its most critical phase with the triggering of a major zoonotic pandemic. The ecological imbalance collapsed the so-called virosphere, considering that

[77] Nobre (2014), pp. 23–24.

[78] Nobre (2014), p. 26.

[79] Nobre (2014), p. 27.

[80] Nobre (2014), p. 27.

[81] Nobre (2014), p. 27.

viruses are losing their millennial natural hosts and are increasingly approaching urban centers in a dangerous process of migration to the human body.[82] The great anthropogenic crisis previously described, in 2020, directly affected humanity with the uncontrollable COVID-19 pandemic, which, as of the time we wrote this paragraph (12.06.2021), according to official data, has already claimed 14.9 million human lives.[83,84]

Updated data from the Ministry of Environment and Climate Change of Brazil report that the consolidated deforestation rate in the Amazon in 2022/2023 is 9064 km^2. This shows a significant decrease in deforestation in the Amazon, according to data from the PRODES system, from the National Institute for Space Research (INPE). The number represents a decrease of 21.8% compared to the 2022 rate, from August 2021 to July 2022 (11,594 km^2).[85] INPE also released the deforestation data for the Pantanal, presenting a consolidated area of 723 km^2 for the two member states[86] located in the biome, from August 2022 to July 2023. This number represents a decrease of 9.2% compared to the 2022 rate (August 2021–July 2022).

Despite a decrease in deforestation in the Amazon and the Brazilian Pantanal, the numbers still do not inspire optimism because the speed of climate change requires a zero-deforestation stance to avoid the point of no return that will lead to the savannization and desertification of extensive areas of the North and Central-West regions of Brazil.

The remediation of the damages caused by the chaos of the Anthropocene has become an urgency for the salvation of the human species itself, and any attempt in this direction must start with a review of the way humans conceive knowledge, being, and their relationship with nature, so the next chapters of this work will be dedicated to Ontology and Ethics.

References

Alley R (2012) The carbon control knob. Island Press, Washington DC. (The National Climate Seminar 4) Ebook

Bonneuil C (2015) The geological turn: narratives of the Anthropocene. In: Hamilton C, Bonneuil C, Gemenne F (eds). The Anthropocene and the global environmental crisis: rethinking in a new epoch, Routledge, New York. Ebook

[82] Campello et al. (2020).

[83] Organização Panamericana da Saúde. https://www.paho.org/pt/noticias/5-5-2022-excesso-mortalidade-associado-pandemia-covid-19-foi-149-milhoes-em-2020-e-2021.

[84] CNN Brazil. https://www.cnnbrasil.com.br/saude/2021/05/08/mortes-por-covid-19-no-mundo-podem-ser-o-dobro-do-estimado-segundo-estudo.

[85] Gov.br. https://www.gov.br/mma/pt-br/assuntos/noticias/taxa-consolidada-de-desmatamento-na-amazonia-em-2022-2023-e-de-9-064-km2 . Accessed 16 March 2025.

[86] Mato Grosso do Sul and Mato Grosso.

Borre L (2013 abr 24) Harmful algae blooms play Lake Erie again. National Geographic. http://voices.nationalgeographic.com/2013/04/24/harmful-algae-blooms-plague-lake-erie-again/. Accessed 10 June 2025

Campello LGB, Oliveira AFd, Amaral RDd (2020) O direito fundamental à saúde na intersecção da crise ambiental com a pandemia da COVID-19. Revista Jurídica, Curitiba, PR, Unicuritiba 5(62):596–634 http://revista.unicuritiba.edu.br/index.php/RevJur/article/view/4989/371373121. Accessed 10 June 2025

Campello LGB (2006) Desertificação, governança e sustentabilidade. Dissertação (Mestrado) – Faculdade de Direito de Campos, Campos dos Goytacazes, RJ. http://www.livrosgratis.com.br. Accessed 10 June 2025

CCD Steering Committee 20 jun (2007) Colony Collapse Disorder Action Plan. https://www.ars.usda.gov/is/br/ccd/ccd_actionplan.pdf. Accessed 10 June 2025

CNN Brasil (2021) Mortes por Covid-19 no mundo podem ser o dobro do estimado, segundo estudo. https://www.cnnbrasil.com.br/saude/2021/05/08/mortes-por-covid-19-no-mundo-podem-ser-o-dobro-do-estimado-segundo-estudo. Accessed 10 June 2025

Cramer LJ (s.d.) The effects of climate change on the syrian uprising. In: Clark KA, Shaul TR, Lower BH (eds) Environmental science bites, Ohio State University, Columbus, OH. Available on https://ohiostate.pressbooks.pub/sciencebites/. Accessed 10 June 2025

Crutzen PJ, Stoermer EF (2000) The Anthropocene. Global change newsletter, the international geosphere-biosphere programme (IGBP). Stockholm 40:17. http://www.igbp.net/download/18.316f18321323470177580001401/1376383088452/NL41.pdf. Accessed 10 June 2025

Davison N (30 de maio 2019) The Anthropocene epoch: have we entered a new phase of planetary history? The Guardian. https://www.theguardian.com/environment/2019/may/30/anthropocene-epoch-have-we-entered-a-new-phase-of-planetary-history. Accessed 10 June 2025

Degrowith. (2025) https://www.degrowth.info/en/what-is-degrowth/. Accessed 10 June 2025

Gov.br Convenção sobre Diversidade Biológica. (2025) http://www.planalto.gov.br/ccivil_03/decreto/1998/anexos/and2519-98.pdf. Accessed 10 June 2025

Gov.br Taxa consolidada de desmatamento na Amazônia em 2022-2023 é de 9.064km^2. https://www.gov.br/mma/pt-br/assuntos/noticias/taxa-consolidada-de-desmatamento-na-amazonia-em-2022-2023-e-de-9-064-km2. Accessed 10 June 2025

Haktanir K, Karaca A, Omar SM (2004) The prospects of the impact of desertification on Turkey, Lebanon, Syria and Iraq. In: Marquina A (ed) Environmental challenges in the Mediterranean 2000–2050, Springer, Dordrecht

Hamilton C (2015) Human destiny in the Anthropocene. In: Hamilton C, Bonneuil C, Gemenne F (Eds) The Anthropocene and the global environmental crisis: rethinking in a new epoch, Routledge, New York, Ebook

Instituto Nacional de Pesquisas Espaciais (2008) Monitoramento da cobertura florestal da Amazônia por satélites. http://mtc-m16c.sid.inpe.br/col/sid.inpe.br/mtc-m18@80/2008/04.28.13.43/doc/Relatorio.pdf. Accessed 10 June 2025

Instituto Nacional de Pesquisas Espaciais. Advances and perspectives of the monitoring system of INPE. http://www.obt.inpe.br/OBT/assuntos/programas/amazonia/prodes/pdfs/2020_03_SistMonitINPE_English.pdf. Accessed 10 June 2025

Kassiola JJ, Guo S (Eds) (2010) China's environmental crisis: domestic and global political impacts and responses. Palgrave MacMillan, New York

Khoiyangban RS, Gupta N (Eds) (2012) Introduction to environmental sciences. TERI, New Delhi. Ebook

Kurz W (2011) Sinks and sources: the role of forests in carbon sequestration and why it matters. In: FORESTS at risk: climate change and the future of the American West, ACES, Aspen, CO. https://islandpress.org/resources/9781610914246_optimized.pdf. Accessed 10 June 2025

National Research Council (2007) Status of pollinators in North America. The National Academies Press, Washington, DC. https://doi.org/10.17226/11761. Accessed 10 June 2025

Nobre AD (2014) O futuro climático da Amazônia: relatório de avaliação científica. São José dos. ARA;CCST-INPE;INPA, Campos, SP. http://www.ccst.inpe.br/o-futuro-climatico-da-amazonia-relatorio-de-avaliacao-cientifica-antonio-donato-nobre/. Accessed 10 June 2025

OCDE (2020). Environment at a glance. OECD Publishing, Paris. http://www.oecd.org/env/environment-at-a-glance-19964064.htm/. Accessed 10 June 2025

Organização Panamericana da Saúde (2025) https://www.paho.org/pt/noticias/5-5-2022-excesso-mortalidade-associado-pandemia-covid-19-foi-149-milhoes-em-2020-e-2021. Accessed 16 June 2025

Pham Phu, ST (2014) Research on the correlation between chlorophyll-a and organic matter BOD, COD, phosphorus, and total nitrogen in stagnant lake basins. In: Kaneko N, Yoshiura S, Kobayashi M (eds) Sustainable living with environmental risks, Springer, Tokyo. Available on https://scholar.google.com/citations?user=A8z7zAkAAAAJ&hl=en. Accessed 10 June 2025

Plataforma Agenda (2030). http://www.agenda2030.org.br/os_ods/. Accessed 10 June 2025

Six D (2011) Climate, forests and insects: from Montana whitebark pine to South African e*uphobia*. In: FORESTS at risk: climate change and the future of the American West, ACES, Aspen, CO. https://islandpress.org/resources/9781610914246_optimized.pdf. Accessed 10 June 2025

Sulainis BL (s.d.) Warming oceans cause coral reef bleaching. In: Clark KA, Shaul TR, Lower BH (eds) Environmental science bites, Ohio State University, Columbus. https://ohiostate.pressbooks.pub/sciencebites/. Accessed 10 June 2025

United States Geological Survey (USGS) Nutrients and eutrophication (2025). Available on https://www.usgs.gov/mission-areas/water-resources/science/nutrients-and-eutrophication?qt-science_center_objects=0#qt-science_center_objects. Accessed 10 June 2025

United States Geological Survey (USGS) Water-quality loading to the Gulf of Mexico from October 2019 to May 2020 (Preliminary). https://nrtwq.usgs.gov/mississippi_loads/#/GULF_PRELIM. Accessed 10 June 2025

Wang M, et al (2019) Excess nutrient loads to Lake Taihu: opportunities for nutrient reduction. Sci Total Environ 664. https://www.sciencedirect.com/journal/science-of-the-total-environment/vol/664/suppl/C. Accessed 10 June 2025

Waters CN, et al (2016 Jan 8) The Anthropocene is functionally and stratigraphically distinct from the Holocene. Sci 351(6269):aad2622http://science.sciencemag.org/content/351/6269/aad2622. Accessed 10 June 2025

Wood AT (s.d.) The mysterious case of colony collapse disorder. In: Clark KA, Shaul TR, Lower BH (eds) Environmental science bites, Ohio State University, Columbus, OH. https://ohiostate.pressbooks.pub/sciencebites/. Accessed 15 June 2025

World Animal Protection Pesca fantasma: o impacto nos animais do Brasil e ao redor do mundo. https://www.worldanimalprotection.org.br/pesca-fantasma. Accessed 15 June 2025

Chapter 2
The Paradigm Shift

The traditional notion of science in Western culture arises to satisfy the human need to know how things are constituted, with the purpose of achieving an ever more comfortable standard of living for the human being. To know reality, on which human existence is based, as it is, and not as one would like it to be, the episteme emerged as an understanding of reality from the data it provides; therefore, it is different from the concept of doxa, that is, mere opinion.[1]

The episteme is based on the exercise of reason, which engenders reasoning from the observation of the sensible world—a knowledge that is also critical, as it must be constantly revised. In this sense, for Thomas Kuhn, the sciences are based on a disciplinary matrix, which he named paradigm, that is, a structure shared by the natural and physical sciences of a certain era.[2] Suze Piza observes that the concept of paradigm is polysemic and was already used before Kuhn's work, but, influenced by this author, it became known and current in contemporary epistemological discourse as the meaning of disciplinary matrix.[3]

In this line, paradigm can be understood as a structure shared by practitioners of the same discipline and "composed of symbolic generalizations, axioms, definitions, laws, shared values, consensus, models and standards accepted by the scientific community, all the procedures and effects of the procedures that a specific field at a given historical moment is willing to accept."[4]

Kuhn explains that the so-called scientific revolutions can be understood as non-cumulative episodes of development, in which the older paradigm is replaced, totally or partially. He compares this to political revolutions, which occur because a segment of the political community comes to understand that existing institutions

[1] Cupani (2017), pp. 34–35.

[2] Kuhn (2012), p. 51.

[3] Piza (201), p. 170.

[4] Piza (201), p. 170.

R. D. d. Amaral, *The Principle of Harmony with Nature as a Legal Foundation*,
https://doi.org/10.1007/978-3-032-05475-3_2

have ceased to adequately address problems. Similarly, scientific revolutions are triggered because a growing understanding is formed within a specific segment of the scientific community that the prevailing paradigm has ceased to function adequately. Both in the political world and in the scientific one, the evaluation of the malfunctioning of the prevailing paradigm triggers the crisis, which is the prerequisite for the revolution.[5]

Although there is a current understanding that Kuhn's theory of scientific revolutions and paradigm change is restricted to the natural sciences, Suze Piza explains that, like Kuhn, Michel Foucault also defends the idea of the possibility of knowledge production and truth from the notion of what he called "concrete or historical a priori,"[6] that is, each knowledge must be evaluated in its form of constitution by its own truth criteria—that is, the conditions of knowledge of its field and its time. Foucault calls this *epistémê*, while Kuhn calls it a paradigm or disciplinary matrix. Piza explains that Foucault's *epistémê* is "an epistemological soil full of discourses that serve as a reference for the validation of everything that is considered at a given historical moment or in a given way of life: a delimited field."[7]

In this line, the *epistémê,* Foucault's concept, denotes the knowledge of an era, the ground on which this knowledge flourishes, and the fundamental codes of a culture that govern social practices, customs, and traditions. This concept of *epistémê* is crucial to discerning ruptures between ideas and the theory for the birth of new knowledge. This paradigm shift of Kuhn, or Foucault's *epistémê* change, can occur in both natural and physical sciences, as well as in social sciences.

The environmental crisis described in the first chapter is enough to raise reflection on the inadequacy of the anthropocentric and dualistic paradigms, already described, which has dominated all branches of knowledge, including natural and social sciences.

Indeed, to this day, anthropocentrism has triumphed as an understanding that human beings enjoy a special meaning, a privileged and central *status*—a belief that permeates everyday thinking, guiding an attitude toward other animals, toward nature, and in the very relationship with divinity, as the Western human being has forged a God in his likeness. Anthropocentrism in religion has corrupted the very conception of the divine. Spinoza already denounced this human imposture, arguing that God is free from passions and is not affected by any emotion, joy, or sadness.[8] By attributing to God intellect, will, joy, and sadness, the human being has only molded a God in his own image.

Anthropocentrism is deeply rooted in all branches of knowledge. The discipline responsible for knowledge itself, epistemology, has anthropocentric bases. Likewise, metaphysics (ontology) and ethics also flourished on anthropocentric ground.

[5] Kuhn (2012), pp. 180–181.

[6] Piza (201), p. 170.

[7] Piza (201), p. 137.

[8] Spinoza (2014), p. 79.

Epistemology and ontology, even when dealing with language, are centered on the human being, as the only language considered intelligible is human. The ontology forged in the West took on an anti-realist aspect and established an understanding of the world from the human mind, as if this mind created the world itself through language.

This anthropocentric epistemological ground, in whose layers lie the various humanities that have succeeded in the West since the establishment of human reason as the only lens through which it is possible to see the sensible world and convert it into concept, into language, has severely impacted nature, starting with the misconception about a supposed inexhaustibility of the vital energy of the soil, waters, flora, and fauna.

Human groups that economically dominate the planet have already caused irreversible damage to nature, decreeing the extinction of thousands of species of animals and plants. However, the damages are not minor for the human species itself. The voracity for economic development and wealth generation to benefit a small percentage of humans is carried out at the expense of climate changes that can compromise the very existence of humanity.

The ecological imbalance that already compromises the sustainability of the planet, as well as the dignity and well-being of its human and non-human inhabitants, already makes human existence extremely painful in poor and developing countries. However, global warming, ocean acidification, soil impoverishment, scarcity of rainfall, and desertification will make life on Earth inhospitable for all humans, including the restricted club of the very rich.

The anthropocentric paradigm, which supports natural, physical, and social sciences, does not present real and effective means of reversing the environmental crisis to ensure sustainability on the planet, considering that the root of the problem lies in the very essence of anthropocentrism. Thus, in the face of the crisis, a few decades ago, silently, a "scientific revolution"[9] has been engineered, which already permeates various fields of knowledge in search of a broader view, allowing us to see the world beyond the narrow lenses of anthropocentric rational idealism, through the window of the reality of the biosphere where the conditions of life pulsate. In this sense, Leena Vilkka predicts a new enlightenment: "The second enlightenment must be the revolution of nature. This must extend the principle of equality to the non-human world."[10]

The cornerstone of the paradigmatic change in the human being's view of his relationship with nature lies in the value of the natural world for the human being. For the prevalent anthropocentric view, nature has only an instrumental value; it is nothing more than an economic resource useful for human purposes. In this line, the relations between the human being and the nature are merely technical, industrial, commercial, recreational, and esthetic. In anthropocentric horizons, the only being on Earth whose value is intrinsic—that is, valuable in itself—is the

[9] Kuhn (2012), p. 180.

[10] Vilkka (1997), p. 52.

human being itself, a view that is rooted in the symbolic order, which was built either from the revelation of the divine, which would have bequeathed to the human being his own image and likeness, or in the *logos*, as rationality and language.

However, in the twentieth century, slowly, a new conception of the value of nature emerged; thinkers dissonant from anthropocentrism, which until then was almost unquestionable, began to understand that nature has a value that is its own, regardless of its usefulness to human beings. That is, a philosophical and ethical movement was established for the recognition of the intrinsic value of animals, plants, and ecosystems.

Leena Vilkka discusses the three currents that emerge in this sense, establishing, as a methodological criterion of distinction between them, the degree of extension of recognition of the intrinsic value of other non-human beings.

Thus, zoocentrism recognizes the intrinsic value of superior animals, that is, vertebrates—beings that are considered sentient and capable of feeling pain and suffering. This current proposes the ethical consideration, the welfare, and the rights of sentient animals.[11]

Biocentrism, whose etymological root is "*bio*," meaning life in Greek, postulates respect for life, whose meaning is not limited to the biological aspect but includes life in a broader sense, within the social and ethical context. Biocentrism values the flourishing of various forms of life, biodiversity, and individual lives as well. This concept dates back to Bergson's vitalist theory, Albert Schweitzer's ethical conception of life, and James Lovelock's Gaia Hypothesis.[12]

Vilkka enumerates the main ideas of ethical reverence for life in Schweitzer's thought: (1) Life is sacred; (2) all living beings belong to each other; and (3) reverence for life includes real values such as sympathy and love. This biocentric current recognizes intrinsic value and extends ethical consideration to every living being. Thus, Vilkka explains that biocentrism encompasses "ethics being extended to responsibility for everything that has life. If I consider my life an intrinsic value, I understand that other lives will live and have intrinsic value."[13]

Arne Naess and George Sessions, founders of the so-called deep ecology movement, are the precursors of the ethics for life, as they propose ethical consideration and welfare for all forms of life on Earth. They postulate that all forms of life have value in themselves, regardless of their utility to humans. Paul W. Taylor proposes a biocentric theory that focuses on the living individual. It recognizes inherent value and ethical consideration for each individual living organism.[14]

Finally, ecocentrism, whose precursor is Aldo Leopold, assigns intrinsic value also to ecosystems. It is based on the notion of a biotic community and extends

---

[11] Vilkka (1997), p. 39.

[12] Vilkka (1997), p. 58.

[13] Vilkka (1997), p. 60.

[14] Vilkka (1997), pp. 60–62.

ethical consideration not only to living organisms, like animals and plants, but to the Earth, waters, forests, rivers, and mountains.[15]

Before delving deeper into the ecological-philosophical currents that combine to form a new non-anthropocentric paradigm, it is necessary to examine the reflections of this paradigmatic change in various branches of science and, above all, in ecology.

The rational, dualistic, anthropocentric paradigm is giving way to the emergence of new scientific models, which are structured from systems theory. Examples of these new models in the epistemological horizon of the twenty-first century are Ilya Prigogine's new alliance, also called the metamorphosis of science, Fritjof Capra's new physics, Konrad Lorenz's sociobiology, and all the new trends that postulate the end of the dichotomy between natural sciences and social sciences.[16]

Cirne-Lima, when dealing with the themes of causality and self-organization, observes that Ludwig Von Bertalanffy's systems theory, born in the field of biology in 1945, radiated to various branches of science, becoming a general theory of all sciences. The systems theory became the creative womb of Norbert Wiener's cybernetics, Uexküll and Weizsäcker's ecology, Maturana and Varela's neurophysiology of knowledge, Buckley's psychology, Gray, Duhl, and Rizzo's medicine and psychiatry, Prigogine's chemistry, Lee Smolin's physics, and finally, Niklas Luhmann's sociology and law.[17]

The systems theory, born in biology, was the driving force behind the change in the epistemological paradigm consolidated in modernity and will continue to influence human thought in the centuries to come, to the point that physicist Lee Smolin identifies it as a unifying theory, which reconciles quantum mechanics with the theory of relativity.[18] For Cirne-Lima, this most universal general theory, which permeates the natural sciences, also reverberates in philosophy, enabling the development of a general ethical system that encompasses the ecological issue.

Cirne-Lima identifies, in the essence of Bertalanffy's systems theory—which introduced the scientific concept of self-organization—the ancient monist theory of Neoplatonic philosophers: Plotinus, Nicolas Cusanus, Spinoza, Goethe, Schelling, and Hegel. Thus, the great scientific revolution brought about by the concept of self-organizing systems would be an organic continuation of pre-Aristotelian monism, which was developed by the Neoplatonics from the idea of *causa sui*, that is, *self*-causation. Investigating this possibility, Cirne-Lima finds that Bertalanffy dedicates his work, General Systems Theory, to Nicolas Cusanus and Goethe, recognized Neoplatonics. This note of gratitude reinforces the hypothesis of the collaboration of the Neoplatonic monist conception of immanence and *causa sui*—that is, self-causation[19]—in the formulation of Bertalanffy's concept of

---

[15] Vilkka (1997), p. 72.

[16] Santos (2009), p. 40.

[17] Cirne-Lima (2012), p. 153.

[18] Cirne-Lima (2012), p. 153.

[19] *The expression* ***causa sui*** *seems to have been introduced into medieval philosophical literature through Latin translations of Alfarabi. It has also been indicated that it was first used in the 12th*

systematic self-organization. From this point, the Brazilian philosopher Cirne-Lima develops the theory of a general ethics, built on the foundations of Neoplatonic monism, which rescues the concept of self-causation and reconciles it with the idea of contingency and free will. This will be examined in later topics as the foundation of an applied ecological ethics reconciling human beings with nature.[20]

The emergence of these scientific models, gestated by systems theory and corroborated by the revision of the anthropocentric paradigm itself, as well as by the so-called ontological turn proposed in anthropology through Viveiros de Castro's perspectivism and Philippe Descola's[21] metatheory of the four ontologies, opens the way for new ontological horizons and, above all, for a new ethics, which privileges the valorization of the real world, life in its fullness, and the human being as a member of an ecologically balanced earthly community.

Hans Jonas, who is also a follower of philosophical monism, observes that the possibility of considering a value in itself and inherent rights for the biosphere could no longer sound absurd, but this change:

> [...] would require substantial changes in the foundations of ethics. This would mean seeking not only human good, but also the good of extra-human things, that is, expanding the recognition of "ends in themselves" beyond the sphere of the human and including care for these in the concept of human good. No previous ethics (other than religion) prepared us for a role of faithful custodian - and the scientific view of nature, even less.[22]

Jonas continues his explanation about the threats of technique and human action on the vital world, whose silent claims we should attend to as a mandatory requirement sanctioned by natural laws themselves. However, he emphasizes that the adoption of this posture brings a theoretical implication that "would compel us to extend the reflection on the mentioned changes and go beyond the doctrine of action, that is, of ethics, to the doctrine of existence, that is, of metaphysics, in which all ethics must ultimately be founded."[23]

---

century. ***Causa sui*** *was used by Saint Thomas, Suárez, and many scholastic authors, as well as by Descartes and especially by Spinoza. Originally,* ***causa sui*** *did not refer to God (God was rather the* ***principle sui****).* ***Causa sui*** *could apply to man as a free man, indicating that he determined himself freely. However, it was said that nothing is* ***causa sui****, since every being is as it has an origin distinct from itself, that is, it is caused. God was presented as* ***causa sui*** *by Descartes in his proof (which Kant called ontological) of the existence of God. Spinoza began his ethics with the definition of the concept of* ***causa sui****: 'By cause of itself I understand that whose essence involves existence, that is, that whose nature cannot be conceived except as existing'. It can be said that in Descartes and Spinoza there is a positive definition of* ***causa sui****, unlike the medieval scholastic definition, which was rather negative, since it affirmed that a being is causa sui when it has no external cause (external to the being considered).* (Ferrater Mora (2004), p. 432.

[20] Cirne-Lima (2012), pp. 154–155.

[21] The intellectual project of Philipe Descola starts from the study of the humanization of the animal and plant world by indigenous peoples toward the conceptual expansion of nature, as a *continuum*, that integrates humans, animals, and plants. Descola (online).

[22] Jonas (2006), p. 41.

[23] Jonas (2006), p. 42.

Starting from this reflection by Jonas, in the sense that before the doctrine of action—that is, of ethics—one must inquire about the ultimate foundation of everything that exists, the doctrine of existence, metaphysics, or ontology, this work adopts as a premise the understanding that the change of the legal paradigm on which the relationship of the human being with nature is based must have its starting point in human thought itself about existence, about access to "being" and the conditions of life, to, in a second moment, advance on ethics and, finally, open new horizons in the sphere of law.

2.1 The Search for a New Ontological Paradigm of Life as a Starting Point for Overcoming the Environmental Crisis

Considering that this work starts from the premise that the reversal of the environmental crisis involves the ethical and legal revision of the human relationship with nature, it is deemed necessary to examine the new ontologies to re-signify the interaction of the human being with the natural world, and thus propose a new ethos that underpins the legal norms regulating the relationship of the human being with the biosphere.

Hans Jonas observes that the human being, in his first attempts to interpret the nature of things, saw life everywhere and in himself. Existence was permeated by a soul, which was in everything. This is called animism or panvitalism; that is, the world is a living being, and life and being are always in a coextensive relationship.[24] Anthropologist Philippe Descola, in his ethnographic work on the Achuar people, consolidated his theory on animism based on the worldview of these people, for whom animals, plants, and other beings see themselves as human, with a human soul. This attribution of subjectivity—that is, soul or consciousness—to plants, animals, meteorological phenomena, and objects is what is called animism.[25]

This animistic or panvitalistic view persists among some indigenous peoples. At this point, it is appropriate to make a brief digression to tell an illustrative story of what animism is in the worldview of the Krahô people, inhabitants of the state of Tocantins in Brazil. This is the story of the Kàjre hatchet. Among the Krahôs, there is an element of community harmonization, the Kàjre hatchet, which, in the 1940s, was taken by anthropologist Harald Schultz to São Paulo and incorporated into the collection of the Paulista Museum of the University of São Paulo (USP), where it remained for approximately forty years. However, in 1986, the Krahôs discovered that the Kàjre, which they considered missing, was in the said museum. So, they headed in a delegation to São Paulo, where they

[24] Jonas (2004).

[25] Sztutman (2009).

stayed for more than ninety days negotiating with the rectorate of USP so that the hatchet would be returned to them.[26]

For the Krahôs, Kàjre, the hatchet, is a sacred mythological being—a singing being—used in rites of passage. Di Felice and Pereira report that they went to the Pedra Branca Village, where the Kàjre is, on which occasion Martinho, a member of the Krahô people, told them about its meaning for his people. He explained that many years ago, there was a hunter named Hartant, who one day went hunting with other indigenous people. After an unsuccessful journey, they stopped in the forest to rest, when they heard a song. The indigenous people asked Hartant where the song was coming from, and he explained to them that it was Kàjre, the hatchet, which was with its owner and therefore sang. Hartant went to the owner and asked for the hatchet. The owner told him that there were two hatchets: one male and the other female. Hartant had to choose one of them, and he chose the male hatchet. Before leaving, Hartant learned all the songs to continue singing with his hatchet.

As can be seen, for the Krahô people, life permeates everything; even an entity that, for Western rationality, is a mere object, for them, is a being with a soul. There was a time when the ancestors of Western culture were also animists. However, later, matter came to be understood as "non-life," considering that the essence that gave it shape and life only existed in the intellect of the agent. With the advancement of natural sciences in modernity, the human being has been distancing himself from the ontology of life and delving into the "ontology of death."[27] The scientific methodology, based on analysis and measurement, defines a standard of cognizability more suited to deal with dead matter than with life, as living things do not submit to precise mathematical analysis—so much so that the human body only becomes intelligible through the study of the corpse.[28] From the consolidation of modernity, the way Westerners began to access the world is predominantly materialistic: The world is matter, and a dead and empty matter, a view that led humanity to a misunderstanding of life.

Enrique Leff warns that to think of a solution to the current environmental crisis, it is not enough to just measure the dynamics of climate change and its effects; it is necessary to understand how the modes of understanding life and knowledge have mobilized human actions that induce the acceleration of entropy processes. That is, the search for a solution to the environmental crisis begins by thinking about thought itself and the way of accessing the "being" and life.[29]

Leff places the ontology consecrated in the West as the ultimate cause and the origin of the environmental crisis, of the violence practiced against nature, and proposes a new way of thinking about the conditions of life. It is not about thinking constructed only from the truths offered by physical sciences, nor by the truth revealed by phenomenological reduction; the author throws the challenge of

[26] Di Felice and Pereira (2017), pp. 41–48.

[27] Jonas (2004), p. 22.

[28] Jonas (2004), p. 21.

[29] Leff (2018), p. 42.

deconstruction and redefinition of a constellation of concepts and notions about life, whose meanings have been covered up. Indeed, many concepts engendered in modernity were already born covered by an exacerbated idealism, solipsistic and detached from reality, or by the ontology of matter, by scientific reductions, and their technological applications.[30]

Leff proposes the search for a new ontology to investigate that which precedes the "being," that is, life itself, which sustains the "being."[31] in. this task, he returns to the pre-ontological thought of Heraclitus and elects, as his travel companion, the obscure philosopher of Ephesus, Martin Heidegger, the great interpreter of Heraclitus, who, in the 1940s of the twentieth century, delved into the fragments of Heraclitus in search of the doctrine of the *logos* to rescue the fullness of the "being."[32] Leff uses the handrails left by the philosopher of the Black Forest to descend into the depths of the doctrine of the *logos* pre-ontological, but in search of what precedes the very "being": life.[33]

To redefine the relationship between human beings and nature in ethics and law, it is first essential to understand the serious implications of the history of Western metaphysics in relation to the environmental crisis, which, as Leff presents it, is a crisis of the very understanding of the conditions of life. Thus, it becomes necessary to examine and reflect on the pre-ontological thought of Heraclitus of Ephesus, considering that this thinker built a doctrine of being and life before the institution of dualism and anthropocentrism. Leff undertakes this archeological work using the tools provided by Heidegger's existential ontology of "being," but his goal is to go a step beyond Heidegger, aiming to find in Heraclitus the tip of the guiding thread for the reconstruction of an ontology of life and thereby reverse the anthropogenic environmental crisis.[34]

From the philosophical thought of Martin Heidegger, Leff warns that the alienation of metaphysics in modernity did not only cause a forgetting of "being," but it produced, above all, a misunderstanding about the conditions of life on Earth. This alienation regarding life, the biosphere, was established with the very emergence of language, which, granted by the *logos*, by rationality, created our symbolic conceptual world. It was at the moment when the human being felt the need to name beings and the world itself that the reflection about "being" arose. By saying "is" of what presents itself and establishing a differentiation between "being" (what is) and "entity" (what presents itself), the so-called human reason—the *logos*, which also comes to be called *ego* or *cogito*—encoded the human symbolic order as the only possible image of the world.[35]

---

[30] Leff (2018), p. 49.
[31] Leff (2018), p. 59.
[32] Heidegger (2018).
[33] Leff (2018), p. 429.
[34] Leff (2018), p. 51.
[35] Leff (2018), p. 434.

In this encoding of the symbolic order by language, the human being arrogated to define nature as mere matter, placing it in an ancillary position, with mere instrumental value, an inexhaustible resource for the fulfillment of his desire for power. This ontological view is reflected in ethics and, consequently, in law. In the same vein, Di Felice asserts that:

> The phonetic alphabet, written language and much of Western rational thought contributed to the construction of an architecture of thought that created the premises of the contemporary environmental catastrophe, spreading an anthropocentric conception that made it impossible, with very few exceptions, to think of the world beyond man.[36]

In other words, the human being gave meaning to reality according to his rationality, forged a projection of the real world constituted by his language, and within this symbolic order organized knowledge and society with its ethical, political, social, and economic rules. However, this worldview, apprehended by rationality, was already deformed by its will to power and to dominate the natural world. This caricature of reality was formalized by the grammar of language and was elevated to the *status* of epistemology, metaphysics, ethics, esthetics, natural science, politics, and legal science.

This conceptual, theoretical, and representative world, constituted by the *logos*, separated from the real world and deformed by the desire for power, was being created by the language of the various overlapping humanities, which forged our worldview. In Hebrew culture, the creative language was legitimized in the revelation of one God, who created the world itself and bequeathed it to a single species arbitrarily elected as heir and continuator of his creation, considering that this species was created according to the image of the Creator himself. Greek culture instituted the symbolic world, that is, conceptual, legitimizing it in an exalted rationality exclusive to the human being, dissociated from the natural world, and enthroned man as the master of all other beings, the legitimate interpreter of truth by Aristotelian philosophy, which placed him at the apex of the great chain of being.

But does this symbolic, conceptual world, which we instituted by language—whether legitimized in revelation or legitimized in reason—correspond to the real world, to the true "being," and to life itself, which sustains "being"?

Leff points to an abysmal mismatch between the real world and the world conceptually instituted by the *logos*, and attributes this distancing to the alienation of metaphysics and sciences in relation to life, to the fact that scientific rationality has been configured in the objective order of a technique guided only by a human will for the destructive appropriation of nature, which, throughout modernity, has interfered in such an intense way in the real world to the point of being considered an element of alteration of the planet's geological and climatic structure, triggering the current anthropogenic chaos, which we now call Anthropocene.[37]

---

[36] Di Felice (2017), p. 24.

[37] Leff (2018), p. 454.

In this regard, Leff warns that the great challenge for humans is to make a critical review of their own thinking, not only to rediscover the truth of "being," as proposed by Heidegger,[38] but to forge another beginning—a new paradigm that surpasses the very metaphysics that underlies our culture—to decipher and rethink an ontology of life, which "reactivates the power of nature, from the consideration of the principles of thermodynamics, the ecology of life and the existential ontologies of the original peoples that were disregarded in the construction of Western thought."[39]

This invitation from Leff to consider the existential ontologies of the original peoples dialogs with the critique that Boaventura de Sousa Santos makes of the "indolent reason that underlies, in its various forms, the hegemonic, philosophical and scientific knowledge produced in the West over the last two hundred years."[40] Santos, when discussing this lazy reason, observes that it manifests in four different ways: (1) the impotent reason, which is not exercised because it thinks there is nothing it can do; (2) the arrogant reason, whose flaw is not feeling the need to exercise because it sees itself unconditionally free; (3) the metonymic reason, whose flaw is considering itself the only possible reason and, thus, claiming itself as the only form of rationality, so it does not bother to know other forms of rationality; and (4) finally, the proleptic reason, which does not tend to think about the future, as it believes it knows everything about it and conceives it as a constant, linear, automatic, and infinite improvement.

Of all these manifestations of "indolent reason," the metonymic and proleptic forms stand out at this point, considering that these forms of "indolent reason," forged in the consolidation of the liberal state in Europe and the United States, with the industrial revolutions and the development of capitalism, began to organize, preside over, and monopolize the philosophical and epistemological debates of the last two hundred years, delegitimizing all other knowledge or ways of accessing "being" thought by the original peoples of the Southern Hemisphere.[41]

This detachment of Western reason from the existential reality of the ontologies and epistemologies of the peoples of the South, denounced by Boaventura de Sousa Santos, dialogs with the discourse of Enrique Leff, when he points out the need to reconstruct a new ontology, in which the symbolic order of language considers "the negentropic forces of life in which the imaginaries, habits and practices of these peoples, of their ways of existence that redirect the flows of matter and energies on Earth, where the meaning of life is rearticulated."[42]

After making an incursion into the philosophy of Heraclitus of Ephesus to understand how pre-metaphysical Greek man conceived nature and related to it, this work will make a brief incursion into pre-Hispanic Andean thought and

[38] Heidegger (2015).
[39] Leff (2018), P. 56.
[40] Santos (2009), p. 95.
[41] Santos (2009), p. 95.
[42] Leff (2018), p. 56.

"Amerindian perspectivism"[43] to verify what is common between these cosmologies and Greek thought before the dualists Plato and Aristotle. Thus, in this meeting or crossing of cosmological paths, perhaps one can glimpse an ontological horizon that signals the reconciliation of *logos* and myth, of human beings and nature.

2.2 A Return to Nature and to the Logos in Heraclitus of Ephesus in Search of the Fire of Life

Leff proposes, as a path to overcoming the environmental crisis, the investigation and reflection on the difference between nature and reason, drawing from the seminal thought of Heraclitus and Heidegger's meditation in search of the truth of "being," to arrive at a perspective of truth, the reality of life, and its significant aspect. The first step on this path of returning to the genesis of Greek metaphysical thought begins with the following questions: Where is the truth of being? Where is the truth of life? Is this differentiating and emerging power found in reason, as language or human knowledge, or is it inherent in nature itself?

For Leff, the truth of being and life, this differentiating power of everything that exists is not in the human psyche or in rationality; it is a differentiating power that emerges from nature itself, which engenders the reality of life. In other words, the potentiality of "being" and of life emerges from nature, in its real existence, and not from human understanding, based on a conceptual symbolic order arbitrarily granted by language.

It is only possible to understand the triggering of metaphysical events that culminated in the environmental crisis by examining this crisis while taking into account the forgetfulness and misunderstanding of the original conditions of life and their effects on the degradation and entropic death of the planet. For such an endeavor, it is not enough to merely recognize the mismatch between reason and nature, resulting from the disjunction of the theoretical symbolic with the natural world, but it is necessary to think about the serious problems of the Anthropocene resulting from this disconnection, deconstructing "the lie that nestled in reason, which perverted and interrupted the possibility of a technique based on nature, inspired by the way life organizes itself in the facticity of life itself."[44]

In search of an ontology of life, Leff starts from Heidegger's concept of the facticity of life, which aimed to overcome both the mode of access to the experience of Kant's transcendental idealism, as well as the scientific and materialistic mode of knowledge of life that was constituted in the nineteenth century with empiricism. He observes that the understanding of life, in Heidegger's thought, derives directly from the phenomenology of his master, Edmund Husserl, who

[43] Castro (1996), pp. 115–144.

[44] Leff (2018), p. 543.

intended to overcome the Cartesian representative model and Galileo's science to find, in the intentionality of the subject, the most authentic way of apprehending things themselves. However, Heidegger ventured into other horizons, as he reconstructed an ontological foundation different from the Husserlian phenomenological perspective and thus opened his own path, outlining the first categories of his fundamental ontology. In this initial phase, his reflections on the facticity of life, the genesis of the Dasein, emerge. But what is the facticity of life in Heidegger's fundamental ontology, and why does Leff scrutinize it in an attempt to find an ontology of life?[45]

In the philosophical tradition, the term "facticity" was coined by Fichte, as Theodore Kisiel clarifies:

> [. . .] he was not referring to empirical fact or a collection of them, but to the central "fact" of the tradition of modern thought, which starts from Descartes' famous regression to the "fact of I think", understood as the irreducible limit of reflection behind which one cannot question.[46]

Kisiel explains that the Cartesian "fact of I think" became the ground on which all modern philosophy is based. The "fact of I think" is an unquestionable starting point, which is taken as truth by modern philosophers. Thus, it turned into a contingency of the very thinking of modern philosophy, and it is in this sense that the expression "facticity" should be understood in modern philosophy.[47]

Ferrater Mora clarifies that the sense of "fact" for Heidegger is different from the current sense attributed to the term; it is a fact in the "existential" sense, that is, facticity:

> Heidegger distinguishes the facticity of facts in a "normal" and "natural" sense and the facticity of Dasein [. . .] Facticity is a dimension of Dasein as "being-in-the-world", and it is the "fact" of being thrown among things and situations [. . .]. Thus, for example, without facticity, consciousness could choose its connections with the world in such a way that "I could determine to be born bourgeois or as a worker". In other words, what we call "fact" determines the way I will be in the world, but it cannot determine my being.[48]

Leff observes that when Heidegger speaks of the "facticity of life," this life referred to is not yet life itself, natural life, but a factual life—a mere conceptual resource—which is at the base of his ontology of "being," which aims to deconstruct the metaphysical understandings of entities that were proclaimed by previous philosophers:

> The hermeneutics of the facticity of life that Heidegger intends does not inquire into the Being of Life as a pre-ontological order of real life, of the thermodynamic order from which the fabric of the ecosystem that sustains human life emerges, but the order of transitive and intransitive meanings of the verb to live.[49]

[45] Leff (2018), p. 193.

[46] Kisiel (2014), p. 37.

[47] Kisiel (2014), p. 37.

[48] Ferrater Mora (2004), p. 1001.

[49] Leff (2018), p. 195.

The facticity of life in Heidegger is still restricted to the order of language and does not aim to touch life in its concreteness; therefore, despite having advanced to overcome the alienation of "being" characteristic of materialistic scientific empiricism and transcendental idealism, it still limits itself to dealing with "being" only on the plane of language—a "being" that inhabits the symbolic order, which does not touch the biosphere, where the biological dimension of the human being is sustained, making him a brother to all other beings.

Although Heidegger intends to search for the fundamental meaning of "being," which was forgotten by the previous ontology that stopped at the superficiality of "being," Leff notes that Heidegger's "being" is still detached from the conditions of real life. Indeed, Heidegger's main concern was to go beyond the sciences, which are only concerned with beings and their formal concepts but ignore the "being" of entities in its deepest, original sense—that is, "being" as such. However, Heidegger does not touch the organic, biological being; his metaphysics is alienated from the body and the organic world. For Jonas, Heidegger failed to overcome the dualistic tradition.[50]

Thus, faced with the insufficiency of transcendental idealism and the existentialist ontology of Heidegger's "being"[51] in. thinking about life itself in its organic dimension, Leff asks: "Could there be a phenomenological access to the truth of life, about the real of life, about the constitution of metabolism and sustainability of life arising from cosmic order and disorder?"[52]

With the aim of answering this question, Leff returns to the pre-metaphysical Greece of Heraclitus, and he does so still guided by the handrails built by the philosopher of the Black Forest. Perhaps there lies the great legacy of Heidegger for our time, marked by the anthropogenic crisis: his archeological interpretation of Heraclitus' thought before the establishment of the cosmological vision instituted by the rationality of Platonic and Aristotelian ontology.

Leff clarifies that Heidegger distinguished two meanings for the two ways of manifestation of nature: (1) φύσις ὄντα and (2) Τέχνή ὄντα. The second meaning is the form of being of nature seen only as a natural resource to be used by reason, by technique. The first meaning has a broader and more original sense; it is the pre-ontological sense of nature, before human interference—that is, before being touched by thought, by the first principles of the grammar of language, and by the human hand itself. In this sense, Heidegger presents it as the *φύσις* (*physis*) and compares its unveiling with the opening of the vault of heaven, of the stars, of the ocean, and of the Earth—a powerful and ambivalent presence that, despite threatening the human being by the indomitable force of its emergent potency, protects, feeds, sustains, and supports him. This nature is indomitable and prevails by its own will, regardless of the will of the human being.[53]

---

[50] Jonas et al. (1994), pp. 820–821.

[51] Heidegger (2015), pp. 98–99.

[52] Leff (2018), p. 707.

[53] Leff (2018), pp. 264–265.

Leff seeks in Heraclitus the origin of this pre-ontological nature described above, *φύσις*. For the philosopher of Ephesus, this nature, the *physis*, is uncreated and was not shaped by a demiurge, as Plato reports in Timaeus; nor was it created by the Abrahamic God of revelation. It simply exists as an eternal fire, as reported by Heraclitus: "This **Κόσμος**[54] is always the same through everything, and neither a god nor a human being created it, on the contrary, this **φμσις**[55] always was, always is and always will be an eternally incandescent fire, burning and extinguishing according to its measure."[56]

Leff considers that in Heraclitus' thought are the answers, not only for the ontological differences between the "being" and the "entity," as Heidegger thought, but also to explain how the disjunction between the real world of nature, *φύσις*, and the theoretical symbolic world created by *λόγος*, the reason, with the respective unfoldings of this original dichotomy, led humanity to the ontology of technique, in which nature began to be seen objectively, only as matter in motion, mere natural resource managed by economic rationality.[57]

This objectification of nature by the rationality of the technical order "interfered not only in the meaning of human life, in the right of the original peoples to live according to their own ontologies, their worldviews, it also interfered in the metabolism of the planetary biosphere."[58]

Nature, in its pre-ontological conception, at the dawn of Western thought, as glimpsed in the philosophy of Heraclitus, emerges as the fire of life:

> [. . .] it is not a being illuminated by an external light, human reason; on the contrary, physis emerges as Light itself. In this view, φμσις not only generates the density of beings that are unveiled by light and driven by the emerging power, but also carries within itself the Light, the fire of life.[59]

If Heidegger draws from the source of Heraclitus to establish an ontology of "being" through the understanding of the unveiling of nature, φύσις, to human reason, Leff seeks more than an ontology of "being"; he seeks that which precedes and sustains "being":

> In this sense, φμσις is not just an ontological category, a way of understanding the being of that which emerges from presence while keeping its essence hidden, but a "mode of production" of entities characterized by their power of emergence, which is kept hidden from understanding. It is in this sense that φμσις names, in its original form, an "ontology of life", a primordial way of understanding the way of being of life and the way of thinking about life.[60]

[54] Cosmos, world.

[55] *Physis*, before the translation into Latin.

[56] Leff (2018), p. 265.

[57] Leff (2018), p. 429.

[58] Leff (2018), p. 498.

[59] Leff (2018), p. 498.

[60] Leff (2018), p. 500.

What Heraclitus calls nature, modern science calls autopoiesis or emerging complexity. Nature is the emerging power of all entities of the order of matter and the organization of life. In this sense, nature is the way of thinking about the ontology of life, the sustaining of life, the negentropic potential, and the resilience of life in the decline of the biosphere caused by the intervention of technique.[61]

From the moment that the human being found a sign to name this living, contingent, and creative emergency force, such as φμσις, physis, and nature, there was already an intervention of human reason; this was the first appropriation of man over the emergency force of nature, and hence the urgent need, as expressed by Leff, to recover and understand what Heraclitus meant by φμσις.[62] This can only be inferred from what remains of the fragments of his thinking, unveiled through the lens of a language archeologist, Martin Heidegger. It is about making an archeological incursion into the meanders of the sign φμσις to find its meaning and significance before metaphysics, which constituted the symbolic order, the world of forms, the language, which Heidegger came to consider as the house of being[63]; however, wouldn't it be more appropriate to consider it the siege of life?

Life, as a generative power, was imprisoned in language through several overlapping layers by the humanities that followed, ever since the institution of the so-called conceptual symbolic order. The work proposed by Leff is to carefully remove each of these theoretical layers that imprison life, until reaching what Heraclitus named φύσις, this self-causal emergent force that, centuries later, was glimpsed by Karl Ludwig von Bertalanffy in his systems theory.[64]

Leff warns that "the environmental issue calls for deconstructing the first intuition of life in the thought of φμσις."[65] But the truth is that it is not possible to understand the meaning and significance of φμσις for Heraclitus. The fragments of his texts present the signs that encode what Heraclitus thought, but his understanding of the sign φμσις will always be an interpretative construction mediated by his interpreters, who only make assumptions. This is what Heidegger did. Therefore, it is from his interpretation that Leff seeks the original meaning of the sign φμσις to construct his own interpretation of nature, understood as φμσις (physis) by Heraclitus, in order to reconstruct an ontology of life closer to the real world—the reality of the biosphere and its processes of autopoiesis.

For Heidegger, the sign φύσις, physis, is the fundamental word at the origin of metaphysical thought and signifies the perpetual emergent.[66] This interpretation demonstrates that the meaning of the original concept of nature, φύσις, in Heraclitus, is much more than the modern conception of nature as an objectified entity, that is, mere natural resource. Nature, φύσις, in the fragments of Heraclitean

[61] Leff (2018), p. 505.

[62] Leff (2018), p. 429.

[63] Reale and Antiseri (2018), p. 449.

[64] Leff (2018), p. 433.

[65] Leff (2018), p. 502.

[66] Heidegger (2018), p. 85.

text can be understood as the eternal emergence of life that, despite the intervention of reason and technique, persists as a genuine expression of the real world, of the biosphere, as a creative and autopoietic force.

Heidegger also scrutinizes Heraclitus' doctrine of the *logos*, unraveling the origin of the sign λόγος, reason, pointing to the existence of a dual logic for this sign: (a) the understanding of the way of being of nature, φύσις, in its emergence; and (b) the way of thinking about how nature, φύσις, emerges and is witnessed by the human being.

This dual logic extends to the difference between what emerges from the real, from the physis, φύσις, and what is humanly produced, that is, what emerges from the τέχνη (technique), which, for Heidegger, signifies human production, bringing forth a form, something that was hidden—a discovery.[67]

In this conception, nature, φύσις, refers to that which surges from the emergent force, from the chaos of the universe and the realm of life, something that does not belong to what is properly human. On the other hand, technique, τέχνη, in Heraclitus' original conception, is human production from the potency of nature. But this nature is not yet objectified, as will occur in the unfolding of the history of technique in modernity.[68]

Heidegger unveils in Heraclitus' thought the organization between the modes of reference of reason and nature. Leff considers that there is a clue left by the emergence of logical knowledge, of physical sciences, and thus the first traces of how human rationality began to think about nature and impact it. Metaphysical thought, in which the senses of reason and nature were forged, determined the modes of human intervention in life. This is the beginning of a line to understand in what way, to what degree, and in what sense human knowledge, established and developed within a symbolic order of language, influenced over millennia the power of negentropy[69] of nature as an emergent force or the artificial acceleration of its entropy.[70]

[67] Heidegger (2018), pp. 62–164.

[68] Leff (2018), p. 468.

[69] To understand the meaning of negentropy, it is first necessary to understand entropy. According to Odum and Barrett, energy should be understood as the ability to perform work. Thus, the behavior of energy is described in two laws of thermodynamics: i) first law of thermodynamics, or law of conservation of energy, in which energy can be transformed from one form to another, but cannot be created or destroyed; ii) second law of thermodynamics, or law of entropy, according to which "no process involving energy transformation will occur spontaneously unless there is a degradation of energy from a concentrated form to a dispersed form. For example, the heat in a hot object will tend, spontaneously, to disperse into the colder surroundings." Thus, entropy can be understood as the measure of an unavailable energy resulting from transformations; the term can also be understood to refer to the general index of disorder associated with energy degradation. In this way, organisms, ecosystems, and the ecosphere itself present as an essential thermodynamic characteristic: "[. . .] they can create and maintain a high state of internal order or a condition of low entropy (a low amount of disorder)." Odum and Barrett (2020), p. 78. The term negentropy is used by Léon Brillouin to refer to negative entropy, that is, the reduction of entropy and energy loss. Brillouin (1964), p. 14.

[70] Leff (2018), p. 500.

Leff draws attention to the fact that human knowledge, in the metaphysical transformation of technique within the regime of rationality of modern science, for the technical and economic appropriation of nature, has directed, mobilized, and directly impacted the real world. In this sense, he points out that reason is not only the human way of apprehending and collecting information about what emerges from nature, but also the way of producing from the vital potency of nature itself—a way of producing oriented by the meanings attributed by rationality itself to logical, ethical, and technical knowledge.[71]

The alienation of the real conditions of life by metaphysics, physical sciences, and ethics made it impossible for the human being to formulate a technique consistent with nature, inspired by the way life organizes itself. In Heraclitus' original conception, technique, τέχνη, is a kind of knowledge that guides human production from nature, but not from an objectified nature, typical of modern technique.[72]

In the face of the ecological failure resulting from the disjunction between the real world—that is, the biosphere—and the conceptual symbolic order, Leff proposes a new ontology of life, which takes into account the laws of thermodynamics, as well as the entropic and negentropic processes of the biosphere. In this path, in the subsequent topics, this work will make a brief reflection on other ontological possibilities, built outside the dualistic model, and their contribution to the reversal of the anthropogenic environmental crisis.

2.3 Plato's Unwritten Doctrine and the Ontology of Life in Cirne-Lima's Evolutionary Dialectic

Enrique Leff's proposal to seek a new ontology of life perfectly dialogs with the philosophical system proposed by Cirne-Lima, which is based on the monist ontology contained in Plato's unwritten doctrine, from which Plotinus, Proclus, Augustine Aurelius, Spinoza, Fichte, Schelling, Hegel, and Teilhard de Chardin's Neoplatonism blossomed—a philosophical current that, in Brazil, was adopted by Cirne-Lima.[73] The Platonic monism dissected by Cirne-Lima 73 rests on the concept of the immanence of nature; therefore, it could have forged another destiny for the biosphere by allowing the consideration of its entropic and negentropic processes as an emerging force of life.

Cirne-Lima explains that, although Plato appears to be dualistic, considering the dichotomy of the world of things and the world of ideas that permeates his entire philosophical system, there is a philosophical current suggesting that Plato was, in

[71] Leff (2018), p. 57.

[72] Leff (2018), p. 535.

[73] Cirne-Lima (2017), pp. 32–35.

fact, a monist. Cirne-Lima defends Plato's monistic philosophical system, using internal arguments identified in the dialog itself, "*Sophist.*"[74]

He points out that in the dialog "*Sophist,*" Plato teaches that ideas are organized in a pyramidal structure. At the top of the pyramid are placed, in two pairs, the supreme ideas: (1) sameness—otherness; (2) rest—movement. These supreme ideas are subordinate to a single first principle from which everything derives, which explains everything, and to which everything returns. Therefore, given this premise established by Plato in the dialog "*Sophist,*" Cirne-Lima questions how this passage of the dialog could fit into a supposedly dualistic view. He argues that the unifying force of this being, this one, to which the supreme ideas are subject, eliminates any possibility of dualism.[75]

Cirne-Lima clarifies that the monist Platonism current, which developed in the School of Tübingen,[76] collated the testimonies of the monistic Platonic philosophical system that is part of the so-called unwritten doctrine—an esoteric doctrine of Plato, which would have been orally passed on only to a more restricted group of initiates. The main testimony of Plato's unwritten doctrine originates from a text by his disciple Aristotle, who referred to it several times and criticized it.

Mesquita observes that the validity of the written dialogs does not diminish the relevance of the "unwritten teaching, but rather is indebted to it." Plato left written the prescription of what should be done, but the realization, the concretion of this doing, was carried out in the very orality of the unwritten dialogs: "The to–do, which for Plato constitutes the essential and, ultimately, the only purpose of

[74] Cirne-Lima (2020), p. 47.

[75] Cirne-Lima (2020), p. 48.

[76] *What became known in Platonic studies as the Tübingen School emerged and consolidated from the research initiated in the mid-twentieth century by Hans Krämer and Konrad Gaiser and continued by Thomas A. Szlezák, at the University of Tübingen, to which researchers from the Centro di Ricerche di Metafisica of the Catholic University of Milan joined, founded by Giovanni Reale, who, from the 1980s, made such a significant contribution to the development and dissemination of this research as to justify the designation of the Tübingen-Milan Platonic School. Within this school, it became usual to speak of 'hermeneutic paradigms', which would have succeeded in the history of Plato's interpretations. According to Giovanni Reale who created this terminology adopted by the school, there would have been in the history of Plato's interpretation three hermeneutic paradigms, in addition to the one that was born with Plato himself and was consecrated by his direct disciples in the ancient Academy, namely: the middle and Neoplatonic paradigm, which prevailed for about a millennium and a half, from the third century AD; the paradigm formulated by Schleiermacher in the Introduction of his imposing translation of the Platonic work carried out between 1804 and 1828; and, finally, the paradigm of the Tübingen-Milan School. The paradigm proposed by the Tübingen-Milan School, in contrast to the Schleiermacherian paradigm, is characterized by bringing back to the fore the need to resort to Plato's oral teaching to properly understand, both from a historical point of view and from a doctrinal point of view, the set of his writings. According to this paradigm, Platonic writings are not self-sufficient, that is, they cannot be understood only from themselves, neither in their entirety nor in part; from them a unity is not inferred, since this is found underlying them, insofar as it was entrusted to dialectical orality, so that the key to access the totality of Plato's thought must be sought in the indirect tradition, which transmits to us the unwritten doctrines.* Perine (2011), pp. 153–154.

philosophizing, is not done just in writing or by writing. It is done by doing and this doing essentially escapes writing."[77]

In the so-called unwritten doctrine, the Platonic philosophical system is organized around two principles: the principle of unity and the principle of multiplicity. Thus, the relationship between the one and the multiple is the central theme of Plato's metaphysics. Although dualists interpret these two principles as antagonistic, for the monist current, of which Plotinus, Proclus, and Hegel are followers, the principles of unity and multiplicity intertwine. As Cirne-Lima explains, "they overlap dialectically, constituting a single great Principle. I think, in summary, that the Principle of Unity is the thesis and the Principle of Multiplicity is the antithesis and that the synthesis of both is made through what I call the Principle of Coherence."[78]

Later on, Cirne-Lima's aforementioned principle of coherence will be examined when addressing the issue related to general ethics, which precedes the proposal of ethics applied to ecology. At this point, it is of interest to outline an ontology, based on the contours of Neoplatonic monism, which considers life immanent in all beings, deeming this to be more suitable for the formulation of an ethics applied to ecology, one that recognizes the intrinsic value of non-human beings, with the consequent repositioning of these beings into another legal category, distinct from that of things.

The monistic Platonic system will be assimilated and developed by the so-called Neoplatonists, some of whom will work on the synthesis of the principles of the one and the multiple, in a "great dialectical synthesis," that is, the play of opposites; others will work on the idea of unfolding everything that exists from the one.[79]

The relevance of the dialectical monist synthesis, or the unfolding of the one, reverberates in the way of explaining life itself. The Neoplatonic system postulates that all things lead to a first principle that rules everything, and from this first principle descends everything that exists in the sensible world—all beings. This first principle, in ontology and in the logic of the Neoplatonic monist system, is called the original egg. From this original egg, the principle of unity, everything that exists unfolded—all the variety and plurality of beings and things—that is, the principle of multiplicity. Thus, the universe was contained in the initial egg, the first principle. It emerged from this one, unfolding in all its beauty, variety, and complexity, which reveals the principle of multiplicity.[80]

In this line, within the Platonic monism of the unwritten doctrine, which was developed by Neoplatonism, "being" is the synthesis of two opposing pairs that govern the architecture of the universe, as taught by Cirne-Lima:

[77] Mesquita (2018), p. 70.
[78] Cirne-Lima (2001), p. 49.
[79] Cirne-Lima (1998), p. 295.
[80] Cirne-Lima (1998), p. 296.

> The Being, synthetic, is the One, which is everything and within which the opposite poles unfold. Within the Being polarize rest and movement, sameness and otherness. The Being is synthesis, it is the great synthesis. And this Being is not only the Being that is One and that is the All, **Hen kai Pan**, it is the good. The Unwritten Doctrine was compiled by his students in the form of a dialogue about the good **Peri tou Agathou** . This dialogue was never written by Plato personally, it was put to parchment by his students. It is the merit of the Tübingen School, in our century, continued by the Milan School, to have emphasized the esoteric doctrine and to have reconstructed in its general lines the content of Plato's central work, the most central of all. For it is through it that we understand what the dialogues insinuate, but do not clearly say, it is from it that all Neoplatonic tradition derives: the triadic process and the idea of Universal evolution.[81]

Unlike dualism, which underpins Aristotelian, scholastic thought of Thomas Aquinas and moderns, and which established the dichotomies of form/matter, subject/object, and nature/culture, Cirne-Lima emphasizes that the Neoplatonic monist system presents a logic in which the entire universe results from a process of evolution, in which all things and beings emanate from the same creative source. Moreover, "with the ontological inclusion of all things in the initial egg, the logical inclusion of all things in the first principle is also being affirmed."[82] Thus, the task of philosophy is to deduce all things from the first principle, which is self-caused.

In this line, the Neoplatonic monist philosophical system establishes a dialog with biology, not only with the theory of evolution but also with the general theory of systems, which allows formulating an ontology of life itself. Understanding life in a systemic way, that is, interrelated, Cirne-Lima teaches:

> Life is an organism, which is the name we give to the hierarchical harmony of the relationships existing between the various parts that constitute a living being. Beyond the laws of Physics and Chemistry, we have to think something more, namely, the organization, that which orders the relationships between the parts. And as by definition, the living being is that which reproduces, to understand life, we have to consider as central structure that form of organization that reproduces itself, that is, that organizes itself, which is, in itself, self-organization.[83]

The Neoplatonic monist philosophical system was defended in scholastic theology by Augustine Aurelius, later supplanted by the Aristotelian dualism of Thomas Aquinas, which reverberated in rationalist modernity, in empiricism, and even in Kantian transcendentalism. In theology, the last great monists were Spinoza and Teilhard de Chardin, both supporting the immanence of God—the one, in nature—which removes it from the mere position of creature at the service of the human species. However, Spinoza was harshly accused of pantheism by the Hebrew clerics who were his contemporaries.[84] The monist voices of divine immanence in the emerging force of life were silenced, and a God triumphed

[81] Cirne-Lima (1998), p. 296.

[82] Cirne-Lima (2001), p. 65.

[83] Cirne-Lima (2012), p. 159.

[84] Cirne-Lima (2012), p. 65.

who, although transcendent, is quite anthropomorphic, since he delegated the exploration of created and objectified nature to the human being, who became the greatest antagonist of life.

Cirne-Lima, in his work *Dialectics for Beginners,,* returns to monism to deal with evolution through the lens of dialectics and makes a proposal for the reconciliation of the conceptual symbolic order and the real world, to overcome the dissociation denounced by Enrique Leff, which is at the origin of the alienation of nature and that has entangled us in the abyss of the anthropogenic crisis.

The philosophical system project supported by Cirne-Lima is forged in Neoplatonic philosophy and, therefore, has three parts: logic, nature, and spirit. This triad is governed and unified by a first great principle, which is at the root of all speaking and thinking. The principle of non-contradiction, established by Aristotle, is a fundamental principle that inaugurates the Western symbolic order and contains, in Cirne-Lima's dialectical proposal, three principles: the principle of identity, the principle of difference, and the principle of coherence.

According to Cirne-Lima, the philosophy of nature is also governed by the same principles that govern logic (language) and the spirit (human self-consciousness). The principles of identity, difference, and coherence, derived from the principle of non-contradiction—which is at the root of all thinking and speaking—permeate logic, nature, and spirit, reunifying the harmony broken by analytical dualism.

This unifying synthesis in logic, nature, and spirit, by the principle of coherence proposed by Cirne-Lima, opens a door for the inclusion of nature in the ethical community as a being with intrinsic value, and not a mere instrument, thus presenting itself as an adequate ontology to underpin an applied ecological ethics, and for this reason, it will be revisited in greater depth in the topic dedicated to ethics.

2.4 Hans Jonas' Integral Monism

Hans Jonas' ethics of responsibility has been one of the most invoked theories in recent decades when the topic is the ecological crisis; however, less is discussed about the rich Jonasian ontology that underpins the ethics of responsibility. As Jonas himself warns, ethics does not dispense with metaphysics, and so, in this topic, where possible ontologies for a new ecological ethics are analyzed, it is a methodological imperative to dedicate a subtopic to the examination of Jonas' biological ontology in the work *The Phenomenon of Life*, translated into Portuguese with the title *The Principle of Life.*[85]

Jonas proposes an ontology that aims to overcome not only Cartesian dualism but also post-dualist monisms, that is, monist materialism, which he calls physicalism, and also Kantian and existentialist idealisms. These post-dualist monisms imprisoned the "being," either in the province of matter, subjecting it to the despair

[85] Jonas (2004).

of a deterministic and necessitarian fatalism, or on the plane of a transcendent idealism detached from reality, as an empty existence because it is separated from the biological reality of the "being," as Heidegger did.[86]

So Jonas proposes a biological philosophy that reconciles matter and spirit, an integral monism that considers matter and spirit as original dimensions of the same real being.[87]

Jonas argues that life cannot be considered either as pure matter, as materialist evolutionism intends, or as epiphenomenalism.[88] Viana highlights that Jonas, in an article published in 1951 titled "Materialism and the Theory of Organism," as well as in "The Phenomenon of Life," already harshly criticized the Darwinist and neo-Darwinist interpretation of life for having reduced the spirit to matter through the random and genetic variations of natural selection.[89] Jonas understands that the living organism is constituted by a system, a whole, whose parts are interconnected in harmony by a "higher principle," and identifies in the organism the systematic characteristics pointed out by von Bertalanffy, that is, openness, self-regulation, growth, regeneration, adaptation, and the ability to achieve objectives through deviations.[90]

This harmony in the composition of each organism, from the simplest to the most complex, is so fundamental that its compromise can lead the organism to destructive collapse. He draws a distinction between the principle of unity in living systems and mechanical systems, clarifying that, in living systems, life depends on the harmonious interconnection of each part with the whole, which is guaranteed by a higher principle of unity. Every living being is under constant threat of death and, to preserve itself, needs to "want" or "intend" the balance and harmony between the parts—a purpose of self-preservation that is realized, according to Jonas, by metabolism.

Metabolism should be understood in Jonasian ontology as being a more complex process than the simple exchange of matter and, in addition, it still differentiates metabolism in closed mechanical systems, machines, and open organic and living systems. In machines, we do not speak of metabolism, as they are closed systems with a defined identity, and thus, when they consume fuel for their operation, they do not alter their material constituents.[91]

The metabolism in the living organism operates in an open system, which preserves the unity of the parts and maintains continuous interaction with the environment to guarantee its own existence. This is what constitutes the *telos* of

---

[86] Heidegger (2015), pp. 98–109.

[87] Viana (2014), p. 393.

[88] The doctrine according to which mental activities are only accessory elements of neural processes, having no influence on them. Michaelis. Available at: https://michaelis.uol.com.br/moderno-portugues/busca/portugues-brasileiro/epifenomenalismo. Accessed on: April 20, 2020.

[89] Viana (2014), p. 39.

[90] Jonas (2004), pp. 3–84.

[91] Viana (2014).

the organism; that is, it is teleologically driven to achieve the harmony necessary for its existence. All parts of the organism are focused on a common end: self-preservation, a goal that is achieved through metabolism.[92]

This metabolism, however, cannot be reduced to mere mathematical and physicochemical functions. For Jonas, metabolism establishes in nature the entry of the spirit; that is, there is self-determination of the organism in the process of metabolism to choose what will be ingested. Organisms, even the simplest ones, choose the nutrients that will be beneficial for their nutrition and discard what is useless. How is this choice triggered? There is no physical or chemical predetermination; therefore, there is autonomy, an independence of the organism itself in the choice and use of the nutrients necessary for its existential continuity.[93] In this, Jonas already glimpses a degree of freedom, a certain free will—a freedom guided by its own necessity, as the organism has the freedom to choose the nutrients but does not have the freedom not to choose, since it is driven by the biological need to live.[94]

This freedom is inversely proportional to the need: If the freedom to choose nutrients increases, the need decreases; however, with a greater freedom of action by the organism in the choice of its nutrients, there is the risk of erratic choices and, consequently, of death from bad choices. Thus, it can be seen that the organism is neither only matter, with a predetermined metabolism, nor only spirit, freed from the need for exchanges with the organic environment.

If there is a minimum degree of freedom in plants, how does the entry of the spirit occur in these plant organisms? How is the material world animated by the spirit that allows degrees of openness to contingency, to freedom, and to free will, from the most elementary organisms to human self-consciousness?
Viana explains that Jonas hypothetically considers:

> [...] that the spirit is a latent reality since the "primordial explosion". "Latent reality" does not mean that the spirit was a **logos** cosmogonic present in act in inorganic matter, which characterizes the panpsychisms from Heraclitus to Whitehead. Jonas observes that there was no information, a **logos**, the spirit in act, permeating matter from the primordial chaos, determining the progress of being in a programmed way. [...] Jonas denies that the spirit was present from the beginning, but affirms a tendency in matter itself towards the appearance of the spirit. More than a **logos** cosmogonic, there would be an **eros** cosmogonic, represented by two "laws" that merge with the first developments of matter itself: the law of conservation and transcendence.[95]

For Jonas, from the beginning, matter potentially carried degrees of interiority and intentionality. As can be seen, this Jonasian hypothesis of the formation of the cosmos both refutes the dualism of substances (form, idea *vs.* matter), since the spirit is the immanent element in matter itself and not something in the plane of ideas, a transcendent form, as well as rejects materialism, considering that matter

[92] Jonas (2004), p. 85.
[93] Jonas (2004), pp. 98–101.
[94] Viana (2014), p. 397.
[95] Viana (2014), pp. 397–398.

carries within itself, in an immanent way, the power of intentionality. This power of intentionality, this needed freedom supported by Jonas,[96] dialogs with the principle of difference proposed by Cirne-Lima, considering that it can trigger the contingent; therefore, it has the potential to characterize a rudiment of free will of the organism in the search for life, a free will that will gradually increase according to the complexity of the organism.

Unlike the closed system of machines, which has a predetermined identity, the open system of the organism constructs its identity continuously in this exchange of matter with the environment, so that it is subject to contingency.

There is a dimension in every organism that is spiritual and that cannot be reduced solely to matter. However, this spiritual dimension is not separate and independent from matter, as Descartes maintained with his *res cogitans* separated from *res extensa*. This spiritual dimension is gradual in its degree of freedom, according to the complexity of the organism. Viana comments on two texts by Jonas, in which he explains this gradation of the spirit in organisms and makes the bridge from the animal body to the conscious spirit. These texts are as follows: Der Adel des Lebens and *Homo pictor: von der Freiheit des Bildens*.[97]

When commenting on Der Adel des Lebens, which was originally published with the title *Nobility of sight*,[98] Viana emphasizes that, for Jonas, in humans, it is the sense of vision that facilitates the transition from the physical organism to consciousness and makes human consciousness more expansive and robust compared to non-human animals. In examining human behavior in prehistory, Jonas points out that humans distinguished themselves from other animals, demonstrating a high degree of consciousness, because they already had the ability to produce tools, tombs, and figures. In the text Homo Pictor: von der Freiheit des Bildens, Jonas details the human ability to, in addition to satisfying their biological needs, draw figures—that is, produce symbols and reproduce the world through pictorial representations—to satisfy demands that go beyond metabolism. Jonas explains that humans have the ability to reproduce the shape of objects, landscapes, and people in their drawings because they have the ability to distinguish things as similar and enduring; non-human animals, on the other hand, would not have this ability, as "where we see pure similarity, the animal sees one equal or another."[99] Humans, however, are capable of capturing the essence (form) of objects and representing them in a figure through vision; this ability to distinguish the real world from the figure allows humans to reformulate their own world, as they can dispose of the essence even without the presence of the object. Jonas calls this "mediability."[100]

---

[96] Jonas (2004), p. 101.
[97] Viana (2018), pp. 151–163.
[98] Viana (2018), p. 156.
[99] Viana (2018), p. 157.
[100] Viana (2018), p. 158.

Regarding the interconnection between spirit and matter, for Jonas, "there are not two independent things, one spiritual and another material, but one thing with two different dimensions." Thus, just as an object has three physical dimensions, such as height, width, and depth, and none of these dimensions can be reduced to the others, Jonas considers that living organisms also have a spiritual dimension, which organizes matter and gives it various functions.

In Jonas's view, it is the spiritual dimension that organizes the matter of organisms and gradually assigns them functions according to the complexity of the organism: In plants, this function is metabolism; in animals, it assigns perception and movement; and in humans, it is responsible for self-awareness.[101]

These functions are carried out within an interiority or subjectivity—not a mental subjectivity—as Jonas begins his gradation from organisms that do not yet manifest an ipseity, that is, that are not yet subjects, but have a psyche, which is an attribute of all organisms, from the simplest to the most complex, as it relates to the mere impulse for metabolic nutrition. Ipseity is an attribute of beings that, although not conscious, are more evolved on the scale of subjective gradation, as they present an individuality, which already allows them to be considered subjects. It is through this organic interiority, called subjectivity, that the organism communicates with the world to seek the nutrients necessary for its self-preservation.[102]

The interiority of the organism can be glimpsed from its own identity, that is, from its separation from the world as a system. Interiority is experienced internally by the organism itself, while identity is what differentiates it as a being. Thus, interiority and identity are thesis and anti-thesis, which synthesize in the unity of the living organism.

In this communication of the organism's interiority with the external world, mediated by metabolic activity, Jonas identifies the organic intentionality to continue to exist. At this point, his concept of "needed freedom," of self-affirmation, emerges. For Jonas, this movement of the being flows toward its existence; therefore, it is teleological, that is, always animated by an end, which is the continuity of life, and for this, the organism needs to constantly open up to the world in a transcendent movement.[103] This transcendence referred to by Jonas is explained as being the horizon beyond the "punctiform identity" of the organism:

> [. . .] self-interest, driven by necessity, also opens a temporal horizon, which encompasses not the external present but the imminent interior: the imminent future, towards which at each moment the organic continuity is heading to satisfy the need of precisely this moment.[104]

Thus, Jonas classifies organisms on an ascending scale according to their complexity and dimension of freedom. For example, this freedom in plants is metabolism and photosynthesis; in animals, it is motility and perception; and in humans,

[101] Viana (2018), pp. 158–159.

[102] Jonas (2017), pp. 311–313.

[103] Jonas (2017), pp. 311–312.

[104] Jonas (2017), p. 110.

self-awareness. However, in all organisms, there is a psyche and, therefore, a degree of subjectivity that grants them the necessary freedom for existential maintenance. This subjectivity, or free will, is gradual according to the degree of complexity of the organism and is present in all beings, to a lesser or greater extent, from the fern to the human being.[105]

As Viana highlights, the emergence of the organism's subjectivity in Jonasian ontology represented a significant "qualitative leap" toward the construction of a new ethics based on responsibility.[106] Indeed, while it overcomes Aristotelian dualism, which forbids any freedom to nature, it also corrects materialist monism. From the moment that human subjectivity is no longer reduced solely to matter and its deterministic laws, as monist materialism would have it, space opens up for free will and responsibility. This is not a free will detached from reality, floating in Kantian transcendental idealism, but Jonas places the human being as the holder of free will, guided by a freedom oriented by the need to maintain the conditions of life itself, as an emerging force that pulses in all beings.

From this perspective, the organism is both matter and spirit, which self-determines in its vital journey through metabolism, with a greater or lesser degree of freedom, on an ascending scale, at the base of which Jonas places plants, followed by animals and, at the top, the human animal, which, by having the greatest degree of freedom, is subject to the greatest risk of death, so that its erroneous choices cause not only its death but that of all other beings, and for this reason, its responsibility should be exacerbated and asymmetrical in relation to other species.[107] It is precisely this point of Jonas's biological ontology that will root his ethics of responsibility.[108]

2.5 The Dialog Between Neoplatonic Monism and pre-Hispanic Inca Thought

The logic of the Neoplatonic monist philosophical system presents itself as a possibility for overcoming the subject–object, nature–culture dichotomy, which relegates nature to the position of a mere natural resource. This monist view of the world, although it has been ostracized by Western dualist philosophical systems, can be glimpsed in the cultural imaginaries and regional symbolic orders of indigenous peoples in various parts of the planet.

Thus, with the aim of formulating an understanding of these different ontologies, which this work considers necessary for the construction of a new applied ecological ethics that ensures the harmony of the human being with nature, it is

[105] Jonas (2004), pp. 124–125.
[106] Viana (2014), p. 398.
[107] Jonas (2004), p. 123.
[108] Jonas (2004), p. 131.

necessary to take a brief look at the ontology of the Andean peoples, extracted from the ancestral conception of *sumak kawsay*, or *buen vivir,* and its possible dialog with Plato's so-called unwritten doctrine.

Salazar Calderón Galliani establishes an intercultural dialog between the monist philosophy of Plato and the thought of the indigenous peoples of the Andes through the hermeneutic-phenomenological analysis of symbols present in the myths of Inca culture, more precisely in relation to the Andean worldview of parity between human beings and nature, embodied in the concept of *yanantin.*[109]

Salazar Calderón Galliani starts with the ideas of the Inca-origin writer and philosopher Garcilaso de la Vega, who was the first Neoplatonist in the Americas, to establish a connection between pre-Hispanic Andean thought and Plato's unwritten monist doctrine—that is, the unwritten dogma developed by the Tübingen School. He employs the concepts of the one and the dyad as a bridge toward the Inca notion of parity between the human being and nature, which is encapsulated in the concept of *yanantin*. In this endeavor, he explains that the dyad in Plato, as the root of the principle of multiplicity, is the ineffable, the infinity. The one and the dyad, in Plato's unwritten doctrine, represent the being of the entity—the unity within multiplicity.

In addition to the one and the dyad, Salazar Calderón Galliani highlights in the Platonic monist doctrine the existence of a third sphere, whose ontological nature is different from the one and the dyad and which, at the same time, participates in both. This principle is Eros, which is conceived in the *Symposium* as the principle of life and continuous movement, engendering the unfolding of multiplicity, as the creative principle of everything that exists. For Salazar Calderón Galliani, the Platonic protology, which is established on the principles of the one, the dyad, and Eros—this as perpetual creative movement—dialogs with the Inca concept of *yanantin.*[110]

Yanantin in the Quechua language can be translated as *pareja* in Spanish or pair in English. This concept represents the recurring overlap in Andean culture between the symbols of light and darkness, day and night, sky and earth, and the feminine and the masculine. The principle of *yanantin* proposes an analogy between the cosmos and the human body, which symbolically is expressed in the symmetry of male and female bodies. The concept assumes the complementation of opposites. Galliani associates *yanantin* with Plato's Eros as a generative force, whose dual structure presents a relationship of mutual belonging or complementarity. Just like Eros, yanantin is the driving force that binds couples to procreate a new being and also fosters the unity of opposites in a relationship of complementarity.[111]

Salazar Calderón Galliani identifies a dialog between Andean thought on the deeper relational and parity significance of the concept of *yanantin* and

[109] Salazar Calderón Galliani (2015), pp. 128–131.

[110] Salazar Calderón Galliani (2015), p. 130.

[111] Salazar Calderón Galliani (2015), pp. 128–130.

Greek symbolic thought, since both have a dual and, at the same time, complementary understanding of the cosmos. That is, every reality that presents itself assumes a dual aspect, but this duplicity unfolds from the one. Thus, it is different from the Aristotelian-Thomistic duality that has prevailed from scholasticism to modernity, and that separated the soul from matter, the subject from the object, and nature from culture. The Platonic dyad in the unwritten doctrine and the complementary duality of Inca culture have another connotation: the *complexio oppositorum*, that is, the unity of opposites.[112]

In this line, the singular reality is just an expression of incompleteness, of the half that needs the other, symbolically described by Aristophanes in the *Symposium*, when he describes the incompleteness of the human being who, due to arrogance, was condemned to the eternal desire for belonging, to the nostalgia of oneself. Similarly, the mountains, the rain, the sea, and even we humans are all implicated in a dual reality, so that the cosmos is not just a chaotic set of atoms or a void, but rather a relational whole, articulated by an androgynous principle—in the mythology of the *Symposium*, Eros; in Inca culture, *yanantin.*[113]

Salazar Calderón Galliani concludes in his research that both the unwritten Platonic philosophy and the pre-Hispanic Andean thought propose the encounter, that is, a fusion of horizons with the principle by which it exerts both on the one and on the *other* the transformation and creative regeneration of both:

> This is because this liminal dimension of the encounter of thikuy,[114] as we have seen, apart from unity and diversity, has its own ontological consistency, since without being neither one nor the other, it participates in both, orders, gives unity to the plurality, as complexio oppositorum.[115]

This seemingly contrary but complementary and parity double, pointed out by Salazar Calderón Galliani in Inca thought, is inferred from the concept of *yanantin* as the "primordial act of the relational condition of transformation."[116] It is also possible to identify it in Western culture in Heraclitus' enantiodromia,[117] in. Plato's unwritten doctrine, in the Renaissance Neoplatonists, in Hegel's dialectic, and, finally, in the ethics of coherence proposed by Cirne-Lima.[118]

---

[112] Salazar Calderón Galliani (2015), p. 133.

[113] Salazar Calderón Galliani (2015), p. 137.

[114] Principle of Andean culture understood as the fusion of horizons.

[115] Salazar Calderón Galliani (2015), p. 140.

[116] Anjos and Fehlauer (2017), p. 106.

[117] "Run to the other opposite" or "go to the contrary."

[118] Cirne-Lima (2017), pp. 98–112.

2.6 The Macro-Principle of Relationality in Inca Ontology and Its Common Points With Plotinus's Neoplatonism

Josef Estermann deeply examines the so-called relational ontology of the Andean peoples, establishing a comparison between certain aspects of the ontology forged in the Inca cultural crucible and the ontology developed in the West, originating from Greek culture.

Introductorily, Estermann states that speaking of an Andean rationality would already be a philosophical imposition, considering that the concept of rationality is fundamentally Western, represented by the Greek sign λόγος, that is, *logos*. He explains that reason is not a cultural constant, much less a supracultural one, but an "invention," a construction based on the "foundational myth" of Greek philosophy, and that although there are homeomorphic equivalents in other cultures, the concepts carry different meanings.[119]

Even in the West, the concept of reason has undergone a long transformation and a true transculturation. Estermann explains that Western reason has a predominantly cognitive origin. Its foundation was built on the graphic linguistic structure, symbolized by the word structured by grammar, which is the mold of the logical paradigm of concept and proposition.

For Andean philosophy, reality is not logical or linguistic but symbolic, structured in a complex of concrete and material signs that relate to each other. For example, the land worked by the farmer is not an amorphous, inert, and objective reality but rather a living, celebratory reality.

Estermann makes a comparison between Andean philosophy and the Western philosophy of the dualist system, inaugurated by the dualists Plato and Aristotle, whose predominant component is cognitive and founded on dichotomies: subject x object; reality x appearance; truth x falsehood; exterior x interior; and temporariness x eternity. Since the Socratic anthropological turn, the Western world has been divided into a free, autonomous, and sovereign subject and a determined and manipulable object. The author clarifies that, for Andean philosophy, the conception of reality is different from this dual view of the world, as reality for the Andeans is present or presents itself symbolically and not conceptually, as occurs in Western culture.[120]

The first desire of the Andean *runa/jaqui* (person) is not the acquisition of theoretical and abstract knowledge of the world around them, but the "mythical insertion" and the symbolic ceremonial representation of this mythical insertion. Reality, in the Andean indigenous worldview, is revealed in celebration and ceremony. The symbol is the representation of reality—not a cognitive representation, but a symbolic experience.

---

[119] Estermann (2006), p. 99.

[120] Estermann (2006), pp. 104–107.

From the Western point of view, this non-conceptual way of conceiving reality is qualified as "magical," "numinous," and primitive. The fundamental problem of the West's limitation in understanding this Andean way of conceiving reality is the dualist paradigm founded on the subject–object dichotomy, which prevailed as the "foundational myth" of Western thought. This paradigm makes it difficult to understand a non-dichotomous, non-objective rationality. Estermann emphasizes that even Western idealist philosophers, who focused more on the question of identity, could not transcend the "subject-object" gnosiological scheme.

The Western dualist philosophical system was built based on the graphic linguistic structure, presenting itself as a logical linguistic code. For Andean philosophy, reality itself is not logical or linguistic but mythical. The preferred symbol is not the word, nor the concept, but reality itself, in its celebratory and semantic dimension. Reality is present as a symbol, as a complex of concrete and material symbols. The land that the peasant (*runa/jaqui*) works is not an objective and inert reality, a thing, but a living and present symbol of the cycle of life, fertility, and retribution, a symbol of cosmic and ethical order. When the *runa/jaqui* (peasant) looks at the land he tills for planting, he sees it as a symbol, in which all existential reality is represented, in its multiple dimensions.

In this worldview, the Earth is not a thing, nor an instrument for production; it is not a cognitive reality, but the representation of a cosmic order, of the whole, and the act of planting is a ritualistic and ceremonial relationship, imbued with respect and reverence. The *runa/jaqui* (peasant) feels part of the cosmic reality, which reveals itself as a holistic set of symbols significant for everyday life.[121]

Estermann takes as a starting point, to explain the difference between the Western and Andean worldview, our understanding of the foundation of everything that exists—that is, the irreducible foundation and principle of reality, the so-called *arjé* or *arché*.[122] Western philosophy has been scrutinizing this ultimate principle of reality (*arjé* or *arché*) since Thales of Miletus; for Westerners, it is an entity conceived as a substance, whether finite or infinite.[123]

This conception of substantiality is another foundational myth of Western philosophy, whose gnosiological paradigm is based on the ultimate principle that all things and all beings are substantial. For Thales of Miletus, the principle of all things was water; for Anaximander, the principle of everything was infinite, the *ápeiron*; Anaximenes understood that the *arjé* or *arché* was air; Heraclitus of Ephesus maintained that the principle of everything would be fire; the Pythagoreans understood that all things derived from numbers; Parmenides inaugurated conceptual philosophy, establishing the basis of what came to be the theory of being, ontology, later developed by Aristotle; Leucippus, Democritus, and Epicurus attributed the principle of everything to the atom.[124]

[121] Estermann (2006), pp. 107–109.

[122] Estermann (2006), p. 107.

[123] Reale and Antiseri (2003), p. 18.

[124] Reale and Antiseri (2003), p. 18.

Estermann explains that, in Andean philosophy, the principle of everything is not a substantial entity but a relationship. The relationship is the true substance of the Andean worldview. For Western philosophy, more precisely for Aristotle, the relationship is accidental; that is, a characteristic of substances, external and non-essential. First, something exists, then that something relates to another equally existing something.[125]

In the Western worldview, the relationship presupposes the substantial existence of subjects and objects. What Western ontology calls an "entity" (substance) in the Aristotelian sense, for Andean rationality, is a "node of relations," a transition point, a relational concentration. In the Andean view, a stone, for example, is not simply a separate entity existing in itself, but a concentration point of certain force and energy relations. The relationality, as the "founding myth" of Andean philosophy, manifests itself, above all and explicitly, on the anthropological level.[126]

In Western philosophy, the individuality and autonomy of the human being are very important traits, especially due to the influence of the Semitic worldview. Greco-Roman philosophy does not emphasize individuality; it does not position it as a transcendental value. The introduction of individuality and personality as transcendental values occurred, for theological reasons, during the Middle Ages. Estermann emphasizes that, at this point, there was a certain incompatibility between the Greco-Roman and Semitic paradigms, with the Semitic view prevailing in the end.[127]

Estermann observes that ancient and medieval human beings felt inserted in an ordered cosmos and saw themselves as occupants of a place in the "great chain of being," which Glen T. Martin[128] calls a "static holism." However, gradually, during the Middle Ages, there was a denaturalization of the human being and a dehumanization of nature, whose culmination was Cartesian dualism in modernity. The emergence of the concept of the autonomous individual powerfully impacted the conception of life and reality in the Western view. The human being came to be seen not only as the subject of responsibility but also as the main axis of knowledge.

For Andean philosophy, the individual as such is nothing (a non-entity) if not inserted into a network of multiple relations. If a person does not belong to a local community because they were expelled due to their own actions, it is as if that person no longer exists. An unrelated person is dead because disconnecting from natural and cosmic bonds means, for the *runa/jaqui* of the Andes, signing their own death sentence.

The Cartesian *arjé* or *arché* of an individual substance (*cogito ergo sum*) is, for Andean philosophy, an existence without foundation. For Andean philosophy, when a human being uses their thinking, actions, and judgment solely from

[125] Estermann (2006), p. 108.

[126] Estermann (2006), p. 111.

[127] Estermann (2006), p. 110.

[128] Martin (2008).

themselves, believing that they are the foundation and sufficient norm, they no longer "are" in the strict sense, because they are reduced to a world without relations. The true *arjé* or *arché* in Andean thought is the relationality of everything—the network of connections and bonds—which is the vital force of everything that exists. This relationality, which manifests itself at all levels and fields of existence, is the axiom of Andean philosophy.[129]

All the principles that guide the Andean cosmogony unfold from the macro-principle of relationality and aim ultimately at the harmony of the human being with other living beings, both human and non-human, and with Mother Earth.

Is the principle of relationality also present in Western ontology? Is it possible to establish a dialog between the macro-principle of relationality and the Neoplatonism of Plotinus? Laura Westra conducts a comparative analysis of the main pillars of Plotinus' thought with Earth ethics and deep ecology and highlights three fundamental concepts in Plotinus' ontology: unity, freedom, and value.[130]

Unity is the central point of Plotinus' thought, as for him, the "one" is the source of everything that exists. There is a visceral connection between the "one" and the natural creation that is engendered from it, which establishes a bond, a brotherhood among all beings that make up this unfolded plurality of the "one," so that the human being, within this plurality of creation, has a kinship with everything that exists. This means that from the principle of unity, from which plurality unfolds, there arises a membership of the human being with all beings.[131]

Westra reports that, in the treatise titled "What are the causes of the stars?," Plotinus develops an argument, from the description of the functioning of an organism to the functioning of the whole; that is, if the eyes are part of the human body, which is a whole, our body is also part of a larger whole.[132]

David Fideler, in the same vein, observes that this view of Plotinus, in describing the *nous*, establishes points of contact with fractal geometry, which currently provides us with efficient tools for a deeper understanding of nature.

For Plotinus, the *nous* is the living harmony of uniformity and differentiation, unity and multiplicity. This intelligence, this universal being, synthesizes equality and difference, unity and multiplicity, the finite and the infinite. Thus, the universe that manifests itself is rooted in this *nous*; that is, it is a living organism, in which the parts are interrelated with the whole, which is articulated in the parts, and which holographically reflect the nature of the whole. He cites, as an example of a model of fractal geometry—which was already conceived by Plotinus' theory of the *nous*—the small leaves of a fern, which reproduce the exact model of the twig on which they are bundled, and this twig has the same model as the fern as a whole.[133]

---

[129] Estermann (2006), p. 111.
[130] Westra (2002), p. 29.
[131] Westra (2002), p. 34.
[132] Westra (2002), p. 30.
[133] Fideler (2001), pp. 107–109.

Unity was described by Plotinus as the interconnection between all things, so that organisms are intimately united in a relationship of sympathy and correspondence. Thus, the many forms of life, although they have their individuality, are encompassed within a unity, in which each part has a function. The functions of each part are interconnected, so that each being gives and receives something from the other. In this way, the global functioning of the universe is governed by a "law of justice," which establishes "order" and the "power of the controlling force." In this perspective of Plotinus, "the other is our co-generation by the One and our co-dependence on it."[134]

This conception of a holistically structured cosmos, upheld by Plotinus in the third century, dialogs perfectly with the Inca ontology described by Josef Estermann in Andean philosophy. Despite Estermann, in a footnote, refuting the dialog of the principle of relationality, or holistic principle, as the *arché* of Andean ontology with monism in the Hegelian dialectic established between part and whole, there is a great similarity between the principle of relationality and the ontology of Plotinus when he discusses the *nous.*[135]

Estermann asserts that one cannot compare the principle of relationality with Hegelian monist metaphysics, because holism in the principle of relationality is not conceived in a metaphysical and chronological sense, but rather in an axiological and experiential sense. In addition, he further emphasizes that the distinction between substantiality and accidentality, typical of Western ontologies, does not apply to the ontology of Andean relationality, given that in the Inca worldview, relationality is not a subsequent, external, and accidental aspect, but is the very *arché*, since beings only gain concreteness and existence as they interrelate.[136]

He also emphasizes that the conception of Andean relationality is *sui generis*, as it implies a variety of non-logical forms and sub-principles, such as reciprocity, complementarity, and correspondence, which influence affective, ecological, ethical, and esthetic aspects.

Despite the differences pointed out by Estermann, reciprocity and correspondence are also present in the ontology of Plotinus as a development of unity. The principle of reciprocity in Plotinus manifests itself as "cosmic justice"; all beings are connected and relate by giving and receiving from each other.[137] The principle of correspondence in Plotinus, as mentioned, was identified as a precursor to contemporary fractal geometry.[138]

Estermann describes the principle of correspondence in the Andean worldview as a corollary of the principle of relationality. There is a correspondence between the micro- and macrocosm, between the cosmic and the human, the organic and the

[134] Westra (2002), p. 31.

[135] Estermann (2006), p. 126.

[136] Estermann (2006), p. 126.

[137] Westra (2002), p. 32.

[138] Fideler (2001), p. 108.

non-organic, and life and death.[139] It seems that the idea is quite similar to the correspondence in Plotinus and fractal geometry.

Regarding reciprocity, Estermann explains that in the interrelations between humans and non-humans, between humans and nature, and between the human and the divine, there is a cosmic ethic that governs the exchange of goods, feelings, and people. Reciprocity "says that different acts condition each other (interaction) in such a way that the effort or 'investment' in an action by one actor will be 'rewarded' by an effort or an 'investment' of the same magnitude by the receiver."[140]

Regarding the problem of necessitarianism in monist ontology, raised by Estermann as a factor of incompatibility with the principle of relationality in Andean philosophy, as will be demonstrated later, Cirne-Lima solves this problem in his ethics of coherence, which, despite being founded on the monism of Plotinus, corrects the necessitarianism of Hegelian monism. Similarly, Hans Jonas, in his integral monism, which underpins the ethics of responsibility, preserves the concepts of contingency and free will, corrections that further affirm the possibility of a dialog between the said ontologies for the construction of a holistic planetary ecological ethic based on the concept of harmony.

Westra explains that, for Plotinus, nothing truly dies; things and beings simply return to a new form. The particular dissonances compose a comprehensive harmony of the whole, of the opposites, which rise in the synthesis of harmony. For Plotinus, before inquiring about right or wrong, it is necessary to understand the unity of the cosmos, its regularities, and laws, as the basis of our moral understanding lies in the awareness that we are interdependent and dependent on the one.

Westra highlights that this holism in Plotinus' ontology is the basis of his proposal for ecological ethics in the principle of integrity, of Aldo Leopold's Earth ethics,[141] and, to some extent, influenced the deep ecology of Arne Naess. Westra's ecosystemic approach to the principle of integrity is based on a unitary understanding of the biosphere and each ecosystem; that is, each system is considered as one and as a functional whole, which provides life support to its parts. Thus, the cosmic interconnection and the primacy of unity have been the basis of various ecocentric theories.[142] Aldo Leopold, in Earth ethics, already emphasized that the human being is part of the biota of ecosystems.

Despite Estermann[143] emphasizing that Andean relationality is not a Hegelian totality, nor a Levinasian transcendence, nor a Feuerbachian immanence, he does not compare Inca ontology with Plotinus' ontology. Although there are many differences—and there should be—there is a lot of similarity. There is evident holism in both worldviews, which is also found, to some extent, in the perspectivism of

[139] Estermann (2006), p. 138.

[140] Estermann (2006), p. 145.

[141] Leopold (1949).

[142] Westra (2002), pp. 33–34.

[143] Estermann (2006), p. 133.

Amazonian Amerindian peoples[144]: a holism that allows the moral consideration of nature, which can be the ontological basis for the construction of a planetary ecological ethic, like the synthesis that forms at the meeting of the horizons of the North and the South, of the old and the new, toward the becoming of life, which is shared by all human and non-human beings—a holism based on harmony as the guiding thread of life on the planet.

2.7 Ontological Turn and Amerindian Perspectivism

It can no longer be forgotten that access to being is not a monopoly of Eurocentric Western culture, given that anthropology has broken the homogeneous and objective concept of nature and is moving toward the so-called multinaturalism[145] or ontological turn, which recognizes the possibility for indigenous peoples from various parts of the planet to access the "being," thus validating their ways of describing the world. This "ontological turn," provided, among others, by the theory of perspectivism by Viveiros de Castro, the metatheory of the four ontologies by Philippe Descola,[146] and the alternative models of Bruno

[144] Castro (1996), pp. 116–118.

[145] Sztutman (2009), p. 14.

[146] Anthropologist Philippe Descola, holder of the Chair of Anthropology of Nature at the Collège de France, argues that nature or the natural world is seen and defined in different ways by different ontologies. (i) The Western ontology based on naturalism conceives of nature in an objective, external, and unique way. For this view, there are various ways for the different cultures to perceive this objective and unique nature from an external and partial perspectives. This variation of partial and external views of nature is called multiculturalism. (ii) From the study of the worldview of the Achuar people, Descola identified an animist ontology. For the Achuar, kinship relations encompass plants and animals. For example, Achuar women are considered the mothers of the plants grown in their plantations, and they are the creators of these plants and have a blood kinship relationship of motherhood with them. Men, on the other hand, are hunters and as such maintain a kinship relationship by affinity with hunting animals, and they are brothers-in-law of hunting animals. In the animist ontology, social relations extend to the natural world. This continuity between humans and non-humans does not occur by sharing a biological physical body, but rather by the "soul" (*wakan*, in the Achuar language). In the Achuar cosmogony, all beings share the same soul that makes them human; this animistic communion between animals, plants, and human beings was established in the so-called time of myth, when all were humans with the same form, before the speciation that gave different forms and bodies to humans; thus, some came to occupy the body of the jaguar, others of birds, fish, and plants. But, despite this change in bodily forms, the soul remains the same, so they can still communicate through enchantments called *anents*. (iii) Another ontology is totemism, present among the indigenous peoples of Australia. Unlike his master Lévi-Strauss, for whom totemism was merely a classificatory logic, Descola identifies in the totemism of the indigenous peoples of Australia a true ontology. It is totemism that establishes a mode of identification between the human being and the natural world. For the totemic ontology, there is an identification between humans and non-humans both from the point of view of subjectivity (soul) and physicality. There is a sharing of physiological and psychological properties between the totem (natural species) and the

Latour,[147] challenges the naturalist ontology that has always predominated at the base of Western scientific thought. For the naturalist ontological current in Western thought, there is only one objectively conceived nature, and the relationship between humans and this nature is limited to the material plane. The only thing humans have in common with animals and plants is their material constitution; however, this communion is disrupted by the cultural aspect, as humans possess minds, souls, cognition, language, and morality that differentiate and separate them from nature.

This view of discontinuity on the cultural plane is the basis of naturalist ontology, which underpins the sciences within a Eurocentric view and restricts access to "being" only to thinkers congregated on this ontological basis. Other thinkers, originating from peoples whose thoughts were forged in different ontologies, would not be legitimized to epistemologically present their ways of accessing "being" and life itself.

The proposal of the so-called ontological turn is to recognize that there is not just one nature subject to various representations or views, that is, to various cultures, as suggested by multiculturalism and naturalist ontology. There are,

---

members of the totemic group, who share moral and material characteristics, which define the essence of their identity. Thus, the members of the totemic group share the same humanity. The totem, a plant or an animal, is named with an abstract property, which is shared by the entire totemic group. Sztutman (2009), pp. 5–7. Analogism is an ontology that differentiates human beings and non-humans from the point of view of interiority (soul) psyche, subjectivity, and from the physical point of view. (Sá Júnior (2014), p. 20.

[147] *CULT—Can you explain your theory about the network of actors and how it differs from traditional sociology as a new form of sociology? BL—'The network of actors' is something that we developed, my colleagues and I, for simply practical reasons. The sociological explanation of scientific activities that is provided to us does not get us anywhere. Therefore, after trying hard to explain things socially, we realized that the lack was in the very social theory implicit in traditional sociology, from Durkheim. If we could never explain science it is because science is not, itself, social, in the sense that its collectivities are full of flaws. Instead, the sociology we use can describe their associations. We call this alternative sociology to Durkheimian sociology, 'actor-network theory', and then we place it under the rubric of Gabriel Tarde, as many of these ideas had already been developed by Tarde over 100 years ago, without us realizing it before. These ideas were therefore already part of the early days of sociology. Anyway, one of the pioneers in rediscovering the work of Gabriel Tarde is a Brazilian, Eduardo Vargas, who has long been publishing on the subject. Therefore, the theory of the actor-network consists of doing on the social side what the anthropology of sciences does on the side of nature. The symmetry that I used earlier made me realize that both nature and the social (society) are similar. This division between nature and culture is a way of doing politics, of gathering things into two collectivities, for reasons that come from modernity. Everything I do in science studies (**science studies**) is to show that this grouping of beings that we call nature, this amalgam of independent beings, is a poorly constituted collectivity. The concept of 'nature' makes no sense, as there is no such thing as nature. Today, we have proof with the works of Descola and others. But what interests me in sociology (which is different from what Descola does) is the other collectivity: society. We can show that society is poorly constituted, disorganized, unfit. As we now dissolve this dichotomy between nature and society, we have interesting things left to do, like investigating their associations, their connections and their grouping policies: this is what interests me.* Latour (2009), p. 14–17.

indeed, various natures, various worlds, accessed by different ontologies, such as, for example, Amerindian animism, identified by Viveiros de Castro and defined as "all the inhabitants of the cosmos are people in their own department—potential occupants of the deictic position of the first person or subject of cosmological discourse."

The relevance of this turn in ontology, as emphasized by Renato Sztutman, should be transformative:

> The recognition of other ontologies and modes of existence, almost always threatened by hegemonic orders - see the effort of modern Science in stabilizing its own concepts of nature and scientific fact (Latour, 1991) -, is initially a political act that jeopardizes this hegemony. It is in this direction that Viveiros de Castro (2014) assumes that the "Ontological Turn" is, above all, "turn" or the "turn" of the native.[148]

Relationality is also present in the so-called Amerindian perspectivism, a conceptual synthesis which Eduardo Viveiros de Castro and Tânia Stolze Lima propose to examine Amazonian philosophy regarding the relational nature of beings and the composition of the world. Viveiros de Castro explains that, for many indigenous peoples of South America, the world is inhabited by different types of subjects or people, both human and non-human. For these indigenous peoples, the way humans see animals and other subjectivities, such as gods, spirits, the dead, inhabitants of other cosmic levels, meteorological phenomena, etc., is different from the way these beings see them and see themselves.

For these indigenous peoples, especially those from the Northwest Amazon, animals are people or see themselves as people. The visible form, the material body of each species, is a simple garment that hides an internal human form, which is visible only to members of the same species or to the so-called trans-specific beings, such as shamans. The internal form, the spirit of the animal—which is similar to the subjectivity or intentionality that we humans call human consciousness—is substantiated in a human body, hidden under the skin, as well as in the external form of the animal. Thus, an anthropomorphic essence of spiritual nature is highlighted, that is, a consciousness common to all beings, and a variety of sensitive bodily forms, which are considered only as garments that can assume various forms, characterizing a transformational world.[149]

In this ontology of the Amazonian indigenous peoples, a differentiation between the human and the animal—by culture, by spirituality, by intellect, as in Western evolutionary cosmology—is not conceived. On the contrary, "the original condition common to humans and animals is not animality, but humanity [...] The common reference to all beings of nature is not man as a species, but humanity as a condition."[150]

In our naturalist ontology, what makes us similar to other non-human beings is our material, biological dimension; in Amerindian perspectivism, the idea is the

---

[148] Sztutman (2020), pp. 186–187.

[149] Castro (1996), pp. 116–117.

[150] Castro (1996), pp. 116–118.

opposite. Humans and non-human animals do not share the same biological dimension, as each one has a body—a different garment—and what unites us is our common humanity. This humanity shared by all beings is the spiritual dimension, a common consciousness that unites all forms of life.

At this point, Viveiros de Castro highlights the relevance of the difference between the human species and the human condition in understanding the perspectivist ontology of these indigenous peoples. The various animal forms with symbolic and practical roles, such as large predatory animals, which are rivals of humans, and animals that are prey to humans, are covered in different physical forms, but all have a single spiritual "essence." This common consciousness is the humanity shared by these non-human animals and humans.[151]

In naturalist ontology, the interconnection of humans with nature is biological; that is, "humans are here organisms like others, object-bodies in 'ecological' interaction with other bodies and forces, all regulated by the necessary laws of biology and physics."[152] in. the animist ontology, humans and non-humans are members of a sociocosmic community, shared by partaking in a single animic dimension, a single culture, that is, a single spirit.

Viveiros de Castro questions whether animism would also fall into a form of anthropocentrism, as it extends to animals a subjectivity common to human beings—a humanity. The author answers this question:

> [...] self-references of the type "people" mean "person", not "member of a human species"; and they are personal pronouns, recording the point of view of the subject who is speaking, and not proper names. To say then that animals and spirits are people is to say that they are persons; it is to attribute to non-humans the capacities of conscious intentionality and of "agency" that define the position of the subject. Such capacities are reified in the "soul" or "spirit" that these non-humans are endowed with. It is the subject who has a soul, and has a soul who is capable of a point of view [...] Every being to which a point of view is attributed will thus be a subject, spirit; or better, wherever there is the point of view, there will also be the position of the subject.[153]

Viveiros de Castro highlights that while, for our ontology, "the point of view creates the object," for Amerindian perspectivism, "the point of view creates the subject." He emphasizes that shamans explain that these non-human beings are placed in the perspective of subjects who see themselves culturally as humans. The nature of the subject is forged in culture, by a subjectivity shared between humans and non-humans.

In Western ontology, if, on one hand, humanity is a species among other animals, and animality is a province that includes humans by their biological dimension, contradictorily, this same humanity is posited as a moral condition, which excludes non-human animals. Thus, in Western cosmology, the concept of "human nature" claims a physical continuity (biological) and a metaphysical

---

[151] Castro (1996), p. 119.

[152] Castro (1996), p. 121.

[153] Castro (1996), p. 126.

discontinuity (cultural) between humans and non-humans. Amerindians, on the other hand, postulate a spiritual, cultural, and subjective continuity between humans and non-humans, and a physical discontinuity, since, despite each one assuming a differentiated physical body, they share a common soul.[154]

The worldviews of the Amerindian indigenous peoples reveal a relational ontology aimed at the sustainability of life conditions, which is demonstrated in negentropic practices reducing the impact of accelerating entropic processes, thereby questioning the future of all living beings and, equally, that of the human being.

This relational vision of social interdependence between the human being and non-human beings, founded on a kinship relationship, which is proposed by Amerindian perspectivism, also presents itself as an ontological assumption for the construction of an ethics rooted in responsibility, care, and reverence for life in its fullness. An ethics that recognizes the intrinsic value of non-human beings and ecosystems, capable of grounding the theoretical basis for the recognition of subjectivity and the rights of nature itself, and that enables indigenous peoples as legitimate representatives of plants and animals, as subjects of law in the wheel of discourse.

Borrowing the metaphor from Hans Jonas, the change in ontology is Ariadne's thread that will take us out of the anthropogenic chaos.[155]

As can be inferred from the previous items, the analytical and dual ontology that was inaugurated with Aristotle, by conceptualizing substance and separating matter from form or essence, was the starting point for our erratic understanding of nature, which reached its borderline mistake with the concepts of *res cogitans* and *res extensa* of Descartes. Thus, the first step for change is the rupture with the very analytical and dualistic ontological paradigm that served as the basis for anthropocentrism and also for the reductionist view of the biosphere.

Neither does the pure and simple adoption of post-dualist monisms solve the problem, be it the so-called physicalist materialism, which reduces nature to the condition of pure matter, or the transcendental idealism of Kant, or Heidegger's existentialism, which envisage a nature detached from the reality of the biosphere.

The change in the ontological paradigm that is proposed is the adoption of a contemporary Neoplatonism in dialog with the worldviews of the original peoples, the so-called epistemologies of the South,[156] and the Earth system sciences.

In this sense, the Neoplatonic monism of Plotinus harmonizes perfectly with the general ethics of coherence of Cirne-Lima and with the ethics of responsibility of Hans Jonas, and, to some extent, with the worldview of the original peoples; therefore, it presents itself as a new ontology suitable to underpin the foundations of an applied ecological ethics of harmony with nature.

---

154 Castro (1996), pp. 126–129.

155 Jonas (1966), p. 3.

156 Santos (2009).

References

Anjos JC, Fehlauer TJ (2017) Para além do "pachamamismo": *Pachamama* e *Sumak Kawsay* como potência cosmopolítica andina. Tellus, Campo Grande, MS, Universidade Católica Dom Bosco (UCDB), 17(32):106. jan./abr Disponível em https://www.tellus.ucdb.br/tellus/article/view/442/401. Accessed 05 Apr 2025

A Antropologia da natureza de Philippe Descola. Entrevista de Philippe Descola para Andrea Daher Disponível em https://www.scielo.br/pdf/topoi/v14n27/1518-3319-topoi-14-27-00495.pdf. Accessed 05 Apr 2025

BRILLOUIN L (1964) Scientific uncertainty and information. Academic Press, New York

Castro EVd (1996) Os pronomes cosmológicos e o perspectivismo ameríndio. Mana, Rio de Janeiro 2(2):115–144. out. Disponível em https://www.scielo.br/scielo.php?script=sci_arttext&pid=S0104-93131996000200005. Accessed 20 Apr 2025

Cirne-Lima CRV (2017) Dialética para principiantes. Escritos Editora, Porto Alegre

Cirne-Lima CRV (2012) Causalidade e auto-organização. In: Luft E, Cirne-Lima CRV (eds) Ideia e movimento. Civilização Brasileira, Rio de Janeiro

Cirne-Lima CRV (2001) Platão: o uno e o múltiplo. In: Feltes HPDM, Zilles U (Org) Filosofia: diálogo de horizontes: *Festschrift* em homenagem a Jayme Paviani, Caxias do Sul EDUCS; EDIPUCRS, Porto Alegre

Cirne-Lima CRV (1998) A explicação do mundo. In: Ulmann RA (Org) Consecratio mundi: *Festschrift*em homenagem a UrbanoZil-les. EDIPUCRS, Porto Alegre

Di Felice M, Pereira ES (2017) Formas comunicativas do habitar indígena: a digitalização da floresta e o net-ativismo nativo no Brasil. In: Di Felice M, Pereira ES (Org) Redes e ecologias comunicativas indígenas: as contribuições dos povos originários à teoria da comunicação. Paulus, São Paulo, pp 41–58

Estermann J (2006) Filosofia andina: sabiduría indígena para un mundo nuevo, 2nd edn. Instituto Superior Ecuménico Andino de Teología (ISEAT) (Teología y Filosoía Andinas, 1), La Paz Bolivia

Ferrater Mora J (2004) Dicionário de filosofia, vol 2, 2nd edn. Loyola, São Paulo

Fideler D (2001) Neoplatonism and the cosmological revolution: holism, fractal geometry and mind-in-nature. In: Harris RB (ed). Neoplatonism and contemporary thought: part one. State University of New York Press. (Studies in Neoplatonism: Ancient and Modern, 10), Albany, NY

Heidegger M (2018) Heraclitus: the inception of occidental thinking and logic: heraclitus's doctrine of the *logos*. Tradução de Julia Goesser A, Montegomery Ewegen S. Bloomsbury Academic, New York, *E–book*

Heidegger M (2015) Ser e tempo, Tradução de Márcia Sá Cavalcante, 10th edn. Petrópolis RJ, Bragança Paulista SP (eds) Editora Universitária São Francisco, Vozes

Jonas H (2017) Os fundamentos biológicos da individualidade. In: JONAS H. Ensaios filosóficos: da crença antiga ao homem tecnológico. Tradução de Wendell Evangelista Soares Lopes. Paulus (Coleção Ethos), São Paulo

Jonas H (2006) O princípio responsabilidade: ensaio de uma ética para uma civilização tecnológica. Tradução de Marijane Lisboa e Luiz Barros Montez. Contraponto; PUC Rio, Rio de Janeiro

Jonas H (2004) O princípio vida: fundamentos para uma biologia filosófica. Vozes, Petrópolis

Jonas H (1966) The phenomenon of life: Toward a philosophical biology. Harper & Row, New York

Jonas H, Hannum H, Hannum H (1994) Philosophy at the end of the century: A survey of its past and future. Social Research, Baltimore, MA, The Johns Hopkins University Press, 61(4):820–821. Winter. Disponível em https://www.jstor.org/stable/40971061. Accessed 12 Feb 2025

Kisiel T (2014) Hermeneutics of facticity. In: Davis BW (Ed) Martin Heidegger: key concepts. Routledge, Abingdon, UK

Kuhn TS (2012) The structure of scientific revolutions. 4th edn. The University of Chicago Press. (50th anniversary edition), Chicago

Latour B (2009) Entrevista para Marcelo Fiorini. Revista Cult, Ano 12(132): 14–17. fev. Disponível em https://revistacult.uol.com.br/home/entrevista-bruno-latour/. Accessed on 12 Mar 2025

Leff E (2018) El fuego de la vida: Heidegger ante la cuestión ambiental. Siglo Veintiuno, México, DF

Leopold A (1949) A Sand County almanac: With other essays on conservation from Round River. Oxford University Press, New York

Martin GT (2008) Revolutionary holism: the principle of harmony and the rule of law in human affairs. [For upcoming publication in a volume on Harmony from the Institute on Global Harmony, Sardarshahar, India]. Disponível em https://www.radford.edu/~gmartin/Harmony%20and%20the%20Rule%20of%20Law.June14.pdf. Accessed 20 Apr 2025

Mesquita AP (2018) Doutrinas não-escritas. In: Cornelli G, Lopes R (Org) Platão. São Paulo; Coimbra: Paulus; Imprensa da Universidade de Coimbra. Disponível em https://digitalis-dsp.uc.pt/jspui/bitstream/10316.2/44236/1/Platao.pdf. Accessed 04 Mar 2025

Michaelis (online). Disponível em https://michaelis.uol.com.br/moderno-portugues/busca/portugues-brasileiro/epifenomenalismo. Accessed 20 Apr 2025

Odum EP, Barrett GW (2020) Fundamentos de ecologia. Tradução de Pégasus Sistemas e Soluções. Cengage, São Paulo

Perine M (2011) O *Filebo* de Platão e as doutrinas não escritas. Educação e Filosofia, Uberlândia, **Edufu**, 25(49):153–154. jan./jun. Disponível em http://www.seer.ufu.br/index.php/EducacaoFilosofia/article/view/13340/7630. Accessed 26 Apr 2025

Reale G, Antiseri D (2018) Filosofia: idade contemporânea. Tradução de Ivo Storniolo. vol (3). Paulus, São Paulo

Reale G, Antiseri D (2003) História da filosofia: filosofia pagã antiga, vol 1. Paulus, São Paulo

Sá Júnior LC (2014) Philipe Descola e a virada ontológica na antropologia. Ilha, 16 (2): 7–36. ago./dez. Disponível em https://periodicos.ufsc.br/index.php/ilha/article/view/2175-8034.2014v16n2p7/29164. Accessed 20 Apr 2025

Salazar Calderón Galliani, F O (2015) Entre Eros y Wiracocha: un encuentro dialógico entre la filosofía griega y el pensamiento andino. Tesis (Licenciado en Filosofía) – Facultad de Letras y Ciencias Humanas. Universidad Nacional Mayor de San Marcos, Lima, Perú, 2015. Available on http://cybertesis.unmsm.edu.pe/bitstream/handle/20.500.12672/4395/Salazar_go.pdf?sequence=1. Accessed 20 Apr 2025

Chapter 3
A New Ethical System, Guided by Coherence and Responsibility, for the Recognition of Intrinsic Value in Nature

The need to dedicate two chapters of this work to ethics stems from the premise that value preexists the legal norm. Before the established norm, there is always a value. Just as the recognition of human rights went through a "*dynamogenesis* of values," as a result "of a succession of direct and indirect battles for the opening of spaces before the established power," the struggle for the rights of nature also goes through a "*dynamogenesis* of values" that must be examined.[1]

In this line, considering that this work aims at the recognition of the legality of the principle of harmony with nature as a legitimizing foundation for the recognition of subjectivity and personality for plants, animals, ecosystems, species, and the biosphere, it is imperative to scrutinize the principles of a general ethics that underpin the proposal of an ethics applied to ecology, capable of supporting the recognition of legal subjectivity for plants, animals, ecosystems, species, biodiversity, and the biosphere.

This ethics, applied to ecology, in addition to unfolding from the dialog of Neoplatonic monist ontology with the ontologies of the original peoples, should be able to guide action not only in relations between human beings but also between human beings and animals, plants, ecosystems, species, and the biosphere. That is, this applied ecological ethics needs to start from the recognition of intrinsic value and subjectivity in non-human beings and organic holistic entities with which humanity shares life.

With this purpose, the dialectical coherence ethics of the Brazilian philosopher Cirne-Lima and the ethics of responsibility of Hans Jonas will be examined in the following items: as a foundational and legitimizing proposal of an applied ecological ethics that recognizes the intrinsic value of non-human living beings and organic holistic entities and, consequently, enables the extension of rights to these non-human beings and organic entities, placing them as members of a community

[1] Silveira and Rocasolano (2010), p. 185.

R. D. d. Amaral, *The Principle of Harmony with Nature as a Legal Foundation*,
https://doi.org/10.1007/978-3-032-05475-3_3

of subjects that share a cosmic supraconsciousness, which is immanent to all beings and confers upon them the title of dignity.

Before detailing the ethical systems of Cirne-Lima and Hans Jonas, it is urgent to briefly explain the reasons why dualistic ethical systems of Kantian root, despite having represented a great advance in the progress of humanity, do not prove adequate to justify the moral consideration of animals, plants, and ecosystems.

3.1 The Insufficiency of Dualistic Ethics in the Face of the Ecological Crisis

Cirne-Lima explains that at the beginning of our civilization, the ought-to–be, which is the central theme of ethics, was formulated within the family sphere. The *pater*, through the sacred song of the family in the ritual of the sacred fire, redefines the actions of the members of the family group, defining good and evil. Ethics, in what is called Western civilization, arises in the religion of the Greek patriarchal family. Over time, issues related to action go beyond the family sphere and begin to permeate the interests of the larger social group in the city, in the *polis*. At this point in the history of ethics, in ancient Greece, the question arises about what is a just or unjust law, which will be the theme of the sophists, Plato, and Aristotle, and shows us the relevance of ethics and values in the genesis of legal institutions.[2]

This question of the ought-to–be was first addressed by Socrates, who said in his dialogs that virtue is what ought-to–be. This is the starting point of Plato's philosophy: the world that "is" and the world that "ought to be"; it is from this that a doctrine about correct action arises.[3]

Plato establishes as an ethical criterion the hierarchy of values in a pyramidal structure, at the apex of which is the supreme good. Aristotle proposes as an ethical criterion the so-called right reason, which will prevail in Thomistic scholasticism and even in Kantian ethics. The ethics based on right reason will gain depth, as well as the vigor that will reverberate to our days, with Kant.[4]

In modernity, when Kant constructs his ethical system, he starts from the factual assumption that all peoples, at any time and place, have a sense of what ought-to–be; this "ought-to–be," Kant calls the fact of reason. From this starting point, he poses the transcendental question: What is the necessary condition of possibility for such a fact, that is, for all peoples at any time and place to have an ought-to–be? What is the condition *sine qua non* for this fact? Cirne-Lima unravels the question proposed by Kant:

[2] Cirne-Lima (2017), p. 147.

[3] Cirne-Lima (2017), p. 147.

[4] Kant (2017).

> What is the conditio **sine qua non**? For all peoples in all places to have such an Ought-to–be, there must exist an **a priori** structure, there must exist a practical transcendental self guided by a single general principle. There is, therefore, a transcendental Principle of Practical Reason which is a necessary **a priori** condition and the common denominator of multiple local ethics. This practical Principle, Kant calls the categorical imperative: Always act in such a way that the norm of your action can be elevated to the status of a Universal law. This great moral imperative is devoid of content, yes, but in compensation it is valid for all[5].

As can be seen, Kant's critique of practical reason was a great advance in the general theory of ethics, but it presents some problems that hinder its use as a general ethical system capable of underpinning an applied ecological ethics. The first critique is aptly made by the philosopher Cirne-Lima and lies in the fact that Kant split theoretical reason, where descriptive propositions are formulated, from practical reason, where normative propositions are formulated. This duality creates a problem raised by Cirne-Lima: An ethics that aims to be general should indicate how to make the transition from descriptive propositions, from the world of "is," to normative propositions, to provide a foundation for the ought-to–be that avoids the so-called naturalistic fallacy—that is, to provide a foundation for ethics in laws of nature. As Cirne-Lima teaches us:

> Normative propositions are not something that can be given or measured by sensory experience; in the sensory world things are what they are and how they are, there is no Ought-to–be that can be perceived there. But, if we do not form the Ought-to–be from sensory experience, if this is not a criterion of the same, where does the Ought-to–be come from? If it does not come from the sensory world and **a posteriori**, does it mean that it is something **a priori**? And can this be demonstrated or at least shown?[6]

This issue, indeed, presents itself as tormenting because, if the natural laws that exist in the sensory world of the "being" are treated by theoretical reason through descriptive propositions, how will they be apprehended by the ought-to–be, through normative propositions that deal with acting in practical reason? Thus, in the formulation of the normative propositions of practical reason, which deal with acting, will it never be possible to regulate this acting in harmony with natural laws? Then, will all our ethics be devoid of ecological contents? Since entropic and negentropic ecological processes are in the world of "being," can they never be dealt with by the ought-to–be? Indeed, the duality of theoretical and practical reasons established by Kant makes an applied ecological ethics unfeasible, as Cirne-Lima points out:

> In addition to these two issues, which are fundamental, several others arise. The most important of them refers to a crucial problem of our times, Ecology: How to construct an ethics that, prevailing among men and for men, founded exclusively on the dignity of the human person, shows and justifies the ecological obligations that today no one denies as being an important part of our Ought-to–be? In addition, how to construct an ethics that being universal and, therefore, necessarily formal, can have material contents? How to

---

[5] Cirne-Lima (2017), p. 150.

[6] Cirne-Lima (1999), p. 944.

reconcile, in such ethics, the a priori and the a posteriori? And also, how to reconcile the universal validity of ethical principles and the legitimate plurality of many cultures?[7]

Cirne-Lima is right when he points out the insufficiency of the anthropocentric Kantian ethical system to serve as a foundation for applied ecological ethics. In addition to the duality that created an apparently insurmountable abyss between descriptive and normative propositions, which generates a formalist ethics devoid of ecological material contents, it also established a contractualist symmetry that excludes non-human beings from moral consideration, toward whom human beings have only an indirect ethical duty.

When analyzing contemporary deontological ethics based on Kant, such as the contractualism of John Rawls,[8] it is observed that its foundations are the concepts of original position and overlapping consensus, which underpin justice as the result of a choice deliberately made in a hypothetical original contract, the ultimate basis for all other agreements, pacts, and contracts; however, animals, plants, and ecosystems cannot be part of this social agreement, as justice can only be discussed in relations between "autonomous beings capable of mutual recognition as moral equals."[9] From this Kantian premise, non-human beings are excluded from Rawls' contractualist ethical community.

Brian Baxter also discusses the problematic issue of non-human beings being covered by Rawlsian ideas of ethics and justice, considering that they would not be able to occupy the so-called original position, since the participants of this must have cognitive capacity, language, and self-awareness. Similarly, they could not participate in the consensus, as they do not have a sense of justice. Indeed, Rawls' consensus presupposes bilaterality and symmetry of responsibilities among its participants. Thus, his contractualist ethics also proves inadequate as the basis for an ecological ethic.[10]

Similarly, the discourse ethics of Apel[11] and Habermas[12] do not offer a solution to the ecological crisis. Despite the advancements in relation to Kantian and Rawlsian ethics, discourse ethics still does not provide foundations for an applied ecological ethic. Indeed, Apel and Habermas work with two principles: the principle of discourse and the principle of universalization. This, called the "u" principle, corresponds to Kant's categorical imperative; that is, it has the normative role of a duty-to–be. However, this principle is functionalized by the principle of discourse, which confers historical and contingent contents to the principle of universalization. That is, Apel and Habermas work with speech acts to create a hypothetical wheel of rational discourse, in which the themes of good and evil

7 Cirne-Lima (1999), p. 943.

8 Rawls (2008), pp. 173–174.

9 Baxter (2005), p. 155.

10 Baxter (2005), pp. 156–158.

11 Apel (2000).

12 Habermas (1999).

are debated in a non-violent environment and in which everyone is represented to, thus, define if a certain interest is ethical.[13]

Xabier Etxeberria, when dealing with the theme of ethics in the face of the ecological crisis, points out difficulties in discursive ethics in offering a moral solution to the crisis. Firstly, although Habermas and Apel intend to formulate an opening for ecological problems, they cannot disentangle themselves from anthropocentrism, nor from dualism. At this point, Etxeberria cites the objection made to Habermas by Henning Ottmann, in which he asserted that the communicative rationality proposed by Habermas did not overcome access to nature as a mere instrument—that is, an object of human dominion—so it does not offer any possibility for a cosmological ethic that recognizes intrinsic value in nature.[14]

In reply to Ottmann's objection, Habermas reaffirms that, from the cognitive and scientific points of view, it is only possible to access objectified nature. Etxeberria emphasizes that Habermas' discourse ethics allows humans to continue treating nature instrumentally to meet their emancipatory interests. For Habermas, there is a difficulty in overcoming the fragmentation of the relationship between human beings and nature because, as a debtor of Kant, he does not admit a unified reason; he also does not accept a return of ethics to metaphysics. Apel, in turn, bases his ethics on the concept of intersubjectivity of co-responsible subjects in a communicational community. It happens that this communicational intersubjectivity is based on the concept of reciprocity; therefore, it restricts the community of co-responsible and solidary actors to the community of humans.[15]

Both Apel and Habermas cannot unfold this responsibility and solidarity toward non-human living beings, as they are tied to the Kantian conception that non-human beings are objects, so humans have only indirect duties toward them. Apel even mitigates this position, recognizing a limited reciprocity of communicative competence in relation to nature, but not enough to overcome the ties of contractualism to which he is bound.[16]

The origin of Habermas's epistemological objection to extending the circle of ethical consideration to include non-human beings lies in his work that differentiates the concepts of work and interaction.[17] Habermas considers that human work necessarily objectifies nature through the use of science and technology. This relationship of human dominion over nature, reducing it to a mere instrument, is legitimized in the interest of the human species in its own reproduction and survival.

Work, which is a strategic issue for survival, is realized through the mastery of nature. The interaction occurs in the social sphere, governed by the ethics of public

[13] Cirne-Lima (2017), p. 158.

[14] Etxeberria (1994), p. 4.

[15] Etxeberria (1994), p. 4.

[16] Etxeberria (1994), p. 4.

[17] Habermas (2007), p. 189.

discourse, whose ultimate goal is mutual understanding among the members of the ethical community: the human beings.

In this regard, Habermas considers that attributing an end value to nature would be a return to the pre-modern period, a renunciation of the achievements of the enlightenment which, through the mastery of nature, would have bequeathed to humanity full emancipation. Habermas even admits that humans would have a "quasi-moral" responsibility, based on communicative action, toward animals that interact with humans through non-linguistic gestures, because these animals would be establishing an intersubjective relationship with the human community. However, this "quasi-moral" responsibility would not be extended to plants, ecosystems, and animals without communicative ability.[18]

As can be seen, Habermas places epistemological obstacles ahead of the most urgent ethical issue in the history of human thought: the salvation not only of the human species but also of the conditions of life on the planet. The epistemological objections raised by Habermas only make sense to those who are tributaries of the dualistic philosophical system, of which his ethics, separated from metaphysics, is an heir.

Despite having advanced in the direction of constructing a discursive democracy, which ensures the speaking place of socially minority human groups in peaceful discourse, it fails when it detaches from a reality that affects the entire social structure, serving as an insurmountable obstacle to the well-being of humanity. The ecological crisis will inevitably compromise the discourse of non-violence extolled by Habermas. It can no longer be denied that climate change, the desertification of large areas of once-productive land, and the lack of rain are driving millions of people to seek refuge in search of the bare minimum for existence, and this, evidently, exacerbates conflicts and social inequality.

Democracy, as the egalitarian reciprocity of the members of a society, will only be possible on a planet where there are conditions of sustainability, considering that the harmony between the human being and nature presents itself as a basic prerequisite for any project of ecologically sustainable discursive democracy.

3.2 The Dialectical Coherence Ethics of Cirne-Lima as a Proposal Capable of Supporting an Applied Ecological Ethics

As already mentioned, Cirne-Lima proposes a dialectical ethical system based on the resolution of the great theoretical problems that the analytical and dualistic ethical systems, already analyzed in the Sect. 3.1, could not solve.

There are five major issues: (i) How to make the transition from merely descriptive propositions pertinent to theoretical reason to normative propositions

[18] Habermas (2007), p. 189.

of practical reason without falling into the naturalistic fallacy?; (ii) establishing the first major principles that should govern the ought-to–be, to define what is ethically right or wrong; (iii) the issue concerning the transition from the particular to the universal, or vice versa, that is, how to construct an ethics that, even though formal (universal), has concrete contents?; (iv) How to reconcile the universal validity of ethical principles and the legitimate plurality of many cultures?; and (v) How to construct an ethics based solely on the dignity of the human person, capable of justifying ecological obligations?

In dealing with the first issue, that is, how to make the transition from merely descriptive propositions pertinent to theoretical reason to normative propositions of practical reason, without falling into the naturalistic fallacy, Cirne-Lima emphasizes that this issue is intertwined with the second, that is, establishing the first major principles that should govern the ought-to–be, to define what is ethically right or wrong.

He points out that, for Plato, the first major principles of ethics are based on the great laws that govern the cosmic universe—that is, the laws that govern the stars, nature, and the entire universe, and that also discipline the soul of the human being. However, as can be quickly seen, by basing ethics on the laws of nature, Plato fell into the naturalistic fallacy. Aristotle, on the other hand, distinguished and separated descriptive propositions from prescriptive ones, so he escaped the naturalistic fallacy. Nevertheless, he had difficulties in grounding the ought-to–be of virtues. First, he proposed tradition as the legitimizing foundation of the good, the right. But it is known that tradition is not always a suitable ethical criterion, as there are many bad traditions. Later, he adopted the *mesótes*, that is, the middle term. However, Aristotle himself, when analyzing the virtue of courage, concluded that the middle term is not always precisely the middle way. For him, courage is the middle term between cowardice and recklessness, but he concluded that courage is closer to the extreme of recklessness than to cowardice. So, understanding that the *mesótes* could not be the founding principle of his ethics, Aristotle proposes the right reason resulting from well-conducted discourse, *orthòs logos,* as the foundation. However, the first issue remained pending for Aristotle: How to make the transition from descriptive propositions to normative ones?[19]

Cirne-Lima asserts that this problem was not solved by Aristotle, nor by Thomas Aquinas, and not even by Kant, considering that, by separating theoretical reason from practical reason, it continued to leave the ought-to–be devoid of concrete content. Cirne-Lima emphasizes that the first major mistake was to place the problem of the foundation of general ethics in the justification of the transition from descriptive propositions to normative propositions. He questions why we should justify normative propositions, which govern human action, with descriptive propositions, which describe phenomena. Why would the descriptive discourse have a prominence of certainty, truth, and rationality over the normative discourse? He then asserts that the correct path should be the opposite, considering

[19] Cirne-Lima (1999), pp. 943–945.

that the set of normative propositions is more comprehensive and contains the descriptive propositions, as our daily propositions in the concreteness of life, despite having descriptive elements, are always full of values or disvalues.

Purely descriptive propositions are rare, usually only obtained after the abstraction of the value-laden charge that permeates most propositions. Thus, our daily certainties in the concrete world are permeated with values, with descriptions that are sometimes valued and sometimes devalued.

Following this line of reasoning, he points out that the central problem in ethics is not to make the transition from descriptive to normative propositions, but rather to justify the ought-to–be present in our propositions, which are predominantly normative. So, what are the first major principles that should govern the ought-to–be to define what is ethically right or wrong?

To answer these unsettling questions, Cirne-Lima proposes the ought-to–be not only as the great modal operator of ethics but also of all philosophy.

To ground the ought-to–be as a modal operator of all philosophy, he returns to the first principle of being and thinking, the founding of our conceptual symbolic order, the principle of non-contradiction formulated by Aristotle: "It is impossible to predicate and not predicate the same predicate of the same subject under the same aspect and at the same time." This is an unquestionably true and universally valid principle; however, when examining it, Cirne-Lima points out a mistake by Aristotle in formulating the principle of non-contradiction. His error was to assert that contradiction is impossible. Cirne-Lima explains that contradiction is non-sense, it is erroneous, it is irrational, but strictly speaking, it is feasible, it can exist and does exist, so it is not impossible—it is something that can occur on the ontic plane. Thus, the modal operator "impossible" was used by Aristotle inappropriately when he formulated the principle of non-contradiction.[20]

The correct thing, according to Cirne-Lima, would have been to say the contradiction "ought not to be." Aristotle should have used the deontic modal operator "ought-to–be."

In this vein, Cirne-Lima explains that the principle of non-contradiction, which is the basis of thought and being, "does not say that it is impossible to say or write contradiction, it only says that we should not do it, that contradiction should be avoided." Thus, the correct formulation of the principle of non-contradiction is the "Principle of Contradiction to Be Avoided."

In this order of ideas, the primary foundation of the ought-to–be posited by Cirne-Lima as the basis of general ethics is the "Principle of Contradiction to Be Avoided: One should not predicate and not predicate the same predicate of the same subject under the same aspect and at the same time."[21]

Cirne-Lima demonstrates that the ought-to–be that underpins general ethics resides at the root, at the beginning of all knowledge, even of logic, in the formulation of the principle of non-contradiction by Aristotle. This means that

[20] Cirne-Lima (1999), pp. 943–949.

[21] Cirne-Lima (1999), p. 950.

the first principle of all speaking, thinking, and all our rationality—non-contradiction—is a principle of ethical nature, formulated with the deontic modal operator "ought-to–be."

In light of Cirne-Lima's proposal, the transition from descriptive to normative propositions is just a false problem, considering that it has been demonstrated that the set of normative propositions, governed by the modal ought-to–be, is the broadest and contains the set of descriptive prescriptions.

Cirne-Lima explains that this supra-ethics, which is rooted in the deontic modal of the ought-to–be in the principle of non-contradiction, permeates all philosophy: logic, nature, spirit, ethics in the traditional sense, esthetics, and philosophy of history. Finally, he asks to what extent this great ethical principle of non-contradiction governs human action in the social sphere, in intersubjective relations, and in relations with nature: "What does the correct use of predicates have to do with the ethicality of our actions and with ecology? Isn't there a huge distance between one point and the other?"[22]

He answers affirmatively and asserts that this distance exists but must be overcome. He emphasizes that, first, it is necessary to understand that every philosophical system begins with logic because, at the beginning of every process, there is a need for logical justification, considering that it orders the course of thinking, speaking, and all principiological formulation. This logic is not formal logic in the modern sense but Hegel's logic, the one that:

> [...] in shedding light on the first principles or rules that constitute thinking, it immediately raises the question, whether these rules are only rules of thinking or are they also rules of being. Is this logic also an Ontology? Are the necessary connections that traverse thought necessary relations existing in the world of things? Are the first principles of a deep grammar of thinking and speaking also the first principles of the grammar of being?[23]

Cirne-Lima responds positively to these inquiries and warns that the first principles of thinking, those that establish the symbolic conceptual order, must necessarily also be principles of "being," of access to "being"; otherwise, there would be no truth in our thinking and speaking.

Thus, the first principles of speaking and thinking are also principles of being, even though, at a later stage, the rules derived from these first principles may be different and specific to logic and ontology. Cirne-Lima explains that there is a radical connection between logic and ontology, a connection already affirmed by Plato and Aristotle, and that Hegel reconstructed this connection in his philosophical system—an idea that prevailed for a long time, from Plato to the early Wittgenstein.

To resolve the second proposed question, that is, to establish the first major principle that should govern the ought-to–be, to define what is ethically right or wrong, he refers to the first principle of being and thinking, the principle of

---

[22] Cirne-Lima (1999), p. 952.

[23] Cirne-Lima (1999), p. 953.

non-contradiction formulated by Aristotle, and explains that this first founding principle of the symbolic order has the same meaning as Plato's principles of the one and the dyad. He adds that Plato's principles of the one and the dyad[24] can be understood in a more didactic way as the principle of identity (one), the principle of difference (dyad), and the synthesis of both, the principle of coherence (non-contradiction). Thus, the one, the dyad, and their synthesis are summarized in the great principle of universal coherence, or, in other words, non-contradiction.

In other words, the first fundamental principle of all thinking and all being, proposed by Aristotle and accepted as such to this day, is the principle of non-contradiction. Plato also proposed non-contradiction as the basis of thinking and being; however, instead of using the expression "non-contradiction," he used two principles for the same purpose: the one and the dyad, and their synthesis, which is non-contradiction itself. Cirne-Lima identifies the principle of the one with the principle of identity; the principle of the dyad is the principle of difference. The synthesis between both, that is, non-contradiction, is referred to as the principle of coherence.

The philosopher dissects the principle of identity—the one, first in logic—as follows:

(i) Simple identity, represented by the sign "A," that is: "Whoever says a word or writes a sign is exercising simple identity."[25]
(ii) Iterative identity is the serial repetition of identity in its simple form, represented in logic by A, A, A ... to infinity.
(iii) Reflexive identity is the bending of the sign onto itself, symbolized in logic by A=A. It is in this last form of identity that reflection is established; formal logic arises from reflexive identity.

Next, he discusses the dyad, the principle of difference in logic—that is, the "emergence of the new," that which is not contained in the simple identity "A," nor in the iterative identity A, A, A ... and not in the reflexive identity A=A.

The principle of difference is the emergence of something new and contingent. It is realized with the emergence of the different, represented in logic by a "B," a "C," a "D," or any other that is not "A." Cirne-Lima explains that the principle of difference introduces something new, which is not:

> [...] inherently seminal in identity and therefore cannot be derived from it a priori. The principle of difference is the ground from which, later, the concept of contingency,

[24] For Plato, everything derives from the unfolding process of the universe, starting from two primary principles: the principle of unity (one) and the principle of duality or multiplicity or plurality. Thus, everything begins in unity, in a single being. In the beginning, there was only one being, it is the whole and everything, the *hen kai pan*. The one has in its essence the seed of multiplicity, that is, it carries within itself the other. This alterity is seminal in the one. Within the one there is a pair of opposites: the being-one and the being-other. The being-one is the identity, it is the thesis; the being-other is the difference, the multiplicity, it is the antithesis. The synthesis of both forms the triad. Cirne-Lima (1998), p. 296.

[25] Cirne-Lima (1999), p. 954.

> freedom and historicity will sprout. Without difference, there would only be formal logic, a world in which everything that is possible is also always necessary; a world in which there is no existence, in which neither contingent things nor their history exist.[26]

The third principle is that of coherence, which becomes relevant with the appearance of the contingent—that is, the new brought by the principle of difference. With the emergence of the new, in logic represented by "B," which is different from "A," from A, A, A ... and from A=A, there are two possibilities: (i) "B" can be compatible with "A," then we will have a synthesis, an adaptation; (ii) "B" can be incompatible with "A," so there will be an exclusion, an elimination of one of the opposing poles. Thus, coherence has two perspectives, namely: (i) it can mean the elimination of contradiction, when the opposing poles are exclusive; (ii) it can also mean conciliation, the synthesis, when the opposing poles are possible to reconcile and adapt.

It can be seen, therefore, that the principle of coherence is, in fact, the principle of non-contradiction, formulated by Aristotle in the establishment of the symbolic conceptual order, from which all Western rationality unfolded. Cirne-Lima concludes that the operations made to reestablish coherence between "A" and "B" constitute the ought-to–be:

> Thus, formulated as we have done above through the deontic operator, the Principle of Coherence synthesizes within itself identity and difference, reconciles both, and ensures that, if it obeys it, it will remain rational and comprehensible, without the conflict of mutually exclusive poles throwing it into a world where there is no longer any reason and in which nothing makes sense.[27]

Moving from the field of logic to the sphere of nature, Cirne-Lima explains that the principles of identity, difference, and coherence also prevail in ontology and the philosophy of nature, and shows the application of these principles of logic in biology and in the theory of evolution.

As can be seen, the theory developed by Cirne-Lima to explain the principle of non-contradiction—that is, the principle of coherence as a deontic principle, based on the ought-to–be—also applies to the theory of evolution in biology.

An individual existing in the natural world is represented by the simple identity principle: "A." This individual reproduces in the natural world, so it is represented by the iterative identity principle: A, A, A ... What is common in the qualitative internal structure of distinct individuals is called species: a unit that contains the plurality of individuals and is represented by the reflexive identity: A=A.

However, the philosopher warns that if it stopped here, there would be nothing new and contingent; there would be no variety of beings and forms of sensible life. That is, life would not expand as an emerging force toward perpetual becoming. Therefore, for the synthesis of life, the principle of difference is needed to engender contingency, genetic mutations, and evolution itself. The principle of difference is the otherness that breaks the sameness. However, these mutations can be good or

[26] Cirne-Lima (1999), p. 954.

[27] Cirne-Lima (1999), p. 958.

bad, as it will depend on the reconciliation of opposite poles in identity and difference. If the new introduced is compatible and coherent, the mutation will be a success, which means adaptation. If, however, there is incoherence between the mutant (altered by the new) and the environment, there will be elimination. Nature itself eliminates the contradictory pole. This is natural selection in biology and is repeated in the cosmic order of coherence that governs the universe. Thus, Cirne-Lima demonstrates the deontic character, based on the ought-to–be, of natural selection as the principle of coherence applied to nature:

> The Principle does not say that bad mutations are impossible; no, it is deontic and allows against fact. Only after it comes into action is the incoherence noted, it punishes with wasting, disease, and death everything that is incoherent, that is, everything that cannot adapt within the universal coherence of Nature.[28]

However, the principles of identity, difference, and coherence also apply to the so-called realm of the spirit. Cirne-Lima teaches that among living beings in the world of nature, there are those who are capable of reflecting on themselves and on the totality of which they are parts; they are beings endowed with self-awareness. In the current state of the art, it is considered that only humans are endowed with self-awareness. Thus, in their intersubjective relations, they are also governed by the principles of identity, difference, and coherence, as the human being contains both logic and nature: "The man, Spirit that is, it is Logic that has become Nature and vice versa, Nature that has become Logic."[29]

The same principiological structure shapes logic and nature and repeats itself in the human spirit. However, while in nature, other beings, as far as current science indicates, do not have self-awareness of the new, of alterity, in the human spirit, there is consciousness and free will for free decision-making, for creativity and self-determination and, most beautifully, for the principle of responsibility as discussed by Hans Jonas. Thus, he warns:

> [. . .] this is the consciousness of the coherence or incoherence of the free decision with other decisions, those already past, which constitute this person in the construction of their freedom, as well as the coherence or incoherence with future projects, with other people - starting with the closest ones - with all beings and all things of Nature and, finally, with the entire Universe. Man, when deciding freely and thus engendering, through difference, his personality, can and should measure his decision and the consequence of his actions through the standard of measure that is given by the Principle of Coherence: Am I, with this free decision, in coherence with myself, with others, with Nature, with the Universe?[30]

In the human spirit, the principle of difference represents the contingent, free will, the necessary freedom for the flourishing of responsibility. In the principle of coherence, good and evil are constituted—the latter in incoherence, the former in coherence.

[28] Cirne-Lima (1999), p. 957.

[29] Cirne-Lima (1999), p. 958.

[30] Cirne-Lima (1999), p. 958.

For Cirne-Lima, the assessment of the coherence of a concrete decision in everyday life is made at three levels: (i) First, it is necessary to verify internal coherence, which is done by examining one's own consciousness; (ii) then, inquire about coherence with the environment, and establish a dialog with the people around—such as the family, the community, and the society; and (iii) finally, check universal coherence, so as to expand the circle of discourse of the real world in which we live to a broader and ideal circle, which includes all human beings and other beings in the universe.

Along these lines, an action will be ethically approved if it is coherent at all three levels. Despite acknowledging the similarity between his method and the ethics of discourse of Apel and Habermas, as well as Kant's own categorical imperative, he notes that there is a significant distinction, given that his proposal encompasses the rules of good living on the journey from the individual self, the internal coherence of the subject, toward the universal self. Thus, his principles are not merely formal, as are the principles of universalization and discourse of Apel and Habermas, since the principle of difference is necessarily permeated by material contents.[31]

Finally, to solve the third problem concerning the transition from the particular to the universal, or vice versa—that is, how to construct an ethics that, even though formal (universal), has concrete contents—he emphasizes that, despite adopting the principle of universalization, it is not the Kantian universal, which is merely formal and devoid of content, but the concrete universal of Hegel. He explains that for Kantians and formalists in general, such as Apel and Habermas, the ultimate criterion for establishing an ethic is the possibility of universalization; so, if an action can be universalized, then it is ethical. That's why lying and killing cannot be considered ethical, as their universalization would lead to chaos. In these two Kantian examples, the criterion of universalization works very well, but he notes that there are several other hypotheses where the criterion fails. Thus, he considers it a mistake to think of the principle of universalization as an abstract universal—that is, mere subsumption to an abstract concept or a class.[32] He explains that the correct way is to think of the principle of universalization as a concrete universal, as the Neoplatonists and Hegel did. Then, he explains his concept of the principle of universalization:

> If we speak of the Principle of Universalization in the sense of the Concrete Universal, then being universal means, not the fact of being subsumed under an abstract concept or class, but rather the fact of fitting harmoniously or not harmoniously into that Whole which is the Universe. If Universalization is thought of in this way, that is, with harmonious insertion into the Universe, then it really is a criterion of ethicality and coincides exactly with what we have called the Principle of Universal Coherence above. Thus, just as the piston of a car engine cannot be harmoniously inserted into a wristwatch, so too certain decisions and actions cannot be harmoniously inserted into a family, a society, a state and, ultimately, the universe. This, yes, is the ultimate criterion of ethicality: universalization understood as the

[31] Cirne-Lima (1999), p. 960.

[32] Cirne-Lima (1999), p. 961.

possibility of harmonious insertion into the Totality, layer by layer, through all mediations, until reaching the Concrete Universal which is the Universe. This is the third principle of my system project, the Principle of Universal Coherence.[33]

As can be seen, universal coherence is the touchstone of the general ethics proposed by Cirne-Lima, a coherence that permeates logic, nature, and the human spirit, and it is precisely this that allows it to be adopted as a theoretical foundation for an applied ecological ethic. Human beings must be coherent in the realms of logic, spirit, and nature, which allows for the inclusion of animals, plants, and ecosystems as the ultimate recipients of ethics.

Kantian general ethics, on the other hand, views nature merely as a means, in such a way that it does not accommodate the notion of intrinsic value for nature:

[...] Nature only enters this relationship as an intermediary. This evidently transforms Ecology into its opposite, as Nature is only thought of as a means, never as an end in itself. That's why, as a result of this stance, ecologists are sometimes treated with the condescending but cautious kindness with which one treats a gentle madman.[34]

As can be seen, Cirne-Lima's proposal for general ethics adopts the principle of universalization, not as an empty universal resulting from mere subsumption to a class or abstract concept, but as a concrete universal. This means that for a behavior to be considered ethical, it is not enough to pass through the sieve of universalization, of generality; it must also present content, substance—it must be a concrete universal. The substance of this universal is harmony: "If Universalization is thought of in this way, that is, **with harmonious insertion into the Universe**, then it really is a criterion of ethicality and coincides exactly with what we have called the Principle of Universal Coherence"[35] (our emphasis).

Thus, harmony, which Cirne Lima calls the principle of universal coherence, is the substantial criterion for assessing the ethicality of human conduct, whether internally, in relation to the human being itself, in relation to the society in which it lives, or in relation to the cosmos, understood as the larger community where all beings live.

Every specific ethics of a sphere of human action must be guided by broader principles of a general ethics. In this way, we have bioethics and the various professional ethics, all rooted in a general ethical system, from which they unfold to radiate into specific areas. Applied ecological ethics, as a doctrine of human action in relation to non-human beings and the cosmos itself, finds no foundation in the general ethics of Kant and his contemporary followers, simply because it does not accommodate the attribution of an end value to non-human beings and holistic organic entities (ecosystems, species, biodiversity, and biosphere). Indeed, as Cirne-Lima observes, from the perspective of the Kantian contractualist view, it sounds absurd to consider moral consideration, intrinsic value, subjectivity, and rights for non-human beings and holistic organic entities.

---

[33] Cirne-Lima (1999), p. 962.

[34] Cirne-Lima (1999), p. 963.

[35] Cirne-Lima (1999), p. 962.

However, in the monistic model of universal coherence ethics presented by Cirne-Lima, the ethical consideration of non-human beings and holistic organic entities is a natural development, since coherence occurs at three levels: coherence with oneself, coherence with society, and coherence with the entire cosmos. Thus, non-human beings, ecosystems, and the biosphere are in the cosmic sphere as the ultimate recipients of ethical consideration.

This moral consideration, this recognition of intrinsic value, as a result of cosmic coherence, which should govern both relations among humans, as well as the relations of human beings with non-human beings and with the cosmos itself, has the advantage of dispensing with the establishment of criteria such as motility, perception, emotion, intentionality, language, and self-awareness for the attribution of intrinsic value to non-human beings and holistic entities.

Cirne-Lima explains that his ethics is evolutionist, as they understand the human being and the universe as a continuous evolutionary process. However, it is not an evolution that privileges the strongest; it is an evolution that rewards the most coherent, the one that is in harmony with the universe. Nor is it a necessary evolutionary process, as it harbors contingency and free will and, consequently, safeguards freedom.[36]

Cirne-Lima proposes to solve the intricate issue of free will in his ethics of coherence, based on the understanding that in the universe there are strong laws that structure life, like the concrete beams of a construction. Within these strong laws lies the necessary causality, where free will cannot interfere. However, in the interstices of these "beams," where determinism does not operate, there is space for contingency and for the exercise of free will and responsibility.[37]

This theory of interstitial spaces, adopted by Cirne-Lima, is supported by Charles Taylor when discussing his understanding of Hegel's phenomenology of spirit:

> We must avoid a mistake that can easily arise here. Hegel is not saying that everything that exists happens and comes to us out of necessity. He is talking about the basic structure of things, the chain of levels of beings, the general form of universal history. These are manifestations of necessity. **But within this structure, there is not only room for contingency, but contingency as such** [...].[38]
> (emphasis ours)

Cirne-Lima notes that Hans Jonas also supports an explanation of the world, reconciling the concepts of necessity and freedom.[39] Indeed, Jonas, when dealing with the theme of freedom and the necessity of the organism, argues for the existence of a gradual freedom that perfects itself in the self-aware organism:

> In the concept of freedom, we have a guiding concept capable of guiding us in the task of interpreting life. [...] Therefore, "freedom", in this descriptive sense, is a fundamental

---

[36] Cirne-Lima (1999), p. 964.

[37] Cirne-Lima (2017), p. 183.

[38] Taylor (2014), p. 44.

[39] Cirne-Lima (1998), p. 304.

> ontological trait of life itself; and also, as it is proven, the continuous principle - or at least the constant result - of its advance towards higher degrees, where at each step freedom is built upon freedom, superior freedom upon inferior freedom, richer freedom upon simpler freedom [. . .].[40]

As can be seen, the understandings of Cirne-Lima, Charles Taylor, and Hans Jonas converge in the sense that there exist strong natural laws that are insusceptible to change by human beings. However, in the space between these laws, there are interstitial gaps that allow the exercise of freedom—a freedom that has degrees and reaches its peak in the human being, allowing him to exercise free will and assume responsibilities. By bringing this theory of interstices to the field of applied ecological ethics, it can be observed that there are several strong laws in the fields of biology, physics, and thermodynamics, which, like concrete beams, do not allow human beings to interfere in some inevitably entropic processes. However, in the gaps of these strong laws of causality, there are malleable spaces where it is possible for human beings, as organisms endowed with self-awareness, to exercise free will, to make correct, responsible choices, opting for an ethic of universal coherence that engenders negentropic behaviors and thus privileges life over the death of non-human living beings and holistic organic entities.

3.3 Hans Jonas's Ethics of Responsibility as a Basis for Applied Ecological Ethics

Hans Jonas begins his theory of the ethics of responsibility by asserting that the boundary that existed between the *polis*, which was once an enclave in the natural world, and nature itself, has been broken. The human being has made the world a universal artifact and usurped the place of nature:

> Once it could be said **fiat iustitia, pereat mundus** - "let justice be done even if the world perishes"—, where "world" evidently meant the renewable enclave in the imperishable totality; this phrase can no longer be used even rhetorically, when the perishing of the totality has become a real possibility because of human deeds, just or unjust. Questions that have never before been the subject of legislation enter the circuit of laws that the global "city" must formulate, so that there can be a world for the next generations of men.[41]

Jonas explains that ethics, in its traditional conception, was restricted to inter-human relations in a given space, in an immediate present time. The relationship of the human being with the extra-human world through technique, with the exception of medicine, was foreign to the provinces of ethics. This traditional inter-human ethics was limited to disciplining human action in the past and present and dispensed with theoretical and scientific inquiries, so that moral action was

[40] Jonas (2004), pp. 106–107.

[41] Jonas (2006), p. 44.

dissociated from cognition, as Jonas emphasizes,[42] reminding us that Kant himself[43] asserts that it would not be necessary to know science or philosophy to know what is good or evil, considering that to be an honest and good person, wise and virtuous, a common intelligence and the desire to act according to the moral law would suffice.

However, in the face of man's mastery of technique and his brutal interference in nature during the twentieth century, this traditional, merely formal ethics became inadequate—or perhaps even obsolete—in the face of the complexity of the environmental crisis. Thus, Jonas postulates and presents a new ethics, capable of encompassing the relations of the human being with the extra-human world, an ethics that projects into the future—something unprecedented because, until Kantian thought, ethics served to regulate action pertinent only to past and present acts.

Jonas asserts that modernity has increased technique and given absolute primacy to *homo faber,* a hypertrophied individual, fascinated by the continuous and incessant progress of technique and, at the same time, empty of the "being" lost in the ontological and ethical vacuum, as a great artifact devoid of values, among many others engendered by the very rational and linguistic construction of what is called modernity.[44]

He emphasizes that Kantian ethics, based on the rationality and will of the human individual, has become insufficient to balance the devastating effects of the technical intervention of *homo faber* on the extra-human world and the very existence of humanity. Kant's ethics does not make a judgment about the existence or non-existence of humanity and the non-human world, as it is limited to intersubjective relations in a given social space, whether in the present or past of acting.[45]

However, in the face of massive technical intervention, which was based on what he identified as the "Baconian program" and whose impact has already altered the very geological structure of the planet, the new ethical imperative proposed by Jonas is appropriate, as it assumes that "the future of humanity is the first duty of collective human behavior in the age of technical civilization, which has become 'all powerful' in terms of its potential for destruction."[46]

Hans Jonas takes a decisive step by breaking away from the dualist, analytical, and contractualist tradition of Kantian ethics to propose an asymmetric responsibility of the human being toward nature, and he does so based on the data of the reality of the severe entropic acceleration of ecological systems caused by rampant human interference on planet Earth. As a profound scholar of metaphysics, he bases his ethics on a vitalist ontology. Jonasian responsibility ethics is guided by human compassion, which emerges from the very nature of the "being" as the

[42] Jonas (2006), pp. 36–37.

[43] Kant (2005), preface.

[44] Jonas (2006), pp. 41–43.

[45] Jonas (2006), p. 47.

[46] Jonas (2006), p. 229.

holder of a purpose: the care for other beings and for the sustainability of life itself.[47]

Thus, he follows the middle path between conventional anthropocentrism, which treats non-human beings and nature as mere instruments or objects of human interests, and radical biocentrism, which postulates, in addition to the recognition of intrinsic value for non-human beings, an egalitarianism among species. Jonas seeks balance and adopts a weak anthropocentrism, which means that, while rejecting the instrumental view of nature and accepting the recognition of end value, he makes a gradation of the level of consciousness of living beings, based on *De anima* by Aristotle.[48]

Coyne observes that Jonas, in his understanding of life, believes that each living being has its own teleology—that is, an existential purpose that is realized in its own interiority—from which it projects to the world as a being with individuality. Taking as a starting point this interiority experienced by all living beings, even the simplest, Jonas makes an adaptation of the *scala naturae* of Aristotle, creating an ascending chain of existential freedom for living beings in terms of the degree of manifestation of interiority and individuality, which is expressed through greater motility, perception, and thought. This gradation of evolutionary levels culminates in intellection and human self-consciousness at the top.[49]

The high point of Jonasian ethics, for this work, is the attribution of an asymmetric responsibility to the human being in relation to other beings. In this sense, it is noted that Jonas distinguishes two types of responsibility: (a) being responsible for the effects of one's own action, because the effects were caused by one's own action; and (b) being responsible not only for an action already consummated but also for an action that needs to be carried out. Here, the object of responsibility is not an act already carried out but something that must be done, that is, a responsibility oriented toward the future. As Ballet and Bazin point out, Jonas proposes "a philosophy of action, where successive generations defend a duty of solidarity (intra and intergenerational justice) derived from their close relationship with a fully inclusive natural world—their biosphere."[50]

Wellistony C. Viana explains Hans Jonas's thought by making the distinction between responsibility for present and past acts and responsibility initiated for the future:

> Thus, it would not be respect for the Law the ethical sentiment par excellence as Kant affirmed, but the Responsibility for the good. According to Jonas, two types of responsibility can be admitted: one is that which concerns the effects of my action. I am responsible for something in the measure that I provoked this or that effect with my action. But there is another type that concerns, not the action carried out, but an action that must be carried out. In this type, I am responsible not so much for the effect produced, but for the cause that

[47] Ballet and Bazin (2017), p. 176.

[48] Ballet and Bazin (2017), p. 182.

[49] Coyne (2017), pp. 303–304.

[50] Ballet and Bazin (2017), p. 177.

> must produce such an effect. On one side there is the "ought to exist" of an object (**Seinsollen**) and on the other, the "ought to do" (**Tunsollen**) of the subject capable of producing such action.[51]

To exemplify the second form of responsibility—that is, responsibility for something that must be done—Jonas cites the responsibility of parents for their children and the responsibility of politicians for the conduct of public affairs. Both are marked by a common characteristic: the care for an objective good, the survival of the human person (in the case of the father's responsibility toward the child and the politician's responsibility toward the human community). Viana emphasizes that, in both models, the good considered is life itself, an intrinsic good that underpins all value and moral norms. Thus, responsibility is prior to all action, as it "stands before an absolute value that imposes itself as a duty to be."[52]

Jonas also places the life of non-human beings at the center of his ethical discourse and proposes a fundamental duty toward the future, a duty that deviates from the classic standard of reciprocity. This is an asymmetrical, non-reciprocal duty, similar to the duty parents have toward the life of their children. The actions that must be engendered to ensure the future existence of humanity surpass the interests and will of present humanity.

The ethical foundation of this asymmetrical responsibility lies in metaphysics—a metaphysics of the meaning of "being," which must break the limits of conventional anthropocentrism. By embarking on an investigation into value and purpose, he concludes that the purpose, the goal of his ethics, is what answers the question "for what?"

> What we must demand from our principle cannot be demanded by the traditional idea of rights and duties - by the idea based on reciprocity -, according to which my duty is the reflected image of the other's duty, which in turn is seen as the image and likeness of my own duty, so that, once certain rights of the other are established, my duty to respect and, if possible (adding an idea of positive responsibility), promote them is also established. This does not serve our purposes. For claims only arise from what claims - from what, above all, is. All life claims life, and this may be a right to be respected. What does not exist makes no claims, and therefore cannot have its rights violated. Let it have them when it exists, but not on account of the possibility that it will exist someday. [...] The claim to existence only begins with existence. But the desired ethics deals exactly with what does not yet exist, and its principle of responsibility must be independent of both the idea of a right and the idea of reciprocity - so much so that it is appropriate to ask the playful question, invented by virtue of that ethics: "What has the future already done for me? Does it respect my rights?"[53]

In his ethics of responsibility, Jonas postulates the revision of Kant's imperative, "act in such a way that the maxim of your action becomes universal," for a new imperative, which ensures a duty to exist not only for humanity but also for nature

---

51 Viana (2010), p. 113.

52 Viana (2010), p. 113.

53 Jonas (2006), p. 89.

itself: "act in such a way that the maxim of your action allows the perpetuation of human beings on the planet."[54]

The ethics of responsibility proposed by Hans Jonas and the ethics of universal coherence by Cirne Lima prove to be suitable to underpin a proposal for applied ecological ethics, capable of supporting the postulation of the recognition of subjectivity and rights by nature.

Both Cirne-Lima and Hans Jonas do not follow ontological dualism or the post-dualist monisms of materialist and idealist necessity, as they adopt a libertarian type of Neoplatonic monism, which recognizes intrinsic value in nature without resorting to contingency, free will, and responsibility.

3.4 The Applied Ecological Ethics of Harmony with Nature

This work proposes an applied ecological ethics capable of addressing practical issues, in which the conflicts of interest of the recipients of this ethics are involved, so it should follow realistic criteria and be connected with biological and ecological sciences. The recipients of this ethics are all living beings, human and non-human, and also ecosystems, rivers, mountains, species, and the biosphere itself. The tone of this ethics, applied to the life of its recipients, should be the reconciliation of self-conscious beings with all other non-human beings, ecosystems, rivers, mountains, species, and the biosphere.

Therefore, this theory of action, applied to the relations between human beings, all non-human organisms, and nature itself, is henceforth called the ethics of harmony with nature, considering that harmony, as already explained, is the content of the principle of universalization, resulting from the synthesis of the tensions of opposing forces in Cirne-Lima's general ethics of coherence, which radiates and unfolds to constitute the applied ecological ethics of harmony with nature.

The applied ethics of harmony with nature starts from the premise that all non-human living beings and holistic organic entities, from the simplest to the most complex organisms, including plants and animals, as well as ecosystems, rivers, mountains, and species, have intrinsic value. Like humans, these beings have legitimate interests, moral consideration, and intrinsic value, and therefore should be recognized as moral and legal subjects.

This extension of the ethics of harmony with nature, in addition to recognizing rights for non-human living beings and holistic organic entities, also aims to strengthen human rights already achieved, considering that it ensures the human right to a healthy and balanced biosphere—a right that is the foundation of the flourishing of all other human rights. Indeed, without the guarantee of the future existence of a healthy and balanced environment,

[54] Jonas (2006), pp. 47–48.

human life and freedom are at risk. We must not forget that, even now, there are thousands of refugees wandering the planet due to the environmental crisis, and that thousands of human beings, at this moment, have their lives cut short by a biological tragedy triggered by the spillage of a zoonotic virus, SARS-CoV-2—a tragedy that is deeply connected with the anthropogenic environmental crisis.[55]

The ethics of harmony with nature not only locate intrinsic value in the well-being and individual flourishing of living organisms but also recognize the intrinsic value of holistic organic entities that sustain the systemic communities that integrate biotic life.

The applied ethics of harmony with nature is, above all, a theory of loving action to guide human relations with their own body, as an extension of the Earth on which meadows, forests of large angiosperms or conifers, and savannas thrive, from this Earth that gestates the seeds of wheat, rice, beans, and corn that feed humanity, which will return to it. It is a proposal for reconciliation with the water of streams, rains, and seas; if the human body is made up of 70% water, when water is poisoned, one kills one's own body. For health, humans need to harmonize with the water that falls from the sky onto their roofs, that flows in streams back to the sea, that underlies the subsoil, and that animates the life of plants and animals, with which they must live in a respectful relationship, even within the biological reality of the food chain.

It is a proposal for harmonious life with all non-human living beings: the bee that pollinates plants and the worm that fertilizes the soil, small and large mammals, birds, and fish; it is the recognition that, despite being different, we are the unfolding of Plato's One, which diversifies into multiplicity to compose the great web, the synthesis of life.

The applied ecological ethics of harmony with nature aims to teach boys and girls that the poisoning of the bee is the moral weakening of today's human being and the interdiction of the human being of the future, but that the human being, as a complex and self-conscious being, is free to change the outcome of this story. This is the great power of *Homo sapiens* within the Earth community.

3.4.1 Key Concepts for the Applied Ethics of Harmony with Nature

For a better understanding of the applied ecological ethics of harmony with nature, it is necessary to address key concepts such as metaethics, moral consideration, intrinsic value, and inherent value.

---

[55] Campello et al. (2020), pp. 596–634.

3.4.1.1 Metaethics

As previously discussed, the main issue when it comes to the discourse of ethics is the problem of constructing moral judgments from natural facts, the so-called naturalistic fallacy; thus, it is necessary to elucidate this issue because the applied ecological ethics that is sought in this work, as the axiological foundation of the legal norm of recognition of intrinsic value and subjectivity to animals, plants, and holistic organic entities, must be realistic and cognitivist. Therefore, it is a methodological demand to preliminarily resolve the issue of the naturalistic fallacy.

In simple terms, the naturalistic fallacy was the name Moore gave to the moral conception that uses naturalistic facts, that is, empirical ones, to construct moral judgments.[56] This reasoning, for example, is recurrent in evolutionary biology in the attempt to construct an evolutionary ethics. Among the various criticisms received, one stands out, pointing out that the self-awareness of the human being and his self-determination do not allow him to be considered merely as an evolutionary consequence.

Hume[57] was one of the first to reject this naturalistic ethics, pointing out that from the descriptive language of factual premises, it is not logically possible to derive prescriptive propositions, which is the proper language of ethics, that is, the language of ought-to–be, deontic:

> [...] in every system of morality that I have hitherto met with, I have always noticed that the author proceeds for some time in the ordinary way of reasoning [...] when suddenly I am surprised to find, instead of the usual copulations of propositions, is and is not, I meet with no proposition that is not connected with an ought or an ought not. This change is imperceptible, but is of the last consequence [...] it would be necessary to give a reason for something that seems entirely inconceivable, namely, how this new relation can be deduced from others that are entirely different.[58]

However, this is not the only criticism of naturalistic ethics. The main objection comes from Moore, who warns that it would be a fallacy to define what is good based on natural properties, because good, by its very nature, would not be susceptible to definition.[59] It is seen that there were two objections: one of logical order, by Hume, and another, the conceptual fallacy, by Moore.[60]

Ferry and Vincent, in the same vein as Hume, warn:

> Either we reduce the normative to the descriptive, the right to the fact, the morality to the history and nature that determine it; however, in this case, it is necessary to renounce the idea of normative ethics and limit oneself to describing moral behaviors in a neutral way, as is done with animal behavior. Then, there is no longer ethics, only ethology, which,

[56] Moore (1993).

[57] Hume (2010).

[58] Chediak (2006), p. 148.

[59] Chediak (2006), p. 149.

[60] Chediak (2006), p. 149.

without value judgment, limits itself to showing why and how animals, human or not, conduct their lives.[61]

As previously demonstrated, the general ethics of universal coherence by Cirne-Lima, from which the applied ecological ethics of this work unfolds, addresses and resolves the metaethical issue raised by Hume, Ferry, and Vincent. Cirne-Lima overcomes the logical objection of the naturalistic fallacy, since, unlike making everything descriptive language, as naturalists do, he demonstrates that the ought-to–be is the great modal operator, not only of ethics but of all philosophy and all knowledge.

Cirne-Lima's metaethical proposal makes the problem of the transition from descriptive propositions to normative ones a false problem, considering that it demonstrates that the set of normative propositions, governed by the modal "ought-to–be," is the broadest and contains the set of descriptive prescriptions.[62]

Indeed, as the philosopher from Rio Grande do Sul observes, all descriptive propositions contain a value charge. For example, one cannot deny a charge of judgment in the following propositions: (1) Smoking causes lung cancer; (2) the burning of the Amazon Rainforest affects the rains in the center-south of South America; and (3) the silting of the Taquari River compromises the Pantanal ecosystem.

All these descriptive propositions deal with natural phenomena, are empirically verifiable, but one cannot deny the charge of judgment present in them, so they implicitly contain a normative command. They are factual descriptions that motivate human action. Thus, Cirne-Lima is correct when he points out that the set of normative propositions is larger and contains the descriptive propositions.

Nussbaum, from an essentialist view, makes an explicit intertwining of descriptive discourse with normative discourse, arguing that the conception of the human being is, in itself, a normative conception, considering that it involves highlighting certain functions as more basic than others.[63] This statement by Nussbaum corroborates Cirne-Lima's ethical system in the sense that the set of prescriptive propositions is broader and contains the set of descriptive prescriptions, considering the normative nature of the human being, who is essentially a formulator of strong evaluations, as proposed by Charles Taylor.

Thus, the concern of Ferry and Vincent is overcome by the metaethical proposal of Cirne-Lima.

It remains to continue the examination of Moore's objection, which opposes the definition of moral terms, such as the concept of good. Attfield emphasizes that this stance of Moore was widely adopted and led some philosophers not only to deny the possibility of measuring the good but also to refute the possibility of finding the truth of moral statements. For this current, no moral knowledge would be possible, and this resulted in the so-called "non-cognitivism" in morality, which unfolded

[61] Chediak (2006), p. 150.

[62] Cirne-Lima (2001), p. 65.

[63] Nussbaum (1993), p. S53.

into three currents: (i) Hume's emotivism, in which morality is driven by passions; (ii) prescriptivism, for which moral discourse is merely the universalization of precedents—similar cases with equal judgments; and (iii) projectivism, which reduces moral judgments to mere projections onto the world made by people, based on their feelings, interests, and activities.[64]

As can be seen, for moral non-cognitivism, moral statements do not present any realistic objectivity; they are just a projection of emotions and interests, so that the speech act of the moral statement does not transmit information—it only explicates feelings, attitudes, and subjective motivations formalized in commands destined for others.

Nevertheless, Attfield points out that the non-cognitivist argument—that fact statements are alien to moral language—is also weak, considering that, for example, when someone states inside a zoo: "a tiger has escaped from the cage." This orientation, in fact, will surely guide people's actions, even more than a genuinely normative proposition. This argument by Attfield is deepened by Cirne-Lima in his theory, in the sense that all propositions are prescriptive—some to a greater extent, others to a lesser extent—that is, the set of prescriptive statements contains the set of propositions describing facts.

Thus, deontic normative propositions can indeed derive from facts and, consequently, carry truth value. This deconstructs the thesis of moral "non-cognitivism," which does not provide any security, as it falls into deep subjectivism, considering that it relates moral properties to the evaluations of groups of people and societies. This could lead humanity to dark times, as occurred in the last century with the Jewish Holocaust. Indeed, subjecting moral judgments to emotions, feelings, and the interests of individuals or groups of people represents a great risk to the life of humanity, non-human beings, organic entities, and the biosphere itself.

This moral discourse of "non-cognitivism" does not serve to guide an applied ecological ethic. Indeed, today, despite the existence of incontrovertible scientific data and satellite images, there are people who, for subjective and biased reasons such as greed and easy profit, deny global warming, the existence of fires, and the acidification of the oceans, for example. Therefore, it is necessary to base the ecological ethical discourse on moral realism, grounded in facts and scientific reports.

For moral realism, real moral properties are independent of the mental state or the spirit of the people who attribute them. When it is said that something is morally right, it is because there are objective reasons to do so, and not just because of people's feelings and emotions about it.

Attfield also refutes the argument of non-cognitivists in the sense that it would not be possible to admit the existence of moral facts, and even if they existed, attitudes diverge on many topics, such as abortion, euthanasia, monogamy, and polygamy, which would not allow a consensus to establish a moral truth. The fact that disagreements exist is not sufficient to refute the existence of moral facts, since

[64] Attfield (2012), pp. 172–174.

disagreements are also recurrent in the descriptive language of sciences and history itself.[65]

For moral realism, disagreements in the formation of moral judgments are not an issue that affects the truth; they are about cultural clashes, emotions and interests, or even epistemological deficiencies. When it comes to the formation of value judgments in the ecological sphere, most of the divergences come from clashes of economic interests of people or groups who do not want to stop making exorbitant profits with the accelerated entropy of the planet, or from uninformed people who, due to an epistemological deficiency, deny the existence of the environmental crisis.

In the sphere of ecological morality, knowledge is fundamental to supporting moral assertions. In this vein, an applied ecological ethic is primarily realistic—that is, formed by moral propositions rooted in facts, whose truth judgment is verifiable by statistics and environmental impact studies.

3.4.1.2 Moral Consideration

What entities matter morally to human beings when making their decisions? What are the things that are important in themselves?

These questions have a strong ethical impact. For Kantians, rational beings matter, as well as humans with cognitive deficiencies and children. For Hume, an ethical non-cognitivist, who bases moral choices on feelings and passions, the recipients of moral consideration could be humans and sentient animals, as the latter also have emotions and feelings. Mill and Bentham, utilitarians, could say that all beings that feel pain are worthy of moral consideration.[66]

Attfield explains that the basic criterion for attributing moral consideration to an entity is to recognize that it has its own good that is independent.[67] For Paul Taylor,[68] all living creatures have their own good. In the view of Aldo Leopold[69] and Arne Naess,[70] in addition to living creatures, ecosystems, rivers, mountains, and species also have their own good.

Robin Attfield[71] clarifies that Kenneth Goodpaster, the creator of the term "moral consideration," makes a distinction between moral rights and moral consideration. Indeed, in his seminal article on the topic, Goodpaster restricts the use of moral rights to human beings—that is, self-aware beings—while the term moral consideration is used more broadly to encompass non-human beings.

65 Attfield (2012), p. 192.
66 Attfield (2012), p. 72.
67 Attfield (2012), p. 46.
68 Taylor (2011), p. 85–94.
69 Leopold (1949), p. 194.
70 Naess (2008), p. 56.
71 Attfield (1995), p. 8.

Goodpaster[72] explains that he makes this distinction to avoid unnecessary complications to his concept of moral consideration, considering the lack of consensus on the concept and scope of moral rights. He asserts that, for some authors, rights are something broader, while for others, they are quite strict. For example, he cites that, for Warnock,[73] rights are synonymous with moral relevance, while other authors believe that to hold rights, one must meet more demanding requirements, such as rationality. In this vein, the thought of John Passmore[74] is cited, who believes that the concept of rights does not apply to non-humans. Goodpaster makes it clear that he does not adhere to this understanding:

> I doubt it is so clear that the class of rights holders is or should be restricted to human beings, but I propose to suspend this issue entirely, framing the discussion in terms of the notion of moral consideration (following Warnock), except in texts where there is reason to think that the broader sense of "rights" is being used.

As can be seen, Goodpaster does not distinguish the concept of moral consideration from rights by denying non-human beings the possibility of holding rights, but he does so with the purpose of placing his concept of moral consideration outside the discussion zone about the ownership of rights by non-human beings—a topic that will be addressed later.

David DeGrazia explains that recognizing the moral status of a dog means admitting that it has moral importance in its own right, and not merely in view of human interests. In this perspective, an animal cannot be mistreated except if there is a good reason for it. A good reason, for example, would be mistreating a dog to defend the physical integrity of a child. However, even among people who admit that animals have moral status, there are different ways of considering the moral rights of animals. DeGrazia points out three understandings: (i) In a more vague and loose sense, saying that a being has moral status is to admit that it has rights, albeit minimal and on a differentiated scale. For this current, a dog has moral status, which assures it some rights, but not in an egalitarian way compared to a human being. (ii) For a second, stricter interpretation, recognizing moral status in animals means that their interests carry equal weight to human interests. For this current, a dog's interest in avoiding its own pain and suffering is as morally important as a human's interest. (iii) There is also a third, stronger current regarding the recognition of moral status and rights, which surpasses the notion of utility to justify, in itself, the interest in having guaranteed rights. Thus, if someone has a right to something, it means that, as a rule, this right must be guaranteed, even if this may imply a disadvantage for society as a whole, for example, the right that humans have to due process. DeGrazia clarifies that Tom Regan considers the interest of animals in having their rights guaranteed in this sense, regardless of any utility or human interest. For this current, recognizing the

---

[72] Goodpaster (1978), pp. 308–325.

[73] Goodpaster (1978), p. 308.

[74] Goodpaster (1978), p. 311.

moral status and rights of animals means guaranteeing their vital interests in an almost absolute way.[75]

Mary Ann Warren observes that the concept of moral status has long been a subject of debate. For instance, in ancient Greece, women, enslaved individuals, and people from other cultures were often placed in a morally ambiguous category, as they were regarded as inferior by many scholars of that era. Today, entities such as fetuses, animals, plants, biological species, and ecosystems are situated in a similarly contested space of moral consideration.[76]

Baxter deeply considers the moral status of non-human living beings, ecosystems, and nature, and points out that the first substantive issue to be addressed in an approach to ecological justice is the restriction of moral status only to sentient organisms. Baxter criticizes this line of thought, as he believes that the recognition of moral status should be extended to all non-human living beings and even to ecosystems.[77] He critically analyzes the thoughts of Peter Singer and David DeGrazia, authors he considers the most resolute in defending the restriction of moral consideration only to sentient non-humans. He examines DeGrazia's perspective, which, based on Singer and Regan, defends in summary: (1) equal moral consideration for sentient non-humans; (2) the extension of moral status to sentient non-humans does not imply the concession of identical rights for sentient non-human animals and humans; and (3) adoption of Rawls' reflective equilibrium metaethical position.[78]

Baxter points out that DeGrazia successfully refutes many arguments offered against the extension of moral status to sentient non-humans. The first common argument against egalitarian consideration is that only beings capable of establishing obligations with others, members of the community, may have recognized moral *status*. DeGrazia refutes this argument, reflecting on humans who are not fully rational, such as fetuses, babies, people in comas, and mentally ill individuals.[79]

Despite these humans being unable to form contractual relationships, they are not denied moral *status*. DeGrazia also refutes the argument that it is the special feelings of connection, or bond, that give humans a good reason to privilege their companions to the detriment of non-humans. He also refutes the current that moral *status* should be restricted to moral agents. From this perspective, beings incapable of reciprocating duty, as is the case with non-humans, would not be due moral consideration. The lack of reciprocity in fulfilling duties would be an obstacle to the recognition of moral consideration. DeGrazia deconstructs this thesis, demonstrating its failure in the face of hypotheses involving humans deprived of full reason (babies, people in comas). Now, if humanity extends moral *status* to these

[75] Degrazia (2002), pp. 29–31.

[76] Warren (1997), p. 12.

[77] Baxter (2005), p. 123.

[78] Baxter (2005), pp. 78–79.

[79] Baxter (2005), p. 79.

humans, even when deprived of reason, why does it deny it to non-human beings? In this sense, DeGrazia asserts that the thesis of reciprocity in fulfilling duties as a condition for the recognition of moral *status* is inconsistent. If humanity recognizes the moral *status* of humans incapable of assuming duties, denying sentient animals moral *status* on this basis would amount to "speciesism."[80]

Baxter recognizes the vigor of DeGrazia's ideas but considers them insufficient, as they restrict consideration only to sentient animals and individuals. For Baxter, a theory of moral recognition needs to be more comprehensive, addressing the issue of species survival and also supporting all forms of life, sentient and non-sentient.[81]

Warren, in turn, develops a pluralistic theory, for which there is not a single property that all entities must have to be holders of a certain degree of moral *status*. The author lists the following intrinsic and relational properties that human common sense supposedly sees as sufficient for the attribution of moral *status* to an entity: (1) intrinsic properties: being alive, having consciousness, having sentience, being a "subject of a life," having the capacity for rational agency; (2) relational properties: being part of an ecosystem, being an important part of an ecosystem, being part of a community, being an endangered species, being part of the human community.

Warren argues that it is possible to attribute some degree of moral *status* to an "entity," both based on the possession of an intrinsic property and taking into account a relational property, or both. For Warren, it is not only the capacity for rational agency that authorizes the possession of moral *status*; therefore, her theory refutes the anthropocentric thesis that only human beings count morally.[82]

For Warren's pluralistic theory, the possession of one or another property, both intrinsic and relational, is already sufficient for the recognition of moral *status*. To strengthen her thesis, she also uses the argument that some humans do not possess rational agency (newborns, people in comas) but are part of the human community, and by this purely relational criterion, they are guaranteed the highest degree of moral *status*. For Warren, moral *status* can be acknowledged in degrees.[83] Thus, different types of entities can have varying degrees of moral *status* and, therefore, can demand different types of obligations from those who are full members of the community—the moral agents, the human beings.[84]

The basic idea of this principle is that it imposes on moral agents (human beings) the need to take into account certain types of interests that entities have by virtue of possessing the properties that confer upon them moral *status*. Thus, being a living organism grants the right to a minimum degree of moral *status* and requires that moral agents consider its interest in continuing to live fully and

---

80 Baxter (2005), pp. 80–81.

81 Baxter (2005), p. 93.

82 Warren (1997), pp. 122–123.

83 Warren (1997), pp. 182–183.

84 Baxter (2005), p. 104.

naturally for its species. So, if you are a living organism, you cannot be harmed, nor can your life be ended gratuitously without a good moral reason.[85]

Baxter notes that Warren's theory of moral *status* is insufficient because it does not attribute moral *status* to holistic organic entities, such as ecosystems and species, despite leaving open the possibility for such, provided it is proven that the ecosystem is a living entity. He believes that the weakness of Warren's theory lies in the point where it sets, as a condition for the recognition of moral *status,* a series of intrinsic and relational requirements that, although listed in a plural list—which is positive—still constitute an arbitrary selection of legitimizing criteria for moral *status*, as they are subject to "human moral sense."[86] He cites Callicott's criticism of plural lists of conditions for the recognition of moral *status*, because multiple ethical principles are applied to the same moral situation.

Indeed, Warren does not base her theory of moral *status* on a single ethical theory, such as utilitarianism or Kantian deontology. Instead, she mixes criteria—some ethical, others deontological, others axiological—and ultimately, her theory relegates the recognition of moral *status* for non-human living beings to human discretion.[87]

In various anthropocentric or non-anthropocentric ecological ethical currents, there is a consensus on the concept of the moral agent, restricting it to rational human beings. However, several divergences arise when the discussion is about who the moral patients are. For the current identified as zoocentrism, the moral patients are only sentient human beings and animals; for the biocentrism current, all living beings, human and non-human, are moral patients; for ecocentrism adherents, in addition to human beings, all non-human living beings, ecosystems, mountains, rivers, oceans, and species are recipients of moral consideration; therefore, they are moral patients.

This work proposes the recognition of moral *status* not only for the holders of moral obligations, called moral agents, that is, adult human beings endowed with full mental faculties. If children and adults with reasoning compromised by mental illnesses, despite not being subjects of moral obligations, are moral patients—that is, recipients of respectful treatment and consideration by moral agents—likewise, individual non-human living beings and holistic organic entities, such as ecosystems and species, should be covered by moral *status* as moral patients, or moral subjects, as Paul Taylor prefers.

The recognition of moral *status* for non-human living beings and holistic organic entities, such as ecosystems and species, should be based on the principle of universal coherence proposed by Cirne-Lima, considering that the approach of a coherent attitude restores the idea of harmony that should permeate the necessary

[85] Baxter (2005), p. 104.

[86] Baxter (2005), p. 106.

[87] Baxter (2005), p. 107.

relations between moral agents and moral patients. Cirne-Lima's principle of universal coherence also legitimizes the assumption by moral agents of a unilateral responsibility, as proposed by Hans Jonas,[88] and exacerbated by the risks created by humans in the Anthropocene.

The fact of being a holder of moral consideration can be confused with the fact of having value. Although there is a connection between moral position and having value, strictly speaking, they do not mean the same thing, considering that there are entities and creatures that are valuable or desirable, but only because of their instrumental function, and not because they are considered as possessing their own good. Thus, the concepts of moral consideration and value do not always coincide.[89]

In addition to delimiting the concept of moral consideration, it is important, for an applied ecological ethics, to reflect on the good in nature. When thinking about goodness, there is intrinsic goodness—something that is good in itself—and extrinsic goodness, which can be instrumental and transformative goodness or systemic and relational goodness. A sharp knife is instrumentally good; instrumental goodness is the "good for," different, therefore, from the good in itself.[90] This is a relevant metaethical issue as a starting point for an applied ecological ethics: should non-human beings and ecosystems be conserved because they are good for humans or because they are good in themselves?

The understanding that the conservation of biodiversity of animals, plants, and ecosystems is justified only in view of human interests attributes to nature a merely instrumental goodness, so it does not justify the recognition of moral consideration for non-human living beings and holistic entities, such as ecosystems and species. On the contrary, if it is understood that non-human living beings, ecosystems, and species are good in themselves, they will be considered recipients of moral recognition, regardless of their utility to humans.

In this last perspective, even if there were not a single human on Earth, bees, whales, springs, and leafy trees would all be good for a value that is inherent to them and completely independent of human evaluation. From this view, it would be very presumptuous to think that rivers, like the Nile and the Amazon, exist solely for the human being. If humans did not exist, they would still be there, essentially beautiful and good; therefore, they are intrinsically good.

---

[88] *Causal power is the condition of responsibility. The agent must answer for his actions: he is responsible for their consequences and will answer for them, if necessary. At first, this must be understood from a legal point of view, not a moral one. [. . .] Only the living being, in its needy nature subject to risks—and therefore, in principle, all living beings -, can be the object of responsibility. But this is only the necessary condition, not the sufficient one for such. The distinctive mark of the human being, of being the only one capable of having responsibility, also means that he must have it for his fellow men—they themselves, potential subjects of responsibility -, and that he always really has it, one way or another: the faculty for such is the sufficient condition for its effectiveness.* Jonas (2006), p. 165 and 176.

[89] Attfield (2012), p. 47.

[90] Vilkka (1997), p. 21.

Some also speak of systemic goodness, which satisfies functional and relational requirements in the functioning of nature as a whole. The adherents of the biocentric current understand that rivers, mountains, and ecosystems do not have an intrinsic goodness, but a systemic goodness, as they are at the base of the life of living beings. For ecocentrism, the rocks, plankton, rivers, ecosystems, and species have more than just a merely relational and systemic value, considering that they have intrinsic value, that is, essential. Thus, instrumental goodness is utilitarian, systemic goodness is relational, and intrinsic goodness is essential.[91]

It is the goodness found in nature that impels the human being, in the capacity of a moral agent, to consider it morally, as taught by Leena Vilkka:

> From the axiological point of view, the varieties of goodness in nature are related to what people should seek and protect. The goodness of nature must have a moral position. All non-human beings that possess goodness should be considered morally relevant beings. Their goodness is a morally significant characteristic that obliges us. When we say that non-human beings possess axiological goodness, we do not mean that plants and animals are moral agents, but that their goodness should count in our moral concern. They are the object of our morality.[92]

This value, which we must recognize in the goodness of nature, is one of the values that the human being, as a moral agent capable of evaluating, must seek outside of himself, in the world, to guide his choices, always guided by the principles of coherence (Cirne-Lima) and responsibility (Jonas).

3.4.1.3 Intrinsic Value

Despite the truism, something has value if there is a reason to value it. Some emotional states are considered valuable, such as, pleasure, happiness, and flourishing. These states are considered valuable not for what they cause but for themselves and, therefore, are called intrinsic values. For many philosophers, for something to have value, it depends on the existence of someone who is an evaluator, and thus there would be no value without evaluation made by a rational being. However, this is a mistake, as Attfield points out: "One cannot confuse what is valued with what is valuable. There are many valuable things that are not valued due to the epistemological deficit of the human being. On the other hand, there are things not valuable that are valued, for example rise and fall of fashion."[93]

In this line, the conditioning of all value to a rational evaluator is part of an anthropocentric view, which does not fit with the ecological ethics applied from harmony with nature, so it is necessary to distinguish intrinsic value from extrinsic value.

---

[91] Vilkka (1997), p. 22.

[92] Vilkka (1997), p. 24.

[93] Attfield (2012), p. 47.

There are many types of values; some things are valuable because they facilitate or provoke others. However, there are entities that are valuable by their very nature. So, it does not matter if they are valuable for another reason beyond themselves, and thus they are considered intrinsically valuable; therefore, they have intrinsic value.

Other things are valuable only for serving as instruments for valuable results. Attfield observes that ecosystems, rivers, and mountains are valuable because they enable valuable and prosperous lives, represent the preconditions for the flourishing of other valuable entities, and, for this reason, many ethicists consider them to have systemic value—that is, a form of relational value for enabling valuable lives to prosper. This is a relational value and not instrumental, as many argue, because, as Attfield observes, it is not appropriate to consider ecosystems, rivers, and mountains as simple human instruments.[94]

Before advancing the considerations on the understanding of the various currents that recognize the intrinsic value of non-human living beings, whose variation lies in the degree of coverage, it is necessary to understand the meaning of intrinsic value as an objective value within the four aspects that deal with the topic. Leena Vilkka[95] points out four major groups regarding the basic meaning of intrinsic value:

1. Intrinsic value (objective) in the conception of Clarence Lewis Irving;
2. Intrinsic value (objective) in the philosophy of Aristotle and Kant;
3. Weak intrinsic values (objective); and
4. Strong intrinsic (objective) values.

The first group, led by Clarence Lewis Irving, considers intrinsic value as an experienced or felt value. This perspective is followed by Michael Zimmerman, with his theory of the intrinsic value of pleasure, and Archie J. Bahm, who differentiates three types of intrinsic value: (a) pleasure; (b) satisfaction; and (c) preferences. Ultimately, for this perspective, pleasure, pleasant, and happy experiences are intrinsically good, and in this way, the source of intrinsic value is consciousness; that is, intrinsic value is necessarily experienced by consciousness. In this line, for the defenders of anthropocentrism, only the human being can have intrinsic value, for being endowed with consciousness that allows states of experience. Later, Eero Paloheimo extended the intrinsic value in terms of states of experience to all sentient animals. From his studies with ladybugs (*Coccinellidae*), Paloheimo argued that these small beings are endowed with sense organs; therefore, they would be subjects of states of experience and, therefore, possessors of intrinsic value.

For the second group, whose foundation lies in Aristotelian and Kantian philosophies, intrinsic value is inherent value. Although the expression "intrinsic value" is not found in the texts of Aristotle and Kant, the conception that there is something good in itself arises in the Aristotelian dichotomy of the existence of something that is an end to be pursued for itself, and something that is only a means

[94] Attfield (2012), p. 48.

[95] Vilkka (1997), pp. 27–30.

pursued for an end. In the first category, something that is an end to be pursued for itself is the intrinsic value. In the second, there is the instrumental value—entities that only have value if they have value for something else. Following the Aristotelian perspective, Thomas Aquinas argued that only the intellectual nature of the human being would have value in itself; everything else would be instrumental values at the disposal of humanity. Kant maintained "that animals are only a means to an end, that end is humanity."[96] In this anthropocentric philosophical root, only the human being is the possessor of intrinsic value, for being the possessor of language, intellectuality, and rationality.

As can be seen, intrinsic value, as an inherent value, is initially identified as an anthropocentric value, but from this root, two interpretations of intrinsic value arise: (i) the Kantian view of self-worth or self-esteem; (ii) the zoocentric view, which considers animals as subjects of their own lives.

When Kant speaks about human value, he uses expressions such as "inner value" and "dignity," that is, "people in their highest self-esteem are above any price."[97] Kant's conception brings the idea of an end: the human being, a person who should not be valued as a means but as an end in itself, because they have dignity and inner value that are absolute. Due to the fact that people perceive their own value as an end value, and absolute (intrinsic), they are capable of seeing the same value in others. If the human being has the capacity to value themselves, to recognize their own value as an end in itself, they also have the capacity to value various states and things. Hence derives the Kantian notion of intrinsic value, that is, self-worth, as an end value.

In the third group of the classification proposed by Vilkka are the weak intrinsic values, which are classified as follows: i) exclusivity value; and ii) inherent value (*inherent value*). For this current, the inherent value is located in objects apart from states of consciousness. The inherent value (*inherent value*) opposes the detected value; the latter exists in the state of consciousness of an evaluator, while the inherent value (*inherent value*) resides in the thing itself. This is the value of works of art, historical buildings, battlefields, and wonders of nature. Weak anthropocentrism places pets in this category. This value, although inherent to the thing and outside states of consciousness, is considered objectively weak, as it still depends on an evaluator. A work of art only has inherent value (*inherent value*) because there is someone with consciousness valuing it—an evaluator—and thus its objective or intrinsic value is weak.[98]

In the fourth group, Vilkka deals with strong intrinsic (objective) values. In this group is the *inherent worth*, as an objectively strong value, which is independent of an evaluator and, therefore, differs from *inherent value*, which is an objectively weak value, as it requires an evaluator.[99]

---

[96] Vilkka (1997), p. 28.

[97] Vilkka (1997), p. 28.

[98] Vilkka (1997), p. 29.

[99] Vilkka (1997), p. 59.

Returning to the fourth classification of intrinsic value as a strong objective value, the *inherent worth* is based on the empirical fact of a being having its own good that must be realized for its flourishing and existence. Indeed, for the existence of a living entity, it is better that its good be realized than not realized, regardless of what evaluators think. For example, for the existence of an angiosperm, it is better that photosynthesis is performed, regardless of what humans think. It is understood, therefore, that *inherent worth* is completely "separated from the values of any other beings and their merits."[100] Photosynthesis, as an *inherent worth* of a plant, has its own nature and belongs to it constitutively.

Some philosophers express skepticism about the existence of objective end value, whether in the form of Kantian intrinsic value or *inherent worth*, as they consider that everything in the world only has value because this value is derived from an evaluator's assessment. For these thinkers, only extrinsic value would exist: inherent (*inherent value*), instrumental, and contributory. However, as Attfield points out, this is a contradiction, because if everything had derived value, how would an evaluator, a reference to derive value, exist? Therefore, for logical reasons, it is imperative to recognize the existence of entities with strong intrinsic value; otherwise, we fall into the void of nihilism.[101]

The anthropocentric ethical paradigm is in transition and is slowly giving way to a new *ethos* that recognizes end value objectively, whether intrinsic in the Kantian mold or the *inherent worth* of other beings besides humans. However, Attfield observes that recognizing intrinsic value in an entity does not automatically imply the recognition of rights. When it is said that an animal's health has intrinsic value, it is not yet being said that it has rights; it is only being affirmed that there are reasons to protect the health of this animal for what it is. However, there may be reasons to act otherwise, such as prioritizing a person's need to eat, to also ensure their intrinsic value.

Vilkka methodically organizes the disagreements about the recognition of intrinsic value according to the degree of ethical extension: (i) The anthropocentric current limits the recognition of intrinsic value to the human being; (ii) zoocentrism extends the recognition of intrinsic value to reach sentient animals; (iii) biocentrism places the issue of life as the central point, therefore recognizing end value, whether as intrinsic value in the Kantian mold or the so-called *inherent worth* of Paul Taylor, to living beings; and (iv) ecocentrism adopts a more holistic position and is dedicated to the issues, concepts, and values of ecosystems and species.[102]

Zoocentrism targets vertebrate animals with its ethical concern, as it arose in the context of activism for animal rights. Its concern is to avoid the suffering of animals in human societies. The struggle of the zoocentric current is waged against the use of animals in laboratory testing by the pharmaceutical and cosmetic industries, the commercialization of meat and animal skins, the commercial

[100] Vilkka (1997), p. 30.

[101] Attfield (2012), p. 49.

[102] Vilkka (1997), p. 37.

exploitation of animals in general, and the breeding of animals in captivity, subject to cruelty. The struggle of the zoocentric current is the search for respect and the well-being of animals.

Throughout the history of humanity in the West, animals have been treated as mere instruments and models for the cure of human diseases or even as raw material for the human economy. They have been seen only as instruments and sources of inputs, such as skin, fat, wool, leather, musk, and proteins for the human diet. To oppose this enslavement of non-human animals by human animals, the animal liberation movement emerged. In modern times, this movement defends the intrinsic value of animals considered individually, as sentient beings, who feel pain, so that humans should respect the well-being of animals.

For zoocentrism, animals have their own well-being, completely independent of and different from human well-being; thus, they have intrinsic value. In addition, within zoocentrism, there are currents such as the so-called animal mentalism, which supports the subjectivity of animals:

> [...] animal consciousness and suffering exist at the cognitive and emotional levels. Vertebrates deal with their environment in an emotional way. They can suffer pain and feel pleasure and well-being. The ability of operant learning means that animals are capable (more or less reliably) of controlling how to obtain food or escape danger. An animal detects order in its environment, and its brain does so emotionally.[103]

Finally, from the view of zoocentrism, the well-being of animals has intrinsic value, considering that suffering is intrinsically bad for sentient beings, so people should recognize the suffering and well-being of animals based on their abilities to formulate value judgments as moral agents.

Biocentrism, in turn, goes further in ethical extension to encompass life itself as the scope of human morality. But how should the meaning of life be comprehended in this context? Leena Vilkka points out that the answer to this question depends on the attitude adopted toward life. She explains that the following pairs are synonymous: alive/not alive; animate/inanimate; and organic/inorganic. Thus, one must first scrutinize the difference between being alive, being animate, and being organic, and correspondingly, not being alive, being inanimate, and being inorganic. What is the appropriate semantic field of these neighboring words? Living entities, such as animals and plants, are also organic; however, not every organic entity is alive, such as humus. In this line, the meaning of life depends on the vision—the attitude one has toward life itself. For deep ecologists, water, soil, and even rocks are living entities. However, for most thinkers, only animals and plants are living and animate entities, while rocks, in addition to not being alive, are inanimate. Living and animate refer to active entities, but living also reminds us of vitality and organicity. According to Vilkka:

> [...] a new hierarchy for the terms "organic", "alive" and "animate" would be that organic entities would include the largest groups of entities, such as ecosystems and even the entire earth, while animate life would include only animal life. For many people, to animate is

[103] Vilkka (1997), pp. 40–41.

> synonymous with life, including flora and fungi. [...] A distinction can be made between "being alive" and "having a life". Having a life requires complex mental abilities. Being alive, the opposite of being dead, is a notion of biology, while having a life is a notion of biography. People and animals have their lives in the biographical, historical sense: they have a past and a future, they have hopes and fears about their own lives. Non-human sentient animals are subjects of biographical lives. In this biographical sense, "having life" cannot be attributed to plants, although plants are living beings. Plants have a biological life, but not a biographical one.[104]

However, within the concept of life, one cannot forget the relevance of biodiversity, such as the diversity of genes, species, and ecosystems. The concept of diversity dates back to Arthur Lovejoy's principle of plenitude, which, although dualistic and anthropocentric, brought to light the idea that the world will always be better the more diversity it contains—a conception that provoked a reflection on diversity being a good in itself and, in a way, contributes to the recognition of intrinsic value to biodiversity.[105]

Within the biocentric perspective, due to the diversity of understanding about the meaning of life, there are more restricted currents that limit the recognition of intrinsic value to the flourishing and well-being of living organisms, individually considered. Other thinkers, following Aldo Leopold's land[106] ethic, recognize the intrinsic value of the flourishing of holistic entities such as ecosystems, species, and the biosphere itself.

Attfield locates intrinsic value in the well-being and flourishing of living creatures. In answering the question of what constitutes the well-being and flourishing of a living creature, he explains that each species has a type of flourishing and raises another question about what is common among members of various species, pointing out essential capacities. The essential capacities of a species are those whose absence, in most members of a species, would characterize it as such. For example, if most ferns lost the ability to photosynthesize, the species would be disfigured. Therefore, photosynthesis is an essential capacity for the flourishing of ferns, and consequently, one can locate in photosynthesis an intrinsic value.[107] The same can be said of the motility and smell of wolves and self-determination in humans. These are examples of essential capacities for the flourishing of these living beings, and in them lies intrinsic value. As for ecosystems, Attfield argues that, although they present a vital importance for life systems on the planet, in his conception, they do not present a value in themselves, or a good of their own, considering that their value depends on the beings they sustain; therefore, it is a mere relational systemic value and not intrinsic.[108]

In the biocentric perspective, one of the most prominent voices is that of Paul Taylor; however, for methodological reasons, this work dedicates a specific topic

---

[104] Vilkka (1997), p. 55.

[105] Vilkka (1997), p. 55.

[106] Leopold (1949).

[107] Attfield (1995), pp. 45–46.

[108] Attfield (1995), p. 51.

to this author to better explain the nomenclature adopted by him to name the end value of living beings. Paul Taylor does not adopt the expression "intrinsic value" but "inherent worth," and also differs from others by not adopting the expression "moral patient" and preferring "moral subject."

Finally, the ecocentric current attributes intrinsic value to all living beings, species, ecosystems, and the biosphere. Ecocentrism places philosophical and ethical discussions, concepts, and the value of ecosystems at the center of discussions. Ecocentrism recovers the organicist understanding of nature and the holistic view of life itself, in a way that, for ecocentrism advocates, it is not enough to defend the intrinsic value of the well-being and flourishing of animals and plants individually; it is also necessary to include, within the scope of morality, and defend as an intrinsic value in itself, the integrity of forests, mountains, rivers, biomes, and the biosphere as a whole, holistic, and interrelated entity.

In this more holistic perspective, Rolston III unfolds the defense of the intrinsic value of ecosystems from the following statement by Aldo Leopold: "One thing is right when it tends to preserve the integrity, the biotic community. It is wrong when it tends otherwise. [...] This land is a community, it is the basic concept of ecology, but this land must be loved and respected, it is an extension of ethics."[109]

Rolston III teaches that to locate the intrinsic value of ecosystems, one cannot focus on the individual organism, which he calls the organismic position, but rather on the systemic and holistic function of ecosystems, even though they are composed of parts in an apparently chaotic and non-homeostatic interaction:

> [...] ecosystems will count more than any of the component organisms, because the systemic processes have generated and continue to support and integrate tens of thousands of member organisms. The appropriate unit for moral concern is the fundamental unit of development and survival.[110]

This work adopts the notion of intrinsic value as an end value, derived from the conception rooted in Kantian thought, of self-value—something that is good in itself because it has dignity. Thus, it recognizes end value in all living beings, human and non-human, as well as in holistic organic entities, a matter that will be explored further in the chapter addressing the concept of biological dignity.

At this point, it is worth remembering Jonas's gloss, which, when dealing with the principle of responsibility as an asymmetric duty of humans toward nature, takes as an example the duty of care of parents toward their children—a duty that escapes the bilaterality of contractualism. This example is the typical case of the exercise of duty and responsibility of moral agents toward a being that is a moral subject without moral agency.

Taylor, similar to Jonas, understands that non-human living beings, despite not having moral agency, are moral subjects in relation to whom moral agents have duties and responsibilities.

---

[109] Rolston III (2020), p. 167.

[110] Rolston III (2020), p. 168.

In this line, the good of living beings, as moral subjects and possessors of inherent worth, is a fundamental value, which imposes on the human being, as a moral agent, an attitude of respect and recognition of the legitimate claim to the flourishing of living beings. For Taylor, the human being will only have a respectful attitude toward nature, considering it morally, if he recognizes this value that is inherent to it (inherent worth).

3.4.1.4 Paul Taylor's Inherent Value

Initially, Taylor[111] asserts that his concept of inherent worth does not confuse with the concept of "good of a being." He points out that the proposition "a being has its own good" is merely descriptive, while the claim that it should or should not be treated in a certain way employs prescriptive, deontological language. For Taylor, the fact that an animal or plant has its "own good" is not enough to impose a duty on moral agents to respect that animal or plant. Thus, it is necessary to have more than the recognition of a good of its own for an entity to claim its benefits from moral agents. This "something more" is what Taylor calls inherent worth.

However, before proceeding, it is necessary to clarify that Taylor adopts the theory of values of Clarence Lewis Irving,[112] according to which, in summary, values can be classified into two large groups: intrinsic value and extrinsic value. For Irving, intrinsic value is a value directed toward states experienced by consciousness, that is, satisfaction, pain, pleasure, joy, sadness, and well-being. It is a value that is not derived from another, a value in itself, but always an "experienced value." It should be noted that this concept of intrinsic value, as defined by Irving, does not coincide with the concept of intrinsic value in the sense given to the expression by deep ecologists, who adopt the Kantian conception of the concept of intrinsic value, that is, the Kantian[113] self-value. In Irving's classification, adopted by Paul W. Taylor, extrinsic value is a type of value that derives from something that has intrinsic value. Extrinsic value can still be of three types: (a) inherent value; (b) instrumental value; and (c) contributory value.

Firstly, Irving's inherent type of extrinsic value will be addressed, which Taylor describes as inherent value. It is a value that is attributed to an entity by its own characteristics. For example, Michelangelo's Pietà has an inherent value of the type *inherent value* type. This value is located in the entity itself, outside of conscious states. The value of the Pietà is inherent to the fact that many admirers of Renaissance art value it for its esthetic perfection. Note that this type of inherent

[111] Taylor (2011), p. 86–90.

[112] Irving (2011), p. 380.

[113] *The Kantian argument is as follows: intrinsic value refers to the idea that we have the ability to value ourselves. I have the ability to value different types of states and things. Furthermore, I have the ability to value myself. Therefore, I have intrinsic value. This argument can be applied to animals, who have the ability to value themselves and, therefore, have intrinsic value in terms of Lewis's 'experienced value' and Kant's 'self-value'.* Vilkka (1997), p. 29–30.

value proposed by Irving results from the relationship between an evaluating subject and the evaluated entity, so it is a derived value. In this concept, an animal can also be the recipient of inherent value (*inherent value*) because it receives the esteem of its guardian. This type of inherent value, according to Irving, is relative, as it depends on someone's appreciation. He classifies this type of value as inherent because it is a value resulting not from economic importance, but from aesthetic, poetic, affective, or historical significance.

Following this classification of Irving's values, for whom intrinsic value is a value experienced by states of consciousness, Taylor had to create a different nomenclature for end value, so he uses the expression *inherent worth* to name a type of value that is recognized only in entities with their own good. It is noted that, in practical terms, Taylor's *inherent worth* is equivalent to the intrinsic value of Kantian origin. When Taylor says that an entity "X" has *inherent worth*, it means recognizing an end value distinct from that *inherent value* proposed by Irving, as this entity has this value regardless of any evaluator. If an entity has its own good, and if it is better for this good to be realized than not, then the entity has a value of the type *inherent worth.*

The assertion that a living being has *inherent worth* raises two implications: (a) This entity is deserving of concern and moral consideration, as it is a moral subject; and (b) all moral agents have the primary duty to promote and preserve the good of the entity as an end in itself.

As can be seen, Taylor, like Tom Regan, also works with the concept of a moral agent to refer to adult humans with mental aptitude. However, while Regan refers to animals as moral patients, Taylor uses the expression "moral subject" to refer to living beings as holders of *inherent worth.*

Taylor proposes, as a criterion to recognize the *inherent worth* of a non-human being, the same criterion that is used to establish the truth of the assertion that a human being has *inherent worth.* He argues that it is a matter of coherence that each human, as a rational, conscious, and autonomous being, considers himself a holder of *inherent worth* out of self-respect, so that, as a matter of coherence, he cannot deny the same value to other humans. The same reasoning must be applied to recognize the truth of the assertion that all animals and plants have *inherent worth*, as this is the only coherent view within a biocentric belief system, which is based on respect for nature and maintains that each living being has its own good.[114]

Vilkka explains that, for Taylor: "Inherent worth is the foundation of the moral considerability of each living organism. This is based on each living being having a good of its own, which is the objective perspective of inherent worth. The good of a living being is an empirical fact of that being."[115]

Taylor points out that the various theories of environmental ethics converge in the sense that a moral agent is a being with capacities that allow him to act morally

---

[114] Taylor (2011), p. 94.

[115] Vilkka (1997), p. 62.

or immorally and, in this way, to be a holder of duties and responsibilities. Among these capacities are those of formulating judgments of right and wrong and of acting with the willpower to fulfill the decision that he deems appropriate. Not all humans are moral agents, but it may be that non-humans with moral agency will still be identified. There are humans without moral agency, such as babies and people with cognitive limitations. However, although they are not moral agents, they are moral subjects.

In explaining his concept of the moral subject, he stresses that humans can be both moral agents and moral subjects. This is because humans not only have duties and responsibilities toward others but are also recipients of duties and responsibilities from other humans, and in this position, they are moral subjects. In the role of a moral agent, a human can act justly or unjustly, while in the position of a moral subject, he can be the recipient of a just or unjust action. Thus, all moral agents are moral subjects, but not all moral subjects are moral agents. A newborn, for example, is not a moral agent, but is a moral subject, to whom moral agents have duties.[116]

In this line, the good of living beings, as moral subjects and possessors of an end value of the type *inherent worth*, is a fundamental value, which imposes on the human being, as a moral agent, an attitude of respect and recognition of the legitimate claim to the flourishing of living beings. However, the human being will only have a respectful attitude toward nature by acknowledging its inherent worth.

3.4.1.5 The Concept and Extent of Value Suitable for the Applied Ethics of Harmony with Nature

This work considers it suitable for the applied ethics of harmony with nature to adopt the concept of intrinsic value in its Kantian conception—of end value, internal and absolute—which is located in the well-being and flourishing capacity of individual living beings, as well as in organic holistic entities, such as biodiversity, ecosystems, species, and the biosphere, since all living organisms, including humans, are organically and systematically inserted into ecosystems.

In this sense, the thought of Rolston III is highlighted, for whom ecosystems should count more than the individual organisms that make them up, considering that the systemic processes of ecosystems generate, support, and integrate tens of thousands of member organisms, configuring a fundamental unit of development and survival, so they represent an appropriate unit to be the recipient of moral consideration.[117]

Despite not adopting Paul Taylor's expression of inherent worth to name the objective value of non-human living beings (animals and plants), ecosystems,

[116] Taylor (2011), p. 29–34.

[117] Rolston III (2020), pp. 168–169.

biodiversity, species, and the biosphere, it is considered, however, appropriate to adopt the expression "moral subject," from Taylor, instead of "moral patient," to refer to all beings and entities that are recipients of moral consideration and recognition of intrinsic value by moral agents, that is, rational human beings.

Moral agents—rational and cognitive human beings—in addition to respecting each other, since they are simultaneously moral agents and moral subjects, should respect and consider not only human beings who lack moral agency due to the absence of cognition, but also non-human living beings, ecosystems, species, biodiversity, and the biosphere, which are moral subjects because they possess intrinsic value. In addition to human beings, as moral agents, being subject to the "ought-to–be" of coherence in their actions in relation to the well-being and freedoms of human and non-human moral subjects, they should also assume the ethical responsibility of practicing beneficial actions that ensure the flourishing and well-being of these beings in the present and the future. This responsibility is unilateral, in the manner proposed by Hans Jonas, considering that it is intergenerational and interspecies.

3.4.2 *The Applied Ethics of Harmony with Nature*

Once the key concepts have been established, it now remains to outline the proposal for an applied ecological ethics of harmony with nature to support the following chapters, which will deal with the ownership of rights by non-human living beings, that is, animals, plants, ecosystems, species, and the biosphere.

First of all, it is necessary to conceptualize the word "harmony" for the purposes of applied ecological ethics. The harmony invoked here has its roots in dialectics, especially because the general ethics theory that underpins this proposal for applied ethics is the ethics of coherence of Cirne-Lima, a monist, dialectical, and non-necessitarian theory, as already demonstrated in Section 3.2.

The first mention of harmony used in the dialectical sense was with Heraclitus. The Greek word corresponding to harmony is *ἁρμονία*, which in Greek means "junction." Heidegger, when interpreting fragment 123 of Heraclitus, explicates harmony in that text as the "junction," the point of connection of one thing to another, or better said, the interconnection of two entities in interaction. For Heidegger, Heraclitus is talking about the interconnection between the appearance and the self-concealment of *physis*.[118]

In Fragment 51, Heraclitus says: "They do not understand how the diverse agrees with itself, harmony of the antagonistic as in the bow and in the lyre."[119] This is the foundation of his doctrine called "harmony of opposites." This junction of the bow and the lyre as opposing forces, thesis and antithesis, whose synthesis is

[118] Heidegger (2018), pp. 102–103.

[119] Ferrater Mora (2004), p. 1323.

the musicality, is the metaphor for the starting point of his philosophy. The "unity of opposites" is the principle from which the becoming unfolds.

According to Fritjof Capra, in Confucianism, the Tao is the reality that encompasses everything, the continuous flow of perennial change. This change repeats itself in patterns; the wise being recognizes the patterns and becomes one with the Tao, living in harmony with nature. Its movement is cyclical: "to move away means to return." Everything comes and goes, expands and contracts. The cyclical movement of the Tao expresses itself in the junction (harmony) of opposites, yin and yang. When the yang reaches its peak, it withdraws in favor of the yin. This refers to Heraclitus' thought of the invisible harmony, the union of the concealment and unveiling of the physis. The Tao is that which is sometimes darkness and sometimes the emergence of light, represented in the "diagram of the supreme fundamental." It is the cold and the hot, the movement and the rest; it is impermanence, which does not allow the same man to bathe in the same river twice, as Heraclitus of Ephesus prophesied.

Fritjof Capra points out that, just as in Heraclitus' doctrine, the basis of Taoism is the harmony of opposites:

> It is astonishing to realize that, at the same time that Lao Tse and his disciples were developing their conception of the world, the essential characteristics of the Taoist conception were also taught in Greece by a man whose teachings have come to us in a fragmented form and who was - and still is - often misunderstood. This Greek Taoist was Heraclitus of Ephesus. Heraclitus shared with Lao Tse not only the emphasis on continuous change - which he expressed in his famous statement "Everything Flows" - but also the notion that all changes are cyclical. Heraclitus compared the order of the world to "an eternally living fire, igniting in measure and extinguishing in measure", an image very similar to the Chinese idea of the TAO, which manifests itself in the cyclical interaction of yin and yang.[120]

For Taoism, to act in harmony with nature is to "act spontaneously in accordance with the true nature of each individual." In the Tao, there is a guiding proposition of harmonious action: "Those who follow the natural order flow in the current of the **tao.**"[121]

This means to restrain oneself in actions contrary to natural laws; if there is no contrariness to the natural order of flow, there will be harmony.

Similarly, in the cosmogony of the Incas, every real or conceptual object exists in pairs. Their fundamental concept is not unity but parity, represented seminally by the couple Manco Cápac y Mama Ocllo, symbolically represented by Pachamama (mother-cosmos), whose icon in the ruins of the temples is a circle, and Pachatata, represented by a square geometric figure. In most archeological sites in Peru, these two icons are found. Javier Lajo explains that this iconography, marked by parity, aims to demonstrate relationality, complementation, and proportionality, which guide the parity between humans and the parity of the human being with nature. These forms are also present in the Andean cross or cross of

[120] Capra (1983), p. 92.

[121] Capra (1983), pp. 92–93.

Tiwanaku, an icon constructed by the interlacing of circles and squares to represent the proportionality and complementarity between these geometric figures, which also represent the feminine (circle) and the masculine (square), symbolizing the cosmos as a "duo-verse," a binary cosmos that is different from the Western "universe." This binary cosmos is represented by the so-called Tawa-Chakana, or "route of interrelation" or "path of truth." In the Andean cross, there are two diagonals that cross in the center, representing the path of truth.[122]

This parity of Andean cosmology is apprehended through the concept of yanantin and encompasses the correlation of opposites: yána and yánan, with the suffix tin being the element of junction. In its morphological function as an adjective, yána means dark and, as a noun, boyfriend. Meanwhile, yánan, in its function as an adjective, means white. The suffix tin interconnects the opposites, giving them unity and the sense of complementation of the opposites—a concept similar to Plato's complexio oppositorum, the one and the other at the base of the understanding of the cosmos that seeks balance and harmony.[123]

Cirne-Lima, in his general ethics of coherence, proposes this harmony as the content of the principle of universalization, which is essential for the formulation of ethics, and attributes to it the name of the principle of coherence (or non-contradiction), as the synthesis of the one (identity–thesis) and the dyad (multiplicity–antithesis), that is, the inaugural principle of Western cosmology: Aristotle's principle of non-contradiction, applicable to logic, nature, and the human spirit.

As can be seen, the element of the junction of opposites, harmony, is in the paths of truth of three great ontologies: the Chinese, the Greek, and the Mesoamerican-Andean. This signals and reinforces that the harmony of the human being with nature is a universal and timeless postulate.

What human beings should seek is coherence with themselves, with the immediate environment—that is, with other human beings who form society—or with the mediate environment—that is, nature, where non-human living beings and ecosystems are found. This coherence is good; it is the perfect junction, ἁρμονία, the perfect fit, the harmony of the individual human being with his conscience, with society, and with nature.

While Aristotelian and Kantian ethics deal with the discipline of good human behavior among themselves, that is, in society, the ethics of coherence by Cirne-Lima, from which the applied ethics of harmony with nature unfolds, goes beyond and places the need for the human being to assess whether his relationship with nature is coherent and, therefore, ethical.

At this point, the corroboration of Charles Taylor's concept of strong evaluation proves timely in the sense that the human being, faced with daily choices and decisions, has to measure the coherence of his decisions in relation to society and nature. He will do so as a strong evaluator; that is, his evaluation is internal, as

---

[122] Lajo (2006).

[123] Salazar Calderón Galliani (2015), pp. 128–129.

a self-conscious and evaluative being, a moral agent, but he will seek in the reality of society and nature itself the "logical accounts" that will allow him to measure the coherence of his choices. This is not a subjective and relativistic evaluation based on personal feelings, emotions, and personal interests.[124]

Indeed, the search for harmony, as we have seen, is present in various world-views, and thus, harmony itself can be considered a "logical account" that guides the human being, as a strong evaluator, in assessing the impact of his choices on his relationship with other living beings and ecosystems.

The applied ecological ethics of harmony with nature is a guide for human action, as a moral agent and strong evaluator, in relation to non-human living beings, ecosystems, biodiversity, species, and the biosphere, which have intrinsic value and are considered moral subjects. Thus, the human being, as a moral agent and "strong evaluator," must examine the degree of coherence of his choices, not based on feelings, emotions, and personal interests, but guided by the experience of the reality of the world, which is shared with non-human beings, ecosystems, rivers, mountains, species, biodiversity, and the biosphere, always taking into account the logical account of ἁρμονία, of harmony, of the perfect junction between opposing forces.

References

Apel K-O (2000) Transformação da filosofia: o *a priori* da comunidade de comunicação. Tradução de Paulo Astor Soethe. São Paulo: Loyola, v. 2

Attfield R (1995) Value, obligation, and meta-ethics. Amsterdam: Rodopi. (Value Inquiry Book Series, 30)

Attfield R (2012) Ethics: an overview. Continuum International Publishing Group, London; New York

Ballet J, Bazin D (2017) Hans Jonas: bridging the gap between environmental justice and environmental ethic? Environ Ethics 39(2):176. Summer. Disponível em https://www.pdcnet.org/enviroethics/content/enviroethics_2017_0039_0002_0175_0191. Accessed 05 Apr 2025

Baxter B (2005) A theory of ecological justice. Routledge, New York

Campello LGB, Oliveira AFD, Amaral RDD (2020) O direito fundamental à saúde na intersecção da crise ambiental com a pandemia da COVID-19. Revista Jurídica, Curitiba, PR, Unicuritiba 5(62):596–634. dez. Disponível em http://revista.unicuritiba.edu.br/index.php/RevJur/article/view/4989/371373121. Accessed 20 Apr 2025

Capra F (1983) O tao da física: um paralelo entre a física moderna e o misticismo oriental. Tradução de José Fernandes Dias. Cultrix, São Paulo

Chediak K (2006) O problema da falácia naturalista para o projeto de uma ética evolucionista. Kriterion: Revista de Filosofia, Belo Horizonte, [*online*], 47(113). Disponível em: https://www.scielo.br/pdf/kr/v47n113/31146.pdf. Accessed 20 Apr 2025

Cirne-Lima CRV (1998) A explicação do mundo. In: Ulmann RA (Org). Consecratio mundi: *festschrift* em homenagem a Urbano Zille, Porto Alegre: EDIPUCRS

124 Meijer (2018), p. 64.

Cirne-Lima CRV (1999) Ética de coerência dialética. Veritas: revista de Filosofia da PUCRS, Porto Alegre 44(4):944, dez. Disponível em: https://revistaseletronicas.pucrs.br/ojs/index.php/veritas/article/view/35248/18499. Accessed 20 Apr 2025

Cirne-Lima CRV (2001) Platão: o uno e o múltiplo. In: Feltes HPDM, Zilles U (Org). Filosofia: diálogo de horizontes: *festschrift* em homenagem a Jayme Paviani. Caxias do Sul, EDUCS; EDIPUCRS, Porto Alegre

Cirne-Lima CRV (2017) Dialética para principiantes. Escritos Editora, Porto Alegre

Coyne L (2017) Phenomenology and teleology: Hans Jonas's philosophy of life. Environmental Values, White Horse Press 26(3):297–315. Disponível em https://www.ingentaconnect.com/content/whp/ev/2017/00000026/00000003/art00004. Accessed 20 Apr 2025

Degrazia D (2002) Animal rights: a very short introduction. Oxford University Press, New York

Etxeberria X (1994) La ética ante la crisis ecológica. Cuadernos Bakeaz, Bilbao 5:4, dic. Disponível em: https://www.academia.edu/3318336/La_%C3%A9tica_ante_la_crisis_ecol%C3%B3gica. Accessed 15 Nov 2025

Ferrater MJ (2004) Dicionário de filosofia. 2 edn. Loyola, São Paulo

Goodpaster KE (1978) On being morally considerable. The Journal of Philosophy 75(6):308–325. Jun. Disponível em https://www.jstor.org/stable/2025709. Accessed 22 Feb 2025

Habermas J (1999) Comentários à ética do discurso. Instituto Piaget, Lisboa

Habermas J (2007) Knowledge and human interests, Tradução de Jeremy Shapiro. Polity Press, E-book, Cambridge

Heidegger M (2018) Heraclitus: the inception of occidental thinking and logic: Heraclitus's doctrine of the logos. Tradução de Julia Goesser Assaiante; S. Montegomery Ewegen. New York: Bloomsbury Academic, E-book

Hume D (2010) Tratado da natureza humana. (Tradução de Serafim da Silva Fontes), 2 edn. Fundação Calouste Gulbenkian, Lisboa

Irving CL (2011) An analysis of knowledge and valuation. The Open Court Publishing Company, La Salle, IL

Jonas H (2004) O princípio vida: fundamentos para uma biologia filosófica. Vozes, Petrópolis

Jonas H (2006) O princípio responsabilidade: ensaio de uma ética para uma civilização tecnológica. Tradução de Marijane Lisboa e Luiz Barros Montez. Contraponto; PUC Rio, Rio de Janeiro

Kant I (2005) **Fundamentação da metafísica dos costumes**. Tradução de Paulo Quitela. Edições, Lisboa, pp 70

Kant I (2017) Crítica da razão prática. Tradução de Monique Hulshof. Vozes; Editora Universitária São Francisco, Petrópolis, RJ; Bragança Paulista, SP

Lajo J (2006) Qhapaq ñan: la ruta inka de sabeduría. 2. ed. Quito, Equador: ABYA-YALA. Disponível em: https://digitalrepository.unm.edu/cgi/viewcontent.cgi?article=1357&context=abya_yala. Accessed 22 Feb, Acesso em 22 fev. 2025

Leopold A (1949) A Sand County almanac: with other essays on conservation from Round River. Oxford University Press, New York

Meijer M (2018) Charles Taylor's doctrine of strong evaluation: ethics and ontology in a scientific age. Rowman and Littlefield International, London

Moore GE (1993) Principia ethica. Calouste Gulbenkian, Lisboa

Naess A (2008) The ecology of wisdom: writings by Arne Naess Drengson A, Devall B eds.. Berkeley, CA, Counterpoint

Nussbaum MC (1993) Social justice and universalism: in defense of an aristotelian account of human functioning. **Modern Philology**, University of Chicago 90(S1):S53, May, Supplement. Disponível em: https://doi.org/10.1086/392123. Accessed 04 Mar 2025

Rawls J (2008) Uma teoria da justiça. Tradução de Jussara Simões; Álvaro de Vita, 3 edn. Martins Fontes, São Paulo

Rolston III H (2020) A new environmental ethics: the next millennium for life on earth, 2nd edn. Routledge, E-book, New York

Silveira VOD, Rocasolano MM (2010) Direitos humanos: conceitos, significados e funções. Saraiva, São Paulo
Salazar Calderón Galliani FO (2015) Entre Eros y Wiracocha: un encuentro dialogico entre la filosofia griega y el pensamiento andino. 2015:148. Tesis (Licenciado en Filosofía) – Facultad de Letras y Ciencias Humanas. Universidad Nacional Mayor de San Marcos, Lima, Perú, 2015. Available on http://cybertesis.unmsm.edu.pe/bitstream/handle/20.500.12672/4395/Salazar_go.pdf?sequence=1. Accessed 22 Feb 2025
Taylor C (2014) Hegel y la sociedad moderna. Tradução de Juan José Utrilla. Fondo de Cultura Económica, México, DF
Taylor PW (2011) Respect for nature: a theory of environmental ethics, 25th anniversary edition edn. Princeton University Press, Princeton
Viana WC (2010) A técnica sob o "princípio responsabilidade" de Hans Jonas. Pensando: Revista de Filosofia, Teresina, UFPI 1(2)
Vilkka L, Value Inquiry Book Series, 59 (1997) The intrinsic value of nature. Rodopi, Amsterdam
Warren MA (1997) Moral status: obligations to persons and other living things. Oxford University Press, New York

Chapter 4
The Historical Trajectory of Theories for the Recognition of Rights to Non-Human Beings

The consolidation of the rights of non-human living beings and holistic organic entities, as occurred with human rights, goes through a slow historical process of recognition—the *dynamogenesis*[1] therefore, before entering the juridification of the principle of harmony with nature, another historical cut will be made to deepen the analysis of the evolution of the movements in defense of the dignity and moral consideration of non-human living beings and holistic organic entities. This historical journey begins in ancient Greece with Pythagoras, with the defense of animal dignity, and reaches today with broader ecological movements, such as biocentrism, deep ecology, and the new South American constitutionalism. Throughout the historical accounts, not only the battles fought in science and philosophy will be emphasized, but also the characteristics of these movements and their evolution in the recognition of moral position and intrinsic value to nature.

4.1 Moral Consideration of Animals in Antiquity

The moral consideration of non-human beings in Western cosmogony has its most distant roots in ancient Greece and begins with vertebrate animals, those closest to human beings and capable of showing sympathy, as this consideration arises from affection, from the bond of affectivity, and also from religiosity. Only from the

[1] Theory adopted by Vladmir Oliveira da Silveira and Maria Mendez Rocasolano to deal with the historicity of human rights: "To express the development and recognition of human rights and why institutions are created to guarantee them, we will use the dynamogenesis of values. Through a geometric-axiological model, dynamogenesis explains the process that underlies the birth and development of new rights throughout history". Silveira and Rocasolano (2010), p. 185.

R. D. d. Amaral, *The Principle of Harmony with Nature as a Legal Foundation*,
https://doi.org/10.1007/978-3-032-05475-3_4

twentieth century will broader ecocentric views emerge, which postulate the recognition of intrinsic value also for non-vertebrate animals and for holistic organic entities.

According to Newmyer, in antiquity, Pythagoras defended the notion of kinship between humans and non-human animals. This Pythagorean thought resulted from his doctrine of metempsychosis, that is, the possible reincarnation of the soul of a human person in the bodies of non-human animals and vice versa. For this view, humans should treat animals well, as they could occasionally be the incarnation of a loved one. Pythagoras showed a certain sympathy for animals as suffering creatures and, to endorse this understanding, he referred to the lost work "The treatise on piety," by Theophrastus Peripatetic (371–287 BC). Porphyry also refers to Theophrastus' work when discussing animal sacrifice in his work "*De abstinentia,*" in the third century. Porphyry clarifies that the arguments used against animal sacrifice are supported by Theophrastus, who believed that, just as human beings recognize a kinship among themselves, they should recognize that humans have a kinship with animals, since animals are also composed of flesh, passions, and souls, even though they are different from humans in their way of life. Thus, because of this kinship, humans should not include in their diet the bodies of animals.[2]

As can be seen, in antiquity, the discussion about the moral consideration of animals was limited to the existence or absence of a supposed kinship between humans and non-humans. The Stoics, as will be seen later, vehemently opposed the ideas of Theophrastus, Pythagoras, Porphyry, and Plutarch, who defended the moral consideration of non-human beings. Porphyry reports that, for Theophrastus, humans should not eat the meat of animals, because it causes them the maximum deprivation—that is, the loss of their own lives. This argument by Theophrastus, as Newmyer explains, echoed in the twentieth century, through the voice of Tom Regan, who argued that the death of animals is rationally wrong because it deprives them of the opportunity to experience any future choice, considering that death prevents all possibilities and expectations of flourishing.[3]

Newmyer highlights that Porphyry states that, before the Stoics, Theophrastus had already developed a conception of *oikeiotes* as a complex concept that encompasses kinship, belonging, and relationship between humans and non-humans to advocate for the ethical consideration of animals. Later, the Stoics would revise the doctrine of *oikeiotes* to, contrary to the original meaning attributed to it by Theophrastus, deny any relationship of sympathy between humans and non-humans.

Newmyer asserts that, although the doctrine of *oikeiotes* has been attributed to the Stoics, it was actually developed by Theophrastus, who advocated for the existence of a kinship relationship between human and non-human animals and proposed a sympathetic relationship between species. However, later, the Stoics

[2] Newmyer (2006), p. 20.

[3] Newmyer (2006), p. 21.

appropriated the doctrine of *oikeiotes* and completely distorted Theophrastus's thought, precisely to deny any relationship of kinship or affection between humans and non-humans, and to affirm the non-existence of the duty of respect on the part of humans toward the lives of animals.[4]

The doctrine of Theophrastus, shared by Porphyry and Pythagoras, was not adopted in the following centuries. Sorabji points out that the philosophical break in antiquity, in relation to the discussion about the ethical consideration of animals, was consolidated when Aristotle categorically denied the existence of rationality in animals, as this denial later served as a theoretical basis for the Stoics.

Sorabji clarifies that this Aristotelian rejection of rationality in animals was based solely on natural sciences, without any concern for the moral consequences of his arguments. In the centuries that followed, Aristotle's scientific considerations served as the theoretical basis for the construction of a theory of the moral inferiority of animals in relation to human beings.[5] Mainly, the Stoics and Epicureans saw in Aristotle's ideas of continuous gradation in nature, the so-called *scala natura*, or "great chain of being," the perfect theoretical foundation to position, within the scheme of creation, non-human animals in a distant and much lower position than humans, to justify the reason why human beings did not owe them moral consideration.[6]

This Stoic interpretation of the denial of rationality to animals in Aristotle's work will become the great theoretical basis of the stance of Western Christianity in relation to animals, placing them as creatures to which humans did not owe justice and which, thus, could be used as they pleased for their purposes and interests. Meanwhile, the doctrine sympathetic to animals, supported by Theophrastus, Pythagoras, Porphyry, and Plutarch, fell into oblivion. Newmyer highlights some of Aristotle's statements, exalting human beings at the expense of non-human beings: "*Only human beings could experience hope and expectation for the future*."[7] The Stoic doctrine, following this line of thought, began to argue that the imperfection of the animal soul made any affinity between humans and animals that could consolidate a moral relationship between species impossible. Cicero maintained that humans owed nothing to animals, given that they were not capable of verbalizing a concept of morality and thus could not respect the rights of humans.

According to Newmyer, based on the supposed absence of language in animals, the Stoics began to argue the impossibility of considering them morally. This mistake of Stoicism would resonate in modernity and contribute decisively to the contractualist doctrine that completely excluded animals from the social contract.[8]

---

[4] Newmyer (2006), p. 21–22.

[5] Sorabji (2001), p. 13.

[6] Newmyer (2006), p. 23.

[7] Newmyer (2006), p. 23.

[8] Newmyer (2006), p. 23–26.

In addition to establishing the benchmarks of Western thought in relation to the treatment given to animals, Aristotelian thought will influence the way humans in the coming centuries begin to relate to nature in general. Peter Burdon observes that the ideas of inexhaustible abundance and continuity in the great chain of being led Aristotle to conclude that all quantities and solid surfaces should be continuous in time and space:

> Nature proceeds little by little from things lifeless to animal life, in such a way that it is impossible to determine the exact line of demarcation and on which side an intermediate form should be. Thus after lifeless things, on an ascending scale, come plants and one will differentiate from the other as to its amount of apparent vitality; and, in a word, every kind of plant though devoid of life in comparison with an animal, is endowed with life in comparison with other bodily entities. Indeed, as we have just observed, there is in plants a continuous scale of ascent towards the animal.[9]

It was in Aristotelian philosophy that the organization of all animals on a graded scale, according to a degree of perfection, emerged. This hierarchical chain placed humans at the top and zoophytes at the base of the chain. In this conception, the environment was categorized merely as a tool for human use, such that plants exist to feed animals and animals to feed humans.

The Aristotelian hierarchy served as a theoretical foundation for anthropocentrism. According to Burdon, the hierarchical ordering of the environment was the basis for the development of classical law and property theory. It was the Roman Stoics, building on Aristotle's thought, who undertook the first formulation of private property and laid the foundations of Western law, excluding non-human animals from the social contract.[10]

The Stoics made a connection between reason and language. For them, *logos* is used in Greek to encompass both concepts: language and reason. In Stoic doctrine, reason was bifurcated into an internal reason, which is thought itself, and a pronounced reason, that is, meaningful speech—the ability to express. Thus, as animals did not present, in the Stoic conception, the linguistic ability that externalizes meaningful language, they were considered irrational and, therefore, unworthy of ethical consideration.[11]

In this sense, Sorabji points out that the Stoics were the first ancient philosophers to place reason as a condition for moral responsibility.[12] Newmyer emphasizes that "in Stoic ethics, moral agency is associated with rational consent." Thus, in Stoic philosophy, animals could not be moral agents because they would not be capable of performing moral actions; they would merely be moral patients, and, for Stoicism, only moral agents fell within the scope of human moral consideration.[13]

---

[9] Burdon (2015), p. 19.

[10] Burdon (2015), p. 22.

[11] Newmyer (2006), p. 26.

[12] Sorabji (2001), p. 112.

[13] Newmyer (2006), p. 27.

In Stoic thought and its modern descendants, only beings endowed with reason and language are rational and, therefore, can be moral agents and worthy of ethical consideration by humanity. According to Daniel Dombrowski, Seneca was the only member of the Stoic school who raised his voice to criticize this exacerbated anthropocentrism of Stoicism in his 121st *Epistulae Morales*; however, Newmyer disagrees with Dombrowski and considers that, for the Stoics in general, animals lacked emotions, reason, belief, and intentionality and, consequently, the moral agency necessary for ethical consideration.[14]

Sorabji[15] highlights that the Stoics and Epicureans had a conception of justice, based on Aristotle, that disqualified animals as irrational beings. For the Stoics, justice depended on a process (*oikeiôsis*) of understanding, feeling, and companionship—a process that, in their conception, could only be developed by rational beings, namely humans. The Epicureans arrived at the same understanding, although they took a different theoretical route. For Epicurus, who would later influence Hobbes, justice could only encompass beings capable of making contracts. Thus, in line with Aristotelian philosophy, only humans are rational and capable of assuming responsibility and obligations.

Contrary to the Stoics and Epicureans, Plutarch was the first thinker of antiquity to advocate a mitigated rationality for animals and to establish an ethics of hunting; his ideas were fruitful, so much so that they were revisited centuries later in the modern discussion of hunting ethics.

Newmyer reports that Plutarch (120 AD) wrote a work called "*De sollertia animalium,*" which was organized in two parts. In the first, he defended the thesis of animal rationality to some degree, refuting the Stoic thought, which advocated the total irrationality of non-human animals. Plutarch took a stand on sensitive points, such as the extent of the distance between animals and humans, the nature of animal emotional life, their linguistic capacity, and the ability to establish contact. He argued that the nature of animals includes a type of innate rationality that guides instinctive behavior.

According to Newmyer, Plutarch emphasizes that nature created animals, providing them with the ability to distinguish between what they should avoid and what they should pursue, and in this lies the sense of self-preservation, which makes the mother female feel affection for her offspring.[16] This idea will be revisited and deepened by Baruch Spinoza[17] in his concept of *conatus*; by Henri Bergson[18] in his theory of creative evolution; by Hans Jonas[19] in his ontology of the organism; by Antônio Damásio[20] in his theory on homeostasis;

[14] Newmyer (2006), p. 59–60.

[15] Sorabji (2001), p. 115.

[16] Newmyer (2006), p. 60–62.

[17] Spinoza (2016), p. 108.

[18] Bergson (2010).

[19] Jonas (2004).

[20] Damásio (2018), p. 21.

and also by Paul Taylor in defense of a fourth type of freedom, which all living beings share to defend their "own good."[21]

However, the line of thought regarding respect for animals, defended by Theophrastus, Pythagoras, Plutarch, and Porphyry, did not prevail, as Aristotle's denial of rationality to animals proved pleasing and convenient to Jews and Christians, who exploited and consolidated the anti-animal Stoic view. Justinian, the Byzantine emperor, based his legal codes on this conception and disseminated it throughout the Western world in a systematic and organized manner.

4.2 Moral Consideration of Animals in the Middle Ages and in Renaissance Neoplatonism

Pepper[22] points out that the medieval view (from the fifth to the fifteenth centuries) of the functioning of the universe and the cosmic position of the human being was influenced, in its physical dimension, by the thought of Aristotle. He reports that, around the twelfth and thirteenth centuries, there was an integration of the Aristotelian view of the world with Christian theology. Thus, a geocentric cosmography was established—that is, the world was at the center of the universe. The explanation of the Earth and the universe was physical–theological, as the universe was governed by principles that contributed to the achievement of the goals of God, the Christian God, who was the final cause of everything. Pepper highlights that, despite the prominence of God, the medieval cosmology was anthropocentric, given that it was permeated by "human perspectives imposed on nature." The world was seen from the human experience and, for this reason, many metaphors were used for its interpretation. For example, nature was compared to a book written by the will of God. Thus, the pious person should read two books—the Holy Bible and nature itself—to discover God's designs. In this view, nature did not exist only to satisfy human desires but also to give instructions to human beings through its mysteries: "The diligence of the ant or the bee would be an example. The fly reminded us of the ephemerality of life, and the fireflies the light of the Holy Spirit." It was based on this view that the doctrine of *signatures* was developed, arguing that everything that existed in visible and corporeal things also had an invisible and incorporeal meaning. In this way, plants, leaves, stones, and animals that resembled, in shape, color, or behavior, a human organ or disease could be used in healing.

In this line of thought, milky plants helped mothers to produce milk; spotted herbs eliminated skin spots; and yellow plants cured jaundice. In addition to the metaphor of nature as a great book, there was also another: nature as

---

[21] Taylor (2011), p. 120.

[22] Pepper (2000), p. 167.

a great animal, the so-called organic metaphor, rehabilitated in the twentieth century by deep ecology.[23]

Among the defenders of organic philosophies in the Middle Ages, there was a current called vitalism, led by Paracelsus, who defended the unity of matter and spirit—that is, all parts of the cosmos were alive and were linked in a unity, in a relationship of mutual interdependence.[24] Carolyn Merchant emphasizes that, since antiquity and in various cultures and peoples, nature has always been compared to a woman—the nurturing, sensitive, and living mother. In the Middle Ages, however, around the fifteenth century, a belief emerged in the supposed cosmic and social disorder caused by luxuriant women thirsty for carnal pleasure. The *Malleus maleficarum* (1486), establishing the anti-feminist doctrine of relentless persecution of witches—a persecution that would occur over the next two hundred years—was published. The supposed sexual lust of women was the basis for their punishment and subjugation.[25] During this period, the Earth, which had always been seen as a feminine entity, began to be compared to the luxuriant, uncontrolled, and wild female, who, like women, should be domesticated and subjugated.[26] Francis Bacon, at the dawn of modernity, wrote that nature, similar to a public woman, should be tamed by men, penetrated in her secrets, and, finally, subjugated by the masculine will.[27]

The organicist current of nature, which flourished in pre-modernity, understood the cosmos as a living organism that grew and developed from its own interior, in an integrated unity of structure and function.[28] This philosophy echoed in the American Romantic movement of the nineteenth century, in the works of Emerson, Thoreau, and John Muir.

Merchant[29] explains that the orthodox medieval view of Aristotelian philosophy envisioned a cosmic model organized in a hierarchy centered on Earth, comprising a rigid living chain of beings, which were organized in strata; the members of each stratum shared characteristics with the members of the steps above and below, but without losing their primary particular characteristics. Thus, the human being was linked with the animal world below, with which it shared sensations, and with the angelic world above, with which it resembled in rationality. Similarly, human society was also stratified according to the *status* of people: peasants at the base, king and pope at the top. In this scale, women were below men.

Renaissance Neoplatonism gave a broader interpretation to the Aristotelian chain of being, attributing to nature a soul—the soul of the world. Renaissance Neoplatonist thinkers include Marsilio Ficino (1433–1499), Giovanni Pico

---

[23] Pepper (2000), p. 170–171.

[24] Merchant (2020), p. 138.

[25] Merchant (2020), p. 154.

[26] Pepper (2000), p. 172.

[27] Ost (1995), p. 39.

[28] Merchant (2020), p. 145.

[29] Merchant (2020), p. 120.

della Mirandola (1463–1494), Henry Cornelius Agrippa (1486–1535), Bernardino Telesio (1509–1588), Tommaso Campanella (1568–1639), Giordano Bruno (1548–1600), Paracelsus (1490–1541), and Giambattista della Porta (1535–1615) . There were several organicist currents in the Renaissance, but, according to Merchant, they all shared a premise:

> [. . .] all parts of the cosmos were interconnected and interrelated in a living unity. From the "affinity of nature", consequently, the bond of all things through mutual attraction or love. All parts of nature were mutually interdependent and each reflected change in the rest of the cosmos.[30]

Merchant points out that Tommaso Campanella postulated the existence of feeling not only in animals but also in the entire cosmos. However, although the alchemical thinkers of the Renaissance evoked nature as a companion endowed with feelings and positioned themselves as its humble servants, they did not hide their desire to alter it, and even perfect it, through alchemy—the magical manipulation of matter. This would be done by imitating its organic processes. Later, Francis Bacon replaced the organic processes of the Neoplatonists with the technique of controlling nature and, most seriously, did so without the ethical constraints of Neoplatonism, which considered nature as a living being and still advocated a unity of society with nature.

The mechanists inherited from Neoplatonism the desire to manipulate matter, but they removed the organic cosmology of a living Earth, sensitive to human action. In the mechanistic view, the manipulation of nature ceases to be an individual challenge and moves to the field of general social interests, necessary for the expansion of commercial capitalism. An empirical philosophy of science is unveiled, in which the human being ceases to be the servant of nature and becomes its master, its creator, uncovering its secrets and dominating its operations.[31]

This radical change in the conception of the world, which prevailed in the medieval period, will be called the age of the scientific revolution and will cover the sixteenth and seventeenth centuries, a period that begins with Nicolaus Copernicus, who challenged the biblical and Ptolemaic geocentric view, which had been accepted as an unquestionable dogma for over a thousand years. Copernicus demonstrated that the Earth was not the center of the universe, nor was the human being the central figure of God's creation. After Copernicus, Johannes Kepler brought to light the harmony of the spheres, corroborating Copernicus's theory. However, it is Galileo Galilei who will definitively bury the old medieval cosmology by observing, through his telescope, that Copernicus's hypothesis was a verifiable and valid scientific theory.[32]

However, as Henry S. Salt points out, from the fourth to the seventeenth centuries, from Porphyry to Montaigne, little to no attention was given to the rights of animals.[33]

---

[30] Merchant (2020), p. 124.

[31] Merchant (2020), p. 196.

[32] Capra (2012), p. 52.

[33] Salt (1922), p. 14.

4.3 Moral Consideration of Non-Human Beings in Modernity

Pepper highlights that Francis Bacon was the first thinker of the scientific revolution to establish the implications of a "society-nature" relationship, advocating the belief that scientific knowledge constitutes power over nature. Bacon, just like Descartes, separates humans from nature. Men and women become the subjects who interpret the object, nature. While Descartes used the deductive method, Bacon relied on the inductive method. Pepper compares Bacon's scientific method to a pyramid, at the base of which are the data accumulated through empirical knowledge, and in the ascending direction of the pyramid, the laws of nature overlap, increasing in generality, with the vertex being capped by a universal law that would explain everything.[34]

Thus, the organic conception of nature as a nurturing and feeding mother is replaced by a view of the Earth as a mere natural resource. This shift from the organicist paradigm to the mechanistic one is well delineated in the thought of René Descartes, whose work "Discourse on the Method for Rightly Conducting One's Reason and Seeking Truth in the Sciences," which became a classic of philosophy, aimed to serve as an introductory manual to science. His analytical method was based on the decomposition of thought and problems into distinct parts and components, with subsequent organization in a logical order. Capra notes that the Cartesian method led to a widespread attitude of scientific reductionism—that is, the reduction of all complex phenomena to their smallest constituent parts, with the study of each part. The central point of the Cartesian method is doubt and was expressed in his maxim "*cogito, ergo sum*" (I think, therefore I am). For Descartes, the essence of human nature lies in the ability to think.

Descartes' analytical method became the distinctive mark of modern scientific thought, allowing humans to carry out complex technological projects. As Capra points out: "It was Descartes' method that made it possible for NASA to take man to the Moon."[35]

However, Pepper emphasizes that Descartes expanded the concept of nature as a machine, considering everything that was not measurable to be unreal. In this perspective, the bodies of non-human animals began to be seen as machines, automatons, whose functioning could be mathematically understood, like a clock. From this reductionist view, there is no vital principle necessary for life, since life differs from non-life only by the degree of complexity of things.

For Cartesian dualism, the act of doubting was the process of thought that established the fact of human existence, which makes the human being the subject, while nature and non-human beings were placed solely as cognizable objects and metaphysically separated from human beings.[36]

Capra points out:

---

[34] Pepper (2000), p. 187–188.

[35] Capra (2012), p. 56.

[36] Pepper (2000), p. 185.

> For Descartes, the Universe was a machine, nothing more than a machine. There was no purpose, life or spirituality in matter. Nature operated according to mechanical laws, and everything in the material world could be explained in terms of the organization and movement of its parts. This mechanical picture of nature became the dominant paradigm of science in the period following Descartes. It guided scientific observation and the formulations of all theories of natural phenomena, until 20th-century physics brought about a radical change. The entire development of mechanistic science in the 17th, 18th, and 19th centuries, including Newton's great synthesis, was nothing more than the development of the Cartesian idea.[37].

At the beginning of modernity, a discussion about the dignity of animals arose, motivated by the practice of vivisection.[38] With the emergence of medical science in the seventeenth century, the method of studying the bodies of animals to verify the functioning of their organs was developed; thus, in European universities, dogs, cats, and other animals were nailed alive to a board and had their bodies opened for studies of the circulatory system. Descartes provided vivisectors with the tranquility of a philosophy that emphasized the ethical irrelevance of nature and animals, since they were considered merely insensitive and irrational machines that did not feel sadness, joy, or even pain and thus could be dissected alive in the name of scientific progress.

Nash highlights that it was at the height of Cartesian thought that, curiously, the first record of an animal protection law is found: the so-called Body of Liberties, adopted by the General Court of Massachusetts in 1641. It was drafted by Nathaniel Ward at the request of the General Court of Massachusetts, in the context of the first codification of the colony's statutes. Ward created a list of rights, which included the prohibition of tyranny and cruelty in relation to animals kept for man's use.

Along the same lines, John Locke, a staunch defender of the natural rights of human beings, admitted that animals have the capacity to suffer and that causing them to suffer is morally reprehensible.[39]

On the other hand, an ecological movement began to emerge in the seventeenth and eighteenth centuries within a religious concept of protecting nature as a creation of God. Another significant pre-ecological movement was the philosophy of animism or organicism, that is, the belief in a single, continuous force that permeated all beings and things, and that everything was a large organism. Baruch Spinoza was the exponent of this current, and his thought would reverberate in the twentieth century in ecological awareness and environmental ethics.

From a religious perspective, John Brukner was concerned about the ecological impact of the English people's expansion in the New World. In a philosophical opinion on animal creation, he questioned whether the transformation of the American desert was not breaking the "web of life"; he was the first to use this expression.

---

[37] Capra (2012), p. 57–58.

[38] Vivisection is the act of dissecting a living animal for the purpose of conducting anatomophysiological studies. In its most generic sense, it is defined as an invasive intervention in a living organism, with scientific and pedagogical motivations.

[39] Nash (1989), p. 15.

In 1789, Jeremy Bentham postulated the end of cruelty to animals, pointing out that the day would come when the rest of the animal creation would acquire rights that could never be taken from them. Bentham recognized that animals could feel pain and thus would experience profound unhappiness, which contradicted his ethics of the greatest happiness, or utilitarianism, for which pain was bad and pleasure was good. Bentham extended the logic of maximizing happiness to enslaved human beings and also to animals. He questioned lawmakers as to why laws denied protection to sentient beings and denounced that this unethical action caused more pain and suffering to sentient beings relegated to suffering by the indifference of laws, and he prophesied: "The time will come when humanity will extend its mantle over everything that breathes." This mantle referred to by Bentham is the moral status and legal protection.

Some of Bentham's contemporaries, such as John Lawrence, advanced in recognizing rights for animals, discussing the tyrannical treatment given to animals from the perspective of justice. Lawrence also supported the abolition of human slavery and women's rights. In addition, he wrote a philosophical treatise on horses and man's moral duties toward brute creations. He argued that the life, intelligence, and feelings of animals necessarily imply rights. In 1790, he postulated that all constitutions recognize the rights of non-human beings. Lawrence relied on Bentham's utilitarian philosophy to claim animal rights, especially in relation to horses.[40]

For Henry Salt, Bentham was the first man who had the honor of postulating the rights of animals with authority and persistence. Salt quotes the following passage from Bentham:

> The legislator must prohibit everything that can lead to cruelty. The barbaric spectacles of gladiators undoubtedly contributed to giving the Romans that ferocity they exhibited in their civil wars. One could not expect a people accustomed to despising human life in their games to respect it in the midst of their passions. It is appropriate, for the same reason, to prohibit all kinds of cruelty against animals, whether for fun or to satisfy gluttony. Cockfights, bull baits, hare and fox hunts, fishing and other amusements of the same kind necessarily imply the absence of reflection or a background of inhumanity, as they produce more acute suffering for sentient beings and, most painfully, prolonged death [...] Why should the law refuse its protection to any sentient being? The time will come when humanity will extend its mantle over everything that breathes.[41]

The fight against cruelty to animals, especially the practice of vivisection, reached its peak in England in 1876 with the approval of the British Cruelty to Animals Act, a legal document that required doctors to use anesthetics in vivisection processes.

In 1879, Edward B. Nicholson defended the rights of animals, emphasizing that although the consciousness and feelings of animals are more limited than those of men, humans should recognize their rights, since if humans with mental disabilities

[40] Nash (1989), p. 20–21.

[41] Salt (1922), p. 16.

do not have moral recognition denied by society, equally the limited reason of animals could not serve as a justification to deny their rights to life and freedom.[42] The English movement in favor of animal rights, which included Bentham, John Laurence, and Eduard B. Nicholson, laid the foundations for the concept of an expanded ethical community in the nineteenth century, with the activism of Henry Salt and Henry David Thoreau.

Salt's work, originally published in 1892, was a major milestone in the fight for the defense of animal rights, as it emphasized the need to protect non-human animals due to their proximity and kinship with humans:

> Nor will it ever be possible to obtain full justice for animals as long as we continue to consider them as beings of a completely different order, and ignore the importance of their numerous points of kinship with humanity. [. . .] If we want to do justice [. . .] we must rid ourselves of the outdated notion of a great chasm fixed between them and humanity, and the common bond of humanity that unites all living beings in a universal fraternity must be recognized.[43]

For most humanitarians of the nineteenth century, the issue with the fact that humans are cruel to animals was the cruelty itself, as a violation of human morality and good action; the torture of animals was not reproached with a view to recognizing an intrinsic value or dignity for non-human beings. Humanitarians still did not have a holistic consciousness; however, even so, their concern for the life and freedom of animals is the ideological element that made environmental ethics flourish. However, it should not be forgotten that, in this still humanitarian scenario, John Muir, as early as 1867, already had a broad ecological vision and proposed respect for the rights of nature as a whole.[44]

4.4 The Expansion of the Ecological Circle in the Twentieth Century

From the Greek word *oikos* come the words "home," "economy," and "ecology." The term "ecology" was coined as early as 1866 by Ernst Haeckel[45] and, from its inception, referred to community and systems. Because of its holistic character, ecology presented itself as fertile ground for the flourishing of environmental ethics.

The broader ecological vision of valuing nature as a whole was also influenced by the research of Charles Elton, who, in 1927, coined the term "food chain" in his research on nutritional dependence, which begins with the sun, passes through

---

[42] Nash (1989), p. 24.

[43] Salt (1922), p. 7–8.

[44] Nash (1989), p. 34.

[45] Nash (1989), p. 55.

plants, herbivores, and carnivores. Elton's research showed that the simplest organisms are at the base of the food chain, so that when you remove an animal, like a hawk or a human, who are at the top of the pyramid, the system does not suffer disturbances; however, when you exclude from the chain living beings at the base, like plants and soil bacteria, the pyramid collapses. Charles Elton's theory was useful for demonstrating that humans are quite vulnerable, as they depend on the bacteria that sustain the grass, which sustains the cattle, which provides the meat. This impacted human understanding of nature and strengthened the idea of a community.[46]

Not all ecologists appreciated the terminology "community." Arthur G. Tansley, for example, understood that the word "community" was loaded with anthropomorphic connotations, and so, in 1935, he coined the term "ecosystem," which was quickly adopted by the scientific community. From these notions brought by ecology at the beginning of the twentieth century, the idea of interdependence in the description of nature was increasingly consolidated. This idea of interdependent flow will reverberate in the determination of human conduct in relation to nature.

Thinkers like Alfred Whitehead decisively impacted environmental ethics. Whitehead, in his theory about the interaction of electromagnetic particles as the essence of matter itself, argues that the identity and purpose of each object in the universe arise from its relationship with everything else, and so all things are in flux all the time, such that every organism, every atom, has an intrinsic value resulting from its contribution to the continuous reality of the universe.[47]

Equally impactful was the thought of Albert Schweitzer, a philosopher and biologist who decided to study medicine to attend to the original inhabitants of Equatorial Africa under French colonization. Thus, in 1915, two years after taking up his medical post in Africa, while sailing on a small steamer on the Ogowe River during twilight, his boat passed a herd of hippos. Contemplating them from the deck, he had an epiphany, which led him to the answer he had been searching for years to find regarding his question about what would be the most valid basis for ethics. He concluded that the answer was "reverence for life" and used the German word *Ehrfurcht* to define this reverence, as this word connotes a humble admiration in the face of a vast and mysterious power.

Nash points out that, for Schweitzer, the ethical person "does not break any ice crystal that shines in the sun, does not tear even a leaf from its tree, does not break a flower, and takes care not to crush an insect while walking."[48]

The ecological movement in the twentieth century, which unfolds from humanitarianism, from the organicism of the nineteenth century, from mystical holism, and also from concepts drawn from biology and ecology, will take on

[46] Nash (1989), p. 55.
[47] Nash (1989), p. 57.
[48] Nash (1989), p. 58.

various shades, so that from now on it is didactically necessary to detail the various trends—ecocentrism, zoocentrism, and biocentrism—in order to thus identify their differences and points of contact.

4.5 Aldo Leopold's Land Ethic

Aldo Leopold, in his pioneering work on the ecological study of wildlife in American territory, was one of the first scholars to perceive the connection between ecology and ethics. Thus, he wrote in 1949: "All ethics rest on a single premise: that the individual is a member of a community of interdependent parts."[49]

It was from the research of the Russian Peter D. Ouspensky, especially his work "Tertium Organum" from 1912, that Aldo Leopold concluded that the Earth is "an organism that possesses a certain type and degree of life," and this was a sufficient reason to consider it a "moral being." In light of his observation of the "indivisibility of the earth—its soil, mountains, rivers, forests, climate, plants, and animals," Leopold began to advocate for ethical respect for the Earth "not just as a useful servant, but as a living being."[50]

In 1933, in New Mexico, Leopold presented his paper "The Ethics of Conservation," whose main contribution was the idea of the evolution of ethics, as it draws a parallel between human slavery and the unconditional ownership of land. To this end, he refers to Odysseus, who, upon returning to his Greek homeland, hangs a dozen slaves accused of misbehavior during his absence on a single rope. The slaves were Odysseus's property and thus were outside the ethical community of their master; that is, Odysseus's relationship with the slaves was merely utilitarian, so the decision to punish them was not reached by the judgment of right or wrong but was within the field of mere convenience. Over the centuries, there has been an extension of ethics to encompass the entire human community and abolish the figure of the slave. From this reflection, Leopold warned: "There is not yet any ethics that deals with man's relationship with the earth and with the non-human animals and plants that grow on it. The earth, like Odysseus's slaves, is still property."[51]

Leopold created the paradigm of an ethical system that included nature as a whole, and for this reason, he is considered the father, the founding genius of environmental ethics. In 1933, when he began his work as a professor at the University of Wisconsin, he warned his students that any idea of good or bad species was the result of utilitarian anthropocentrism. In 1944, he wrote the essay "Thinking Like a Mountain." In this article, he recounts a fateful afternoon from the time he worked in the Forest Service; when he was having lunch with his team on a cliff overlooking the New Mexico River, they spotted a wolf crossing the

[49] Leopold (1949), p. 179.
[50] Nash (1989), p. 64.
[51] Nash (1989), p. 62.

river's current and opened fire, as they had the directive to control the overpopulation of wolves in the park. The animal was accurately shot and fell; then, Leopold went to it and could still look into its eyes, in which he saw a green and fierce fire die. This green fire accompanied him for all his days, for thirty years, and made him reflect on the fact that wolves and other predators were necessary to keep hunting animal herds healthy.[52]

Leopold's first work on the ethics of the human relationship with nature was a 1923 article, which was only published in 1979, in which he advocates conservation as a moral imperative. Aldo Leopold went beyond utilitarianism to understand that a wolf was a legitimate part of the southwest ecosystem, so its existence had an ecological and ethical justification, regardless of its usefulness to man. He named this reasoning "thinking like a mountain." His most well-known work, "A Sand County Almanac," introduced the idea of a biotic right in the United States, surpassing the traditional conservationist movement of that country.

Despite Darwinian evolutionists and humanitarians, like John Muir, having glimpsed the idea of a morality that extended beyond human society, it is with Leopold that a well-defined ethic emerges to protect not only individual organisms or superior animals but also ecosystems, the environment, and nature as a whole.[53]

Leopold adopted Schweitzer's principle of reverence for life. In 1948, when he concluded his essay "The Land Ethic" for a local almanac called "Sand County," Leopold argued that a decision about land use "is right when it tends to preserve the integrity, stability, and beauty of the biotic community. It is wrong when it tends otherwise."[54]

As can be seen, Leopold's work surpasses the individual protection of living beings and inaugurates an ecocentric vision of ethical consideration for ecosystems and nature in a broader sense, hence its relevance to the history of ecological ethics.

4.6 Rachel Carson's Silent Spring

In his historical analysis of the evolution of the struggle for the inclusion of non-human beings in the ethical community, Nash cites the work of Rachel Carson, Silent Spring from 1962, considered a milestone in the development of a new ecological ethic. Carson argues that no form of life is a commodity, not even the life of insects, so all deserve ethical consideration. Nash notes that although Silent Spring contributed to the construction of a new environmental ethic, it is still marked by many anthropocentric ideas, such as the division of insects into "friends" and "enemies" of humanity.[55]

---

[52] Nash (1989), p. 61–62.

[53] Nash (1989), p. 68–69.

[54] Leopold (1949), p. 195.

[55] Nash (1989), p. 76–78.

Nevertheless, Rachel Carson's work was fundamental in creating an ecological awareness of the human body. Indeed, her reflections on the interrelationship of humans with the environment and the corresponding impact on human health were crucial in demonstrating the non-existence of boundaries between soil, air, water, and the human organism. Silent Spring demonstrated how vulnerable the human body is to the harmful effects of pesticides. It was her tireless work that led John F. Kennedy to order investigations into the harms of dichloro-diphenyl-trichloroethane (DDT)[56] and other poisons. Two years after her premature death from cancer, the United States Congress passed a law creating the Environmental Protection Agency, and soon after, the domestic use of DDT was banned. However, its export still continues freely, poisoning the soil, air, and water sources of other peoples in peripheral countries.

In her work, Carson describes with moving realism the compromise of the web of life caused by the use of pesticides:

> For each of us, as for the robin in Michigan or the salmon in the Miramichi River, this is an ecology problem, of interrelationships, of interdependence. We poison the caddisflies in a river and the salmon dwindle and die. We poison the insects in a lake and the poison travels, link by link, up the food chain, and soon the birds on the lake's shores become its victims. We spray insecticides on our elms and the springs that follow are silent with the absence of the robin's song, because we did not spray the robin directly, but because the poison traveled, step by step, through our now familiar cycle of elm leaf-earthworm-robin. These are facts that can be recorded, observed, part of the visible world that surrounds us. They reflect the web of life - or death - that scientists know as ecology.[57]

As can be inferred from this passage, Carson advocates a systemic and holistic view of the human relationship as a member of nature—that is, of the biotic community—which she may have inherited from Albert Schweitzer, to whom she dedicated Silent Spring. Carson's moving denunciation, in addition to its direct effects on U.S. environmental policy, also had the great merit, as pointed out by Attfield,[58] of being, along with the work of Aldo Leopold, the driving force for the development of ethics applied to ecology in the decades that followed.

4.7 The Sierra Club Versus Walt Disney Enterprises Case

Nash reports that, from the 1970s onward, a strong academic and scientific movement was triggered to construct an environmental ethic that included non-human beings and holistic organic entities in the ethical community. However, in this profuse scientific production, environmental ethics came to have various meanings, some even contradictory. There was much disagreement about moral eligibility—about

[56] Dichloro-diphenyl-trichloroethane.

[57] Carson (2010), p. 163.

[58] Attfield (2012), p. 114.

who should be included in the ethical community and what the eligibility criteria would be. Some environmental philosophers considered only domestic mammals worthy of moral consideration, while self-proclaimed deep ecologists claimed the extension of moral consideration to all forms of life. In turn, so-called holistic ethicists advocated the inclusion in the ethical community of soil, rocks, air, water, and the biophysical processes that constitute the ecosystem.[59]

In this time of theoretical effervescence for a new environmental ethic in the American academic environment, Nash highlights the work of Christopher D. Stone, a philosophy professor at the University of Southern California. In the midst of the trial of the Sierra Club versus Walt Disney Enterprises case, which dealt with Walt Disney Enterprises' intention to build a ski resort in the valley known as Sierra Mineral King, the Sierra Club, guardian of the region, filed an inhibitory demand. However, the Court of Appeal understood that the Sierra Club had no interest, as it had not suffered any injury. This case inspired Christopher D. Stone, who, reflecting on the issue, created an unprecedented thesis in the sense that it should "give legal rights to forests, oceans, rivers, and other so-called natural objects." Stone's thesis, set out in an essay entitled "Should Trees Stand?," reached Justice William O. Douglas who, in the trial of the case, in a minority vote, stated that the appropriate name for the case would not be Sierra Club versus Morton (Rogers Morton was the U.S. Secretary of the Interior in 1972), but Mineral King *versus* Morton. Justice *Douglas* questioned: "Why not open American courts to rivers, lakes, estuaries, beaches, mountain ranges, woods, swamps, or even air?" He also emphatically pointed out that these entities, to which ethical consideration was being attributed, should be represented by their legitimate spokespersons—human beings with whom they maintained a close relationship.

In this historic Supreme Court trial, Justice *Douglas* proposed intrinsic rights to the environment and mentioned, in his vote, Aldo Leopold's land ethic, which expanded the boundaries of the moral community. Despite being a minority vote, his position was widely disseminated in academic circles and U.S. media. Nash notes that Christopher D. Stone and Justice *Douglas* found a conceptual door for the rights of nature in 1972, and subsequently, philosophers and theorists quickly opened it.[60]

4.8 Zoocentrism: An Animal Liberation Movement

Concern for animal welfare, as seen previously, is quite old, dating back to ancient Greece, was weakened by the prevalence of Stoic and Christian thought in the Middle Ages, but it was reborn with strength in modernity, with Jeremy Bentham as a great advocate for animal welfare.

---

[59] Nash (1989), p. 121–125.

[60] Nash (1989), pp. 125–129.

In the twentieth century, the so-called zoocentric philosophical movement of utilitarian inspiration emerged, whose central concern is vertebrate animals. The scope of this movement is to ensure the welfare of animals and their liberation from suffering caused by humans, who use them as guinea pigs for laboratory experiments, mass-breed them for protein and fur sources, and use them as tools for work and leisure. As access to food consumption and goods grew, humans began to exploit animal life in an unlimited and ruthless way to satisfy their most frivolous consumption desires, as Leena Vilkka observes:

> The central concern has been the protection and care of people, while other animals do not have the same degree of moral protection or lack moral standing altogether. Even animal sciences have focused on human welfare or health. Animals have been treated as instruments and models for human diseases or as raw material for the human economy.[61]

To combat this speciesism, denounced by Vilkka, and ensure the welfare of animals, the animal liberation movement emerged in the twentieth century, postulating the recognition of an end value for non-human animals.

Among these various open doors, the animal liberation movement, based on utilitarian philosophy, stands out, as it harks back to the teachings of Jeremy Bentham and is led by Peter Singer,[62] who advocates for the inclusion, in the moral community, of animals capable of feeling pain and pleasure. Within the criterion established as the limit for the extension of Singer's moral community, the animal must have sufficiently sophisticated nervous systems to feel pain; these are called sentient beings. For Singer, herding is true slavery. Despite the scope of Singer's ethical consideration being more restricted, as it applies only to sentient animals, it made a great contribution to the evolution of ecological ethics, as it brought to the general public the discussion of the important topic of the inadequacy of a merely anthropocentric ethic. Singer postulates the recognition of intrinsic value for non-human animals, adopting as a criterion the mental states that allow feeling pain or pleasure—sentience. That is, he attributes intrinsic value only to the conscious states of sentient beings.

For Singer, similar interests should receive equal consideration, as they have equal value. However, he makes a distinction between equal consideration and equal treatment, noting that, just as people who receive equal consideration are treated unequally according to their inequalities, sentient beings, although they are holders of moral consideration, should not be treated in a strictly equal manner, as they present differentiated needs according to the nature of their interests.[63]

Thus, Singer supports the priority of treatment in relation to the interests of some creatures over others, establishing a scale of satisfaction of interests not only according to the degree of mental complexity of the being but also taking into account the relevance of the interest at stake. For example, in a collision between the interest of a human diner and the interest of a calf to live and flourish, much

---

[61] Vilkka (1997), pp. 37–38.

[62] Singer (2010).

[63] Attfield (2012), p. 51.

more is at stake for the calf than for the human. In this case, although the complexity of the human organism is greater, the interest of the calf should prevail over that of the human.[64]

It is also worth highlighting, in the struggle for the recognition of intrinsic value for non-human animals, the work of Tom Regan. Nash observes that Regan's approach to animal liberation reflects the rhetoric and the arguments of the movements that fought for the civil rights of minorities in the previous decades and is not based on the utilitarian philosophy that inspires Peter Singer.[65]

Regan proposes two criteria for his environmental ethics: (a) ethical extensionism for animals; (b) recognition of inherent value. He explains that he uses the term "inherent value," considering that he postulates a value regarded objectively. That is, in his proposal for the recognition of value, he does not take into account the animal's mental states, such as the ability to feel pain or pleasure. In this context, the recognition of value is independent of the state of consciousness and should take into account the properties of the animal itself, as the recognition of inherent value is, above all, an attitude of respect and preservation.[66]

Vilkka explains that, for Regan, the properties of a being that enable it to have its inherent value recognized are to be the subject-of–a-life. However, Regan himself admits that this is an arbitrary criterion, which does not cover all animals. Regan makes a distinction between intrinsic value and inherent value.[67] For him, the current view that defends the recognition of intrinsic value takes into account the animal's mental states, its ability to suffer and feel well-being, and its mental experiences as an individual. He uses the metaphor of a cup with coffee: whoever recognizes intrinsic value treats the animal as a mere receptacle—the important thing is the content, the mental experiences. In the recognition of inherent value, the value is considered objectively, regardless of the sensations of pleasure, preferences, and satisfactions of the animal.

Regan also makes a distinction between a moral agent, the adult human being in full use of mental faculties, and a moral patient, who is the recipient of moral consideration and the respect of the moral agent. Moral agents have ethical duties not to harm both other moral agents and moral patients, who are the animals, subjects of a life. These moral patients can be subdivided into two large groups: (1) individuals who, although conscious and sentient, do not have other abilities; (2) conscious, sentient individuals who possess other cognitive and volitional abilities. Most mammals are in the second group, while the other animals are in the first group.

When asked about the criterion for considering the non-human animal as a subject-of–a-life, Regan admits that it is an arbitrary choice and, therefore,

[64] Attfield (2012), p. 52.

[65] Nash (1989), p. 249.

[66] Vilkka (1997), p. 31.

[67] Tom Regan does not use the term *inherent worth* used by Paul Taylor; when he speaks of inherent value, he uses the expression *inherent value*.

does not cover all living beings. Vilkka concludes that the recognition of inherent value, according to Regan's theory, is reduced to sentient animals.[68]

In truth, the animal liberation movement is based on traditional American liberal philosophy, where ethics has always been at the service of protecting individual lives in the face of collective entities, such as the state and nation. Liberal philosophy first dealt with the inclusion of all humans in the ethical community, since, for centuries, it allowed slavery. Abolitionist movements of liberal inspiration included all humans in the ethical community of the planet. Finally, the animal liberation movement emerged, led by Peter Singer and Tom Regan, extending ethical consideration to non-human "sentient" animals.

These theories, which limit inclusion in the moral community only to "sentient" animals or "normal mammals," caused some dissatisfaction in the ecological movement, which intends to break with the vision of anthropocentric ethics in a broader way to derive ethical rules about the relationship of humans with the entire environment.

4.9 Deep Ecology

Parallel to the animal liberation school, a broader philosophical movement emerged called deep ecology, whose roots lie in Norwegian philosophy. As early as 1941, Peter Zapffe founded "biosophy," a non-anthropocentric theory of man–environment relations. In 1974, Sigmund Kvaloy, also Norwegian, wrote an article coining the term "ecophilosophy." However, the leading figure of the Norwegian ecological movement was Arne Naess, a survivor of the resistance to Nazism and a mountaineer, who had a strong impact on American environmentalism by proposing "deep ecology" and a new discipline in the ecological field, which he called "ecosophy."[69]

Arne Naess inspired Americans George Sessions and Bill Devall to adopt a broader view, in which ecology involves philosophical and religious principles, establishing a new form of relationship between the human being and the environment. The most impactful aspect of this new paradigm proposed by Naess was "ecological egalitarianism." This same philosophy was also referred to by other philosophers as "biocentrism" or "anti-anthropocentrism." Naess also advocated the establishment of "a central democracy in the biosphere" and the "equal right to live and flourish," which he later called "self-realization."

The philosophy proposed by Naess considered the ethical and moral inherent value not only in all living beings but also in "rivers, landscapes, and ecosystems." Deep ecologists were quite familiar with food chains and the reality of one life having to take another life to sustain itself, so they did not focus on the individual

[68] Vilkka (1997), p. 44.

[69] Nash (1989), p. 144.

being but on the ecological process as a whole. Nash explains that, for Naess and Sessions, environmental impact and even the death of animals would be ethically acceptable as long as they were done to ensure basic vital needs.

For deep ecologists, the concept of "vital" is the touchstone for deriving ethical rules, with the opposite of "vital," within the ecological process, being "excessive." Thus, one of the responsibilities of modern technological civilization would be to understand the "vital" vs. "excessive" dichotomy. Nash explains that, from this perspective, in unmodified ecosystems, such as deserts, for example, predator and prey coexist in a balance of vital needs.

Deep ecologists proposed a critique of human interference in the environment beyond basic vital needs. Nash reports that the premises set by deep ecology provoked concerns and brought forth the following question: Could Homo sapiens be a civilization (which is the human form of self-realization and flourishing) without violating the basic deep ecological principle of ecological egalitarianism? Deep ecologists responded to this question, arguing that, while some impact is permissible, modern humanity has grossly exceeded appropriate levels, just as a lion that killed fifteen antelopes a day would have exceeded.

From this perspective, an environmental ethic became necessary and urgent as a mechanism of self-restraint. Nash observes that if a lion were to kill fifteen antelopes a day, this behavior would be excessive and harmful to the vital balance of the ecosystem, but it is not possible to pass a value judgment on the lion's conduct. However, humans have not only the power but also the ability to formulate judgments about the right or wrong of their behaviors.[70]

In line with deep ecology, the relevant work of the Brazilian theologian and philosopher Leonardo Boff, who, in addition to discussing the crisis of the civilizational paradigm of modernity, prophesies about the new paradigm that will emerge, with the following characteristics: (1) a totality constructed with organically interconnected diversity; (2) reconnection of beings with each other, in a relationship of cosmic interdependent solidarity; (3) an ontological relationality; (4) proposal of a unifying and ordering thread of cosmogenic processes, in the figure of the divine; (5) recognition of complementarity and reciprocity at the base of the original dynamism of the universe, which goes through chaos before reaching the cosmos; (6) delay of the planet's entropy by negentropic human behaviors; (7) recognition of our communion of destinies and future; (8) recognition that the common good is of the entire cosmic community; (9) the recognition that the human being, still as an observer, interferes in the constitution of the world and its contingency, so that, being an ethical subject, can, in the space of freedom, weigh the most valuable interests of the cosmic community to which he belongs, to make responsible decisions; and (10) review of the anthropocentric paradigm, to adopt a holistic, loving, and inclusive attitude toward human and non-human living beings and ecosystems.[71]

[70] Nash (1989), pp. 144–146.

[71] Boff (2004), pp. 53–56.

The principles of deep ecology can be summarized as follows: (a) well-being and flourishing of human and non-human life; (b) recognition of intrinsic value, focused on the well-being and flourishing of all forms of life on Earth; (c) self-realization of all living beings; (d) biocentric equality; and (e) recognition of intrinsic value in natural diversity itself.

4.10 Paul Taylor's Biocentrism

Paul W. Taylor is one of the exponents of the current known as biocentrism. Taylor defends biocentric egalitarianism; that is, he rejects the anthropocentric idea that humans are superior to non-human animals and plants. Despite his denial of anthropocentrism, Taylor is recognizably Kantian and seeks, in Kant's virtue ethics, the concept of respect for nature. However, he emphasizes that the condition for having this respect is moral consideration and the recognition of "inherent worth" in living beings. Taylor's position differs from the holism of deep ecology, which recognizes intrinsic value in ecosystems, as it restricts the recognition of end value only to living beings.

Starting from the idea of recognition of the "inherent worth" of living beings, Taylor supports a moral equality among all living beings. However, when questioned about the possibility of conflicts between the interests of human and non-human beings, he proposes priority principles to guide judicial decisions in resolving conflicts of interest between humans and non-humans. He clarifies that these principles are based on the ethical ideal of an "ideal harmony between nature and human civilization."[72] Taylor's priority principles are as follows: (1) principle of self-defense; (2) principle of proportionality; (3) principle of minimal error; (4) principle of distributive justice; and (5) principle of restorative justice.

Leena Vilkka establishes a comparison between Taylor's biocentric theory and Tom Regan's zoocentric theory to demonstrate the similarities in their ontological foundations. Both agree that some living beings—non-human, sentient animals for Regan and living beings in general for Taylor—have their own good regardless of people. Regan's "subject-of–a-life" criterion and Taylor's "own good" are taken as the standard for locating end value, referred to by Taylor as "inherent worth" and by Regan as "inherent value." Taylor's concept of a moral subject corresponds to Regan's concept of a moral patient. Both concepts refer to beings that are holders of moral concern and respect by humans. Both focus on the good of individuals and do not consider ecosystems or species as recipients of inherent value.[73]

Regan attributes to moral agents a duty toward moral patients, who are sentient animals, while Taylor works with the Kantian view of respect for moral agents toward moral subjects, the subjects of a life, which are all living beings.

[72] Taylor (2011), p. 279.

[73] Vilkka (1997), p. 69.

It clarifies that the meaning of harmony in this context should be understood as follows:

> [...] the preservation of balance between human values and the well-being of animals in natural ecosystems. It is a condition on Earth where people are able to pursue their individual interests and the cultural ways of life they have adopted, while allowing many biotic communities in a wide variety of natural ecosystems to continue existing without interference[74].

As can be seen, Taylor's proposal for ecological justice is much more comprehensive and profound, and, despite restricting the recognition of moral consideration only to living beings, his justice system allows, by reflex, ecosystems to also be protected, considering that he defends "the ethical ideal of harmony between human civilization and nature."[75]

4.11 The Integral Ecology of Thomas Berry—Earth Jurisprudence

Thomas Berry is the creator of the theory of Earth Jurisprudence. He is a persistent critic of the anthropocentric paradigm and its influence on Western laws. He argues that the current legal system "is supporting exploitation instead of protecting the natural world from destruction by a less industrialized economy."[76]

Berry's theory has been studied and developed by Peter Burdon and Cormac Cullinan. In this item, a quick examination of these two authors will be presented to verify the nuances of Berry's Earth Jurisprudence in the thoughts of both.

The great achievement of Berry's theory is to have moved from the field of ethics to the legal sphere. Berry warns that abstract legal categories serve only for the self-assessment of people or political communities, in total disconnection from ecocentric values. In this sense, he presents criticisms of legal positivism: (1) the consecrated notion of private property serving as an authorizing mechanism for human exploitation of nature; (2) the non-recognition of rights outside the human community; and (3) the fact that there is no recognition or provision for the quality of being subjects of rights for non-humans.

Berry[77] categorically asserts that, to achieve a viable community between Earth and humanity, a new legal system must be rethought, with the task of articulating the conditions for the integral functioning of the Earth process.

Burdon, when studying Berry's work, deduces the existence of two types of "laws," organized in a hierarchical relationship: The first order is the so-called great law, which refers to the principle of the Earth community.

[74] Taylor (2011), p. 234.

[75] Taylor (2011), p. 321.

[76] Burdon (2015), pp. 81–82.

[77] Berry (1988).

The second order of law is human law, which represents the binding prescriptions articulated by human authorities.

He points out two issues that characterize the interrelationship between the so-called great law and human law. (1) Human law derives its legal quality and power to bind from the great law. Thus, considering that humans exist as part of an interconnected community with mutual dependence, only normative rules that point toward the common good, within a macrocosmic perspective, have the quality of law. In this line, when faced with decisions whose conflicting interests relate to the environment or to human–Earth interactions, human law must be guided by the great law. (2) Human laws that deal with the environment and do not respect the great law are corrupted and, therefore, unfit to bind the population.[78]

Berry's theory has several points of contact with the doctrine of natural law of Saint Thomas Aquinas. The Thomistic doctrine of natural law is based on the supposed existence of a body of universal and immutable law, and thus, natural law represents a body of superior laws, which serve as benchmarks for examining the moral adequacy of common laws. This superior law is accessed by human beings through reason. However, Burdon clarifies that many advocates of Earth Jurisprudence do not adopt the philosophy of natural law and shy away from the positivism vs. natural law dichotomy.

Burdon emphasizes that Berry reproduced in Earth Jurisprudence the doctrine of Saint Thomas Aquinas of the "Superior Laws." The Thomistic legal theory unfolds four types of laws arranged hierarchically: (1) eternal law, the rules given by God that govern nature; (2) natural law, which is the dimension of eternal law that can be discovered through reasoning; (3) divine law, which is God's law revealed in the scriptures; and (4) human law, which is at the base of the order and consists of rules supported by reason and articulated by legislators.

As can be inferred from Question 90 of the Summa Theologica, Saint Thomas Aquinas discusses the essence of law, defining law as "nothing more than an ordinance of reason for a common good, made by the one who takes care of the community and promulgated it." Burdon compares Earth Jurisprudence with the natural law theory of Saint Thomas Aquinas and emphasizes that, in Berry's doctrine, the equivalent of the great law is the ecological conception of "Earth community." Thus, the great law would equate, within an ecological natural justice, to the human interconnection with nature, as well as to the ecological integrity of the Earth community. However, the term "nature" in "Earth Jurisprudence" has a different meaning from how this word is interpreted in the natural law theory of Saint Thomas Aquinas. In the Thomistic theory, "nature" specifically refers to universal truths unfolded from human reason, being, therefore, different from the meaning of nature in the ecological sense.[79]

Burdon emphasizes that, for Berry, the planet is a unique and interconnected community, so humanity must expand its consciousness to understand and adopt

[78] Burdon (2015), pp. 81–82.

[79] Burdon (2015), pp. 82–86.

the "supremacy of the already existing Earth governance." In this perspective, the Earth is our first teacher and legislator. He also refers to Cormac Cullinan's interpretation of how Berry describes the "great law."

> [. . .] laws or principles that govern how the universe works and notes that they are timeless and unified in the sense that they all have the same source. This law is manifested in the Universe itself and can be witnessed by phenomena such as gravity and alignment of planets, growth of planets and cycles of day and night.[80]

As can be seen, the theory of ecological justice presented by Burdon prioritizes the revision of existing legal systems and governance structures, so that they adopt political and normative measures that strengthen the health and integrity of the Earth community.

His theory strengthens the human interrelationship with the environment, as it suggests a shift from the anthropocentric paradigm, which has privileged economic growth, toward the ecocentric concept of "Earth community." Burdon clarifies that he adopts the expression "Earth community" from Thomas Berry because it expresses the notion that ecosystems involve the individual behaviors of organisms, which are considered members of ecosystems and not isolated parts.

The concept of "Earth community" can represent a value axis to guide the legal system, not only redefining the content of existing laws but also guiding the legislator on the need to prioritize laws that ensure ecological integrity.

Indeed, to readjust the role of nature in legal relations, Burdon takes as a starting point the concept of "ecological integrity" of the terrestrial community. Every law in environmental law, to have material legitimacy, must meet the concept of ecological integrity; if not, citizens will be authorized to reject it through peaceful civil disobedience. The concept of "ecological integrity" can be assessed by meeting some criteria: (1) autopoietic capacity for regeneration and evolution of life over time in a specific location; (2) assessment of climatic conditions and other biophysical phenomena; (3) influence of ecological science on public policies; (4) recognition of intrinsic value in ecosystems; and (5) limitation of human development and exploitation of nature.[81]

Thomas Berry's theory of ecological justice, inspired by Thomistic principles and developed by Burdon, presents itself as a middle way in the search for harmonization between human rights and the rights of non-human beings, as it is rooted in the balance between all beings and ecosystems.

Cormac Cullinan, also a student of Berry, presents a theory of ecological justice, which he calls wild law, from a broader view rooted in the principles that govern the universe. He bases his conception of the great law on the cosmogenetic principles developed by Brian Swimme and Thomas Berry, according to which the evolution of the universe occurs through three means: "(1) differentiation; (2) autopoiesis; (3) communion." Differentiation refers to the diversity, variety, and complexity of the natural world; autopoiesis refers to self-creation, self-organization, and

---

[80] Burdon (2015), p. 86.

[81] Burdon (2015), p. 88.

self-knowledge, while the principle of communion pertains to the interconnectivity of the entire universe.[82]

The great law, in Cullinan's interpretation, should be unfolded from these great cosmogenetic natural principles. At this point, it differs from Burdon because he fills the content of the great law with the concept of ecological integrity.

4.12 The New Latin American Constitutionalism and the Andean Philosophy of *Buen Vivir*

Wolkmer points out that, in the last two decades, a new pluralistic and transformative constitutionalism has flourished in Latin America as a result of political changes, relations between indigenous populations and the state, and, mainly, rights related to the ownership and protection of nature. This constitutionalist movement is marked by three major cycles: (a) legal pluralism; (b) recognition of indigenous peoples; and (c) the right to identity, cultural diversity, and defense of the environment.[83] The apex of this movement is crystallized in the Constitutions of Ecuador and Bolivia, which brought a plurinational, community constitutionalism, where the experiences of "traditional knowledge" coexist with the practices of egalitarian jurisdictional pluralism, in addition to the recognition of collective rights linked to the common goods of nature. We emphasize that the Constitution of Ecuador represents the culminating moment for the "new" Latin American constitutionalism, considering its bold "biocentric turn," as it began to admit rights inherent to nature, the right to *buen vivir,* and the human right to water.[84]

Eduardo Gudynas explains that the discussion about the recognition of intrinsic value and the rights of nature has had its advances and setbacks, but, surprisingly, many of the ideas defended by ecological movements crystallized in the Constitution of Ecuador of 2008, and, for the first time, the intrinsic value of the rights of nature was expressly recognized in a Political Charter. Parallel to the Western biocentric movement, which postulates a break with anthropocentrism linked to modernity, whose philosophical basis is founded on dualist ontology, a concrete break with legal anthropocentrism flourished in Latin America, within the scope of a decolonizing political movement, led by indigenous people and intellectuals. This movement of indigenous ecological resistance is based on positions called relational ontologies, already exposed previously when addressing the change in the ontological paradigm. Gudynas clarifies that, in the paradigm of relational ontology, the dualist distinctions of Western modernity

[82] Cullinan (2011), p. 68.

[83] Yrigoyen Fajardo (2011), pp. 139–159.

[84] Wolkmer and Wolkmer (2014), pp. 994–1013.

disappear. For the so-called relational ontology, humans and non-humans are moral subjects, all members of the same expanded community.

In this line, the Constitution of Ecuador refers to Pachamama and defines it in the following way, in Art. 72, "where life reproduces and realizes." Gudynas emphasizes that, from the point of view of political ecology, this constitutional provision offers a substantial novelty, considering that it values the worldview of indigenous peoples and that the incorporation of the concept of *sumak kawsay* (*buen vivir*) is a substantial step to allow the presence of other worldviews and wisdoms in the construction of environmental policies.[85]

Alberto Acosta, when discussing *buen vivir*, clarifies that it is not an originality nor a novelty of the political processes of the early twenty-first century in the Andean countries. He emphasizes that "buen vivir is part of a great search for life alternatives forged in the heat of humanity's struggles for emancipation and life."[86] That is, *buen vivir* should not be confused with "Western well-being."

In the same vein, Diana Murcia asserts that the understanding of the rights of nature in the Constitution of Ecuador cannot be dissociated from the logic of *sumak kawsay* or *suma qamaña*, called *buen vivir* in the constitutional text. She also points out that the notion of *sumak kawsay* is ancestral, not being a creation of the Ecuadorian and Bolivian Constitutions, but dating back to the worldview of the Andean indigenous peoples, which has only recently been elevated to the *status* of a constitutional norm. Thus, there is a permanent obligation to consult indigenous peoples about the content of the *sumak kawsay*, as stated in the preamble of the Ecuadorian Constitution, which proclaims "a new form of citizen coexistence, in diversity and harmony with nature."[87]

Similarly, Wolkmer, when discussing the new constitutionalism, emphasizes that the concept of *buen vivir*, as the essential core of the biodiversity chapter, establishes an interaction with the worldview of harmony between human communities and nature, in which the human being is part of a community that constitutes Pachamama. He cites Quintero to emphasize that, in this context, nature is visualized as a "space of life" and not as a thing,[88] and also highlights that the movement of the "new" constitutionalism has fostered a reflection and reconstruction of a world view committed to life as an expression of a harmonious relationship between the human community and nature. However, the canons and legal institutes of the new constitutionalism, despite emerging as innovative in the context of Western legal theories, were conceived within the ancient knowledge of the original communities, especially the Andean ones, and, thus, have been transmitted by various generations in their complex and plural interactions with the world. Finally, this way of conceiving and relating to nature emerges in the pluralistic legal movement of the new Latin American constitutionalism,

---

85 Gudynas (2010), p. 52.

86 Acosta (2016), p. 208.

87 Murcia (2009), p. 5.

88 Wolkmer and Wolkmer (2014), p. 1007.

consecrated by the constitutions of Bolivia of 2009 and Ecuador of 2008, as the apex of a continuous multicentennial resistance movement.[89]

As Wolkmer observes, what the West calls "ecological consciousness" as something inherent to modernity, in the context of the original peoples of Latin America, is a tradition of many centuries, which has been perpetuated for generations in the processes of political and cultural resistance.[90] Indeed, the consciousness of respect for nature that the world's largest economies currently postulate at summit meetings to build their multilateral declarations on ecological balance and sustainability, since time immemorial, has been the pillar of the ancestral culture of Latin America, rooted in the principle of rationality and harmony with nature.

References

Acosta A (2016) O buen vivir: uma oportunidade de imaginar outro mundo. In: SOUSA CM (Org). Um convite à utopia, EDUEPB, Campina Grande, pp 203–233. Disponível em: http://books.scielo.org/id/kcdz2/pdf/sousa-9788578794880-06.pdf. Accessed 22 Feb 2025

Attfield R (2012) Ethics: an overview. Continuum International Publishing Group, London, New York

Bergson H (2010) A evolução criadora. Tradução de Adolfo Casais Monteiro. Editora UNESP, São Paulo

Berry T (1988) The dream of the earth. Sierra Club Books, San Francisco, CA

Boff L (2004) Ecologia: grito da terra, grito dos pobres. Sextante, Rio de Janeiro

Burdon PD (2015) Earth jurisprudence: private property and the environment. Routledge, New York, NY

Capra F (2012) O ponto de mutação: a ciência, a sociedade e cultura emergente, 30 edn. Cultrix, São Paulo

Carson R (2010) Primavera silenciosa. Tradução de Cláudia Sant'Anna Martins. Gaia, São Paulo

Cullinan C (2011) Wild law, 2nd edn. Siber Ink. Ebook, Cape Town, South Africa

Damásio A (2018) A estranha ordem das coisas: as origens biológicas dos sentimentos e da cultura. Companhia das Letras, São Paulo

Gudynas E (2010) La senda biocéntrica: valores intrínsecos, derechos de la naturaleza y justicia ecológica. Tabula Rasa, Bogotá, Colombia. Univers Col Mayor de Cundinamarca 13:45–71 jul./dic. Available on https://www.redalyc.org/pdf/396/39617525003.pdf. Accessed 13 May 2025

Jonas H (2004) O princípio vida: fundamentos para uma biologia filosófica. Vozes, Petrópolis

Leopold A (1949) A Sand County almanac: with other essays on conservation from Round River. Oxford University Press, New York

Merchant C (2020) The death of nature: women, ecology, and the scientific revolution, 40th anniversary edn. Harper One, London (Ebook)

Murcia D (2009) El sujeto naturaleza: elementos para su comprensión. Instituto de Estudios Ecologistas del Tercer Mundo, Quito

Nash RF (1989) The rights of nature: a history of environmental ethics. The University of Wisconsin Press, Madison, WI

Newmyer ST (2006) Animals, rights and reason in Plutarch and modern ethics. Routledge, New York (Ebook)

[89] Wolkmer et al. (2019), p. 71–108.

[90] Wolkmer et al. (2019), p. 77.

Ost F (1995) A natureza à margem da lei: a ecologia à prova do direito. Tradução de Joana Chaves, 2. edn. Instituto Piaget, Lisboa

Pepper D (2000) Ambientalismo moderno. Tradução de Carla Lopes Silva Correia. Instituto Piaget, Lisboa

Salt HS (1922) Animals' rights: considered in relation to social progress. G. Bell and Sons, London. Available on https://archive.org/details/cu31924030305332/page/n5/mode/2up. Accessed 13 May 2025

Silveira VOd, Rocasolano MM (2010) Direitos humanos: conceitos, significados e funções. Saraiva, São Paulo

Singer P (2010) Libertação animal: o clássico definitivo sobre o movimento pelos direitos dos animais. Tradução de Marly Winckler. WMF Martins Fontes, São Paulo

Sorabji R (2001) Animal minds and human morals: the origins of the western debate. Gerald Duckworth, London

Spinoza B (2016) Ética: edição monolíngue. Tradução de Tomaz Tadeu, 2. ed., 5. reimpr edn. Autêntica, Belo Horizonte

Taylor PW (2011) Respect for nature: a theory of environmental ethics, 25th anniversary edn. Princeton University Press, Princeton

Vilkka L (1997) The intrinsic value of nature. (Value Inquiry Book Series, 59), Rodopi, Amsterdam

Wolkmer AC, Wolkmer de MFS (2014) Repensando a natureza e o meio ambiente na teoria constitucional da América Latina. Novos Estudos Jurídicos, Itajaí, RS. Univali 19(3):994–1013, set./dez. Available on https://siaiap32.univali.br/seer/index.php/nej/article/view/6676/3811. Accessed 13 May 2025

Wolkmer AC, Wolkmer de MFS, Ferrazzo D (2019) Derechos de la Naturaleza: para um paradigma político y constitucional desde la América Latina. In: Liliana EA et al (eds) La naturaleza como sujeto de Derechos en el Constitucionalismo Democrático. Universidad Libre, Bogotá, pp 71–108

Yrigoyen Fajardo, RZ (2011) El horizonte del constitucionalismo pluralista: del multiculturalismo a la descolonización. In: Garavito R, C (coord.). El derecho en América Latina: un mapa para el pensamiento jurídico del siglo XXI. Siglo Veintiuno, Buenos Aires, pp 139–159. Available on http://professor.ufop.br/sites/default/files/tatiana/files/el_horizonte_del_constitucionalismo_pluralista_yrigoyen.pdf. Accessed 13 May 2025

Chapter 5
The Legality of Harmony with Nature

Considering that, since 2009, the United Nations (UN) has been promoting a series of interactive dialogs on the moral consideration of nature under the heading "Harmony with Nature,"[1] and that Principle 1 of the Rio Declaration also refers to harmony with nature, as well as Article 19 of the American Declaration on the Rights of Indigenous Peoples,[2] and that, in addition, the Earth Charter, in its Principle 1(a), recognizes the intrinsic value of each form of life, this chapter aims to investigate the hypothesis of inferring normative quality from the ethical narrative of harmony with nature.

What will be the legal nature of this harmony among all beings as stated in the context of the UN reports by representatives of states, scholars, and peoples of various origins and traditions? Will it be a political guideline, a principle that is merely moral, or a legal principle?

Although harmony with nature is not expressly stated in international declarations, is it possible to identify legal normativity in the ethical narrative of harmony with nature in the reports of the UN Secretary-General, in Principle 1 of the Rio Declaration, in the Earth Charter, and in Article 19 of the American Declaration on the Rights of Indigenous Peoples?[3] Can harmony with nature be considered an emerging legal principle derived from the natural laws that govern the biosphere and from the ancestral wisdom of the peoples of the planet, as documented in the reports of the UN Secretary-General? If it is a principle, what will be the content of its normative core? The following topics delve into these questions.

The approach to the normativity of harmony with nature will be carried out in six phases: (1) a historical approach to the ethical narrative of harmony with nature in documents produced by the UN; (2) the basis of the legal principle of harmony

---

[1] United Nations, Harmony with Nature, online.

[2] OAS, online.

[3] OAS, online.

R. D. d. Amaral, *The Principle of Harmony with Nature as a Legal Foundation*,
https://doi.org/10.1007/978-3-032-05475-3_5

with nature in the natural laws that govern ecosystems; (3) an analysis of the ethical narrative of harmony with nature in light of the general theory of legal principles; (4) an examination of the ethical narrative of harmony with nature in light of the theory of general principles of law within the scope of international law, to verify the hypothesis of the emergence of harmony with nature as a general principle of law; (5) harmony with nature will then be examined from the specific perspective of the theory of principles in the sphere of international environmental law; and finally (6) the normative core of the principle of harmony with nature will be investigated.

5.1 The History of the Approach to Harmony with Nature in the UN

The UN has played a significant role in environmental issues since 1968, when the General Assembly, under the proposal of the Economic and Social Council, recommended the participation of the UN in discussions on topics of ecological interest. This historic decision culminated in the holding of the Stockholm Conference on the Environment in 1972. Subsequently, the UN created, by Resolution 2997 of 15.12.1972, a special subsidiary body called the United Nations Environment Programme (UNEP), which is responsible for "setting the international agenda on the environment, promoting the coherent implementation of the environmental dimension of sustainable development in the United Nations System and serving as the global environmental authority defender."[4]

On October 28, 1982, the UN issued Resolution 37/7, proclaiming the document known as the World Charter for Nature.[5] In 1983, the Brundtland Commission was established, which, in 1987, published the report "Our Common Future" to emphasize:

> [...] the need for an integrated approach to development policies and projects that, if environmentally sound, should lead to economic development in both developed and developing countries. The report emphasized the need to give higher priority to anticipating and preventing problems. It defined "sustainable development" as development that meets present and future environmental and development goals and concluded that without an equitable sharing of the costs and benefits of environmental protection among countries, neither social justice nor sustainable development can be achieved.[6]

Following the work of the Brundtland Commission, events of fundamental importance were convened for the formation of awareness regarding the need for global

---

[4] UN. About the United Nations Environment Programme (UNEP). Available at: https://www.unenvironment.org/pt-br/sobre-onu-meio-ambiente. Accessed on: May 13, 2025.

[5] World Charter for Nature, October 28, 1982, G.A. Res. 37/7, 37 U.N.G.A.O.R. Supp. (No. 51), at 17, U.N. Doc. A/37/51 (1982). Kiss and Shelton (2004), p. 29.

[6] Kiss and Shelton (2004), p. 29.

environmental sustainability, including Rio 92 and the 2002 World Summit, whose objective was also sustainable development.[7]

Rio 92, like the Stockholm Declaration, made recommendations to the States Parties, establishing a catalog with 27 recommendations, which it called principles.[8] The first principle of the Rio Declaration, despite placing the human being at the center of concerns with sustainable development, thus showing a still markedly anthropocentric stance, makes an unequivocal call for "a healthy and productive life **in harmony with nature**"[9] (emphasis ours).

The fact that the first principle of the Rio Declaration placed harmony with nature as a human right is a relevant milestone for the purpose of this work, and, later on, this theme will be revisited. The Rio Declaration, in terms of its normative content, belongs to the category of soft law, that is, a norm that does not impose binding obligations on the addressees.[10] As Ulrich Beyerlin and Thilo Marauhn point out, the principles included in the Rio Declaration do not have a homogeneous status. Some are customary international norms; others are in a gray area within international law.[11]

The General Assembly, over the years, has been recommending a series of resolutions on the pelagic zone and large-scale net fishing, as well as unauthorized fishing in the national jurisdiction zone. In addition, it has issued resolutions to minimize pollution, waste, and waste disposal, while regulating the use of natural resources shared by two or more states. But what exactly is the normative force of these resolutions? Ulrich Beyerlin and Thilo Marauhn emphasize that international environmental law is a system of heterogeneous concepts grouped into three layers: (1) a layer composed of very abstract ideas; (2) a second layer with denser ideas and less abstract concepts; and (3) a third layer with concrete norms.

They explain that in the first layer are the fundamental ideas, such as international solidarity and international justice—quite abstract and imprecise concepts that, although per se do not regulate the conduct of states, are important sources of ethics that guide the concepts of the second layer.

The key concepts of the second layer function as a "transmission belt" between abstract ideas and the concrete norms of international law. They help transform extra-legal ideas of solidarity and justice into applicable legal principles and rules, which constitute the bulk of international environmental law norms.

The concepts of the first layer are extremely relevant, given that states, which are reluctant to bind themselves to treaty obligations, prefer to make agreements containing more abstract and vague commitments associated with another concept of the second layer.[12]

---

[7] Kiss and Shelton (2004), p. 30.

[8] Beyerlin and Marauhn (2011), p. 29.

[9] Beyerlin and Marauhn (2011), p. 29.

[10] Beyerlin and Marauhn (2011), p. 29.

[11] Beyerlin and Marauhn (2011), p. 45.

[12] Beyerlin and Marauhn (2011), p. 46.

In this line, since 1968, the UN has been declaring principles that, although not binding, have served in an impactful way to guide member states in adopting protective environmental legislation. In this sense, Kiss and Shelton highlight that if the Stockholm Conference had not taken place, it would not have triggered a planetary movement by national governments to enact protective environmental laws.[13]

Since 2009, the UN has spearheaded a movement of ecological reflection, whose value axis is holism and harmony with nature. On April 22, 2009, the United Nations General Assembly, through Resolution 63/278,[14] expressed in language that the Earth and its ecosystems are our home and affirmed the conviction that, to achieve a fair balance between the economic, social, and environmental needs of present and future generations, it is necessary to promote harmony with nature and the Earth. It further reaffirmed that the term Mother Earth is shared by the language of various peoples, at different times and places on the planet, and that this maternal evocation of the Earth, which dates back to our ancestry, reveals the interdependent relationship between humans, other living species, and the planet we all inhabit. Thus, recognizing that Mother Earth is an ancestral and revered cultural entity, April 22 was designated as International Mother Earth Day every year in many countries.

Subsequently, Resolution 64/196 of 2009,[15] by the General Assembly of the United Nations Organization, expressly mentioned harmony with nature. This normative act invited member states, relevant United Nations organizations, and international, regional, and sub-regional organizations to consider the issue of promoting life in harmony with nature as appropriate and to convey their opinions, experiences, and proposals on this matter to the UN Secretary-General. It also urged non-governmental organizations and relevant stakeholders to observe and raise awareness of International Mother Earth Day.

From 2009 to 2020, the UN has intensified multilateral dialog around the approach of harmony with nature, and the conclusions of these dialogs and reflections are detailed in the reports of the Secretary-General.

Upon analyzing the reports, the evolution of multilateral work in favor of holism and harmony with nature is evident. Indeed, the first report was produced to comply with the UN General Assembly Resolution of 2009, Resolution A/64/196 AGNU, which was unanimously approved under the title Harmony with Nature. Since then, each report has received the same title and centers its propositions on sustainable development.

Resolution A/64/196 AGNU of 2009 invited the Secretary-General to express his opinion on the theme "life in harmony with nature" as well as to provide reports on the contributions of states and regional groups regarding this theme. The Secretary-General has since organized and hosted the so-called interactive dialogs

[13] Kiss and Shelton (2004), p. 29.

[14] United Nations, A/RES/63/278, online.

[15] United Nations, A/RES/64/196, online.

on the theme of harmony with nature, with representatives of state parties, experts, scholars, and researchers from various countries participating in these colloquiums.

The interactive dialogs have produced eleven reports since 2010. These documents are hosted on the site *Harmony with Nature*,[16] in the following order:

2010	A/65/ 314	Report I—Addresses the need for sustainable development initiatives to reconnect the Earth community
2011	A/66/ 302	Report II—Proposes changes in the metaphysical paradigm
2012	A/67/ 317	Report III—Criticizes the ontological and ethical basis of Western economic and legal systems
2013	A/68/ 325	Report IV—Highlights the difficulty of understanding the concept of nature in Western culture
2014	A/69/ 322	Report V—Associates the anthropocentric metaphysical and scientific orientations adopted in the West with the consolidation of also anthropocentric legal systems that excluded nature from ethical and legal consideration
2015	A/70/ 268	Report VI—Deepens the concept of intrinsicness between humans and nature
2016	A/71/ 266	Report VII—Establishes the consensus of recognizing intrinsic value to nature, as well as the need for a change in attitude and behavior toward a non-anthropocentric view
2017	A/72/ 175/	Report VIII—Provides an analytical account of legislations from various countries that have recognized the rights of nature in laws and judicial decisions
2018	A/73/ 221	Report IX—The report is based on contributions to the eighth interactive dialog on harmony with nature, held on April 23, 2018, which addresses Earth Jurisprudence in the implementation of sustainable production and consumption standards in harmony with nature and trends in the implementation of Earth Jurisprudence in laws, policies, education, and public engagement
2019	A/74 +236	Report X—Celebrates and highlights the evolving consciousness of humanity in its relationship with Mother Earth, an evolution manifested worldwide through legislation, policy, education, and public engagement, all guided by the urgency to protect Mother Earth and make the transition to an Earth-centered paradigm in the promotion and implementation of the 2030 Agenda for Sustainable Development
2020	A/75/ 266	Report XII—Due to the Coronavirus Disease 2019 (COVID-19) pandemic, the dialog was canceled. The context of this report is, therefore, of a global human health crisis. In the report, the Secretary-General highlights the achievements made in the second half of 2019 and in the first half of 2020, which still demonstrate a paradigm shift from a human-centered society to an Earth-centered society and in the implementation of the 2030 Agenda for Sustainable Development

[16] United Nations, Harmony with Nature, online.

The dialogs, documented in the reports, were initially aimed at preparing UN leaders for the Second Environment Summit, which was held in Rio de Janeiro in June 2012, under the *slogan* Rio+20, deliberately chosen to commemorate the 20th anniversary of Rio 92.

However, after the Rio+20 moment, this work continued and deepened in proposing changes that impact ontology, ethics, science, economy, and, above all, the legal system, as it has been incisive in emphasizing the urgent need for a paradigm shift in attitude and understanding of the world to also reverberate in the legal system.

The "Harmony with Nature" reports are produced in a different way, as they document the dialogs of people from various nations and cultures, state authorities, and also members of civil society and academia. The very procedure for producing the reports is structured based on a proposal of holism and harmony.

Furthermore, when analyzing the ontological and ethical foundations of the reports, it is found that they rest on metaphysical visions that overcome Cartesian dualism and anthropocentrism. The central point of the "Harmony with Nature" reports is sustainability—the sustainable development proposed for humanity since Rio 92. With the aim of achieving this sustainable development, they propose a new ethical orientation to regulate human action in relation to nature, with all recommendations permeated by harmony with nature, an expression that is not just an epigraph for the reports but the very soul of the dialogs of this entire movement, as harmony is the keynote not only of the material content of the reports but also of the procedural methodology adopted.

The analysis of the reports shows that their main concerns are educational research, balance in consumption, sustainable development, human cognitive processes, the economy, a holistic ethic, and, above all, the concept of ecological justice, which is proposed under the title of *Earth Jurisprudence*. In the theoretical framework of the "Harmony with Nature" reports, among others, is Arne Naess's vision of deep ecology.

Another relevant aspect of the "Harmony with Nature" reports is their adherence, albeit implicit, to the so-called "ontological turn,"[17] as they emphasize the search for a holistic view in indigenous cultures—that is, in the cosmogony of the original peoples—as well as in the tradition of the ancient peoples of the West, which was lost on the tortuous path from the Middle Ages to modernity. In this sense, the second report, in paragraphs 79 and 80, stressed the need for a change in the ontological paradigm, with a return to the worldviews of the original indigenous peoples, to ancestry, and to traditional oriental medicine.

The third report,[18] in paragraphs 34 and 38, made severe criticisms of the ontological and ethical basis of Western economic and legal systems. The fourth report,[19] in paragraphs 12, 15, 60, and 64, deepened these criticisms, highlighting

---

[17] Castro (1996), p. 116.

[18] United Nations. A/67/317, online.

[19] United Nations. A/68/325, online.

the difficulty of understanding the very concept of nature in Western culture, thanks to the reductionist duality imposed by the Cartesian paradigm. This report is fundamental, as it brought the relationship between humans and nature to the epicenter of the environmental crisis.

The fifth report[20] advanced in associating the metaphysical and scientific anthropocentric orientations, which were adopted in the West, with the consolidation of anthropocentric legal systems that excluded nature from the circle of ethical and legal consideration. It further progressed in naming as "Earth system science" the metaphysical and scientific conclusions and propositions based on a new holistic paradigm presented in the previous reports. In this new proposal brought by the "Harmony with Nature" reports, the Earth is conceived, in paragraph 11, as a holistic system in which no living being or ecosystem takes precedence over another; it is one, indivisible, continuous, and endless system. In paragraph 12, it completed the study on the scope of the concept of holism and its normative irradiation for sustainable development and proposed something innovative and impactful: the governance of the Earth system based on the Earth's natural laws.

The sixth report,[21] in paragraph 35, deepened the concept of intrinsicality between humans and nature.

The seventh Report[22] presented the differential of not having been provided by the Secretary-General, as had been the case previously. Instead, it was prepared by experts on harmony with nature (A/71/266) and published in 2016. It marked the first virtual dialog on harmony with nature, which began on April 22, 2016, in commemoration of International Mother Earth Day. The "Earth Jurisprudence" experts who participated in this dialog took two important steps: They recognized the intrinsic value of nature, as well as the need to change perceptions, attitudes, and behaviors to non-anthropocentric ones, focused on the Earth. This report sought its foundations in the results of the first virtual dialog of the General Assembly on harmony with nature and made explicit, in paragraph 6, that the world "is not an inanimate object to be exploited, but our common home, alive and subject to a multitude of dangers to its health" (our emphasis).

Subsequent reports have already brought news of changes in various countries, which are amending their legislation to recognize the rights of nature. It is noted that the approach of harmony with nature in these reports and in the respective resolutions that underpin them is not a mere empty slogan; it is a profound approach that permeates the interactive dialogs of the UN, both from a procedural point of view and from a material point of view.

In this sense, by Resolution 68/216, of December 20, 2013,[23] the UN General Assembly invites states to: (a) build a knowledge network in order to promote a holistic method to identify different economic approaches that reflect the factors

[20] United Nations. A/69/322, online.

[21] United Nations. A/70/268, online.

[22] United Nations. A/71/266, online.

[23] United Nations (2013), online.

and values of living in harmony with nature, relying on the latest information to achieve sustainable development and facilitate the support and recognition of the fundamental interconnections between humanity and nature; and to (b) promote harmony with the Earth, as found in indigenous cultures, and learn from them to support and promote the efforts that are being made, both at the national level and in local communities, to reflect on the protection of nature.

On August 01, 2016, a note[24] was issued by the UN Secretary-General on sustainable development and harmony with nature, compiling the understandings established by the experts participating in the virtual dialogs on harmony with nature, promoted to comply with Resolution 70/208.

The said document states that the first step toward the recognition of the rights of nature occurred in 2012 at the United Nations Conference on Sustainable Development, held in Rio de Janeiro, when the heads of the participating states approved the document "The Future We Want." In this document, it was recognized that the promotion of harmony with nature is necessary to achieve a fair balance between the needs of future and present generations.

Subsequently, in Resolution 70/1, dated September 25, 2015, the UN General Assembly approved an action plan for the development of the 2030 Agenda,[25] which includes 17 sustainable development goals with 169 targets. Among these goals, target 12.8 stands out, as it seeks to ensure that people around the world have relevant information and knowledge for sustainable development and lifestyles in harmony with nature.

In the context of the 2030 Agenda, the 2016 virtual interactive dialog[26] promoted the achievement of target 12.8, bringing together scholars from around the world for reflection and consolidation of understandings about an Earth governance project known as "Earth Jurisprudence."

During the 2016 interactive dialog, scholars from various parts of the world observed that, from a perspective that ethically recognizes the Earth, the planet cannot be considered an inanimate object to be exploited. They asserted that this reality requires a reconsideration of our relationship with nature, which can be achieved with support for the so-called "Earth Jurisprudence," whose new vision should prevail in legislation, ethics, institutions, policies, and practices, including respect for the Earth and its natural cycles. They also established the following noteworthy understandings:

(a) Recognition of the Earth as a source of natural laws that govern life
(b) Interdisciplinarity of basic values that should govern the economy, physical sciences, and law

[24] United Nations. A/71/266, online.

[25] United Nations, Civil Society Working Group for the 2030 Agenda for Sustainable Development.

[26] United Nations, Harmony with Nature, online.

(c) The need to develop a new environmental ethic, responsible for deepening our understanding of how harmony with nature brings true meaning and fulfillment to our lives
(d) They proposed the philosophy of "Earth Jurisprudence," founded on four fundamental principles: (i) subjectivity; (ii) community; (iii) legality and order; and (iv) recognition of the wild nature of the Universe
(e) The incorporation into conventional philosophy and ethics of the worldview of indigenous peoples to eliminate the artificial difference between human beings and nature.[27]

The aforementioned document also highlights the presence of the principle of harmony with nature in the Encyclical edited by Pope Francis, the *Laudato Si'*, from which the text infers: (a) recognition of the intrinsic value of nature; (b) respect for the laws of nature; (c) recommendations on overconsumption and anthropocentrism; and (d) relevance of the culture of peoples and indigenous culture to our world.[28]

Regarding the legal aspects per se, the scholars participating in the 2016 interactive dialog established the following understandings:

(a) The importance of recognizing the fundamental rights of ecosystems and species to exist, thrive, and regenerate
(b) That the laws of nature are sources of Earth's rights, and these rights cannot be abolished by human justice
(c) That these rights of nature do not oppose human rights, as we are part of nature, so our human rights are also encompassed by the rights of nature
(d) That the right of each sentient being is limited by the rights of all other beings to the extent necessary to maintain the integrity, balance, and health of larger ecological communities
(e) That recognizing intrinsic value and rights to the Earth does not mean ending property rights, but only making a shift in consciousness in the sense that the title of ownership does not grant the right to destroy ecosystems. Hence, the importance of making decisions based on a hierarchy of needs established from notions of ecosystem integrity and their ability to thrive
(f) The need for an ecological justice institution with judges and courts to adjudicate conflicts between human and non-human beings; and
(g) That the recognition of the rights of nature is necessary, but not sufficient, as we need to prioritize the dignity of the human being and the dignity of the Earth over the personality and interests of corporations or companies.[29]

In addition to the reports on harmony with nature, the United Nations General Assembly, since 2009, has issued resolutions on the subject, which we will analyze in the topic dedicated to the sources of international environmental law.

---

[27] United Nations. A/71/266, online.
[28] Pope Francis (2015), online.
[29] United Nations. A/71/266, online.

This harmony with nature, proposed in the aforementioned reports of the UN interactive dialogs, will only be effective if it enters the legal systems of nations to change the anthropocentric and contractualist tradition, which excluded non-human living beings and ecosystems from the community of moral and legal consideration. Therefore, the next subtopics are dedicated to examining the hypothesis of the normative principality of harmony with nature.

5.2 Harmony with Nature as a Legal Principle: The Basis of the Legal Principle of Harmony with Nature in the Natural Laws that Govern Ecosystems

The human being, as a self-aware being, moral agent, and strong evaluator, inhabits two worlds: a symbolic sphere—the so-called sociosphere and noosphere,[30] created by his own language, and the natural world, the biosphere, considering that his creative consciousness rests on a biological body. Thus, in addition to the spiritual space of free will, in which he exercises his creative freedom and responsibility, he also shares another freedom with all living beings: the freedom of biological flourishing, in such a way that he shares a common language with all beings and ecosystems—the language of the natural laws of life. This is a biological reality that ethics and law can no longer ignore.

To contain the effects of the anthropogenic crisis, it is no longer viable to think of law only as a cultural creation, separate from the laws of nature. Legal systems that ignore the natural laws governing the biosphere are not in line with the applied ecological ethics of harmony with nature, based on the principle of universal coherence.

The Rio Declaration emphasized the importance of ecosystems in its Principle 7: "States should cooperate in a spirit of global partnership to conserve, protect and restore the health of Earth's ecosystems."[31] The Biodiversity Convention, in 2000, adopted 12 principles, the central point of which is the sustainable management of ecosystems. Principle 10 made it clear that: "The ecosystem approach should seek the appropriate balance between the conservation and use of biological diversity and its integration."[32]

In this sense, Kiss and Shelton[33] point out the necessary observance by international environmental law of the "laws of nature," considering that the root of environmental law should be the natural sciences, such as biology, ecology, chemistry, thermodynamics, and physics. This rooting of environmental law in

[30] Chardin (1997).

[31] RIO92, online.

[32] Ecosystem Approach. Available at: https://www.cbd.int/ecosystem/principles.shtml. Accessed on: May 13, 2025.

[33] Kiss and Shelton (2004), p. 13.

the natural sciences is explained by the fact that it regulates human behavior in relation to non-human living beings and ecosystems. Thus, legislators and jurists should make use of scientific knowledge about biological life and Earth system sciences to legislate coherently.

Jørgensen et al. highlight the emergence of ecosystem ecology as a consequence of the change in the environmental management paradigm brought about by Rio 92 and the Convention on Biological Diversity.[34] In this direction, the Convention, in its Article 2, defined an ecosystem as: "A dynamic complex of plant, animal and microorganism communities and the non-living environment, interacting as a functional unit. Humans are an integral part of ecosystems."[35]

As can be seen, the aforementioned definition includes humans as integral parts of ecosystems and emphasizes the interaction between its components, which in itself already denotes a significant change in ecosystem theory. In this vein, Jørgensen et al. propose an ecosystem theory from a new ecological paradigm, which they call "New Ecology." The theory of Jørgensen et al., which applies the principles of thermodynamics to ecological systems, highlights the fundamental natural laws from which the legal principle of harmony with nature emerges—an ethical and legal principle that this work proposes.

The principle of harmony with nature is a relational, systemic principle and, therefore, requires interdisciplinary knowledge. As will be demonstrated, the most impactful legal consequence of the principle of harmony with nature is the recognition of intrinsic value and subjectivity in non-human living beings and organic holistic entities. Thus, necessarily, the principle of harmony with nature calls for an understanding of the systemic conception of life in the biosphere.

Capra explains that this systemic conception of life is based on the awareness that physical, biological, psychological, and social phenomena maintain an essential interrelation and interdependence. He emphasizes that, although there is not yet a conceptual and institutional structure that fully accommodates this systemic view, it is already being worked on and applied by various individuals, communities, and organizations that are adapting based on new ways of thinking, according to these relational and systemic principles.[36]

This work proposes the principle of harmony with nature as the conceptual and institutional structure postulated by Capra[37] to regulate human relations with the environment. The principle of harmony with nature operates as an interdisciplinary bridge between the legal language, which regulates the relations of human beings and their institutions in the so-called noosphere, and the language of the natural sciences, which studies and describes ecosystemic phenomena in the biosphere. This link between the prescriptive language of law and the descriptive language of the natural sciences can enable the legal interpreter to understand and consider the

[34] Jørgensen et al. (2019), p. 11.

[35] Ministry of the Environment (2000), online.

[36] Capra (2012), p. 259–261.

[37] Capra (2012), p. 259–261.

great laws of nature from a systemic and inter-relational perspective, which conceives the world as relations of integration and cooperation.[38]

In this sense, among the great natural laws that govern the terrestrial ecosystem, the second law of thermodynamics, the so-called law of entropy, is of fundamental relevance to life on the planet, so it can no longer be ignored by legislators and law enforcers. This work presents three metaphors to explain the law of entropy: (i) the garden; (ii) the terrarium; (iii) the fantastic Snowpiercer locomotive, from the comic fiction of Jacques Lob, Benjamin Legrand, and Jean-Marc Rochette.

1. The garden receives sunlight every day and is visited by birds, bats, and bees. The birds, brought from the neighboring park, carry seeds of two wonderful trees, which grow and provide shade, oxygen, and nectar in abundance. Different plants are born every day, and there is a constant buzz of bees. The garden is also visited by bats and opossums. If the gardener leaves and returns two years later, this garden will be alive and thriving, with a greater diversity of plants, insects, mosses, and small animals. In thermodynamics, this is the description of an open system, which receives energy—solar radiation—and mass: water from precipitation, insects, birds, and animals originating from the external environment. The energy received every day generates work, which triggers more vitality and biodiversity, taking the system further away from thermal death. The openness of the system is essential for the maintenance of life, as it requires an energy input, which is only possible in non-isolated systems.[39]
2. A retired engineer has kept a plant alive inside a sealed bottle for over 40 years, according to the British newspapers *The Sun* and *Daily Mail*. The plant, planted inside the container in 1960, was last watered in 1972—the same year that a cork was placed in the bottle and has never been removed—said the publications about the 80-year-old "gardener," David Latimer. The plant survived because a "self-sufficient ecosystem" was created inside the bottle, with soil, bacteria, and organic material coming from the leaves and the structures of the plant, according to the *Daily Mail*. Of the genus *Tradescantia*, the plant was the only one of four seeds inside the bottle that survived.[40] This report describes a closed system; although it does not exchange mass with the external environment, it receives a continuous flow of energy from the sun. Closed systems are viable because they receive energy, which is converted into work to maintain order and life inside.
3. Lastly, metaphorically, the fictional experiment *Le transperceneige* by Jacques Lob, Benjamin Legrand, and Jean-Marc Rochette is presented to describe an isolated system. Everything starts when an experiment to prevent global warming fails, and a new ice age takes over planet Earth. The only survivors are aboard a huge revolutionary locomotive, the Snowpiercer. The Snowpiercer is

[38] Capra (2012), p. 259–261.

[39] Jørgensen and Svirezhev (2004), p. 17.

[40] G1 (2013), online.

> a locomotive designed to function as an isolated thermodynamic system. In fiction, the Earth was deprived of its energy source, the Sun, and the planet itself was converted into an isolated system, heading toward thermodynamic equilibrium. Engineers, from a limited initial energy, set the Snowpiercer in motion; its friction on the tracks became the only energy source to keep its system running, as there was no more Sun. Inside the Snowpiercer, a fragile biological and thermodynamic system was created to generate energy and produce food for the crew and passengers. The energy obtained from the friction of the tracks produced the work to generate more energy: vegetables, fruits, grains, and protein for the last humans. However, being an isolated system, the fragile living and social system of the Snowpiercer will inexorably head toward entropic death unless the Earth starts receiving the Sun's energy again. Isolated systems tend toward greater entropy, according to the second law of thermodynamics, which leads isolated systems inevitably from order to disorder until the collapse—the so-called thermodynamic equilibrium. As there is no external source of energy, the limited internal energy degrades and no longer produces more work within the system, generating disorder and death. If a system is isolated, it inevitably moves toward death, as it has no gradients to work with.

In thermodynamics, the semantic content of the word "equilibrium" refers to the non-existence of energy, mass, and information exchange—a situation that leads the system to complete energy degradation and, consequently, the impossibility of producing work to maintain life.

Thermodynamic, or thermal, equilibrium in an ecosystem is not desirable, as it represents the maximum degree of entropy, which leads the system to collapse. This occurs when two bodies or substances reach the same temperature. The word "thermodynamics" refers to the spontaneous transfer of heat; a hotter body transfers heat to a colder body. For example, the Sun transfers heat to the Earth, providing it with energy to fuel the life cycle through photosynthesis. Plants absorb 1% of solar energy in the photosynthesis process, while the rest is degraded or dissipated through transpiration or vapor release. The degradation of solar energy is proportional to the number of species in an ecosystem, which is why the equatorial region has a greater number of species. In this region, the Sun's rays are perpendicular, and thus, in the equatorial zone, there is a greater diversity of living beings to account for the absorption of the large amount of solar energy irradiated in this area. A young forest degrades less energy than an old forest. The greater the development of an ecosystem, the lower its surface temperature, as the increase in ecosystem complexity increases its ability to degrade the flow of solar energy, so that less energy will remain to be radiated in the form of infrared radiation and generate heat.[41]

In this vein, thermodynamic imbalance is essential for the Earth system, as energy exchange between systems only occurs when there is a difference in their

[41] Filho and Penha-Silva (2005), p. 34–39.

temperatures. Thus, life on Earth is only viable because the Sun radiates its light onto the planet, and this occurs because of the temperature difference between the two systems. The Sun has an approximate temperature of 6000 °C, while the Earth averages 25 °C, which allows a constant flow of energy from the Sun to the Earth, enabling the formation of life on the planet through biological processes.[42]

In this context, the concept of entropy strictly applies only to isolated systems, which naturally tend from order to disorder until they reach the so-called thermodynamic equilibrium. However, Jørgensen et al. clarify that often the term is used metaphorically to refer to all types of systems, even to closed and open systems that are far from thermodynamic equilibrium.

The concept of entropy was created by Rudolf Julius Emanuel Clausius in 1865 and denotes the idea of the passage of time and the direction of transformation, derived from the concepts of transformation (*τροπη*), evolution, mutation, and confusion (*εντροπη*). This is one of the most fundamental laws of nature, considering "that it addresses the paths we must avoid to keep the Earth alive." The law of entropy shows that there is a statistical tendency, or probability, for disorder, for maximum entropy, with the loss of information and availability of usable energy, which can lead a system to thermal death—what Clausius called thermodynamic equilibrium—the death of biological systems and ecosystems through the destruction of diversity.[43]

Therefore, living beings cannot exist in conditions of thermodynamic equilibrium. To keep life away from this deleterious stage, systems need to receive external energy, matter, and information and, thus, self-organize the material and energetic flows received from outside the system, under different conditions of temperature and energy.

Jørgensen and Svirezhev describe the planet's energy cascade in a chain of systemic reactions, which is open to solar energy and almost closed to the materials that transit through the solar system:

> **1. Source**: solar radiation → (2) **anabolism** (charging phase): incorporation of high-quality energy, with embedded work capacity (information), into complex biomolecular structures, causing the anti-entropic system to move away from equilibrium → (3) **catabolism** (discharge phase): deterioration of the structure involving the release of chemical bond energy and its degradation to lower states of utility for work (heat) → (4) **dissipator**: dissipation of degraded energy (low entropy), energy released as heat to the environment (to Earth, to deep space), involving entropy generation and return to thermodynamic equilibrium.[44] (our emphasis)

To better understand this thermodynamic cycle of an open system described by Jørgensen and Svirezhev, this work takes as an example the life cycle of a tree in three stages:

---

[42] Oliveira (2011).

[43] Jørgensen et al. (2019), p. 19–22.

[44] Jørgensen and Svirezhev (2004), p. 57.

1. The leaves of the tree receive solar energy and perform photosynthesis. In this anabolism process, the plant accumulates adenosine triphosphate (ATP), high-quality energy, which it uses for its own growth. To sustain its life with ATP, a tree, according to Peter Wohlleben,[45] stores 20 tons of CO_2 in the trunk, branches, and roots. This is the first phase of the cycle described above by Jørgensen and Svirezhev. As can be seen, photosynthesis is a powerful neutralizer of entropic degradation, as it organizes water and carbon dioxide through solar energy, which has low energy and disordered agitation, into structures, branches, and roots, thereby reducing the entropy of the Earth system.
2. The second stage of the cycle described by Jørgensen and Svirezhev is catabolism. With the death of the tree, the 20 tons of CO_2 that were stored during its life in the trunk, branches, and roots will be catabolized by fungi and bacteria, which digest the wood, degrade the molecules, and release the CO_2 stored in the tree's structure throughout its life. This energy, which the tree used as information and work in the constitution of its own matter, will now be converted into a lower state of energy, that is, heat.
3. The third phase of the cycle, described by Jørgensen and Svirezhev, is dissipation. Peter Wohlleben explains that in this phase, part of the CO_2 will return to the atmosphere after the death of the tree, but most will remain in the ecosystem itself. Slowly, the dead wood is degraded, centimeter by centimeter, by various species of living beings and processed deeper and deeper into the soil. Then, the rain saturates the organic remains. In the depths of the soil, the temperature is milder, and the lower the temperature, the slower life becomes, reaching stagnation. Thus, the CO_2 is trapped in the soil, taking the form of humus and, according to Peter Wohlleben, in the distant future, it may be converted into lignite and coal. In this phase, there is low entropy, as only a part of the CO_2 returns to the atmosphere in the form of heat, while another part is retained in the formation of coal, gas, and oil.[46]

Since the Industrial Revolution, there has been an acceleration in the burning of trees that cover the biosphere, coupled with a gradual increase in the use of fossil fuels and the consequent release of carbon dioxide that has been stored by coal and oil over 300 million years.

When a tree is burned, all the CO_2 stored in its wood is abruptly released into the atmosphere. Thus, in addition to the large increase in the release of carbon stored in the fossils of ancestral trees, which decomposed in the swamps to form peat and later coal that began to be used in industry and human mobility, the carbon dioxide resulting from the burning of present-day trees was added. The fact is that these fires not only released more carbon dioxide into the air but also reduced the forests, which, along with algae, are the major consumers of carbon dioxide.

[45] Wohlleben (2017), p. 87.

[46] Wohlleben (2017), p. 87–89.

This means that, simultaneously with the emptying of the reservoirs of carbon dioxide stored underground in the form of coal and oil, and its release into the atmosphere, there was a reduction in natural carbon sinks. The result of this was the exhalation of an excess of carbon dioxide into the air—that is, energy in the form of heat—which has been altering the planet's temperature to trigger the so-called greenhouse effect.

Jørgensen et al. observe that the vast majority of the energy received from the Sun by the Earth's surface is dispersed; that is, it is reflected, stored in the soil, and absorbed by water. One percent of the Sun's energy is fixed by photosynthesis, which is the metabolic process that plants use to transform solar energy into organic compounds that support the great diversity of living species, whose work decreases entropy and paves the way for evolution, with the perpetuation of living organisms. The Earth system, as an open and living system, evolves with "the continuous and discontinuous flow of negative entropy," that is, external energy, which feeds the carbon cycle and decreases the degree of entropy within the planet. This entropic slowdown is also called negative entropy or negentropy.

However, not all the solar energy that enters the Earth system is utilized. Jørgensen et al. clarify that "every year, the Sun sends to Earth 5.6×10^{24} J of energy, more than 10,000 times the energy that humans consume in a year." A portion of the energy that enters the ecosphere is reflected without being used, a phenomenon called albedo. The denser and larger the biological structure of ecosystems, the more solar energy is captured, and the lower the globe's albedo.[47]

The non-isolation of the Earth system and ecosystems only makes the evolution of life possible because it not only enables the capture of energy by photosynthesis but also the export of generated heat out of the system in order to maintain a viable temperature for vital processes.[48] The fact is that the increase in emissions of greenhouse gases, primarily carbon dioxide, is creating "a partial blanket that retains some thermal radiation from the surface, making the Earth substantially warmer."[49] This disturbance in Earth's temperature, with the increase in heat, is a serious factor of entropic acceleration, given that even in open systems, uncontrolled growth of entropy can lead the system toward the dreaded thermodynamic equilibrium.

The second law of thermodynamics, the law of entropy, is a law of nature that operates at the base of the Earth's system of life. It is a fact of reality that cannot be overlooked in the formulation of ethics and legal norms, as it profoundly impacts the ecological integrity of ecosystems and the well-being of human beings, who are part of the terrestrial biotic community, along with all other living beings. Thus, this work proposes the principle of harmony with nature as an interdisciplinary link between the thermodynamic reality of the biosphere and the legal reality, which lies in the realm of the so-called sociosphere.

---

[47] Jørgensen et al. (2019), p. 23.

[48] Jørgensen et al. (2019), p. 25.

[49] Khoiyangban and Gupta (2012), p. 377.

The principle of harmony with nature, based on the ethics of coherence proposed by Cirne-Lima, is the primary "ought-to-be" that should be observed by humans to inhibit individual and collective behaviors that increase the levels of entropy in the Earth system. In this vein, all human actions that interact with the Earth system should be guided by harmony with nature.

The act of consuming, which has been treated since the dawn of modernity solely within the field of contractual relations between humans and, therefore, governed by the legal principle of good faith, among others, should also be considered as a relationship between the human being and nature—a relationship that should be guided by the ethics of coherence proposed by Cirne-Lima, whose core is harmony with nature itself.

In nature, the quintessence of harmony, as a synthesis of antagonistic forces, is negentropy in favor of life. This is realized through attitudes such as the fair consumption by predators in relation to their prey, with relationships of mutualism, complementarity, reciprocity, and cooperation among all living beings.

All legislation, political, economic, and legal acts of the human community reverberate in some way in the biosphere; therefore, they should be guided by the principle of harmony with nature to reduce the entropy of the Earth's system, thus guaranteeing the human right to an ecologically balanced environment and to life itself.

In this order of ideas, harmony with nature, which consists of a coherent and ecologically balanced action, emerges from the second law of thermodynamics as a necessary principle that imposes limits on the exercise of human freedom. Indeed, the law of entropy can be compared to structural concrete beams in the Earth system. Humans can, in the exercise of free will and their creative nature, implement various changes in favor of socioeconomic development in the interstices of these structural beams, but these main beams, which are the natural laws that govern ecosystems, cannot be tampered with under penalty of collapsing the Earth system. Therefore, the principle of harmony with nature acts as a compass to guide coherent human action so as not to compromise the integrity of the structural beams of the laws of nature, especially the law of entropy.

5.3 The Principle of Harmony with Nature in Light of the General Theory of Principles

As demonstrated earlier, the pursuit of harmony with nature is an ethical narrative present in the cosmology of various peoples, in different places and times on planet Earth, so it presents itself as a value vector that permeates many cultures and, therefore, is capable of guiding an applied ecological ethic. In this task, the applied ecological ethic of harmony with nature was proposed based on the general ethic of universal coherence by Cirne-Lima and the principle of responsibility by Hans Jonas, as the value on which the legal norm of harmony with nature is based.

It is not enough for "harmony with nature" to be a precept about human action in the ethical sphere; it is necessary to advance in the sense of scrutinizing its normative principle character. Just like many other principles, which are recognized by international law and national legal systems, such as the principles of reasonableness, proportionality, legal certainty, and objective good faith, harmony with nature also emerges as a legal principle that is present in the culture of various Western and Eastern peoples and that is already manifested in the jurisprudence of courts of different legal systems, as will be demonstrated below.

Before we proceed, for methodological and didactic reasons, it is appropriate to provide the reader with a brief revisit of the theory of principles, starting with their definition. The elucidation of the concept of principle in the legal sphere is not trivial, given that the concept of principle has varied according to the evolution of theoretical currents on its nature, classification, and function. The theory of principles arose in the field of private law, where, at this stage, principles were devoid of normative force. However, even in the civilist stage of the theory of principles, voices like those of F. de Clemente and Mucius Scaevola already pointed out an autonomy in the existence of principles beyond the positivized texts.[50]

From the first half of the twentieth century, the theory of principles began to be developed within the scope of public law. In this sense, the doctrine of Vezio Crisafulli was decisive, as he formulated a normative concept of principle in his work "La Constituzione e le sue Disposizioni di Principio."[51] Subsequently, a strong doctrine on the positivity and effectiveness of principles in the field of Constitutional Law was consolidated, but its roots have always been grounded in the theory of general principles of law.[52]

The theory of general principles of law went through three significant phases: (i) natural law; (ii) legal positivism; and (iii) post-positivism. In natural law, principles were mere axioms inspiring the postulates of justice, without normative form. Natural law influenced the theory of general principles of law until the emergence of the positivist historical school, for which the principles were only those codified in the codes, and their role was merely a subsidiary normative source. Even when codified in constitutional texts, their nature was only that of supralegal programs and, therefore, lacked normativity. Finally, with the advent of post-positivism, marked by the constitutionalist movement, the constitutions recognized the axiological prominence of the principles, elevating them to the top of the normative construct of legal systems.[53]

Bonavides, citing Bobbio, highlights that the normative force acquired by the principles in contemporary constitutions and in the jurisprudence of the Constitutional Courts was preceded by the interpretative work performed by the International Courts of Justice (ICJs), which, still under the aegis of old legal

[50] Bonavides (2001), p. 231–240.

[51] Bonavides (2001), p. 230.

[52] Bonavides (2001), p. 230.

[53] Bonavides (2001), p. 231–240.

positivism, built a neopositivist jurisprudence of the general principles of law concerning their nature, validity, and content from a fruitful interpretation of Article 38 of the Statute of the Permanent Court of International Justice, which, as early as 1920, declared: "'the general principles of law, recognized by civilized nations' as capable and suitable to solve controversies, alongside treaties and international customs; formula, this consecrated and incorporated literally by art. 38, 1, "c", of the Statute of the International Court of Justice and, then with slight variations, by art. 215, 2 of the treaty that established in 1957 the European Economic Community."[54]

In addition to the fruitful and revitalizing jurisprudence of the ICJs, one cannot forget the decisive role of legal science in the pioneering doctrine of Jean Boulanger and Josef Esser, as well as the thinkers who continued to build a solid doctrine of principles in the field of constitutional law, among whom stand out Vezio Crisafulli, Ronald Dworkin, Robert Alexy, and Friedrich Müller.

Nowadays, there is no longer any doubt about the normative nature of principles, but I could not fail to mention here a definition of etymological inspiration brought by Luis Diez de Picazo,[55] considering that it perfectly dialogs with the proposal of this work to demonstrate the legal principiological nature of harmony with nature, because harmony with nature, before being an ethical account of the peoples of this planet, is also a principle of natural laws that govern the Earth system.

Picazo, drawing from a critique that F. de Castro makes of the functionalist definition of principle constructed by Josef Esser, points out that the definition of principle cannot start from criteria such as the "*ratio iuris*," reason for being, purpose, or function of one or several rules of law, the set of them, or even an institution. He concludes that the idea of principle should be sought in the language of geometry, where the first truths are found, and finishes his thought with an etymological reference: "principles are just because they are at the beginning, they are the premises of a whole system that develops *more geométrico*."[56]

Thus considered, the principles point to truths: objective truths, derived from divine law and natural law. Despite basing the concept of principles on objective truths, and even on natural laws—therefore situated in the plane of being, that is, ontic—subsequently, Picazo points out their normative character, emphasizing the deontic nature of principles.[57]

The theory of Picazo and F. de Castro, which considers viable the possibility of natural laws—those in the ontic language plane—being capable of acting in the plane of ought-to-be as legal principles, perfectly dialogs with the proposal of this work in the sense of deriving, from the second law of thermodynamics, the principle of harmony with nature as a legal principle.

---

[54] Bonavides (2001), p. 237.

[55] Picazo (1983), p. 1267–1268.

[56] Picazo (1983), p. 1267.

[57] Picazo (1983), p. 1267–1268.

As already explained in the chapter that deals with ethics, this work, based on Cirne-Lima's theory, has already demonstrated the overcoming of the obstacle created by the theory of the naturalistic fallacy,[58] according to which it is logically impossible to derive prescriptive propositions from the descriptive language of factual premises, which is the proper language of ethics and law—that is, the language of ought-to-be, deontic, where ethical and legal principles reside.

The Brazilian thinker Cirne-Lima overcomes the logical and linguistic objection of the natural fallacy, since, unlike considering everything that is factual as descriptive language, as naturalists do, he demonstrates that the ought-to-be is the great modal operator, not only of ethics and law but of all philosophy and all knowledge. For Cirne-Lima, the set of normative propositions, governed by the modal ought-to-be, is the broadest and contains the set of descriptive prescriptions.[59]

In this line, the second law of thermodynamics, a phenomenon of the biosphere, when reported in language, becomes a factual occurrence with a certain value load, so that it also enunciates a prescriptive proposition—that is, the duty of the human being to always act in harmony with nature, under penalty of leading the Earth system to thermal death, which, in the end, would compromise the rights to life and human dignity, leading humanity to a fatally unethical and unfair outcome.

Being a mainstay among the natural laws that govern the Earth system, the second law of thermodynamics is necessary and inevitable in its effects on the biosphere and the concrete social reality in which life develops, which forms the basis of all institutions, including legal and economic ones. The inevitability of a natural law on all dimensions of life on the planet would already be, by itself, enough to qualify this natural law as a representation capable of justifying the recognition of a legal principle in the field of regulation of human relations with nature.

The principle of harmony with nature is a prescriptive expression of the second law of thermodynamics, and therefore, this work considers it initially as a pre-legal principle. It is a principle because it brings a precept about the origin of the entire chain of life. It is pre-legal because this precept results from a natural necessity, not from an act of human will, and therefore prescribes duties and asymmetric responsibilities for the human being in his relations with the biosphere.

As can be seen, this necessary, non-derogable precept is intertwined with the most relevant legal institution, the right to life, so that this, by itself, could be enough to justify the recognition of the principle of harmony with nature as a legal principle implicit in Constitutions; however, to avoid the stigma of returning to the old philosophical current of so-called legal naturalism,[60] this work will adopt

---

[58] Cirne-Lima (2001), p. 65.

[59] Cirne-Lima (2001), p. 65.

[60] "The conception of law as a pure phenomenon of reality leads to the idea of legal science as a science of reality and its method as a causal explanation of this reality. The most consequential modalities of this conception are mechanistic naturalism, which interprets legal conceptions as processes originated by external causes and influences (as, for example, classical physics did in

Esser's theory of functional equivalence in the formation of legal principles as a starting point to demonstrate the legality of the principle of harmony with nature.

Esser explains the process of the formation of legal principles as a functionally necessary piece for the solution of concrete problems and presents a functional view of the legal system that, unlike closed dogmatic systems, develops valuation and order principles through jurisprudential legal practice when solving specific and continuous problems over time. Thus, in a system organized from the functional equivalence proposed by Esser, it is not the system itself that is the center of legal thought, but the problems that need to be solved by the legal system.[61]

He also points out that "A clear characteristic of our time is that the examination of problems is increasingly entrusted to specialists. These, in turn, are forced to elevate the principles related to their area of knowledge out of the fossilized figures of the law. Many of these problems are not encompassed by systems of rigid normative structure, a situation that has caused a real crisis in the theory of sources."[62]

Esser's pioneering words still echo with acute realism in the twenty-first century, considering that there are several problems that reverberate in the natural and social dimensions of present-day humanity, and most of the legal systems are not able to bring solutions at the speed imposed on our time by the urgencies triggered by the advent of the algorithm and, mainly, by the climate crisis of the Anthropocene.

The problematic relationship of the human being with the biosphere, which triggered the climate crisis, is not addressed by the vast majority of norms positivized in legal systems, which are still fossilized in the duality of legal anthropocentrism, forged in our contractualist modernity, which separated culture from nature, transforming the latter into a mere natural resource with instrumental value.

Earth system scientists, ecologists, geologists, biologists, and jurists of Earth Jurisprudence do not find support in positive law; even the environmental law of several countries is still based on an anthropocentric paradigm. Faced with this serious problem, which compromises the life and dignity of all species and, also, of human beings, several courts around the world have been consolidating a continuous jurisprudence based on the ethical value of harmony with nature, as will be demonstrated later.

The confrontation of this problem, first by the courts in the judgments of numerous concrete cases involving the relationship of human beings and their institutions with the biosphere, demonstrates how current and vigorous Esser's theory of functional equivalence still is in highlighting the emergence of the principle of harmony with nature as a legal principle recognized by the legal practice of courts in various countries around the world.

---

relation to inanimate nature); and vitalism, which interprets law as a function of biological life, in the mold of biological sciences ..." Wieacker (2010), p. 652.

[61] Esser (2019).

[62] Esser (2019), p. 22.

In his pioneering work, Esser treats principles as sources of law and investigates their origin, nature, classification, and systematization. As Galuppo observes, it was Esser, in his classic work *Grundsatz und Norm in der richterlichen Fortbildung des Privatrechts*, published in 1956, who gave a new direction to the doctrine of legal principles. He demonstrated that principles were more than moral foundations of positive law, considering their function "as a technical means of expanding the legal system."[63]

In the aforementioned work, he examines the hypothesis of recognizing harmony with nature as a legal principle, initially through the lens of Esser's doctrine, considering that his theory served as a starting point for thinkers of both the *common law* system and the Roman–Germanic system.[64] When dealing with principiology in the context of International Law, Esser attributed a universal character to principles—a universality not in the sense that they would be a supranorm, but in the possibility of finding the same principles in different systems and legal orders.

He points out that, in various national legal systems, the coincidences of solutions obtained through different structures attract the attention of comparatists. Despite these structures being influenced by diverse cultures, they produce similar and even identical solutions. He concludes that this can only be explained by the universality of legal needs and by the identical value granted to the same postulate by various peoples.[65]

It is possible to verify, then, that the unity that gives rise to a universal principle does not occur from conceptual categories, but in the communion of problems that repeat themselves in various legal systems over a continuity of time. He explains that this dynamic of principle formation found very favorable ground in the field of international law, considering that Article 38(3) of the Statute of the Permanent International Court has always regarded the international judicial power as a source of law. The creation of international law predominantly followed the jurisprudential method, but in a differentiated way, considering that it did not have the experience of the binding authority of the English precedent, because there is not a mass of repeated cases in the field of international jurisprudence.[66] Thus, this jurisprudence is consolidated by comparing substantially coincident national practices to solve identical problems.

He explains that this universal perspective of law formation allowed the rediscovery of functional laws, which were hidden under dogmas in different institutions of various legal systems, and which provided identical solutions for identical problems experienced in their social realities. He cites, as an example of this phenomenon, the attenuation of the rigor of legal security in legal acts by the requirement to safeguard good faith in contractual relations. This phenomenon

---

[63] Galuppo (1999), p. 227.

[64] Galuppo (1999), p. 227.

[65] Esser (2019), p. 328.

[66] Esser (2019), p. 314.

occurred in various legal systems and resulted in the creation of an equivalent institution in different systems and structures of law: the legal principle of good faith.[67]

Esser also deals with the formation of principles in domestic law, within the systems of Roman–Germanic law, as a result of the symbiosis between the jurisprudence of the courts and the systematization offered by the doctrine. He considers that jurisprudence is as much a source of law as the Legislative Power. He describes the iter of judicial development of principles until they become institutions of their own, before there is legislation and independently of it. He cites, as examples of this formative phenomenon of law, the institutions of abuse of right, non-imputability, and liability without fault in the German legal system.[68]

These new institutions, born from jurisprudential casuistry, can arise due to a gap or even the need to resolve a concrete problem that repeats itself over a continuous period. Thus, the principle is not something discovered—understood as a positive element of the precedent—since the precedent is not the substantial expression of the principle, but the act by which it is formed; that is, the positive reason for the validity of the principle.[69]

Losano observes that, for Esser, it is the casuistry that states the law, considering that the pre-existing principles[70] of positive law need to be embodied in positive legal principles and institutions. Within the system of *common law,* this happens naturally through precedent, while in the continental system, it is through general clauses that jurisprudence evolves and updates the norms "by reference to the principles that are behind the general clauses."[71] Losano also notes that, even as a jurist of the continental system and therefore bound to positive legal norms, Esser manages to demonstrate the possibility of jurisprudence surpassing them, considering the creative and expansive function of general clauses, which allow courts to overcome the limits of this closed system.

Despite Esser not having used more rigorous terminology in his theory of principles, as he even confronts principle with norm, as pointed out by Alexy,[72] it is undeniable that he was a pioneer in recognizing the normative character of principles.

For Esser, principles, as elements of the constitution of the legal system, arise from concrete problems and not from the system itself. Thus, he adopted a problematic model without, however, refuting the systematic model. His theory establishes a cycle of emergence of principles in the following order: (1) a problem, a fact, is observed; (2) this fact is examined in the light of prudence or *phrónesis*, guided by the values shared by a given community, and at this stage, the principle

[67] Esser (2019), p. 342.

[68] Esser (2019), p. 342.

[69] Esser (2019), p. 254.

[70] Losano (2010), p. 260.

[71] Losano (2010), p. 260.

[72] Alexy (2008), p. 87.

already arises; and (3) in the last stage, there is the articulation of the principle in the legal system.[73]

As pointed out by Galuppo, Esser suggests a complementarity between the problematic method, inspired by the topic, and the systematic method; that is, between the induction of the first and the deduction of the second. In this way, he reconciles the need for internal integrity of the legal system without giving up the external connection with the dynamics of problems arising in society; that is, he does not disregard the historicity of law.

Esser emphasizes that the effectiveness of principles does not depend on their provision in legal texts; their justification comes from the nature of things or institutions, as functionally necessary pieces for the solution of concrete problems:

> Hence, principles, given analogous circumstances, are equally well known in all legal systems, even where there is no law explicitly foreseeing them. The necessity, in conjunction with a harmony, not yet sufficiently studied, in ideas about justice formed in the course of history, gives rise, in the face of equal conflicts of interest, to coincident solutions - even in the absence of "law" and doctrinal concepts.[74]

In discussing the source and normative force of principles, which are created from problems in the concrete world, he raises the question of the origin of their legitimacy. At this point, he criticizes both the positivist view and natural law. He criticizes positivism for reducing the legitimacy of principles to provisions in the positive text, conceiving law as a non-historical phenomenon, derived from the legislator's reason and legitimized only by the norm. Similarly, when dealing with natural law, he calls it "terra incognita" due to the absence of well-defined concepts and for presenting a law composed of principles unfolded from a supposed universal human reason. Despite these criticisms of natural law, he admits a "primacy of pre-legal truths." For Galuppo, Esser maintains the preexistence of principles in relation to positive norms, as ethical values. He also admits that some principles have a universal character, as they are present in all legal systems.[75]

Esser's understanding, in the sense of the preexistence of principles in relation to positive norms, as ethical values shared by different peoples, confirms the hypothesis of harmony with nature as a legal principle. Indeed, as already demonstrated in previous chapters, harmony with nature, as an ethical value that intersects with the natural laws of the Earth system, is present in various ancestral cultures of the West and the East, which evidences its character as a pre-legal truth.

Various courts within legal systems around the world, inspired by this ancestral ethical value of harmony with nature, are issuing decisions that recognize the intrinsic value of nature and the dignity of non-human beings and organic holistic entities, such as rivers, forests, and ecosystems. This emerging non-anthropocentric jurisprudence signals the search for a balanced and coherent relationship between human beings, non-human beings, and organic entities, so that, in light of Esser's

[73] Galuppo (1999), p. 227.

[74] Esser (1961), p. 7–8.

[75] Galuppo (1999), p. 19.

theory of principles, this work identifies in this planetary jurisprudential movement the consolidation of the principle of harmony with nature.

Nevertheless, as Bonavides (2001) points out, Esser, despite this fruitful theoretical legacy about the positivization of principles by judicialism, due to his private law training, did not follow the publicist turn of the theory of principles as the cornerstone of the State of Law and the material theory of the constitution. In this new phase of the development of the theory of principles, Ronald Dworkin, with his theory of the connection of law to morality, Friedrich Müller, with his structuring theory of law, and Robert Alexy, with the doctrine of criteria to distinguish rules and principles, will occupy a prominent place.

With the prevalence of constitutionalism, the concept of norm gains other contours, making it necessary to assess the legality of the principle of Harmony with Nature also in light of new normative theories emerging in the field of public law with the advent of post-positivism. Among the various lines that emerge in the post-positivist scene, this work considers Friedrich Müller's methodical structuring theory the most suitable for assessing the normativity of the principle of harmony with nature.

Müller's structuring theory conceives, in the process of constructing the norm, the concrete and social reality. It is a complex theory that has the merit of overcoming the duality that positivism established between the plane of "being" (ontic) and "ought-to-be" (deontic). Precisely for this reason, it supports the principle of harmony with nature, which is based on the ethics of universal coherence proposed by Cirne-Lima. This ethics is of a cognitive nature, meaning it is guided by principles of Earth system sciences, which overcame the duality between "being" and "ought-to-be"—a duality once imposed by formalist thinkers with the fallacious argument known as the naturalistic fallacy, as discussed in the chapter on ethics.

For Müller's structuring theory, the normative text—that is, the linguistic signs that make up the statements conveyed in the laws—are not yet norms; they exist on the plane of virtuality. They are merely a "pre-image," input data, or a starting point in the process of constructing the norm. The normative text, together with the auxiliary interpretative resources, will compose what Müller calls the program of the norm. These auxiliary interpretative resources function as a means of treating the raw normative text and include traditional interpretation techniques, such as grammatical, genetic, historical, systematic, teleological methods, and others specific to the various branches of law, as well as other contemporary interpretation criteria.[76]

Through the program of the norm, which functions as a filter of reality data, the judge will select the facts in social reality, and these data and facts will compose what he calls the normative scope. This selection of data and facts from reality, made by the judge and guided by the program of the norm, must follow a method

[76] Müller (2013).

that requires, above all, the justification of choices to allow the scrutiny of the work of concretizing the norm, which is an imperative of the Democratic Rule of Law.[77]

By integrating the program of the norm with the scope of the norm, a general and abstract norm is created, which, in the process of individualization before the concrete case, gives rise to the norm decision, that is, the individual and concrete norm. It is noticeable that Müller's theory is systemic but proposes an open system that allows a constant dialog with the reality of the world, considering that the data of this reality are constitutive of the norm. However, this opening of the text to the context of concrete reality does not mean the adoption of a free theory of law, since Müller's method establishes a model of praxis theory on the concretization of law, with criteria that fulfill the functions of stabilizing, rationalizing, and facilitating the verifiability of the production of the norm decision.[78]

Through the lens of Friedrich Müller's structuring theory of law, it is possible to understand the process of constituting the rights of nature in courts in various countries, which have concretized protective norms for non-human living beings in their decisions.

The constitutional and local courts of various countries, as will be demonstrated in the next topic, have started from external normative texts—conventions that ensure ecological balance and sustainability—as well as from their internal legal texts, guided by hermeneutic and heuristic criteria that consider the urgency to circumvent the climate crisis, to constitute normative programs capable of selecting, in the reality of the climate crisis, the data and facts integrating a normative scope updated by the urgency of constructing norms concretizing the rights of nature.

The analysis of these decisions rendered by the judiciary of countries on all continents reveals a jurisprudence that arises from normative decisions with very marked common characteristics, both in their normative programs and in their normative scopes.

The normative programs are composed of conventions with the force of soft law and internal laws, some of constitutional status, but most are national, state, and local infraconstitutional laws, whose raw texts are treated with innovative hermeneutic criteria, considering they adopt the ethics of responsibility and harmony with nature, the heuristic of indigenous peoples from various places on the planet and, mainly, from the southern hemisphere. Therefore, in the process of concretizing these norms, normative programs are constituted from a new non-anthropocentric and decolonizing paradigm.

In the analysis of the normative scope of these decisions, it is possible to verify the selection of data and facts that concern the violation of the physical integrity of animals, contamination of rivers and other bodies of water, forest fires, loss of biodiversity, and loss of territories by indigenous peoples due to contamination with heavy metals. However, the distinctive feature of this normative scope does

[77] Müller (2013), p. 194–195.

[78] Müller (2013), p. 234 and p. 236.

not exactly lie in the choice of these data from the reality of the biosphere, as anthropocentric environmental law has been doing this for some time. What distinguishes these decisions concerning the selection of data for the constitution of their normative scopes is the consideration of facts that were previously ignored by legal language, for example: thermodynamic phenomena like entropy and negentropy; ecological facts in the field of interaction of living beings, such as predation and symbiosis; ecosystem management; and the sentience and affectivity of animals.

Traditional environmental law has always constituted its normative scope through the filter of anthropocentric normative programs, both in the raw text of the laws and in the hermeneutic criteria for handling these texts. Thus, various relevant facts and data from the biosphere and the Earth system have always been ignored, because the relevant facts worthy of legal consideration for the constitution of the scope of the norm, in the anthropocentric paradigm, were only those useful to the human being, mainly from an economic point of view.

The old environmental law, forged in the anthropocentric paradigm, is still based on the contractualism of Kantian ethics, for which only the human being has intrinsic value. In addition, this anthropocentric law, developed under the auspices of legal positivism—which separates the "being" from the "ought-to-be"—reduced the normative contents to mere expressions of human will, without taking into account the data of reality and, thus, scientific interdisciplinarity as a cognitive element essential for the realization of normative decisions that involve conflicts in human relations with the biosphere.

Unlike the environmental law of the anthropocentric paradigm, whose holders of protective norms have always been human beings, the emerging jurisprudence of harmony with nature recognizes animals, plants, and ecosystems as holders of the rights to life, to biological integrity, to existential flourishing, and even ensures the affective dimension of animals. What is observed, therefore, is the emergence of a powerful jurisprudential activity of non-anthropocentric inspiration, which has a common foundation in its normative programs, namely: the reconciliation of the human being with nature and not just the protection of the environment as a mere environmental resource.

This work observes, in the dynamics of the movement to realize the rights of nature, a constant dialog between its normative programs and the reality of the biosphere—a tangible reality governed by natural laws, which were not created by the act of will of the human community—and the symbolic world of language, which Teilhard de Chardin called the noosphere. It is an unprecedented normative construction that expanded the circle of coverage of its normative program to include data from the reality of the biosphere, previously not considered relevant by the legal noosphere.

Thus, in the course of realizing these norms, there is a reconciliation between the two spheres of the human dimension, which were separated by scientific and legal positivism. From the perspective of the jurisprudence of harmony with nature, the sphere of language, of culture, of the "ought-to-be" communicates with the sphere of life in its biological dimension, with the being, the living organism of the biosphere, to constitute normative decisions, which place the lives of human and non-human living beings at the center of the interests of a new non-anthropocentric jurisprudence. This new jurisprudence understands the law not only as a construction of human will but also as a cognitive tool for harmonizing the human being, in its social dimension, with the natural world of which it is a part as a being of biological dimension.

The self-reproductive character of this non-anthropocentric jurisprudence of harmony with nature is also observed. These various normative decisions, constituted by the interaction of their normative programs with the normative scope expanded to the reality of the biosphere, generate precedents that feed back into the hermeneutic criteria for handling the raw normative texts for the constitution of new normative programs.

At this point, it is possible to observe a dialog between the structured method of Müller and the theory of principles of Esser, who, despite having adopted a problematic model, never denied the systematic model of the constitution of norms. In his theory, he describes the cycle of the emergence of principles, starting from a problem or a fact, which begins to be examined in the light of values shared by a given community in judicial decisions. These decisions, after some time, generate precedents that can constitute a principle in the legal system.

When analyzing the current jurisprudence of recognition of the rights of nature, one can see the emergence of precedents guided by a common value: the harmony of the interests of the human being and its institutions with the biosphere, that is, the principle of harmony with nature. This principle, constituted by the normative decisions, emerges as a principle that, in its hermeneutic function, will feed back into the system, functioning as an interpretive criterion for the constitution of normative programs in the course of realizing new normative decisions about the relationship of the human being with the biosphere.

Still examining the principle of harmony with nature in the context of the general theory of principles, one cannot fail to pass it through the sieve of Ronald Dworkin's thought, who, when dealing with the concept of principle, establishes a distinction between policies, legal principles, and legal rules. Dworkin distinguishes between principles and policies. He points out that policy is the type of standard that establishes a goal to be achieved, usually an improvement in some economic, political, or social characteristics of the community. A "principle" is a standard that must be observed, not because it will promote or guarantee an economic or social solution considered desirable, but because it is a requirement of justice, equity, or some other dimension of morality.[79]

As can be seen, policies do not have the same legal potential as principles, considering that these are derived from a fundamental concern based on the ideas

[79] Dworkin (2013), p. 44–45.

of justice, equity, and morality. Dworkin uses two examples to differentiate principles from policies. Measures to reduce car accidents are a policy, while the standard, in the sense that it is not acceptable for a human being to profit from their own mistakes, is a principle. What differentiates this latter standard from the former is that it is based on a precept of justice and morality, while measures to reduce car accidents aim at the well-being of a social group.[80]

The principle of harmony with nature emerges as an ethical precept of coherence, therefore fitting Dworkin's criterion. However, as will be seen later, Dworkin restricts principles to the province of individual rights, which poses a hindrance to the hypothesis of harmony with nature as a legal principle, considering its irradiation in the scope of collective and diffuse rights.

Robert Alexy, on the other hand, adopts a broader concept of principle than Dworkin, as he considers that principles can address both individual and collective rights:

> Dworkin's concept of principle is defined more narrowly than this. According to him, principles are only those norms that can be used as reasons for individual rights. Norms that refer to collective interests are called policies by him. The differentiation between individual rights and collective interests is undoubtedly important. But, it is neither required nor convenient to link the concept of principle to the concept of individual right. The logical characteristics common to both types of principles to which Dworkin refers with his concept of principle in a generic sense - and which clearly appear in cases of collisions between principles - indicate the convenience of a broad concept of principles.[81]

The legal principle of harmony with nature resonates in both individual and collective rights, so Alexy's broader understanding, in the sense that principles can deal with both individual and collective rights, proves more appropriate for the purpose of confirming harmony with nature as a legal principle.

As will be verified in the next topic, the jurisprudence regarding the recognition of the rights of nature is inspired by a common value: the balance in weighing the interests of human beings and their institutions against the interests of nature. This balance is the very core of the principle of harmony with nature, which emerges as the axiological axis of various norms and decisions of courts in several countries.

The principle of harmony with nature already functions as a hermeneutic criterion for the treatment of raw normative texts, both internal and external, which will constitute the normative programs for filtering increasingly comprehensive and inclusive normative scopes of data and facts of the biosphere for the concretization of new normative decisions on conflicts between human interests and non-human interests.

---

[80] Dworkin (2013), p. 45.

[81] Alexy (2008), p. 116.

5.4 The Planetary Emergence of the Jurisprudence of the Principle of Harmony with Nature

To demonstrate the evolution of the process of concretizing the principle of harmony with nature, this work lists the following decisions rendered by constitutional courts, regional courts, and single judges in various countries. These decisions are cataloged by the UN on the *Harmony with Nature* UN site.[82]

The purpose of bringing this jurisprudence is to provide a brief summary of the judgments to demonstrate that the judiciary of various countries, on different continents, has faced a common problem—demands whose causes of action deal with imbalance and incoherence in the relations of human beings with the biosphere. Let's see the following:

(a) Decision of the Inter-American Court of Human Rights

The Inter-American Court of Human Rights issued a decision on February 6, 2020, recognizing the protection of the rights of indigenous peoples in the case of the Indigenous Community Members of the Lhaka Honhat Association (Our Land) versus Argentina.[83]

The Inter-American Court of Human Rights declared the responsibility of the Republic of Argentina for the violation of the rights of 132 indigenous communities living in the province of Salta. Upon analyzing the grounds of the judgment, it is found that the court understood, based on Articles 21 and 26 of the American Convention on Human Rights, that the state violated the right to community property, the right to the cultural identity of the original peoples, and the rights to a healthy environment, adequate food, and access to water. The interpretation stands out in a holistic legal analysis of this ruling; it considers the interdependence of the rights to a balanced environment, food security, and access to water with the right to cultural identity of indigenous peoples and their relationship with the Earth.

This was the first time that the Inter-American Court set a precedent on the rights to water, food, a healthy environment, and, most interestingly, associated these human rights with the human right to recognition of the cultural identity of indigenous peoples in relation to their relationship with the land.[84]

In paragraph 203 of the judgment, the court emphasizes that the decision aims to protect nature not only for its "utility" or "effects" on human beings, "but for its importance to the other living organisms with which we share the planet."[85]

Two points of the court's decision directly dialog with the principle of harmony with nature:

[82] United Nations, Harmony with Nature, online.

[83] Inter-American Court of Human Rights (2020), online.

[84] Inter-American Court of Human Rights (2020), online.

[85] Inter-American Court of Human Rights (2020), online.

i. The recognition of the right to live in harmony with nature, under the terms of Article 19 of the American Declaration on the Rights of Indigenous Peoples, which is realized through the relationship of indigenous peoples with the Earth from their cultural identity, as well as the interdependence of this issue with human rights to the environment, water, and food security;[86] and
ii. The recognition of the need to protect the "other living organisms with which we share the planet," not based on a utilitarian and instrumental value, but as an end value.

This ruling is paradigmatic, as it positions the Inter-American Court of Human Rights toward a moderate anthropocentrism. The recognition of an end value to non-human living beings, as well as the express reference to the principle of harmony with nature provided for in Article 19 of the American Declaration on the Rights of Indigenous[87] Peoples, aligns the court's jurisprudence with the principle of harmony with nature.

(b) Argentina

In 2016, Judge María Alejandra Mauricio, when judging the case of the chimpanzee named Cecília, recognized her subjectivity and the status of being a subject of the fundamental right to be born, live, grow, and die in her own environment.[88] The grounds of the sentence evoke Article 4 of the Universal Declaration of Animal Rights, which guarantees the right of an animal belonging to a wild species to live free in its own natural environment—terrestrial, aerial, or aquatic—and to reproduce. This provision, which guarantees the right of animals to live freely in their habitat and in harmony with their natural environment, is a consequence of the principle of harmony with nature, albeit implicitly.

(c) Bangladesh

The Supreme Court of Bangladesh confirmed the 2019 decision of the High Court (in Writ Petition No. 13989), which declared that the Turag River and all other rivers in the country are "living entities" with rights as "legal persons." In this historic decision, the National River Conservation Commission was given the legal role of guardian for the rivers of Bangladesh to protect and conserve them, prevent pollution and encroachment, and ensure that their rights and the riparian ecosystems are protected. In addition, the decision stated that the rights of the rivers can

---

[86] The American Declaration on the Rights of Indigenous Peoples, in its Article XIX, recognizes the "right to the protection of a healthy environment," which includes the right of "indigenous peoples" to "live in harmony with nature and to a healthy, safe and sustainable environment"; to "conserve, restore and protect the environment and the sustainable management of their lands, territories and resources"; and "to the conservation and protection of the environment and the productive capacity of their lands or territories and resources".

[87] OAS. American Declaration on the Rights of Indigenous Peoples. Available at: https://www.oas.org/es/sadye/documentos/DADPI.pdf. Accessed on: February 4, 2025.

[88] Judicial Power Mendoza. Third Court of Guarantees. MENDOZA, November 3, 2016. Available at: http://files.harmonywithnatureun.org/uploads/upload947.pdf, p. 37. Accessed on: February 4, 2025.

be applied to interdict activities harmful to them by private and public (governmental) entities.[89]

(d) Colombia

Colombia has been leading the jurisprudence movement of concretizing the principle of harmony with nature since 2016, when its Constitutional Court issued an unprecedented decision on a case of illegal mining, in which it recognized the Atrato River as a subject of rights.

On June 17, 2020, the Supreme Court of Justice of Colombia declared the Isla de Salamanca National Park a subject of rights to protect it from rampant deforestation. In the grounds of the decision, the court noted that the human being is not superior to nature and, therefore, cannot use it indiscriminately as a mere object. It also pointed out that there is a relationship of interdependence between the human being and nature and that the human being must carry out its economic activities harmoniously to avoid environmental degradation.

On August 28, 2020, the Superior Court of Ibagué declared the Los Nevados Natural National Park a subject of rights for its protection, recovery, and conservation.

In 2019, the following significant rulings were made in Colombia: The Municipal Civil Court of La Plata, Huila, Colombia, recognized the La Plata River as a subject of rights, ordering protective measures for the well-being of the population and the La Plata River.

The Administrative Court of Tolima ordered the end of mining exploitation in the rivers of Coello, Combeima, and Cocora, as well as their basins, recognizing them as subjects of rights to protection, conservation, maintenance, and restoration. The Superior Court of Justice of Medellín recognized the Cauca River, its basin, and tributaries as subjects of rights.

The First Criminal Court of the District of Neiva recognized the Magdalena River as a subject of rights. The decision states that the Magdalena River, its basin, and its tributaries are subjects of rights to protection, conservation, maintenance, and restoration by the state.

The Administrative Court of Quindío recognized the Quindío River as a subject of rights to protection, conservation, maintenance, and restoration.

The Special Jurisdiction for Peace in Colombia recognized Katsa Su, the vast territory of the Awá people, as a subject of rights and a victim of the armed conflict.

The Third Court of Execution of Penalties and Security Measures in Cali, Colombia, recognized the Pance River as a subject of rights. The Court's decision came in response to a tutela citing rights violations due to pollution.

The Regional Court of the Fourth Court of Execution of Penalties and Security Measures in Pereira recognized the Otún River as a subject of rights.

---

[89] Bangladesh Supreme Court Upholds Rights of Rivers. August 24, 2020. Available at: https://mari-margil.medium.com/bangladesh-supreme-court-upholds-rights-of-rivers-ede78568d8aa Accessed on: February 4, 2025.

In 2018, the Supreme Court of Justice of Colombia issued another historic decision by granting rights to the Colombian Amazon region, in the same terms as those granted to the Atrato River.

The Administrative Court of Boyacá, Colombia, declared the Páramo de Pisba (Pisba Plateau) a subject of rights.

The First Criminal Court of the Circuit of Cartagena ordered the State of Colombia to protect and preserve the life of bees as pollinators. In 2017, the Supreme Court of Justice of Colombia established that animals are rights holders, recognizing rights for the Andean bear, also called the spectacled bear or "oso de anteojos" (Tremarctos ornatus).

As can be seen, the Judiciary of Colombia, from its highest court to regional and local courts, has developed consistent jurisprudence based on the principle of harmony with nature.

(e) Ecuador

On January 19, 2022, the Constitutional Court recognized that the Monjas River and the ecosystem to which the river belongs have the right to "full respect for their existence and the maintenance and regeneration of their life cycles, structure, functions, and evolutionary processes." After noting the river's illness and the loss of ecological balance, the court concluded that the Municipality of Quito had violated the river's rights and, therefore, ordered its full repair in accordance with its right to be restored.

Upon analyzing the text of the decision, it is found in topic 116, the reasoning based on Article 71 of the Ecuadorian Constitution, which expressly recognizes nature as a subject of rights—that is, as the holder of the right to have its existence, maintenance, and regeneration of its vital cycles, structures, functions, and evolutionary processes respected.[90]

On September 8, 2021, the Constitutional Court ruled in favor of the Rights of Nature for mangroves, also based on Article 71 of the Constitution of Ecuador. It highlights in Topic 26 that "Nature is not an abstract entity, a mere conceptual category or simple legal statement. Nor is it an inert and insensitive object. When the Constitution provides that the existence of nature must be fully respected and recognizes that it is 'where life reproduces and realizes' it indicates to us that it is a complex subject that must be understood in a systemic perspective."[91]

This evocation of the systemic nature of nature is a legal recognition of the second law of thermodynamics and, therefore, of the principle of harmony with nature, which is deepened in Topic 27 of the decision, when it states that nature is composed of an interrelated, interdependent, and indivisible set of biotic and abiotic elements, which form a community of life.

On November 10, 2021, the Constitutional Court of Ecuador decided that plans for copper and gold mining in a forest within an environmental protection area are unconstitutional and violate the Rights of Nature. The court ruled that the mining

[90] http://files.harmonywithnatureun.org/uploads/upload1165.pdf. Accessed on: February 3, 2025.

[91] http://files.harmonywithnatureun.org/uploads/upload1279.pdf. Accessed on: February 3, 2025.

licenses issued in Los Cedros, a protected area in the northwest of the country, would harm the forest's biodiversity, which is home to spectacled bears, endangered frogs, dozens of rare species of orchids, and the brown-headed spider monkey, one of the rarest primates in the world.[92]

On September 24, 2020, the Constitutional Court of Ecuador issued a decision to ensure the protection of the Rights of Nature for the Alpayacu River, whose waters have been contaminated by poultry, pig, and agricultural companies.[93]

In 2019, a judge in Quevedo, Ecuador, accepted a protection order in favor of the peasants of the province of Los Ríos. The judge granted the protection order and pointed out that GM crops violate the rights to life, health, work, a healthy environment, and the rights of nature.[94]

2019—The court recognized violations of the collective rights of free, informed, and prior consultation, water rights, and the rights of nature and the environment in the community of Sinangoe.[95]

2019—The Constitutional Court of Imbabura ruled in favor of the Protected Forest of Los Cedros, recognizing that mining would violate the Rights of Nature.[96]

2019—The Supreme Court of Ecuador delivered the verdict in a case of crime against fauna and flora, ordering the confiscation of a vessel carrying 6,226 sharks. The grounds for the decision recognize the rights of nature.

The shareholders of a mining company requested a constitutional precautionary measure to protect the rights of nature, which were severely threatened by the inevitable rupture of a dam containing more than 390 million cubic meters of mining waste. The grounds for the petition were based on the violation of the rights of nature.

A judge in Quevedo, Ecuador, granted a protection order in favor of the peasants of the Province of Los Ríos; in the grounds of the decision, he asserted that genetically modified crops were violating the rights to life, health, work, a healthy environment, and the rights of nature itself.

In 2016, precautionary measures were sought and granted for the protection of the rights of nature, considering that, in the city of Alamor, where the San Francisco Recreational Center was located, the upper part of a hill was being

---

[92] http://files.harmonywithnatureun.org/uploads/upload1164.pdf. Accessed on: February 3, 2025.

[93] The Guardian. Plans to mine Ecuador forest violate rights of nature, court rules. Available at: https://www.theguardian.com/environment/2021/dec/02/plan-to-mine-in-ecuador-forest-violate-rights-of-nature-court-rules-aoe. Accessed on: February 3, 2025.

[94] Judicial Function. Trial No: 12283201802414, SECOND INSTANCE, entry number 1. August 16, 2019. Available at: https://www.derechosdelanaturaleza.org.ec/wp-content/uploads/2019/07/Sentencia-OGM.pdf Accessed on: Feb 03, 2025.

[95] Judicial Function. Multicompetent Judicial Unit Based in the Gonzalo Pizarro Canton, of the Sucumbios Province. 07/17/2019. Available at: https://www.derechosdelanaturaleza.org.ec/wp-content/uploads/2019/07/SENTENCIA-PRIMER-NIVEL-COF%C3%81N-SINANGOE.pdf. Accessed on: Feb 03, 2025.

[96] Judicial Function. Multicompetent Chamber of the Provincial Court of Imbabura. July 25, 2019. Available at: https://www.derechosdelanaturaleza.org.ec/wp-content/uploads/2019/08/SENTENCIA-APELACI%C3%93N-CEDROS.pdf. Accessed on: Feb 03, 2025.

destroyed with the use of heavy machinery by the Municipal Prefecture of Puyango.

In 2013, a judge ordered the Ministry of the Environment to exercise oversight actions in the civil bidding and award process of La Clementina Farm, with the aim of guaranteeing the rights of nature and the forest.

In 2012, a decision was issued by the Constitutional Court, which focused on the constitutional aspect of a law that prioritizes conservation over the constitutional right to internal migration.

In 2011, the Vilcabamba River achieved its first victory in the so-called Court of the Rights of Nature.

As can be seen, the Judiciary of Ecuador has given broad effectiveness to Article 71 of the Constitution of Ecuador, which enshrined the principle of Harmony with Nature in that country by expressly safeguarding the rights of nature, or Pacha Mama. The enshrined constitutional text considered nature, or Pacha Mama, as it is recognized by the original peoples of that country, as the dimension "that reproduces and realizes life." As can be seen, the 2008 Constitution broke with the anthropocentric colonialist tradition that placed nature in the legal category of a commodity. Gudynas points out that the 2008 Constitution incorporated the perspective of *buen-vivir*, or Sumak Kawsay in the Kichwa language.[97] This vision of the original peoples of the Andes about the relationship with nature is the quintessence of the principle of harmony with nature.

Acosta explains that the *buen-vivir* "is about building a life in harmony of human beings with themselves, with their peers and with Nature," then quotes the Bolivian philosopher Fernando Huanacuni, who, when explaining the meaning of "*sumak kawsay*," highlights the deepest sense of the term "*sumak*" as the concrete realization of what is ideally beautiful and good. The word *kawsay* "is life itself, in reference to a dignified life, in harmony, balance with the universe and the human being."[98]

(f) Guatemala

On November 7, 2019, the Constitutional Court of Guatemala issued a historic non-anthropocentric decision that, in addition to recognizing the spiritual and cultural relationship between indigenous peoples and the element of water, also recognized water as a living entity. In this sense, it declared the unconstitutionality of the Agrarian Transformation and Mining Laws for excluding the sacred character of water and, thus, making it impossible for water to be recognized as a living entity—a subject deserving of rights—which is why it cannot be killed by contamination. The decision highlighted that water is a living being that has cycles and connects with the cosmos, and moreover, for the Mayan people, water is a sacred being.[99]

---

[97] Gudynas (2019), p. 94.

[98] Acosta (2016), p. 89.

[99] Constitutional Court. Republic of Guatemala. Partial General Unconstitutionality. Available at: http://files.harmonywithnatureun.org/uploads/upload958.pdf Accessed on: Feb 03, 2025.

(g) India

On May 1, 2022, the Madras High Court in India declared Mother Nature a living being. Similarly, the Madurai court, through the ruling of Judge S. Srimathy, decided that nature holds fundamental/legal rights and constitutional rights aimed at ensuring nature's survival, security, sustenance, and resurgence to maintain its *status* and to promote its health and well-being.[100]

In 2019, the Punjab and Haryana High Court granted the *status* of "legal person or entity" to animals in Haryana, recognizing them as having the "rights, duties and corresponding responsibilities of a living person."[101]

In July 2018, the Uttarakhand High Court granted the *status* of legal person or entity to animals in the northern state.[102]

In April 2017, the Gangotri and Yamunotri glaciers of the Himalayas received the *status* of living entities, including waterfalls, meadows, lakes, and forests.[103]

The second court in world history to declare a river as a legal person was the High Court of the province of Uttarakhand, in India. In the case between Mohd. Salim v State of Uttarakhand and others (Writ Petition (PIL) No. 126 of 2014), Judge Rajiv Sharma recognized the Ganga and Yamuna Rivers, two of India's most sacred rivers, as subjects of law.[104]

In 2012, in the case TN Godavarman Thirumulpad *vs.* Union of India and others, it was expressly recognized, on the grounds of the votes of Judges K.S. Radhakrishnan and Chandramauli Kr. Prasad, that environmental justice could only be achieved by moving away from anthropocentric principles.

(h) Mexico

In 2018, the prohibition of cockfighting, within the framework of the Animal Protection Bill of the State of Veracruz, was challenged by a local entity that benefited from cockfighting, alleging that there would be a violation of the right to culture and property, among other human rights. A Supreme Court decision stated that "no practice involving mistreatment and unnecessary suffering to animals can be considered a cultural expression protected by the constitution (federal)." The Supreme Court decision set a precedent for the recognition of the rights of non-human animals.[105]

---

[100] Before the Madurai Bench of Madras High Court. W.P.(MD)Nos.18636 of 2013 and 3070 of 2020. PRONOUNCED ON: 19.04.2022. Available at: http://files.harmonywithnatureun.org/uploads/upload1274.pdf Accessed on: Feb 03, 2025.

[101] In the High Court of Punjab & Haryana at Chandigarh. Date of decision: 31.05.2019. Available at: https://www.livelaw.in/pdf_upload/pdf_upload-361239.pdf Accessed on: Feb 03, 2025.

[102] In the High Court of Uttarakhand at Nainital Writ Petition (pil) no. 43 of 2014. Available at: http://files.harmonywithnatureun.org/uploads/upload706.pdf Accessed on: Feb 04, 2015.

[103] In the High Court of Uttarakhand at Nainital. Available at: http://files.harmonywithnatureun.org/uploads/upload662.pdf Accessed on: Feb 04, 2015.

[104] Writ Petition (PIL) N°. 126 of 2014. Available at: https://www.yumpu.com/en/document/view/58002817/writ-petition-pil-no126-of-2014. Accessed on: Feb 04, 2025.

[105] Amparo en Revisión 163/2018 Complainants: Mexican Commission for Gallistic Promotion, Civil Association and Efraín Rábago Echegoyen. Available at: http://files.harmonywithnatureun.org/uploads/upload993.pdf Accessed on: Feb 04, 2025.

As we will see, the Supreme Court of Brazil has also issued a similar decision regarding vaquejada, a recreational activity that involves the mistreatment of cows.

(i) South Africa

On June 20, 2022, a petition to the High Court of South Africa, in the Gauteng-Pretoria Division, sought the release of three elephants known as Lammie, Mopane, and Ramadiba from the Johannesburg Zoo.

The demand was brought by the NGO Animal Law Reform South Africa, the EMS Foundation, and others against the Johannesburg City Parks and Zoo and other government institutions involved with the zoo. The case is awaiting judgment.

In 2018, the Supreme Court of Appeal issued a judgment on June 1, recognizing the customary rights of the indigenous Dwesa–Cwebe community to harvest mussels on the east coast of South Africa according to their ancestral custom.[106]

(j) United States

In 1972, Sierra Club versus Morton (405 U.S. 727) is known for the dissenting opinion of Judge William O. Douglas, who stated that the Sierra Mineral King Valley should have standing to bring a lawsuit for its own protection.

(k) Brazil

The jurisprudence of the Brazilian Supreme Court has taken a stance for the protection of animal welfare since 1990, when it ruled on the Case of the Farra do Boi (RE 153.531/SC) and established that the state's obligation to ensure the full exercise of cultural rights, promoting the appreciation and dissemination of manifestations, does not exempt it from observing the constitutional norm that prohibits subjecting animals to cruelty. The decision resulted in the prohibition of the Farra do Boi, an old practice in the member state of Santa Catarina.[107]

In 2007, the Supreme Court of Brazil overturned state norms of the member state of Santa Catarina (ADI 2514), considering cockfighting a cruel practice and, therefore, unconstitutional. This 2007 decision served as a precedent for other actions against laws of member states that supported cockfighting. In 2011, in the judgment of ADI 1856, the rapporteur, Minister Celso de Mello, pointed out that the practice of cockfighting "is inherently cruel, as the birds of the fighting breeds are subjected to mistreatment in competitions," and rejected the arguments that cockfights would be sports practices or cultural or folkloric manifestations.[108]

---

[106] The Supreme Court of Appeal of South Africa Judgment. Reportable Case N°: 1340/17. Available at: http://files.harmonywithnatureun.org/uploads/upload697.pdf Accessed on: Jan 31, 2025.

[107] STF. Special Environment: the STF and the defense of animal rights Court prohibited their use in product tests and the slaughter of seized animals. June 12, 2023. Available at: https://portal.stf.jus.br/noticias/verNoticiaDetalhe.asp?idConteudo=508,720&tip=UN#:~:text=Farra%20do%20Boi,pr%C3%A1tica%20antiga%20de%20Santa%20Catarina. Accessed on: Feb 06, 2025.

[108] STF. Farra do Boi. Available at: https://portal.stf.jus.br/noticias/verNoticiaDetalhe.asp?idConteudo=508,720&tip=UN#:~:text=Farra%20do%20Boi,pr%C3%A1tica%20antiga%20de%20Santa%20Catarina. Accessed on: Feb 06, 2025.

In 2016, in a historic decision, the Supreme Court of Brazil, in the judgment of ADI No. 4.983, declared the unconstitutionality of a law from the member state of Ceará, which regulates the vaquejada.[109] The Plenary of the Supreme Federal Court (STF) judged this direct action of unconstitutionality, filed by the Attorney General of the Republic against Law No. 15.299/2013, from the member state of Ceará, which regulates the vaquejada as a sports and cultural practice in the state. The majority of the ministers of the Brazilian Supreme Court followed the vote of the rapporteur, Minister Marco Aurélio, who considered there to be "intrinsic cruelty" applied to animals in the vaquejada. The judgment of the matter began in August 2015, when the rapporteur, while voting on the demand, stated that the duty of environmental protection (Art. 225 of the CF) overrides the cultural values of the sports activity.

When analyzing the foundations of the votes of the court members in this judgment, arguments are already aligned with the biocentric turn. In this sense, Minister Rosa Weber based her vote, highlighting the existence of dignity also for non-human living beings in the following excerpt from her vote: "the present evolutionary stage of humanity imposes the recognition that there is dignity beyond the human person, so the task of welcoming and introjecting the ecological dimension to the Rule of Law is present."[110]

In 2019, the Superior Court of Justice (STJ) of Brazil, in the judgment of REsp n. 1.797.175/SP, adopting an ecological perspective based on the principle of human dignity, issued a historic and paradigmatic decision that recognizes the principle of affectivity in the relationship between human beings and non-human animals, and also established the recognition of animals as subjects of law. The decision also addresses the need to change the anthropocentric legal paradigm and replace it with biocentric thinking, which promotes the interconnection and close relationship between humans and nature and also recognizes the intrinsic value of nature.

In 2021, the Plenary of the Brazilian Supreme Court decided to prohibit the slaughter of wild, domestic, or domesticated, native or exotic animals seized in situations of mistreatment. The Court declared the unconstitutionality of interpretations of provisions of the Environmental Crimes Law (Law 9.605/1998) and Decree 6.514/2008 (infractions and administrative sanctions to the environment),

---

[109] "Vaquejada is a competitive activity in which two cowboys on horseback have to knock down a bull. The animal is pulled by the tail and needs to fall between two painted lines on the ground. One cowboy is responsible for directing the bull to the line area and aligning the animal with the other cowboy, who pulls the bull's tail with his hands to knock it down. It is estimated that the practice originated in the Northeast between the 17th and 18th centuries, from certain traditions: the separation parties, which gathered cowboys to separate the herds; the bull tracks, where animals that escaped from the herd were captured; and the mourão races, where cowboys chased bulls on farms." Senate News (2016), online.

[110] STF. Direct Action of Unconstitutionality 4.983 Ceará. Oct 06, 2016. Available at: https://redir.stf.jus.br/paginadorpub/paginador.jsp?docTP=TP&docID=12,798,874 Accessed on: Feb 06, 2025.

as well as other infraconstitutional norms that authorize the immediate slaughter of these animals.

Minister Gilmar Mendes stated that, according to the correct interpretation of the Brazilian Environmental Crimes Law, the seized animals should preferably be reintegrated into their natural habitat or delivered to suitable institutions, such as zoos and foundations. He also emphasized that the Constitution of Brazil imposes on the public authorities the duty to protect fauna and flora and prohibits practices that subject animals to cruelty.[111]

Similarly, in 2021, the Brazilian Constitutional Court, when judging the Direct Action of Unconstitutionality (ADI) 5995, validated provisions of a law of the member state of Rio de Janeiro that prohibit the use of animals for the development, experiments, and tests of cosmetic products, personal hygiene items, perfumes, and cleaning products.[112]

In 2024, the Federal Supreme Court (STF) of Brazil once again considered the constitutional adequacy of the vaquejada, given that the Brazilian Parliament had promulgated Constitutional Amendment No. 96/2017, which added § 7º to Article 225 of the Federal Constitution to stipulate that sports practices involving animals are not considered cruel, under the conditions it specifies. The judgment is currently suspended; however, the vote of the Reporting Justice, Dias Toffoli, represents a setback in the Court's stance on animal cruelty, as he deemed Constitutional Amendment No. 96/2017, which legalizes the vaquejada, constitutional, arguing for the prevalence of cultural rights.

As will be demonstrated in the chapter that deals with the reaffirmation of human rights by the principle of harmony with nature, when faced with a conflict between the interests of human beings and non-human beings, it is necessary to evaluate the relevance of the interests at stake and to give weight to the basic interest. The theory of priority principles by Paul Taylor, which this work adopts, proposes that the satisfaction of non-basic human interests, which are intrinsically incompatible with the basic interests of other living beings, is a serious disregard for the dignity of living organisms, as it reinforces the idea of the instrumentality of nature.

Taylor cites examples of non-basic human interests, intrinsically incompatible with a respectful attitude toward nature, such as recreational hunting, fishing, and bullfighting. As can be seen, such activities are rooted in human culture; however, the interest in maintaining this cultural expression is a non-basic human interest intrinsically incompatible with the basic interest of animals, which is physical integrity and dignity itself.

[111] STF. Farra do Boi. Available at: https://portal.stf.jus.br/noticias/verNoticiaDetalhe.asp?idConteudo=508,720&tip=UN#:~:text=Farra%20do%20Boi,pr%C3%A1tica%20antiga%20de%20Santa%20Catarina. Accessed on: Feb 06, 2025.

[112] STF. Farra do Boi. Available at: https://portal.stf.jus.br/noticias/verNoticiaDetalhe.asp?idConteudo=508,720&tip=UN#:~:text=Farra%20do%20Boi,pr%C3%A1tica%20antiga%20de%20Santa%20Catarina. Accessed on: Feb 06, 2025.

In this vein, the vote of Justice Dias Toffoli, in recognizing the constitutionality of § 7, added by Amendment No. 96/2017, superimposes the culture of vaquejada, a non-basic human interest intrinsically harmful to animals, on the basic interest of physical integrity and biodignity of the animals involved in the cultural practice of vaquejada. This represents a violation of the principle of harmony with nature implicit in the preamble of Article 225 of the Brazilian Constitution, as will be demonstrated.

Nevertheless, the Supreme Court of Brazil has issued decisions inspired by the principle of harmony with nature, also recognizing the spiritual and identity link of the original peoples with the Earth. In this sense, on April 1, 2020, the STF ratified an innovative judicial agreement for the Ashaninka people of the state of Acre, in the Brazilian Amazon. This agreement guaranteed compensation for the damages suffered due to crimes committed more than four decades ago by a powerful family of timber explorers and politicians from the state of Acre against the Ashaninka people and their forests.

Similarly, in the judgment of ADPF 708/DF (Climate Fund Case), Justice Luís Roberto Barroso, when convening a public hearing, highlighted the autonomy of the rights of nature:

> [...] within the scope of International Human Rights Law, there has been a move towards recognizing the interdependence between the human right to a healthy environment and a multitude of other human rights, as well as affirming it as an autonomous right held by Nature itself (and not just by human beings). In this sense, there are two important decisions of the Inter-American Court of Human Rights (IACHR). In Advisory Opinion no. 23/2017, it established that the right to a healthy environment is "a universal interest" and "a fundamental right for the existence of humanity". And in the case of Indigenous Communities Members of the Lhaka Honhat Association (Our Land) versus Argentina, the first contentious case on the matter, it affirmed that States have the duty of "respect", "guarantee" and "prevention" of environmental damage, as well as the responsibility to ensure everyone's rights to food security and access to water.[113]

In the analysis of Justice Barroso's decision, a nod to biocentrism is observed when he mentions the rights of Nature as an autonomous right and makes explicit reference to the jurisprudence of the Inter-American Court of Human Rights.

In addition to the judgments of the Federal Supreme Court and the Brazilian Constitutional Court, it is important to point out the advancement of jurisprudence toward biocentrism also in the Superior Court of Justice, known as the Citizen's Court, which is responsible for the standardization of the interpretation of federal legislation by regional and state courts.

In 2018, the Fourth Chamber of the Superior Court of Justice (STJ) considered it possible to regulate judicial visits to pets after the dissolution of a stable union. In the grounds of the vote, Justice Luís Felipe Salomão highlighted:

> Seeking to meet social ends, paying attention to the evolution of society itself, regardless of the nomen iuris to be adopted, I think that the resolution should, indeed, depend on the

---

[113] https://redir.stf.jus.br/paginadorpub/paginador.jsp?docTP=TP&docID=767525003 Accessed on: Feb 06, 2025.

> analysis of the specific case, but the idea that we are not dealing with an 'inanimate thing' will be preserved, without extending to it the condition of subject of law. Thus, a third genre is recognized, in which the situation contained in the records should always be analyzed, aimed at protecting the human being and his affective bond with the animal.[114]

> As can be seen, despite not recognizing animals as subjects of law, the rapporteur's vote recognizes their affectivity. The decision represents an advance in recognizing that animals are capable of developing an affective bond, which, in itself, already demonstrates the adoption by the court of a weak anthropocentrism.

The jurisprudence of the Superior Court of Justice has also evolved significantly in consolidating procedural tools that favor the normative realization of nature's rights in reparation actions. In this sense, influenced by Minister Hermann Benjamin, a respected and recognized researcher of nature's rights, the procedural application of the theory of *in dubio pro natura* was developed.

> The legal manifestation of the complexity of ecological processes and the growing ethical, political, and legal esteem for the guarantee of environmental quality, the principle of *in dubio pro natura*, in its procedural sense, finds its remote origins in the traditional principle in dubio pro damnato (= in doubt, in favor of the injured or victim), used notably in the protection of people's physical integrity. No one questions that, as a fundamental right of present and future generations, the ecologically balanced environment demands comprehensive, effective, and efficient judicial protection, not content with rhetorical, cosmetic, theatrical, or fantasy material and procedural initiatives.[115]

The improvement of procedural procedures for the realization of nature's rights demonstrates the inclination of the Superior Court of Justice toward a weak anthropocentrism and, therefore, the realization of the principle of harmony with nature.

Finally, it is worth noting, in Brazilian jurisprudence, a decision of June 11, 2021, from the Sixth Federal Court of Florianópolis that granted an injunction in a Public Civil Action filed by the Research Group on Environmental Law and Political Ecology in Risk Society, Florianópolis (Federal University of Santa Catarina), which aims to recognize Lagoa da Conceição as a subject of rights and develop a new socio-ecological governance for the protection of the ecological integrity of its entire watershed. The injunction ensured the continuity of the action filed on May 20, 2021, ordering the creation of the Judicial Council for the Protection of Lagoa da Conceição and also recognized the rights of Nature in the following terms: "As for the recognition of the rights of Nature, art. 144 of the Organic Law of the Municipality conferred on nature the ownership of rights in its sole paragraph and ordered the Public Power to promote public policies and environmental monitoring instruments so that nature acquires ownership of rights."

---

[114] Superior Court of Justice. SPECIAL APPEAL No. 1.713.167—SP (2017/0239804-9). Available at: https://animaiscomdireitos.ufpr.br/wp-content/uploads/2019/06/stj-guarda-de-animal-de-estimacao-1.pdf.

[115] STJ. SPECIAL APPEAL No. 883.656—RS (2006/0145139-9). Available at: https://scon.stj.jus.br/SCON/GetInteiroTeorDoAcordao?num_registro=200,601,451,399&dt_publicacao=28/02/2012.

The Federal Regional Court of the Fourth Region (TRF4) confirmed, in part, the first-instance decision, making adjustments only in relation to the attributions of the CJ-PLC, deciding that it has a merely consultative character, to advise the judiciary on already judicialized issues.

(l) Pakistan

On April 15, 2021, the Supreme Court of Pakistan confirmed a decision by the Provincial Government of Punjab that prohibited the construction of new or expanded cement factories in environmentally fragile zones. The Supreme Court recognized that these cement factories could cause further depletion of groundwater, among other harmful environmental impacts. As part of its consideration, the court emphasized the need for the government to uphold the precautionary principle to protect the rights to life, sustainability, and dignity of communities around the project areas. In addition, the court recognized the need to protect the rights of nature, stating that "the environment needs to be protected for its own sake" and that "[the]man and his environment need to commit to the good of both and this peaceful coexistence requires that the law treats environmental objects as holders of legal rights."[116]

On May 21, 2020, the Islamabad High Court of Pakistan issued a decision recognizing the rights of non-human animals. In this decision, it ordered the release of the Asian elephant named Kaavan, who was kept in solitary confinement at the Marghazar Zoo, to an ecological sanctuary. The decision by Chief Justice Athar Minallah brings a comforting reflection on the COVID-19 crisis, in the sense that it brought an "opportunity for humans to introspect and relate to the pain and suffering suffered by other living beings" caused by "human arrogance."[117]

(m) Peru

On March 15, 2024, the Nauta Court in Loreto issued a paradigmatic judgment in Peruvian Earth Jurisprudence, recognizing the Marañón River as a legal entity. This decision represented a major victory for the efforts led by the Huaynakana Kamatahuara Kana Federation, a group of indigenous Kukama women from the district of Parinari, in the province and region of Loreto. The judgment established an important precedent, recognizing the inherent rights of the river, such as the right to exist, flow freely, and remain free from contamination. In addition, it highlighted the need to protect water sources, advocating for the involvement of local communities in the protection of the Amazon ecosystem.[118]

These decisions, issued by judges from all continents, bring, as a converging point, the emergence of a non-anthropocentric jurisprudence of harmony with

---

[116] In the Supreme Court of Pakistan. C.P.1290-L/2019. Available at: http://files.harmonywithnatureun.org/uploads/upload1281.pdf.

[117] In The Islamabad High Court, Islamabad (Judicial Department) W.P. No.1155/2019. Available at: http://files.harmonywithnatureun.org/uploads/upload1079.pdf.

[118] Judicial Power of Peru. Notification N° 157-2024-JM-CI. March 15, 2024. Available at: http://files.harmonywithnatureun.org/uploads/upload1475.pdf.

nature. When analyzing their foundations, it is observed that the protective scope of the environment is no longer based on the instrumental valuation of nature as a mere natural resource, a thing, and a commodity. Its normative programs are constituted by non-anthropocentric hermeneutic criteria and by the worldview of indigenous peoples, which allows for a filtering of facts and data from ecology, anthropology, and ethology, among other branches of science, in the constitution of the norm decision. These decisions have been materialized in a new paradigm of interaction between the "ought-to-be" and the "being," the latter represented by the biosphere and the Earth system sciences.

The jurisprudence, which emerges in South America under the axiological auspices of the powerful movement of the *buen-vivir* of the indigenous peoples of the Andes and the Amazon, has been the driving force for the recognition of intrinsic value and subjectivity in rivers, forests, and animals. The jurisprudence of *buen-vivir* communicates with the jurisprudence of the Brazilian courts, which, discreetly, have been making the epistemological and axiological turn toward weak anthropocentrism since the 1990s. This paradigm shift is being built through the interpretation of the Brazilian Constitution of 1988, in a jurisprudential and doctrinal movement of gradual greening of Brazilian constitutional and civil law.

This emerging jurisprudence in the courts of South America has its roots in the principle of harmony with nature, an ancestral and common value of the various indigenous peoples who still inhabit and guard the ecological integrity of the great biomes of South America: from the Andes, the Amazon, the austral forests of Tierra del Fuego, the deserts of Salta and Atacama, the Pantanal, the Cerrado, the Pampas, the Atlantic Forest, and the Caatinga.

The Jurisprudence of Harmony with Nature in South America, before being constituted in the signs of the legal language of the Constitutional Courts, was sung in the dreams of indigenous women and men who, since 1500, have dreamed of liberating Pachamama from colonial shackles. This non-anthropocentric jurisprudence, before being written by judges in the texts of constitutional norms and in the Declarations of Law of international courts, was forged with a powerful amalgam: the sap of thousands of trees felled in the Amazon; the blood of indigenous women, men, and children murdered in the struggle for land; the despair of millions of mammals, birds, reptiles, and insects carbonized by the indiscriminate expansion of the frontiers of agropastoral production; and the vomit of the Earth wounded by the deadly toxicity of mercury from mining.

This non-anthropocentric jurisprudence of the South American Courts, which was born from the enunciative social fact of the degradation of life in forests, fields, deserts, mountains, and swamps, shares a common axiological sense with the jurisprudence that recognizes the rights of the living water in Guatemala, the great rivers in India, Pakistan, and Bangladesh, and the rights of animals in South Africa and Mexico. This sense, shared by courts of such diverse countries on different continents, is the principle of harmony with nature.

All these decisions were guided by a higher value, which is harmony with nature itself, and all have common characteristics: (1) They see the Earth, rivers, forests, water, animals, and ecosystems through a new ontological window, as they overcome the nature/culture dichotomy. This new jurisprudence starts from the ontological premise that humanity is part of nature, that is, it lives in an inseparable relationship of interdependence with other living beings, not only in the biological dimension but also in the affective and spiritual dimensions. (2) These decisions adopt a new ethical paradigm, as they recognize in non-human living beings an end value and not just a means or an instrument, a natural resource at the service of society. (3) This jurisprudence brings a decolonizing seed because it considers the relevance of the cultural identity of the original peoples of the planet for the harmony of the human being with nature. (4) The decisions rendered by these courts, from such diverse cultural contexts, present a common and innovative legal aspect in legal dogmatics: the displacement of nature, that is, of rivers, forests, seas, and animals, from the legal category of "thing" to that of "subjects of law." (5) All these decisions are animated by a purpose of interconnection between the human being and non-human living beings. (6) These decisions are based on the norms of international environmental law, as well as regional and global declarations of human rights.

These values, which are shared by various cultures, are being adopted as a reason for decision-making by courts of various legal systems when judging conflicts about the relations of the human being with nature, thus consolidating the jurisprudence of harmony with nature.

As can be seen, the courts of various countries, on different continents, are being challenged to solve similar problems, which arose with the crisis of the Anthropocene. Faced with these concrete problems, they are rendering decisions guided by a common hermeneutic principle of harmony with nature, which bundles ethical values shared by original peoples who inhabit such diverse regions of the planet.

This jurisprudential movement is similar to the one that, centuries ago, established good faith as an ethical and legal principle based on trust and coherence to regulate conduct in relations between human beings. In the present century, the courts of various countries are taking a step forward in recognizing the existence of an ethical and legal principle of trust and coherence, intended to guide the relations of human beings with non-human beings and holistic organic entities.

5.4.1 A Brief Analysis of Legal Provisions and Other Official Documents Recognizing the Rights of Nature in Various Countries

In addition to the non-anthropocentric jurisprudence developed in the courts of various countries, there is a global movement to positivize the rights of nature in constitutions, national and local laws, and other normative acts. The United Nations' Harmony with Nature website reports on this legislative movement, briefly explaining the new laws regarding the rights of nature, as well as the influence of social movements in this ongoing evolution of humanity's legal consciousness that also consolidates, in positive law, the principle of harmony with nature:

(a) Argentina National Law/Federal Law: 2020—Proposal for national regulation on the rights of nature.[119]

Local Regulations

2020—On October 13, Representative Valeria López Delzar (CREO-Santa Fé Party) presented an ordinance on the Rights of Nature to the Deliberative Council of the municipality of Santa FÉ.[120]

2020—On November 26, the Municipality of the city of Rosario adopted a decision declaring its support for the recognition of the Paraná River and the Wetlands as subjects of rights. The petition was presented by Dr. Aníbal Faccendini, Director of the Water Faculty of the National University of Rosario, in partnership with the Interdisciplinary Water Center of the Faculty of Political Sciences and International Relations of the same university, along with a significant number of local NGOs and academic institutions.[121]

2020—On November 23, Representative Carlos Del Frade (Social and Popular Front Party—Province of Santa Fe) presented a Bill on the Rights of Nature to the Chamber of Deputies of Santa Fé.[122]

2019—A proposal to amend the Constitution of the Province of Santa Fé to include the rights of nature is currently being debated by members of local government.

2018—The municipal council of the city of Santa Fé approved a local ordinance recognizing, in its Article 4, the rights of nature. The ordinance must be promulgated by the Mayor of the city of Santa Fé. The ordinance was originally submitted to the municipal council by the city of Santa Fé's governmental and citizen security commission.[123]

---

[119] Bill. Protection of the rights of nature. Available at: http://files.harmonywithnatureun.org/uploads/upload1037.pdf. Accessed on: January 31, 2025.

[120] Ordinance project. Rights of nature. Available at: http://files.harmonywithnatureun.org/uploads/upload1038.pdf Accessed on: January 31, 2025.

[121] La Capital. The proposal to declare the Paraná and the wetlands as a legal entity is of municipal interest. November 27, 2020. Available at: https://www.lacapital.com.ar/la-ciudad/es-interes-municipal-la-propuesta-declarar-persona-juridica-al-parana-y-los-humedales-n2626517.html.

[122] Chamber of Deputies of the Province of Santa Fe. The Province of Santa Fe Enacts with Force of Law. November 23, 2020. Available at: http://files.harmonywithnatureun.org/uploads/upload1050.pdf.

[123] Commission of Government and Citizen Security. Available at: http://files.harmonywithnatureun.org/uploads/upload725.pdf.

(b) Australia

National Law/Federal Law

2020—Approval on June 16 of the law called "The Great Ocean Road and Environs Protection Act," which recognizes the Great Ocean Road as "a living and integrated natural entity."[124]

2017—The Victorian Parliament approved, on September 21, the Yarra River Protection (Wilip-gin Birrarung murron) Act of 2017. The law legally recognizes the Yarra as an indivisible living entity that deserves protection. The law also acknowledges the intrinsic connection of traditional owners with the Yarra River and recognizes them as the guardians of the land and waterway they call Birrarung.[125]

Local Regulations

On March 31, 2020, the Blue Mountains Municipal Council of the Government of New South Wales supported a draft from the Mayor and agreed to integrate the Rights of Nature into future operations and planning. The Mayor of Blue Mountains, Mark Greenhill, said: "In practice, embracing the Rights of Nature in law means rejecting the notion that nature is merely human property to be used and, often, abused, but, instead, that it has the right to exist, thrive and evolve—just like us."[126]

On November 24, 2019, Diane Evers, a member of the Parliament of Western Australia, presented the Rights of Nature and Future Generations Bill of 2019. This was the first time that legislation aiming to recognize the rights of nature was presented in an Australian Parliament.[127]

(c) Belgium On May 3, 2019, the Aadewerk NGO for socio-ecological transition submitted a "Voluntary Intervention Petition to Protect Trees" to the French-speaking Court of First Instance. Lawyers Hendrik Schoukens and Gwidje Vermeire presented the petition on behalf of 82 protected trees, postulating the legal recognition of nature.[128]

---

[124] "(Section 1 (a)). The Great Ocean Road is an iconic coastal road along the southern coast of Victoria, with spectacular views over beaches and tall forests, connecting regional towns and national parks and is one of Victoria's major tourist destinations. The legislation also strengthens the involvement of Traditional Owners in the governance of the coast and parks. This legislation is the second statute of its kind in Victoria to recognize part of Nature as a living and integrated natural entity (the first being the Bierrarung/Yarra River, also in Victoria)." Great Ocean Road and Environs Protection Act 2020 No. 19 of 2020. Available at: https://content.legislation.vic.gov.au/sites/default/files/2020-06/20-019aa%20authorised.pdf.

[125] Authorised Version No. 005 Yarra River Protection (Wilip-gin Birrarung murron) Act 2017 No. 49 of 2017. Available at: http://files.harmonywithnatureun.org/uploads/upload1000.pdf.

[126] Council resolves to integrate Rights of Nature into operations and planning. April 15, 2020. Available at: https://www.bmcc.nsw.gov.au/media-centre/council-resolves-to-integrate-rights-of-nature-into-operations-and-planning.

[127] Rights of Nature and Future Generations Bill 2019. Available at: http://files.harmonywithnatureun.org/uploads/upload898.pdf.

[128] Request for voluntary intervention. Art. 813 of the Judicial Code. Available at: http://files.harmonywithnatureun.org/uploads/upload1111.pdf.

(d) Belize

National Law/Federal Law
The adoption of an indefinite moratorium, sanctioned by law on December 29, 2017, to preserve the reef considered a World Heritage site, is based on the prior recognition of nature as a subject of rights.[129]

(e) Bolivia

National Law/Federal Law
Law 300 of 2012
Law 071 of 2010

Other Official Documents
2024—On April 16, at the 23rd Session of the UN Permanent Forum on Indigenous Issues, the Vice-Presidency of the Plurinational State of Bolivia launched the "Plural Wisdoms of Indigenous and Original Peoples Towards a Cosmobiocentric World from the Codes of Good Living" to reaffirm the voices of the world's indigenous peoples and promote their self-determination within the framework of the United Nations Declaration on the Rights of Indigenous Peoples, recognizing them as caretakers of Mother Earth or Nature.[130]

2023—On December 21, the Government of the Plurinational State of Bolivia released the first report of Vivir Bien (Living Well), a life horizon enshrined in the constitution promulgated in 2009 to live in harmony and balance with Mother Earth and people.[131]

2023—On March 23, at the Plenary of the Andean Parliament, the "Declaration for the Assembly of Mother Earth—2024" was adopted. Click on the official document. The supranational representatives of the Parliamentary Assembly of the Plurinational State of Bolivia requested support for the approval of resolutions on regional integration entities "Towards the Assembly of Mother Earth in 2024."[132]

2021—On October 28, the Vice-Presidency of the Plurinational State of Bolivia, through the General Directorate of Geopolitics of Good Living and Foreign Policy, organized the Qutamama Summit. The summit declared Lake Titicaca a subject of rights.[133]

---

[129] In the Court of Appeal of Belize, A.D. 2011. Civil Appeal no. 19 of 2010. Available at: http://files.harmonywithnatureun.org/uploads/upload715.pdf.

[130] Codes of living well. Available at: https://codigosvivirbien.bo/en/.

[131] Report on living well. Bolivia, 2023. Available at: https://www.vicepresidencia.gob.bo/IMG/pdf/informe_del_vivir_bien_epb.pdf.

[132] Andean Parliament. Declaration "Towards the assembly of Mother Earth—2024". Available at: http://files.harmonywithnatureun.org/uploads/upload1518.pdf.

[133] Call of the Q'uta Mama. Available at: http://files.harmonywithnatureun.org/uploads/upload1171.pdf.

(f) Brazil

Municipal Organic Law

Local Regulations

2023—The member state of Mato Grosso do Sul established several protective measures for the Pantanal Biome. Law No. 6160, of December 18, 2023, among other measures, provides the following: (1) prohibition of the cultivation of soy, sugarcane, eucalyptus, and other exotic crops; (2) special protection of capões and cordilleras with tree-shrub vegetation; (3) permission for pasture cleaning for extensive livestock purposes, with authorization from the environmental agency; (4) permission for constructions and buildings related to ecotourism and rural tourism activities; (5) prohibition of the implementation of agricultural projects and intensive livestock; and (6) prohibition of the installation and operation of small hydroelectric plants.[134]

2024—On June 5, the municipality of Goiás (Goiás) recognized the Red River as a subject of rights.[135]

2024—In June, the municipality of Linhares (Espírito Santo) approved a bill recognizing the Waves of the Sea at the Mouth of the Doce River as entities possessing rights.[136]

2024—On April 15, the Mosquito River (Minas Gerais) was recognized as a subject of rights.[137]

2023—On June 11, the Municipality of José de Freitas (Piauí) recognized the Rights of Nature in its Organic Law. The proposal was formalized as a project to amend the Organic Law by the councilwoman of the Municipality of José de Freitas—PI, Yarema Leite Rodrigues de Sousa Alves (Solidarity Party). These measures were promoted by Law Professor Mariana Ribeiro Santiago (University of Marília-São Paulo), Ian Cavalcante, a student in the Master's Program at the same university, and Igor Miranda de Carvalho, a public law specialist from the Motiro/ACERM Association, through its representative Anne Nathyelle de Sousa Silva, by the Municipal Secretary of Urban Policies of the Municipality of José de Freitas—PI, Aerton Ezequiel

---

[134] MS.GOV. Pantanal Law comes into effect, government focuses on enforcement and decree brings first regulations. February 19, 2024. Available at: https://www.ms.gov.br/noticias/lei-do-pantanal-entra-em-vigor-governo-foca-na-fiscalizacao-e-decreto-traz-primeiras-regulamentacoes.

[135] Brazilian River Gains Legal Personhood. August 23, 2023. Available at: https://www.faithinnature.co.uk/blogs/notes-on-nature/brazilian-river-gains-legal-personhood.

[136] Bill No. /2023. Establishes the Rights of the Waves of the Doce River Mouth, in the Municipality of Linhares. Available at: http://files.harmonywithnatureun.org/uploads/upload1510.pdf.

[137] Law No. 2,251, of April 15, 2024. Available at: https://leismunicipais.com.br/a/mg/p/porteirinha/lei-ordinaria/2024/226/2251/lei-ordinaria-n-2251-2024-dispoe-sobre-o-reconhecimento-dos-direitos-do-rio-mosquito-afluente-do-rio-gorutuba-no-municipio-de-porteirinha-e-seu-enquadramento-como-ente-especialmente-protegido-e-da-outras-providencias.

Alves, and by INSOL, an extension project, a solidarity incubator of the University of Marília-São Paulo-UNIMAR.[138]

2024—In March, the Municipality of Santo Antônio do Itambé (Mato Grosso) recognized the rights of Nature in the Serra do Itambé, located in the municipality of Santo Antônio do Itambé, along with its rivers and the Pico da Montanha do Itambé.[139]

2023—On April 17, in the Municipality of Guajará-Mirim (Rondônia), the municipal legislative chamber unanimously recognized the Laje River as a subject of rights. The law was proposed by Indigenous Councilman Francisco Oro Waram, supported by Indigenous Councilman Wen Cacami, and by the NGOs Comvida and Mapas. This is the first river in Brazil with rights and belonging to the Amazon region—a great achievement for the Wari Indigenous Community.[140]

2023—On June 5, the Municipality of Cáceres (Mato Grosso) included the Rights of Nature in its Organic Law. After public hearings to consider Nature as a subject of rights, the proposal was formalized as a project to amend the Organic Law by Councilman Cézare Pastorello (PT). A significant number of civil society organizations participated in the public hearings: Instituto Fé e Vida, Instituto Gaia, Rio Paraguai/Pantanal Committee, ARPA Regional (Regional Association of Agroecological Producers), FORMAD (Mato Grosso Forum for Environment and Development), and Mireni de Oliveira Costa Silva, a doctoral student of the Postgraduate Program at the University of Marília (PPGD/UNIMAR).[141]

2023—On December 4, the Municipality of Alto Paraguai (Mato Grosso) included the Rights of Nature in its Organic Law, recognizing the principle of Harmony with Nature and the Rights of Nature. The bill to amend the law was proposed by Councilman Rozinei Rodrigues da Silva (Mayor), in collaboration with a significant number of high-level authorities, including professors Mariana Ribeiro Santiago (University of Marília-São Paulo), Éverton Neves dos Santos, and Alessandro de Almeida Santana Souza (State University of Mato Grosso), as well as a significant number of academic institutions.[142]

2023—On October 10, the Municipality of Alagoa Nova (Paraíba), within the framework of the reform of the General Organic Law, adopted legislation recognizing the Rights of Nature.[143]

---

[138] Amendment to the Organic Law No. 02/2023. Available at: http://files.harmonywithnatureun.org/uploads/upload1515.pdf.

[139] Proposed Amendment to the Organic Law 001/2020. Available at: http://files.harmonywithnatureun.org/uploads/upload1516.pdf.

[140] Bill No. 007/2023. Available at: http://files.harmonywithnatureun.org/uploads/upload1415.pdf.

[141] Amendment to the Organic Law. Cácares. Available at: http://files.harmonywithnatureun.org/uploads/upload1420.pdf.

[142] Proposed Amendment to the Municipal Legislation-Amendment to the Organic Law of the municipality of Alto Paraguai-MT. Available at: http://files.harmonywithnatureun.org/uploads/upload1514.pdf.

[143] Proposed Amendment to the Municipal Legislation-Amendment to the Organic Law of the municipality of Alto Paraguai-MT. Available at: http://files.harmonywithnatureun.org/uploads/upload1448.pdf.

2022—On June 2, in the Municipality of Serro (Minas Gerais), Councilwoman Karine Roza de Oliveira Santos, President of the Legislation and Justice Committee, with the support of the NGO MAPAS, approved an amendment to the municipality's Organic Law recognizing the rights of nature in its Article 157, no. 1, I, with special reference to the protection and recovery of the Cerrado and the Atlantic Forest, including the maintenance of their conservation units and reforestation, especially on the banks of rivers, aiming at their perpetuity to protect them from mining companies. The official document is available only in Portuguese (see Section IX, Article 157).[144]

2019—The Florianópolis City Council voted to adopt Organic Law 133 of the Municipality of Florianópolis, granting rights to nature. The Organic Law came into effect on November 20, 2019.[145]

2018—Amendment to the Organic Law of the Municipality of Paudalho in the State of Pernambuco adopts the Rights of Nature.[146]

2017—Amendment to the Organic Law of the Municipality of Bonito in the State of Pernambuco adopts the Rights of Nature.[147]

2015—São Paulo—Amendment Project to the Organic Law 04–00005/2015 by Councilman Eduardo Tuma (PSDB).

(g) Canada

National Law/Federal Law

2022—On May 5, the House of Commons of Canada conducted a first reading of Bill C-271, a law to give legal capacity to the St. Lawrence River, provide measures respecting its protection, and establish the St. Lawrence River Protection Committee. The federal bill was introduced by MP Alexandre Boulerice, who participated in the 11th interactive dialog of the General Assembly on Harmony with Nature, held on April 22. The International Observatory on the Rights of Nature (IORN) worked closely with political parties, research centers, municipalities, indigenous nations, and NGOs to support the development of these initiatives.[148]

2022—On May 5, the National Assembly of Quebec conducted a first reading of Bill 990, a law to confer rights to the St. Lawrence River, including the rights to protection, conservation, and restoration, and establishes a council of guardians under the name of "Conseil des gardiens du Fleuve," whose mandate is to protect

[144] Organic Law of the Municipality. Available at: http://files.harmonywithnatureun.org/uploads/upload1282.pdf.

[145] Report of propositions. Available at: http://files.harmonywithnatureun.org/uploads/upload885.pdf.

[146] Amendment to the Organic Law No. 03, of January 5, 2018. Available at: http://files.harmonywithnatureun.org/uploads/upload720.pdf.

[147] Official Gazette. Itamaracá. Available at: http://files.harmonywithnatureun.org/uploads/upload644.pdf.

[148] Bill C-271 Project of Law C-271. Available at: http://files.harmonywithnatureun.org/uploads/upload1277.pdf.

the interests of the river. The provincial bill was introduced by Émilise Lessard-Therrien of the Quebec Solidaire Party. The IORN worked closely with political parties, research centers, municipalities, indigenous nations, and NGOs to support the development of these initiatives.[149]

Local Regulations

2021—In Quebec, a province of Canada, the Innu Council of Ekuanitshit and the Regional County Municipality of Minganie granted legal personality to the Magpie River/Muteshekau Shipu (in Innu) through the adoption of twin resolutions. The river, therefore, was granted nine rights, as well as potential legal guardians primarily responsible for ensuring that these rights are respected. This is the first case of its kind in Canada, made in partnership with the IORN, based in Montreal. Click on the video. Click on the English article.[150]

2020—The First Nations people of Esdilagh (translated as "Where the Land meets the Water") of the Tsilhqot'in Nation documented their rights and responsibilities as traditional caretakers of the Elhdaqox (Sturgeon River, also known as the Fraser River). Endorsed by the Tsilhqot'in Chiefs Council on May 28, 2020, the Esdilagh Sturgeon River Law declares that people, animals, fish, plants, the nen (lands), and the tu (waters) have rights. Click on the article.[151]

2022[152]—On January 19, the city of Sainte-Flavie in Quebec joined the newly launched St. Lawrence River Alliance between cities and indigenous peoples, proposed by the IORN in December 2021. During the period from December 6 to 14, 2021, the cities of Sorel-Tracy and Saint-Catherine in Quebec, as well as the Mamuitun Tribal Council that brings together five Innu Nations, supported the Alliance, eager to present a bill to recognize the legal personality of the river. Click on the article. Click on the official documents of the cities of Sainte-Flavie, Sorel-Tracy, Saint-Catherine, and the Mamuitun Tribal Council.

2023—On April 19, the Assembly of First Nations recognized the legal personality of the St. Lawrence River and directed Chief Picard, Chief of the Assembly, to build an alliance with other indigenous nations living in the Great Lakes watershed to recognize the legal personality of the Great Lakes.[153]

(h) Chile 2022—On March 25, the Plenary of the Constitutional Convention of Chile approved the project report presented by the Commission on Environment, Rights of Nature, Common Goods, and Economic Model that recognized the Rights

[149] Bill No. 990. Available at: http://files.harmonywithnatureun.org/uploads/upload1276.pdf.

[150] Excerpt from the minutes of the regular session of the MRC de Minganie council held by videoconference on February 16, 2021 at 3 p.m. Available at: http://files.harmonywithnatureun.org/uploads/upload1069.pdf.

[151] Tŝilhqot'in Nation. ʔELHDAQOX DECHEN TS'EDILHTAN. Available at: http://files.harmonywithnatureun.org/uploads/upload995.pdf.

[152] Resolution 2022-01-018. Available at: http://files.harmonywithnatureun.org/uploads/upload1161.pdf.

[153] Resolution No. 04-2023. Available at: http://files.harmonywithnatureun.org/uploads/upload1423.pdf.

of Nature (Art. 4): "On the Rights of Nature. Nature has the right to respect and protect its existence, to regeneration, to the maintenance and restoration of its functions and dynamic balances, which includes natural cycles, ecosystems, and biodiversity. The State, through its institutions, must guarantee and promote the rights of Nature in accordance with the determination of the Constitution and Laws." Other approved articles include Waste Management, Environmental Principles, Climate and Ecological Crises, Animal Rights, and Environmental Democracy.[154]

(i) Colombia

Local Regulation
2019—The department of Nariño became the first in the country to recognize nature as a subject of rights by signing Decree 348.[155]

(j) El Salvador

Constitution
2020—The non-governmental organizations Ecología Rebelde, Sí por los Derechos de la Naturaleza, and the Asociación Comunitaria Unida por el Agua y la Agricultura will present a proposal to the Legislative Assembly to amend the Constitution of El Salvador. The constitutional amendment would include the recognition of the Rights of Nature through an article stating: "Nature is also recognized as a subject of rights, as it generates, reproduces and carries out life. It also recognizes the rights to full respect for its existence, to the maintenance and regeneration of its life cycles, structure, functions and evolutionary processes."[156]

National Law/Federal Law
2020—The NGO Sí por los Derechos de la Naturaleza is working on a proposal to recognize the rights of the Río Lempa, the main river of El Salvador, which shares its basin with Guatemala and Honduras.[157]

(k) Spain

National Law/Federal Law
2022—On September 30, the Parliament approved Law 19/2022, recognizing the legal personality of the Mar Menor and its basin, thus becoming the first ecosystem in Europe with its own rights.[158]

---

[154] Official Letter No. 659. Available at: http://files.harmonywithnatureun.org/uploads/upload1195.pdf.

[155] Decree No. 348. Available at: http://files.harmonywithnatureun.org/uploads/upload858.pdf.

[156] Proposal for Constitutional Reform to Incorporate the Rights of Nature. Available at: http://files.harmonywithnatureun.org/uploads/upload990.pdf.

[157] Preliminary Draft of the Declaration and Recognition of the Rights of the Lempa River as a Subject of Rights in El Salvador. July 2020. Available at: http://files.harmonywithnatureun.org/uploads/upload992.pdf.

[158] Law 19/2022, of September 30, for the recognition of legal personality to the Mar Menor lagoon and its basin. Available at: http://files.harmonywithnatureun.org/uploads/upload1287.pdf.

2022—On April 5, the Popular Legislative Initiative (ILP) to recognize the Mar Menor and its entire basin as a subject with rights was voted on by an overwhelming majority in the Congress of Deputies, which approved the start of the processing of a law for the Mar Menor to have legal personality.[159]

Local Regulations

2020—On July 23, the Municipality of Los Alcázares, in Murcia, adopted the ILP to recognize the Mar Menor and its entire basin, the largest saltwater lagoon in Europe, as a subject of rights.[160]

(l) France

Constitution

2018—A constitutional reform to further amend the Constitution (1958) and the Environmental Charter (2004) was initiated on July 10. More than 20 amendments addressing, among other issues, the rights of the living, animal welfare, global commons, the crime of ecocide, and the principle of non-environmental regression were presented by parliamentarians, signaling a trend toward a more Earth-centered constitutional process.[161]

Local Regulations

2023—On June 29, the Assembly of the Province of the Loyalty Islands in New Caledonia, with its strong normative competence in environmental issues and in the application of the unitary principle of life enshrined in 2016 in Article 110–3, enriched the PIL Environmental Code (CEPIL) by adopting regulations on the law of living organisms, creating natural entities subject to law (ENJ), a new category of legal person that does not exist in France or in any other overseas territory. The category of natural entities subject to law (ENJ) was created as the highest category in its nomenclature of protected species and natural areas. Sharks and turtles are the first beneficiaries of this new status. Click on the article. Click on the official document.[162]

2016—The Loyalty Islands, part of the French territory of New Caledonia, inhabited by 90% of the Kanak people, adopted the first phase of their environmental code on April 6, through which certain elements of nature can be recognized in their own rights (see page 7, Articles 110-1 and 110-3).[163]

---

[159] Bill for the recognition of legal personality to the Mar Menor lagoon and its basin. Available at: http://files.harmonywithnatureun.org/uploads/upload1197.pdf.

[160] El País. The municipality of Los Alcázares approves a legislative initiative to give its own rights to the Mar Menor. Jul 23, 2020. Available at: https://elpais.com/sociedad/2020-07-23/el-municipio-de-los-alcazares-aprueba-una-iniciativa-legislativa-para-dar-derechos-propios-al-mar-menor.html.

[161] National Assembly June 22, 2018. Available at: http://files.harmonywithnatureun.org/uploads/upload716.pdf.

[162] The 2nd Edition of the Environmental Code of the Loyalty Islands Province. March 18, 2024. Available at: https://www.province-iles.nc/actualite/la-2e-edition-du-code-de-lenvironnement-de-la-province-des-iles-loyaute.

[163] Official Journal of New Caledonia. June 23, 2016. Available at: http://files.harmonywithnatureun.org/uploads/upload704.pdf.

(m) India

Constitution

2020—The Punjab and Haryana High Court of Chandigarh, on March 2, declared Sukhna Lake a legal entity for its survival, preservation, and conservation, and mandated all citizens of Chandigarh to save the lake from extinction.[164]

(n) Mexico

Constitution

2024—On April 22, International Mother Earth Day, the Congress of the State of Mexico approved the reform of Articles 5 and 18 of the State Constitution, recognizing the Rights of Nature or Biodiversity, as well as native endemic species, as subjects with rights in the State of Mexico.[165]

2021—On July 29, the Local Congress of the State of Mexico unanimously approved elevating the status of the Rights of Nature to the federal constitutional level. The constitutional amendment was presented by Congressman Max Correa in close collaboration with experts from the UN's HwN Program and the Earth Law Center. The proposal will be submitted to the Senate of the Mexican Republic for a vote.[166]

2020—On November 18, 2020, Congressman Fredie Delfín Avendaño (Morena Political Party) presented to the Honorable Congress of the State of Oaxaca (Mexico) the proposal to reform paragraph 39 and to add new paragraphs 40, 41, and 42 of Article 12 of the Political Constitution of the Free and Sovereign State of Oaxaca to include the Rights of Nature. This proposal will be analyzed by the Permanent Commission of Constitutional Studies and is expected to be approved in early 2021.[167]

2019 State Constitution (Federal State)

On June 10, 2019, the Congress of the State of Colima approved an amendment to the State Constitution, recognizing the Rights of Nature.[168]

---

[164] CWP No.18253 of 2009 & other connected petitions. Available at: http://files.harmonywithnatureun.org/uploads/upload994.pdf.

[165] Announcement 2802 April 23, 2024. Available at: http://files.harmonywithnatureun.org/uploads/upload1497.pdf.

[166] National Information. Mexiquense Congress approves initiative that elevates the rights of nature to constitutional rank. Available at: https://informativonacional.com.mx/congreso-mexiquense-aprueba-iniciativa-que-eleva-a-rango-constitucional-los-derechos-de-la-naturaleza-e3TU3NDAwNQ.html.

[167] Morena Parliamentary Group. Available at: http://files.harmonywithnatureun.org/uploads/upload1052.pdf.

[168] Colima makes history: The Rights of Nature are recognized in the Constitution. Available at: https://blancalivier.wordpress.com/2019/06/10/colima-hace-historia-reconocen-los-derechos-de-la-naturaleza-en-la-constitucion/?fbclid=IwAR2izFAuK6Iax4Z5hbXuHnzB5UTPKyTi-_0HEBqy9UempoCzOoRHYJS4y74.

Constitution of Mexico City

On January 31, 2017, the new constitution of Mexico City adopted the rights of nature in its Article 13, paragraphs 2 and 3, page 47 of the constitution. On February 5, 2017, the new constitution was promulgated and came into effect on September 17, 2018.[169]

2014 State Constitution (Federal State)

The Constitution of the State of Guerrero, amended on June 30, 2014, recognizes in its Article 2 the Rights of Nature.[170]

National Law/Federal Law

2013 Environmental Law for the Protection of the Earth.[171]

In the Federal District of Mexico, the Environmental Law for the Protection of the Earth came into effect on October 17, 2013. The relevant sections are highlighted in the document.

Local Regulations

2022—On May 5, in the corresponding commissions of the local Congress of the State of Mexico on the drafting of the bill on the "Promotion and Protection of Native Corn in the State of Mexico," the language proposed by the UN HwN Knowledge Network specialist and Operational Director of ELC Mexico, Claudia Brindis, recognizing the intrinsic value of corn and the inherent rights to exist, flourish, regenerate, evolve, and its rights to restoration, recovery, and preservation, was included. The bill was presented by Congressman Max Correa, who participated in the 11th interactive dialog of the General Assembly on Harmony with Nature, held on April 22. The opinion document is expected to be approved on May 12 at 12:00 p.m. (Mexico City time) in the commissions and on Thursday, May 13, in the plenary of the Congress.[172]

2020—On December 10, Congressman Fredie Delfín Avendaño presented to the Honorable Congress of the State of Oaxaca (Mexico) a bill for the "Defense and Recognition of the Rights of Rivers and Other Water Sources of the State of Oaxaca," in partnership with Congressman Horacio Soza Villavicencio and UN HwN Knowledge Network experts Claudia Brindis and Grant Wilson. The bill is regulatory of the constitutional reform of Article 12 of the Constitution of Oaxaca and establishes that all rivers and other water sources are subjects of rights. The bill will be reviewed by the Permanent Water Commission, and a verdict is expected to be issued in mid-2021.[173]

[169] Political Constitution of Mexico City. Available at: http://files.harmonywithnatureun.org/uploads/upload1288.pdf.

[170] Political Constitution of the Free and Sovereign State of Guerrero. Available at: http://files.harmonywithnatureun.org/uploads/upload665.pdf.

[171] Environmental Law for Earth Protection in the Federal District. Available at: http://files.harmonywithnatureun.org/uploads/upload686.pdf.

[172] http://harmonywithnatureun.org/rightsOfNature/.

[173] Morena Parliamentary Group. DFDA/LXIV/OFIC. 072/2020. Available at: http://files.harmonywithnatureun.org/uploads/upload1078.pdf.

2019—The Local Human Rights Commission of the State of Guerrero agrees to receive complaints about violations of the Rights of Nature in cases presented by citizens regarding animal abuse at the Zochilpan Zoo.[174]

(o) Netherlands

Local Regulations

2023—The municipality of Eijsden-Margraten became the first municipality in the country to approve a motion to locally implement the Rights of Nature.[175]

2019—The Frisian municipality of Dongeradeel, which in 2018 adopted a motion on special rights for the Wadden Sea, merged in 2019 with three other Frisian municipalities into the municipality of Noardeast-Fryslân. On July 11, 2019, the municipal council of Noardeast-Fryslân approved a motion proposing the granting of special rights for the Wadden Sea. In addition, the municipal council requested the appointment of an independent governance authority for the ecosystem. The existing authority cannot be considered independent, as it is part of the local government.[176]

(p) New Zealand

National Law/Federal Law

2017—In March, the Whanganui River was granted legal status as a person.[177]

2014—In July, Te Urewera, formerly a national park, was removed from the national parks system and was legally recognized as "a legal entity" with "all the rights, powers, duties and responsibilities of a legal person" (Section 11(1)). Te Urewera is administered by the new Te Urewera Board, responsible for "acting on behalf of, and in the name of, Te Urewera" (s 17(a)).[178]

(q) Nigeria

National Law/Federal Law

The final stage for the recognition of River Ethiope as a person with legal rights is set, awaiting the final review by the Delta State Assembly.[179]

---

[174] Human Rights Commission of the State of Guerrero. Chilpancingo de los Bravo, Guerrero, December 13, 2018. Available at: http://files.harmonywithnatureun.org/uploads/upload1022.pdf.

[175] Rights for Nature Motion by the Council of the Municipality of Eijsden-Margraten in session on November 7, 2023 Discussing the Program Budget 2024–2027. Available at: http://files.harmonywithnatureun.org/uploads/upload1509.pdf.

[176] Motion Art. 49 RvO. Available at: http://files.harmonywithnatureun.org/uploads/upload974.pdf.

[177] Te Awa Tupua (Whanganui River Claims Settlement) Act 2017. Available at: http://files.harmonywithnatureun.org/uploads/upload711.pdf.

[178] New Zealand Legislation. Te Urewera Act 2014. Available at: https://www.legislation.govt.nz/act/public/2014/0051/latest/whole.html.

[179] Notice of Presentation of a Bill. Available at: http://files.harmonywithnatureun.org/uploads/upload1504.pdf.

(r) Panama

National Law/Federal Law

2024—On June 28, the Minister of Environment, Milciades Concepción, signed Ministerial Decree No. 0123, declaring the new Sagoba National Wildlife Refuge in the Pearl Islands Archipelago a refuge to protect marine turtles, recognizing and defending their rights. This is the first proactive, national-level implementation of Law 287, recognizing the Rights of Nature in Panama.[180]

2022—On February 24, the President of the Republic of Panama signed the law titled "That Recognizes the Rights of Nature and the Obligations of the State related to these Rights." Article 1 of the law states, among other things, that "Nature is a subject of rights and the State and people have the obligation to protect and respect these rights." On September 23, 2020, the bill was initially presented to the National Assembly by Senator Juan Diego Vásquez. Click on the press release (in English, followed by Spanish).[181]

2020—On September 23, Senator Juan Diego Vasquez presented to the National Assembly a bill recognizing the rights of nature, which was officially accepted and will be voted on during 2021. Senator Vasquez drafted the bill in close collaboration with Callie Veelenturf, director of The Leatherback Project and founder of the Rights of Nature, who originally presented the project in conjunction with Felipe Baker, a biology student and part of the Ngöbe-Buglé indigenous community, to Senator Vasquez and the First Lady of Panama, Yazmin Cortizo. The lawyers Irma Hernandez, Juan Diego Infante, and Luisa Pilar Arauz Arredondo collaborated in the development of the bill. The bill has now entered the debate phase before the final vote during 2021.[182]

(s) Switzerland

Constitution

2021—On March 19, National Councilors Jon Pult (SP), Anna Giacometti (FDP), Marionna Schlatter-Schmid (Green), Nik Gugger (EPP), and Beat Flach (GLP), representing five different political parties, submitted a Nature's Rights Initiative to the Swiss Parliament, requesting the recognition of the right to a healthy environment and Nature's Rights. The initiative also requests that the Federal Constitution be amended to recognize nature as a legal entity.[183]

---

[180] Ministry of Environment. Panama creates a new Wildlife Refuge for the protection of Sea Turtles. June 28, 2024. Available at: https://miambiente.gob.pa/panama-crea-un-nuevo-refugio-de-vida-silvestre-para-la-proteccion-de-las-tortugas-marinas/.

[181] Republic of Panama. Law N° 287 (From Thursday, February 24, 2022). Available at: http://files.harmonywithnatureun.org/uploads/upload1168.pdf.

[182] Legislative Procedure 2020–2021. Available at: http://files.harmonywithnatureun.org/uploads/upload1099.pdf.

[183] Right to a Healthy Environment and Rights of Nature. Available at: http://files.harmonywithnatureun.org/uploads/upload1081.pdf Accessed on: February 3, 2025.

(t) Uganda

National Law/Federal Law

2019—In February, the Parliament recognized the fundamental rights of nature to exist, evolve, and regenerate in the 2019 National Environment Act.[184]

Local Regulations

2019—The Local Government Council of Buliisa District signed a resolution on November 22, 2019, in recognition of the customary laws of the custodian clans Bagungu, noting "the concern of the Bagungu clan leaders with Butoka (Mother Earth) and with future generations of all Earth species, and their ancestral responsibility to protect the well-being of their land and the planet." Click on the official document.[185]

(u) United Kingdom

Other Official Documents

2022—On September 1, legal professionals from Ireland and the United Kingdom collaborated to produce a submission to the Citizens' Assembly on Biodiversity Loss, organized by the Irish Government. The in-depth submission, calling for a constitutional amendment to embrace Nature's Rights, is titled "Nature's Rights in Ireland: Towards a Living Island of Rights-bearing Communities." The main authors include representatives from the Queen's University Belfast Law School, Northern Ireland, Environmental Justice Network Ireland, Ecojustice Ireland, and Lawyers for Nature.[186]

2021—On June 24, the Derry City and Strabane District Council of Northern Ireland became the "first in these islands" to recognize Nature's Rights.[187]

(v) United States

Constitution

2014—State Constitution (Federal State)

A State Constitutional Amendment was proposed to the Constitution of the State of Colorado in January 2014, which specifically including the right of municipalities to pass laws establishing Nature's Rights.[188]

---

[184] The Republic of Uganda. THE NATIONAL ENVIRONMENT ACT, 2019. Available at: http://files.harmonywithnatureun.org/uploads/upload834.pdf.

[185] The Republic of Uganda. Available at: http://files.harmonywithnatureun.org/uploads/upload989.pdf.

[186] Rights of Nature in Ireland. September, 2022. Available at: http://files.harmonywithnatureun.org/uploads/upload1286.pdf.

[187] Dear Member of Derry City and Strabane District Council. Available at: http://files.harmonywithnatureun.org/uploads/upload1126.pdf.

[188] Colorado Secretary of State. Available at: http://files.harmonywithnatureun.org/uploads/upload685.pdf.

As already analyzed in this chapter, in formulating the concept of legal principle, Josef Esser emphatically highlights the weight of jurisprudence in the constitution of principles as a source of law, considering that, for his theory of functional equivalence, the normativity of principles depends on the pronouncement of the courts when deciding concrete cases, inspired by the ethical values and justice contained in the principles. This is precisely what allows a constant historical update of the political and dogmatic ideas contained in the principles as "donors of legal meaning to the other norms, not through a hierarchical relationship, but through the integrity they provide to the legal system."[189]

In this line, it was demonstrated through the analysis of the jurisprudence of more than 12 internal courts across different continents, as well as in a recent decision of the Inter-American Court of Human Rights, the emergence of a vigorous jurisprudence recognizing nature's rights, which consolidates the principle of harmony with nature.

The principle of harmony with nature emerges from the jurisprudence of various countries in the judgments of demands that bring in their causes of request a common phenomenological reality, resulting from the objectification of the biosphere and the separation of natural life from culture, in ontology, in ethics, and in law.

These decisions, which have recognized nature's rights, present two striking aspects: some enunciate explicit biocentric value foundations, as occurs in Colombia, Ecuador, India, Pakistan, and Bangladesh, for example. Others deal with similar problems using more pragmatic arguments and are oriented by a weak anthropocentrism, as occurs in Brazil, Mexico, Argentina, and South Africa. Notwithstanding this, all these decisions present a common aspect: They aim to construct solutions for the environmental crisis from a non-utilitarian perspective, which seeks to reconcile human interests with non-human living beings and recognizes in the latter an intrinsic value. Precisely for this reason, this jurisprudence embodies a new legal principle that strengthens the human relationship with natural life.

Even if the principle of harmony with nature is considered a principle only interpretative—that is, one that does not prescribe behaviors, procedures, or specific actions—its normative character cannot be denied, considering that it is already part of various legal systems, representing a relevant legal value shared by the current horizon of legal culture and, moreover, defines an interpretation of human relations with nature as positively justified.

The principle of harmony with nature, similar to the principles of legal security, objective good faith, and reasonableness, emerges as a pre-legal norm, considering that it is rooted in the ethical narratives of various peoples in the West and East, and in the very laws of nature.

In addition to the jurisprudence of courts around the world that recognize the need for a harmonious and coherent relationship between humans and nature, this

---

189 Galuppo (1999), p. 242.

same movement is observed in parliaments. As demonstrated by the analysis of the data obtained from the site *Harmony With Nature* of the United Nations Organization, six countries have already positively recognized the rights of nature in their constitutions. The U.S. member state, Colorado, has also provided rights of nature in its text. Twelve countries have already recognized the rights of nature in national legislation and local laws.

All these laws are inspired by a common axiological axis, a coherent and harmonious attitude of humans toward non-human beings, so they are consequences of the principle of harmony with nature.

5.5 The Principle of Harmony with Nature in Light of the Theory of General Principles of International Environmental Law

In light of the general theory of the principles outlined above, and heading toward the more specific path of international environmental law, this work begins to analyze the methodological proposal of Klaus Bosselmann in his examination of the legal content of the principle of sustainability, for the verification of the hypothesis of harmony with nature as a legal principle within the scope of international environmental law, just as Bosselmann did in relation to the principle of sustainability.

Klaus Bosselmann,[190] when dealing with the principle of sustainability, considers that a legal system cannot, by itself, establish the structure and control of social change but can outline parameters for a change in society; if these guidelines are in tune with the sentiment of society, they will be effective in driving an evolution. Under these conditions, these parameters can come to be considered legal principles. It is noticeable that Bosselmann adopts a historical view, like Esser's, to defend the constitution of the principle of sustainability as a source of environmental law. Indeed, when analyzing his work, there is a historical survey on the evolution of the sustainability theme, to then outline its contours as a legal principle.

Bosselmann also highlights the role of jurisprudence in the juridification of ethical values in the sphere of environmental law, considering that, in the environmental field, there is no homogeneous universal response, given that environmental law operates in various legal systems at national, regional, and international levels, so each system follows its own tradition to define the legal nature of the environment. He takes, as an example to demonstrate this flexibility of the principiological norms in environmental law, the various configurations of the precautionary principle in the legal systems that adopt it. In some legal systems, the precautionary

[190] Bosselmann (2017).

principle is well established in environmental and public health legislation, while in others, it is just a broad approach to guide decision-making.

Bosselmann, in a line of thought similar to that of Verdross and Esser, argues that there is a plurality of principles in the field of international law, beyond the classic sources provided for in Article 38, paragraph 3, of the Permanent Court of The Hague. In this sense, he highlights that, in the field of international law, there is a variety of sources or factors that constitute international environmental law.

In addition to the traditional sources of international environmental law, that is, treaties, customary law, and general principles, there are political approaches, practices, and moral principles, and all of this influences the formation of consensus in international environmental law, so that these understandings shared by various countries evolve and crystallize into principles.

Bosselmann stresses that, although *soft law* is not binding, it is a source of international environmental law, but emphasizes the need to distinguish in the study of sources what is a legal principle from what is a moral principle. He points out that the complexity of legislative sources has led some jurists studying international environmental law to use the term "principle" very vaguely, without investigating the need for legal effects for a moral principle to be considered legal. He argues that, although international environmental law is based on a series of general practices, concepts, and ideas that states take as guidance for their actions, the dividing line between law and non-law should not be weakened, as there are political, psychological, and conceptual advantages in distinguishing between moral principles and legal principles.

Like Esser, he emphasizes the need for the historical process to define the juridical nature of a principle, highlighting that, although moral principles may be referred to in international treaties, such as the mention of the principle of "sustainable development" in the Climate Change Convention, this alone is not enough to convert a moral principle or a political approach into a legal principle, because, prior to legal principles, there is a historical process.[191]

Indeed, in some cases, a legal principle can be created in a single act, such as a constitution, or in international law, in a treaty, or in a historic decision of an international court; but, in most cases, the creation of a legal principle is the result of a slow historical process. In this sense, it is worth bringing the lesson of Vladmir Oliveira da Silveira and Maria Mendez Rocasolano when dealing with the concept of *dynamogenesis* in the consolidation of human rights:

> As we have seen, rights and freedoms were not peacefully achieved, but through arduous struggle, and are historically based on the Western, Euro-Atlantic model. [. . .] Indeed, they are historical acts and facts, ideological positions, philosophical positions, normative texts and institutions that - from the axiological foundation of such a model in Classical Antiquity, through medieval documents and the first declarations of rights to the most recent documents - make up a legal body of institutions and norms of international declaratory character and fundamental constitutional right.[192]

[191] Bosselmann (2017), p. 56.

[192] Silveira and Rocasolano (2010), p. 184.

Similarly, in international environmental law, the rights of nature are forged in the historical process, from moral narratives, political approaches, justice practices of indigenous peoples and ancient civilizations, declarations, *soft laws,* and ethical principles; thus, just as the *dynamogenesis* of human rights occurred, we witness an ethical–legal evolution engendered by the reality of the anthropogenic environmental crisis, in the sense of recognizing the rights of nature, based on the legal principle of harmony with nature.

The UN reports *Harmony with Nature,*[193] the Earth Charter, Principle 1 of the Rio Declaration, the recognition of the rights of nature in the Constitutions of Ecuador and Bolivia, and the various judicial decisions around the world recognizing the rights of animals, rivers, and forests are the genuine expression of this *dynamogenesis* of the rights of nature, so that it is no longer possible to deny the existence of a historical process that calls for the reconciliation of human beings with nature, for the primacy of coherence and respect in human relations with nature. This historical process, driven by the ethics of coherence and respect for non-human beings and holistic organic entities, and by the anthropogenic crisis itself, in the doctrinal line of Esser, Alexy, Dworkin, Bosselmann, Silveira, and Rocasolano, is sufficiently legitimizing of the recognition of juridicality to the principle of harmony with nature.

However, it is still necessary to investigate the legal nature of this principle, its degree of normativity, and its effects on civil law, especially on the legal categories of person and thing. Thus, considering Cançado Trindade's lesson[194] that the principles of international law "constitute the *substratum* of the legal order itself," it is considered pertinent to make a brief analysis of the principle of harmony with nature from the perspective of the doctrine of general principles of law in the field of international law.

For Robert Kolb, the general principles of law are the ferment of the birth and development of intergroup law that came to be known as international law. Since their Roman origin, these principles have symbolized deep values shared by various peoples. In this vein, he points out that the general principles of law have a triple common basis with natural law: (1) rational foundation; (2) supreme legal values; and (3) universality.[195]

In the consolidation of international law, legal doctrine gave ample space to the general principles of law extracted from common Roman law, from which correct reasoning was deduced and, consequently, the principle of good faith, which became a pillar of international law in various treaties.

From the nineteenth century onward, the general principles of law lost their relevance. Kolb attributes this to the preponderance of state will, as postulated by positivism. Legal positivism accommodated the power objectives of national states, so the reference to a universal society began losing ground and giving

[193] United Nations, Harmony with Nature, online.

[194] Trindade (2017), p. 178.

[195] Kolb (2000), p. 12.

way to particular societies, to the force of state internal law, and, thus, there was no longer room for the general principles of a universal law, which were valid regardless of any creative will.

In addition, a large number of treaties began to be celebrated, producing a dense body of rules that occupied the legal space of the general principles of law. At the same time, a strong dualistic distinction between the principles of domestic law and international law emerged. Despite this, several important codifications of civil law did not fail to refer to the general principles of law. Later, with the consolidation of the Statute of the International Court of Justice, the general principles of law returned to the forefront of international law.[196]

However, as Verdross points out, the general principles of law were at the center of the clash between the dualist and universalist (monist) currents regarding the basis of international law. For the defenders of universalism, justice and common necessity should prevail over the arbitrariness of state will, as the principles are superior and prior to the will of the state. For the individualist and dualist current, the state is the only source of law, considering that the law is posterior and inferior to the state.

Authors affiliated with dualist positivism do not accept that the general principles of law are independent sources of rights and reject the possibility of the existence of principles common to various peoples. Monist authors, on the other hand, recognize the quality of the source of law in the general principles of law, either based on the legal consciousness of the peoples, that is, on natural law, or with a foundation in the idea of objective justice.

Verdross, in defending universalism, emphasizes "that the common nature of men and the similarity of basic needs generate and maintain always a minimum of common values that translate into the general principles of international law."[197]

Kolb asserts that the doctrinal currents that deny the general principles of law as autonomous sources of international law aim to render Article 38 of the Statute of the International Tribunal of The Hague a dead letter. In this sense, he criticizes this anachronistic view, which considers only the state as the source of international law, and observes that various institutions, to which competence has been attributed, contribute to the formation of international law.

For Cançado Trindade, the general principles of law inspire the *jus gentium* in its evolutionary process, as they express "the basic considerations of humanity," considering that they are the manifestation of the evolving international legal consciousness:

> These principles are a manifestation of international legal consciousness, they reflect the **status conscientiae** of subjects of international law. Although these principles (as enumerated in art. 2 of the UN Charter) may be open to different interpretations, given their generality, they retain their importance for the correct application of norms and rules, and to guide the evolution of the entire legal system, so that the latter can adjust to the new

[196] Kolb (2000), p. 19.

[197] Kolb (2000), p. 20–22.

> circumstances of international life, respond to the changing needs of the international community, and contribute to the satisfaction of the aspirations of humanity.[198]

As can be seen, Cançado Trindade highlights the role of the general principles of law as a vector of values expressing the consciousness and aspirations of humanity in its evolutionary path. In this sense, it cannot be forgotten that this planetary consciousness is always evolving and cannot be ignored, so that, once crystallized into general principles of law, it will guide the evolution of the legal systems of nations.

Despite the disregard of positivism for the general principles of law, humanity will never do without them, as they are the source from which norms emanate and where they find their meanings, their legitimate ends, such as the common good of all human beings, the meaning of justice, the prevalence of law over force, and the valorization of peace.

For Cançado Trindade, these basic principles have been emerging in accordance with the emergence and consolidation of the various branches of law, and he observes that no matter how specific a domain of law is, its basic principles can be found. He cites, as examples of general principles of international environmental law, the principles of precaution and the polluter-pays principle.[199]

He also teaches that there are some basic principles that are specific to certain areas of law, while others are common to all areas. As can be inferred from Cançado Trindade's lesson, the standard of humanity's justice is constantly evolving, this evolutionary process being driven by the general principles of law, considering that they are above state will and, therefore, serve as the torch that illuminates domestic law toward evolution.

The author emphasizes the relevance of the general principles of law in the formation of normative systems protective of the human person, highlighting them as a genuine expression of the legal consciousness of peoples, at the base of the formation of law itself; therefore, they are peremptory, indispensable, and prior to state will, as they express the notion of an "objective justice" inherent to natural law. For this reason, he recalls the wise words of Verdross at the Hague Court in 1935, when he spoke of the "general principle of *jus cogens,*" rejecting the voluntarist conception of international law.[200]

Thus, in line with Verdross's thinking, this work adopts the understanding that the general principles of law are the expression "of humanity's legal consciousness" and not of the positive law of each State, so that, before being written in texts, they emerge from the very ancestry of peoples.[201]

In this order of ideas, the ethical account of harmony with nature is imprinted in the ancestral consciousness of the peoples who inhabit planet Earth and, thus, emerges as a criterion of justice in Principle 1 of the Rio Declaration, which

[198] Trindade (2017), p. 178–179.
[199] Trindade (2017), p. 180–181.
[200] Trindade (2017), p. 187.
[201] Trindade (2017), p. 207.

provided: "Human beings are at the center of concerns related to sustainable development. They have the right to a healthy and productive life, in **harmony with nature**"[202] (our emphasis).

In the same vein, the UN's *Harmony with Nature* reports and the Earth Charter enunciate harmony with nature as a demand of public consciousness common to various peoples of the Earth, and therefore, capable of legitimizing the principle of harmony with nature as a general principle of law.

As already mentioned, Cançado Trindade teaches that the general principles of law permeate all areas of law, so there are general principles of law that are relevant to the field of international environmental law; thus, the next topic will be dedicated to the analysis of the formation of the general principles of international environmental law, in whose context the principle of harmony with nature will be examined.

5.5.1 The Binding Nature of the Principle of Harmony with Nature in the Scope of International Environmental Law

When dealing with principles in the field of international environmental law, Bosselmann[203] notes that, among international jurists, there is a strong tendency to recognize the relevance of morality in the constitution of principles and cites, as an example, the understanding of Alexandre Kiss and Dinah Shelton, in the sense that international environmental law is shaped by religious and ethical–philosophical foundations important for understanding humanity's relationship with nature.

He also mentions Philip Sand's understanding, in the sense that the concept of sustainable development substantially expands environmental law, and more recently, moral issues, such as intragenerational and intergenerational equity, have also expanded the normative horizons of international environmental law.

When examining the work of Kiss and Shelton, it is found that, indeed, they revolve around the religious origin of environmental protection norms. Specifically, in relation to the Judeo-Christian view, they highlight that there are two opposing currents: (i) one that considers that the creator bequeathed to human beings unrestricted dominion over all non-human beings; (ii) and another, less anthropocentric, that understands the human being as a mere usufructuary of the creator's work and, therefore, should enjoy it with respect and frugality. This latter current evokes passages such as Psalm 24 to justify itself: "The earth is the Lord's, and everything in it, the world, and all who live in it; for he founded it on the seas and established it on the waters. Psalms 24:1,2."[204] in this line, they also cite the *Summa Theologica* and the words of Pope John Paul II:

---

[202] Rio Declaration on Environment and Development. Rio de Janeiro, June 1992. Available at https://cetesb.sp.gov.br/proclima/wp-content/uploads/sites/36/2013/12/declaracao_rio_ma.pdf.

[203] Bosselmann (2017), p. 59.

[204] Kiss and Shelton (2004), p. 09.

> In the **Summa Theologica**, Thomas Aquinas argues that man's dominion over nature includes a competence to use and manage the world's resources, not selfishly, but in the interest of all, should be ready to help others in case of need. Individual property title is seen as imposing a responsibility and trust. On January 1, 1990, World Peace Day, Pope John Paul II stated: "In our days, there is a growing awareness that world peace is threatened not only by the arms race, regional conflicts and ongoing injustices among peoples and nations, but also by a lack of respect for nature, due to the plundering of natural resources and a progressive decline in the quality of life".[205]

The example given by Kiss and Shelton to demonstrate this aspect of the Judeo-Christian view, which emphasizes respect for nature, is reinforced by the recent propositions of Pope Francis in the Encyclical *Laudato Si'*, which presents the life of Jesus as an example of harmony with nature and free from the dualism that separated the soul from the body and the human being from nature:

> Jesus lived in full harmony with creation, to the great wonder of others: "Who is this, even the wind and the sea obey him?" (Mt 8, 27). He did not present himself as an ascetic separated from the world or an enemy of the pleasant things in life. Speaking of Himself, He declared: "The Son of Man came eating and drinking, and they say, 'Here is a glutton and a drunkard'" (Mt 11, 19). He was far from philosophies that despised the body, matter, and the realities of this world. However, throughout history, these battered dualisms had a notable influence on some Christian thinkers and disfigured the Gospel. Jesus worked with His hands, daily coming into contact with matter created by God to shape it with His craftsmanship. It is noteworthy that most of His earthly existence was dedicated to this task, leading a simple life that aroused no wonder: "Is not this the carpenter, the son of Mary?" (Mk 6, 3). Thus He sanctified work, attributing to it a peculiar value for our maturation. [. . .][206]

Kiss and Shelton also examine Islam's view of the human relationship with nature and quote the following excerpt from the document on the principles of Islam for the preservation of nature:

> God's wisdom has ordained to grant man inheritance on Earth. Therefore, besides being part of the Earth and part of the Universe, man is also the executor of God's injunctions and commands. And as such he is a mere steward of the earth and not an owner; a beneficiary and not a distributor or ordainer. Man received this inheritance to manage and use for his benefit and for the fulfillment of his interests. He, therefore, has to maintain and preserve it honestly and act within the limits dictated by honesty.[207]

They also highlight that, in Buddhism, there are principles that underpin a respectful relationship between human beings and nature. In his sermons, Buddha stressed the right to life of non-human living beings:

> Ancient Buddhist chronicles, dating from the 3rd century BC, present a sermon in which the son of Emperor Asoka of India stated that "the birds of the air and the animals have the same right to live and move anywhere on earth as you do. The earth belongs to people

---

[205] Kiss and Shelton (2004), p. 09.

[206] Pope Francis (2015), § 98, online.

[207] Kiss and Shelton (2004), p. 09.

> and all living beings; you are merely its guardian". Subsequently, the King initiated a legal system that continued to exist in the 18th century providing sanctuaries for animals.[208]

Finally, they emphasize that the religions of indigenous peoples share a belief in the spiritual nature and depth of their relationship with the Earth.

In addition to religion, Kiss and Shelton highlight philosophy and ethics as foundations of international environmental law. When analyzing the evolution of international treaties, they observe that these treaties initially presented a utilitarian and human-centered view, with the proposition of norms that treated the environment merely as a useful resource for human beings; the focus of these early treaties was solely on concerns about pollution, as it is harmful to human health.

In this line, even the Rio Declaration on Environment and Development still reflects this utilitarian and anthropocentric approach, as it tries to merge the concepts of economic development and environmental protection. Principle 1 of the Rio Declaration places the human being at the center of environmental concern, a view still corroborated by the Political Declaration of the Summit on Sustainable Development.[209]

Indeed, the concept of sustainable life enshrined in Principle 1 has been widely recognized in national and international legal spheres, assuming a renewed force with the Political Declaration of the Summit on Sustainable Development and representing several achievements in the sphere of human rights, such as the recognition of the human right to have sufficient access to drinking water.

Although the Rio Declaration is still markedly anthropocentric, it cannot be forgotten that it brings, in its Principle 1, the primacy of harmony with nature and can be considered one of the foundations of the principle of harmony with nature. At this point, it is opportune to remember that UNEP, at the sixth session in 1978 in Nairobi, when dealing with the principles of conduct for the use of natural resources shared by states, also regulated the harmonious use of these resources. As can be seen, even though anthropocentric and utilitarian, these two documents already point in the direction of the ethics of harmony with nature.

Kiss and Shelton observe that the idea of equity and justice has underpinned an environment of protection for the relationship not only between human beings of present and future generations but also between human beings and non-human living beings. It is precisely from the ethical foundation of equity between species, defended by ethicists, that the recognition of intrinsic value in nature and the need for a non-hierarchical relationship between humans and other species have unfolded.[210]

These ethical values were already widely shared in 1979, when they were crystallized in the Bern Convention on the Conservation of European Wildlife

---

208 Kiss and Shelton (2004), p. 10.

209 Kiss and Shelton (2004), p. 10.

210 Kiss and Shelton (2004), p. 11.

and Natural Habitats.[211] This was the first document to express a basis for environmental protection founded on the recognition of the intrinsic value of nature, as it expressly acknowledged that wild flora and fauna constitute a natural, esthetic, scientific, recreational, economic, and intrinsic heritage that, therefore, needs to be preserved and passed on to future generations.

Indeed, the text of the Bern Convention emerged as the harbinger of a vision that seeks to harmonize and balance natural heritage, recognizing it as a value relevant to humanity, without, however, diminishing the intrinsic value of nature. Similarly, the Convention on Biological Diversity,[212] from 1992, proclaimed that biological and ecological diversities have intrinsic value. The preamble of the World Charter for Nature,[213] from 1982, in turn, stated that humanity is part of nature and that life depends on the interconnected functioning of natural systems.

The texts of these documents provide evidence of the foundations of an ethical movement that has been consolidating since the beginning of the twentieth century, with Aldo Leopold, Arne Naess, Rachel Carson, Hans Jonas, Thomas Berry, and Leonardo Boff, thus confirming the doctrinal understanding of Kiss and Shelton in the sense that international environmental law is rooted in an ethical movement that recognizes the intrinsic value of nature:

> The intrinsic value of the biosphere is not rejected, but is integrated with an understanding that humans are part of the universe and cannot exist without the conservation of the biosphere and ecosystems, understanding them. From this perspective, all components of the environment have a value not only in their short term, of utility to humans, as the exclusively utilitarian approach proposes, but also as indispensable beings of an interrelated system, which must be protected.[214]

As can be seen, Kiss and Shelton demonstrate the religious and ethical foundations of nature protection and human responsibility, not only for future generations but also in relation to other species. In addition to religious and ethical foundations, they emphasize the visceral connection of international environmental law with the "laws of nature," considering that no branch of law is so rooted in biology, ecology, and physics. This is explained by the fact that environmental law provides rules of conduct for human beings in their relationship with non-human living beings and ecosystems, so legislators and jurists cannot ignore the knowledge of natural sciences in normative formulation.[215]

Another founding element of the principles of international environmental law is the common concern of society and peoples. Every society has, as a cohesive element, a system of common values, which is reflected in religion, philosophy, ideology, and ethics. Principles such as human dignity emerged as a result of values shared by several peoples. It is precisely this common concern of a society

---

[211] Council of Europe (1979), preamble.

[212] United Nations (1992), preamble.

[213] United Nations (1982), preamble.

[214] Kiss and Shelton (2004), p. 13.

[215] Kiss and Shelton (2004), p. 13.

that underpins legal systems. In this sense, Kiss and Shelton record that more and more constitutions around the world proclaim the state's obligation to prevent and combat pollution, erosion, desertification, and ensure the human right to a balanced environment. The recognition that the biosphere is a unique and special place in the universe, in the sense of fostering the emergence of life, is shared by several peoples and corroborates the need to place its protection as one of the foremost concerns of humanity.[216]

As can be seen, the normative principles and even the rules in the sphere of international environmental law have their roots in religious beliefs, ethics, sciences, and common concerns shared by societies, peoples, and humanity itself.

Following this same line, Bosselmann observes that the principles of international environmental law almost never emerge from an ethical vacuum, so their moral grounding cannot be ignored. If the moral dimension of an environmental principle resonates with its legal dimension, that principle must have its legal dimension recognized.[217] This understanding of Bosselmann is in line with Dworkin's thinking, in the sense that, at the root of a legal principle, there is reference to justice, equity, and other forms of morality, and thus, for ideals to be considered legal principles, they need to meet morality requirements.[218]

Nicholas de Sadeleer, in turn, points out that the most relevant principles of international environmental law were created more by bold declarations of *soft law* than by court decisions or treaties. He also shares the understanding that moral principles have the potential to create laws, especially environmental laws.[219]

Nicholas de Sadeleer distinguishes the general principles of law, which he considers typical of modernity, from the set of new environmental principles, which he deems more suitable for adapting to the changing and more complex forms that characterize contemporary environmental law. For Sadeleer, post-modern law is characterized by a context of the emergence of new legal cultures, and environmental legislation has been influenced by these changes more than other legal areas, as these changes shift environmental law from the axis of the direct influence of modern dogma to a new worldview.[220]

For Sadeleer, it is necessary to make a distinction between the general principles of law, which can be extracted through induction and generalization of conventional and customary rules, such as sovereignty and self-determination of peoples, and the general principles of law that emerge in new fields of international relations, such as climate and environment, where problems need to be solved without the handrails of consolidated international precedents in modernity.

Sadeleer points out that, even in the face of the existence of a large number of instruments expressed in the form of declarations of principles in the area of

---

[216] Kiss and Shelton (2004), p. 19.

[217] Bosselmann (2017), p. 60.

[218] Dworkin (2013), p. 44.

[219] Bosselmann (2017), p. 60.

[220] Sadeleer (2020), p. 380–382.

international environmental law, there is still no globally binding international instrument establishing the general principles of international environmental law. He observes that the doctrine has been striving in the identification, elaboration, and development of various general principles of international environmental law. These principles have been deduced from various sources, ranging from *soft law*, such as the Rio and Stockholm Declarations, to arbitral decisions and judicial decisions of the ICJ, some of which merely reflect the application of international law to environmental problems, while others are specific, such as the obligation not to cause environmental damage. However, there are principles within the scope of international environmental law that are recognized and cataloged by an "informal taxonomy of international environmental principles developed by academics," which because they are not grounded "in significant practices through repetitive use in an international legal context cannot give rise to a legal recourse" in the ICJ.[221]

Next, Sadeleer presents his view on the characteristics of the so-called legal post-modernity to outline the meaning of the general principles of international environmental law in this newly emerging legal paradigm. Sadeleer points out the following phenomena as characteristics of post-modernity in the legal sphere: (a) the dispersion of legislative power; (b) the fragmentation of the law; (c) the acceleration of time; (d) the decline of state authority; (e) the increasing dependence on extrajudicial spheres; and (f) the weakening of the very premises of modern law.[222]

The author discusses each of these changes, highlighting their occurrence within the scope of environmental law, given that it is positioned at the intersection between the institutions of legal modernity and the changes brought about by post-modernity.

Unlike modern law, which is structured in general and abstract norms, devoid of precise objectives, environmental laws are guided by concrete objectives, given that most of the international environmental agreements and national environmental codes are characterized not only by the proclamation of legal objectives but also by the incorporation of principles with a precise scope, such as the principles of precaution, polluter-pays, and sustainability.

Thus, when comparing environmental law with other legal disciplines, it is observed that environmental law is oriented toward specific objectives, stated in various principles, which are very different from the general principles of law typical of modernity, given that the principles of environmental law largely derive from declarations.

At this point, it is noted that, unlike Esser, for whom legal principles are formed from the adherence of courts to ethical principles, Sadeleer considers judicial intervention unnecessary for the creation of legal principles as sources of international environmental law.

---

[221] Sadeleer (2020), p. 380–382.

[222] Sadeleer (2020), p. 383–385.

For Sadeleer, the principles of international environmental law establish guidelines for the actions of authorities, mainly legislators. Thus, they confer greater coherence, stability, and balance in the evaluation of conflicting interests, given that they have the functions of activation, guidance, and interpretation, in addition to providing criteria for weighing interests. Like Dworkin, Sadeleer attributes to moral principles a potential for the creation of norms within the scope of environmental law.[223]

Kiss and Shelton, when dealing with the sources of international environmental law, also highlight that the use of *soft law* is predominant in this field. They explain that, formally, *soft law* is not binding and merely expresses a commitment, such as the Rio and Stockholm Declarations. However, precisely because of this, it has a more impactful effect in the field of international environmental law, as most state parties would be reluctant to adhere to binding norms with sanctioning effects; thus, they feel more encouraged to engage with *soft law*.

As already mentioned, international law has its sources provided in Article 38 of the Statute of the Permanent International Court of Justice (PICJ, transformed into ICJ) from 1920, which stipulates, as a condition for the binding nature of normative instruments, the strict observance of the procedure provided there, so that only the following are binding: (a) specialized international conventions and treaties; (b) international custom as evidence of a general practice accepted as law; and (c) general principles of law recognized by civilized nations.

As subsidiary sources, there are international judicial decisions and doctrine. However, Kiss and Shelton assert that this enumeration no longer corresponds to current international practice, considering that it does not cover the texts that, despite not being conveyed in treaties, are adopted by international organizations and whose contribution to international environmental law has been highly relevant.

For Kiss and Shelton, states have preferred non-conventional sources since, due to their non-formally binding nature, they are more advantageous for the state parties. The negotiations of these non-binding instruments are faster and, in addition, their texts do not require internal ratification. Thus, states feel more encouraged to adopt non-binding norms and objectives. Another advantage is that the drafting of non-binding instruments allows the participation of international institutions and non-state actors in the process of creating environmental norms. They cite as examples the World Charter for Nature and the 1979 Bonn Convention on the Conservation of Migratory Species of Wild Animals.

Still within the spectrum of non-conventional sources, they highlight the resolutions and decisions of international organizations that, as a rule, do not have legally binding force, with only three international organizations having the power to issue binding norms: (a) the UN Security Council; (b) the Organization for Economic Cooperation and Development (OECD); and (c) the European Union.[224]

---

[223] Sadeleer (2020), p. 405–406.

[224] Kiss and Shelton (2004), p. 54.

Most international organizations, since their inception in the nineteenth century, have adopted resolutions that are not binding on member states. This procedure of using non-binding instruments is extremely common in international environmental law. The recommendations and declarations of principles at conferences, such as the Stockholm Declaration, or UN meetings, such as those of Vancouver in 1976 and Nairobi in 1978, were decisive for the construction of norms of international environmental law, as they reverberated in the legal systems of nations and triggered significant progress in the domestic legislation of protective norms.

Many resolutions were adhered to by the state parties by consensus and resulted in the adoption of practices, so that, in reality, they are sources of international environmental law recognized by the international legal community. Even though they are not provided for in Article 38 of the Statute of the International Court of Justice, one cannot ignore the relevant role of these resolutions as a technique for the creation of environmental protection norms.[225]

Furthermore, one cannot forget that the directive recommendations that deal with environmental protection have demonstrated a fundamental role in the activities of most intergovernmental organizations for the development of environmental law. The declarations of principles differ from directive recommendations, considering that they do not aim at a specific action to be performed but are corrective guidelines for states, as highlighted by Kiss and Shelton:

> Another function of principles is to establish a fundamental social consensus on the logical basis for a set of laws. In this respect, principles serve the fundamental objectives of any legal system, which must recognize and formulate the emergence of new social values recognized as essential within society. At international level, this can be achieved through declarations adopted and proclaimed by global organizations or international conferences. Principles are widely used in environmental legislation, perhaps more than in any other domain of international law. All major **soft law** texts contain principles.[226]

They also emphasize that, in the field of environmental law, the concept of principles and their value varies in the legal systems of each state. The principles can take on a descriptive feature and indicate the main characteristics of legal institutions, designating fundamental legal norms or filling gaps in positive law. The principles can be fundamental, such as the principles of equality and legal security, or they can be merely technical, like the principle of proportionality. They draw attention to the fact that the principles "can appear in Constitutions and basic laws, as in the fundamental legal tradition or can be of construction."[227]

As can be inferred from the doctrine of Kiss, Shelton, and Sadeleer, the resolutions, although not binding, have a strong creative potential for protective norms in the field of international environmental law, precisely because they are more flexible for the member states.

---

[225] Kiss and Shelton (2004), p. 52–53.

[226] Kiss and Shelton (2004), p. 54.

[227] Kiss and Shelton (2004), p. 54.

Therefore, starting from the lessons of Kiss, Shelton, and Sadeleer that resolutions have emerged as natural creative sources of international and domestic environmental law, the following subtopic examines the United Nations General Assembly Resolutions on Harmony with Nature.

5.5.1.1 United Nations General Assembly Resolutions on Harmony with Nature

(1) First United Nations General Assembly Resolution on Harmony with Nature (A/RES/64/196, of Dec. 21, 2009)[228]

The First Resolution was addressed to member states, relevant United Nations organizations, and international, regional, and sub-regional organizations, and presented the following contents: (a) It called on the recipients to reflect on the importance of promoting actions suitable for life in harmony with nature and to express their opinions, experiences, and proposals on this to the Secretary-General; (b) it encouraged the recipients to make use of International Mother Earth Day in order to promote activities and exchange opinions and points of view on the conditions, experiences, and principles for a life in harmony with nature; and (c) it requested the Secretary-General to present, at the sixty-fifth session, a report on the topic, taking into account the opinions and comments received on the present resolution.

As can be seen, the First Resolution inaugurates an educational movement, extends an invitation to reflection, and opens space for a discussion about the experiences of the recipients, so that they can express what they understand by a harmonious life with nature. These reports were systematized by the Secretary-General.

(2) Second United Nations General Assembly Resolution on Harmony with Nature (A/RES/65/164, of Dec. 20, 2010)[229]

This resolution inaugurated the practice of interactive dialogs, as it requested the Secretary-General to convene, at the sixty-fifth session of the General Assembly, an interactive dialog to be held in two plenary meetings during the commemoration of International Mother Earth Day on April 20, 2011, with the participation of member states, United Nations organizations, independent experts, and other interested parties. These meetings aimed to contribute to and support the efforts of the UN for the realization of the United Nations Conference on Sustainable Development, held in Brazil in 2012. It established the following topics as work objectives: (a) ways to promote a holistic approach to sustainable development in harmony with nature; and (b) sharing national experiences in criteria and indicators for measuring sustainable development in harmony with nature.

This Second Resolution emphasized the need to think about ways of sustainable development in harmony with nature. Formally, it opened a space for the report of

[228] United Nations, A/RES/64/196, online.

[229] United Nations. A/RES/65/164, online.

the participants' experiences and expanded the circle of dialog. It was precisely from these reports, brought by various peoples about their ancestral relationship with nature, that the following resolutions expressed the ethical content of harmony with nature among various nations and peoples.

(3) Third United Nations General Assembly Resolution on Harmony with Nature (A/RES/66/204, of Dec. 22, 2011)[230]

This resolution advanced in the sense of requesting concrete actions from the Secretary-General to: (a) host the second interactive dialog of the General Assembly on harmony with nature to commemorate International Mother Earth Day; (b) issue the third report of the Secretary-General on harmony with nature; (c) strengthen the development of the "Harmony with Nature" website in time for the Rio+20 Conference; (d) encourage all countries and relevant bodies of the United Nations system to develop and strengthen the quality and quantity of basic statistical data on the three pillars of sustainable development; and (e) invite relevant entities of the United Nations system to work with other relevant actors, including non-governmental organizations, experts, and the academic community, as appropriate, both to identify new ways and means to overcome the limitations of gross domestic product in relation to development, and to better measure environmental degradation resulting from human activity.

This resolution presents a more operational character for data mobilization, web implementation of the "Harmony with Nature" site, organization of the space for future interactive dialogs, and also preparation for Rio+20.

(4) Fourth United Nations General Assembly Resolution on Harmony with Nature (A/RES/67/214, of Dec. 21, 2012)[231]

It highlighted the relevance of the first World People's Conference on Climate Change and the Rights of Mother Earth, organized by the Plurinational State of Bolivia in Cochabamba from April 20 to 22, 2010, and the final document of the United Nations Conference on Sustainable Development, held in Rio de Janeiro, Brazil, from June 20 to 22, 2012, entitled "The Future We Want."

It expressed concern about the environmental degradation documented in surveys, the increase in frequency and severity of natural disasters, and the negative impact on nature resulting from human activity. It recognized the need to strengthen scientific knowledge about the effects of human activities on Earth's ecosystems in order to promote and ensure an equitable, balanced, and sustainable relationship with the Earth.

Here, the concern to seek equity, balance, and sustainability in the relationship with the Earth is already noticeable. The use of the word "relationship" as an indicator of moral consideration of nature is noteworthy.

The document also recognized the relevance of ancestral culture for establishing a harmonious relationship with the Earth, emphasizing that many ancient

---

[230] United Nations, A/RES/66/204, online.

[231] United Nations, A/RES/67/214, online.

civilizations and indigenous cultures have a rich history of understanding the symbiotic connection between humans and nature, which promotes a mutually beneficial relationship.

It also acknowledged the importance of the work that has been carried out by civil society, academia, and scientists to draw attention to the weakening of life on Earth, as well as the work of these people in creating more sustainable models of production and consumption.

It further expressed the understanding that sustainable development is a holistic concept that requires the strengthening of interdisciplinary links in different branches of knowledge.

(5) Fifth Resolution of the United Nations General Assembly on Harmony with Nature (A/RES/68/216, of Dec 4, 2013)[232]

The Fifth Resolution requested the following concrete measures from the Secretary-General: (a) organization of the fourth interactive dialog of the General Assembly on harmony with nature to commemorate International Mother Earth Day; (b) invitation to member states to reflect on the existing studies and reports on harmony with nature, including the follow-up of discussions in the interactive dialogs of the General Assembly, such as the one held on April 22, 2013, on different economic approaches, in the context of sustainable development, in order to deepen the ethical foundations of humanity's relations with the Earth and promote new studies on the subject; and (c) encouragement of the appropriate consideration of the issue of harmony with nature in the drafting of the post-2015 development agenda.

As can be seen, this resolution touched on the need for understanding the ethical foundations in the relationship between human beings and the Earth. Here, the notion emerges that achieving sustainable development necessarily involves revising our ontology and ethics.

(6) Sixth Resolution of the United Nations General Assembly on Harmony with Nature (A/RES/69/224, of Dec 19, 2014)[233]

It continued to stress the need for the consideration of more studies and reports to promote a more ethical basis for the relationship between humanity and the Earth.

It encouraged the construction of a knowledge network that facilitates support and recognition of the fundamental interconnection between humanity and nature. It cited indigenous cultures as a reference in promoting harmony with the Earth.

(7) Seventh Resolution of the United Nations General Assembly on Harmony with Nature (A/RES/70/208, of Dec 22, 2015)[234]

The Seventh Resolution invited Earth Jurisprudence experts from around the world to the first virtual dialog in 2016, as well as those who had already participated in the interactive dialogs of the General Assembly. The specific objective of this

---

[232] Available at: http://harmonywithnatureun.org/unDocs Accessed on: May 4, 2025.

[233] Available at: http://harmonywithnatureun.org/unDocs Accessed on: May 4, 2025.

[234] Available at: http://harmonywithnatureun.org/unDocs Accessed on: May 5, 2025.

virtual dialog was to inspire citizens and societies to reflect on how they have interacted with the natural world and, thus, begin an educational effort to implement the sustainable development goals in harmony with nature. From this resolution, the UN began to disseminate the contributions of countries that are recognizing the rights of nature as one of the aspects of promoting sustainable development.

(8) Eighth Resolution of the United Nations General Assembly on Harmony with Nature (A/RES/71/232, of Dec 21, 2016)[235]

It proposed a reflection on the content of the final document of the United Nations Conference on Sustainable Development, held in Rio de Janeiro, Brazil, from June 20 to 22, 2012, entitled "The Future We Want."

It reaffirmed the importance of Resolution 70/1 of September 25, 2015, entitled "Transforming our world: the 2030 Agenda for Sustainable Development," in which a set of universal objectives was adopted to achieve sustainable development goals. It reiterated the need for the commitment of the States Parties to work toward the implementation of the Agenda by 2030. It stressed that the recognition of the need to eradicate poverty in all its forms and dimensions, including extreme poverty, presents itself as a major global challenge, as it is an indispensable requirement for sustainable development. It reaffirmed the commitment to achieve sustainable development in its three dimensions: economic, social, and environmental.

It called on the States Parties to recognize that the planet Earth and its ecosystems are our home, and referring to Earth as "Mother Earth" is common in various countries and regions. It emphasized the contribution of countries that have already recognized the rights of nature in the context of promoting sustainable development. It expressed the conviction that, to achieve a fair balance between the economic, social, and environmental needs of present and future generations, *it is necessary to promote harmony with nature* (our emphasis).

The resolution also highlighted the relevance of Earth system sciences for promoting a holistic approach capable of achieving development in harmony with nature.

(9) Ninth Resolution of the UN General Assembly on Harmony with Nature (A/RES/72/223, of Dec. 20, 2017)[236]

It emphasized the efforts of some countries that are already discussing the possibility of considering a declaration on the protection of nature.

This resolution gave special importance to education in the context of promoting sustainable development and encouraging a holistic approach to expanding public awareness of sustainable development in its three dimensions. It highlighted the emergence of formal and informal educational activities on the rights of nature in the public and private spaces of some countries.

---

[235] Available at: http://harmonywithnatureun.org/unDocs Accessed on: May 5, 2025.

[236] Available at: http://harmonywithnatureun.org/unDocs Accessed on: May 5, 2025.

It underscored the relevance of the work of the experts from the Harmony with Nature Knowledge Network in supporting the UN in bringing to people everywhere the information relevant to the formation of an expanded awareness of the importance of sustainable development and the adoption of a way of living in harmony with nature, in line with Goal 12.8 of the sustainable development goals.

(10) Tenth Resolution of the UN General Assembly on Harmony with Nature (A/RES/73/235, of Dec. 20, 2018)[237]
It reaffirmed the interactive dialog on living in harmony with nature, held on the occasion of the thirteenth meeting of the Conference of the Parties to the Convention on Biological Diversity, in Cancún, Mexico, from December 4 to 17, 2016. It noted the progress of the first decade since the Constitution of Ecuador in Montecristi in 2008, which inaugurated the inclusion of the rights of nature in constitutional text.

(11) Eleventh Resolution of the UN General Assembly on Harmony with Nature (A/RES/74/224, of Dec. 19, 2019)[238]
It encouraged the experts from the Harmony with Nature Knowledge Network to conduct a study on the evolution, over the last decade, of regional, local, and national initiatives for the protection of Mother Earth.

It recognized the need to protect and conserve ecosystems to avoid harmful practices against animals, plants, microorganisms, and inanimate environments, which contribute to the coexistence of humanity in harmony with nature.

As can be seen, the expression "harmony with nature," provided for in Principle 1 of the Rio Declaration, has progressively gained another meaning in the texts of the UN General Assembly Resolutions on Harmony with Nature and in the respective reports produced within the framework of the interactive dialogs proposed to the Secretary-General by the aforementioned resolutions.

In the context of Principle 1 of the Rio Declaration, harmony with nature was inserted into a normative statement of still anthropocentric inspiration. However, throughout the evolution of the interactive dialogs held with people from civil society, the academic world, and representatives of nations and peoples from all over the world, harmony with nature has been gaining the colors and tone of the moral narratives shared by the peoples of the various cultures of the Earth. The interactive dialogs mentioned above unveiled harmony with nature as a dimension of planetary morality shared by various peoples and nations of the Earth for thousands of years—a harmony based on a new epistemological paradigm of valuing holistic and interdisciplinary knowledge and, above all, founded on a new ethic, which shifted from anthropocentrism to the recognition of the intrinsic value of nature.

[237] Available at: http://harmonywithnatureun.org/unDocs Accessed on: May 5, 2025.

[238] Resolution adopted by the General Assembly on December 19, 2019. Available at: https://undocs.org/en/A/RES/74/224 Accessed on: May 5, 2021.

Thus, the principle of harmony with nature, provided for in Principle 1 of the Rio Declaration, underwent a value evolution, gaining an ecocentric meaning in which the ecological morality present in international public consciousness resonates. This catalysis was methodically and democratically carried out by the interactive dialogs of the UN, which opened a planetary agora for the hearing of all peoples, including indigenous peoples, Mesoamerican and Eastern ancestral wisdom, scientists, teachers, and scholars of ethics, law, and Earth system sciences.

In this way, the expression "harmony with nature" contained in the aforementioned resolutions is not just a randomly chosen epigraph but represents the very material content of the reports, which were produced in the period from 2010 to 2019 as a genuine expression of a planetary consensus of various peoples and cultures on the need to erect a harmonizing principle of the relationship between human beings and nature, from a new non-dualistic and non-Cartesian paradigm, but guided by respect for the impulse for life and flourishing, which is shared by all living beings and organic entities.

The reasons for recognizing this principle are similar to those evoked by Vattel, when he discussed the fundamental right of good faith in the execution of treaties for the maintenance of international order: "Everything that is for the common salvation of peoples, for the tranquility and salvation of humanity must be inviolable, it is a sacred thing among nations."[239]

Indeed, good faith can be considered the founding relational principle of trust in relations between human beings and between nations. Obviously, its non-observance would imply the collapse of all legal order, national and international. Without good faith, there would be no possibility for affective, economic, and legal relations between human beings, and for this reason, it is considered a general principle of law endowed with fundamental rights. However, it is necessary to move forward; we cannot ignore the need for regulation of the relationship of human beings with non-human beings, with plants, animals, and ecosystems. Humanity shares the biosphere with non-human living beings, so it is imperative to understand and consider the natural laws that govern this living network of relations, organic and systemic, which are also legal and, consequently, must be guided by the values of coherence and respect for non-human beings and ecosystems.

Thus, as relations between humans, since Roman law, are governed by the principle of trust, embodied in the primacy of good faith, the relationship of the human being with nature must also be governed by trust, coherence, and balance, which emerge from the principle of harmony with nature.

Just as the principle of good faith was founded, from abstract reason, to create a safe environment for the development of human relations and the fruition of national and international institutions, it is time to recognize the existence of a pre-

[239] In the original: "Therefore, anything that, for the common salvation of Peoples, for the tranquility & salvation of Mankind, must be inviolable, is a sacred thing among Nations." Vattel (1758), p. 385.

legal principle, equivalent to good faith, to guide the relations of human beings with non-human beings and ecosystems. This principle is the very harmony with nature enunciated in the United Nations Resolutions previously analyzed.

The principle of harmony with nature emerges as an equivalent of good faith to regulate the relations of human beings beyond the symbolic dimension created by human language. Every human relationship that touches the world of the biosphere must be guided by harmony with nature and its consequences.

Harmony with nature is an ethical value present in all peoples and in natural laws, in the succession of seasons, in the cycles of water, in photosynthesis, in the formation of rain, and in the reproduction of cells. It is a natural principle, but not in the sense of a natural law created by the human being as a fruit of abstract reason; it is natural because it is present in the negentropic processes of the biosphere.

Harmony with nature is not a created principle, but only recognized by the human being, through human language. In this context, Principle 1 of the Rio Declaration, the Earth Charter, and the UN General Assembly Resolutions on Harmony with Nature did not constitute it, but only created the space for the principle of harmony with nature to emerge in human language within an international agora. Thus, despite adopting the understanding of Kiss and Shelton and Sadeleer, in the sense that the resolutions, even if not binding, have creative potential for protective norms in international environmental law, it is argued in this investigation that this creative process does not apply to the principle of harmony with nature. Indeed, the dynamogenic process of the legal principle of harmony with nature is similar to the process of emergence of good faith in the law of nations, since ancient Roman times, as a pre-legal principle, therefore uncreated and only recognized as a logical necessity and, thus, endowed with inalienability and fundamental rights.

Thus, harmony with nature presents the stature and strength of a general principle of law, which resonates not only in the field of environmental law but also in all other branches of law that somehow interfere with the biosphere. Considering also the glosses of Verdross and Esser, in the sense that the general principles of law are not necessarily written in the texts of treaties, since they can derive from the very conscience of justice of the peoples, it can be affirmed with certainty that harmony with nature emerges in international environmental law as a relational principle, which safeguards trust, coherence, and balance in the relations of human beings with non-human beings, as well as holistic organic entities.

But what would be the nature of this principle of international environmental law, and what would be its normative force? Would it be a cogent principle?

As for the degree of normativity of norms in international law, Kolb teaches that it is about determining "to what extent and in what way the content of a mandatory norm influences the process of its interpretation."[240] Sometimes, normativity may be related to a standard that determines the direct applicability of the norm by the legal

[240] Kolb (2000), p. 164.

operator. However, there are legal concepts that are prescriptive due to their substantial richness. According to Kolb, it is in this latter sense that the principle of good faith, for example, has strong normative power in the field of international law.

Kolb reports that, for some authors like C. Tomuschat, objective good faith is one of the most normative general principles of law, as this normativity stems from its axiomatic nature. Indeed, objective good faith within the scope of international law is a fundamental principle, as it is an axiom—that is, a prerequisite necessary for life in society. Without the principle of objective good faith, all legal relations, both domestic and international, would collapse, which in itself is sufficient to confer upon it a strongly imperative character.[241]

In investigating whether objective good faith would or would not be a principle of *jus cogens*, Kolb explains that the concept of *jus cogens* is related to the existence of an international legal order that cannot be confused with the domestic legal order, considering that this limits the scope of foreign judicial and administrative decisions. However, "the international public order, as understood by the vast majority of authors, refers to a set of norms that express the fundamental values of the international legal order and even of the international community."[242] Thus, the norms of international public order that cannot be derogated by the subjects of international law (States) make up what is called *jus cogens*, unlike the so-called dispositive norms, which are derogable.

In this vein, there is a prevalent view that the general principle of objective good faith, considered a fundamental and axiomatic principle, constitutes *jus cogens*, as it is at the very constitutional base of societies. However, Kolb further deepens the explanation about the normativity of the principle of objective good faith, explaining that some general principles of law are characterized by a logical non-derogability, which does not result from simple convention between the States Parties but from the very nature of things, or reason, and are called axiomatic principles. These principles are endowed with a binding and non-derogable nature, which is pre-legal. Thus, *jus cogens* could not prohibit what is already impossible under the laws of reason, the nature of things, and logic. The so-called *jus cogens* applies to situations where derogability is possible but prohibited by values agreed upon as public order. Objective good faith is a principle whose non-derogability stems from reason itself and not from conventions;[243] therefore, it is preexistent to the very concept of *jus cogens*.

Kolb cites the lesson of G. Schwarzenberger in his general course held in The Hague in 1955, in the sense that the principle of good faith is "a fundamental principle that can only be eradicated from international law at the price of the destruction of international law itself, it is a necessary part of the international public order."[244]

[241] Kolb (2000), p. 169.

[242] Kolb (2000), p. 178.

[243] Kolb (2000), p. 179.

[244] Kolb (2000), p. 180.

Similar to the principle of objective good faith, the principle of harmony with nature also presents this pre-legal non-derogability, which comes from the nature of things—that is, from the natural laws of physics, thermodynamics, biology, ecology, and chemistry—whose systematic violation over the last centuries is leading life on the planet to collapse.

If the suppression of the general principle of the law of objective good faith in international legal relations can collapse institutions and lead societies to a state of anomie, the disregard of the general principle of international environmental law of harmony with nature will collapse the biosphere, which supports all social and legal institutions created by humans, considering that the very emergence of life will succumb to the increasing entropy caused by the disregard of this pre-legal principle, which stems from the great laws of the Earth system.

Thus, harmony with nature, like objective good faith, is a general principle of law endowed with non-derogability and pre-legal imperativeness. While objective good faith is a relational principle that operates in the sociosphere to regulate relations between humans, between legal entities created by humans as technical realities, as well as to guide the subjects of international law in the construction of the desired perpetual peace of Immanuel Kant,[245] the principle of harmony with nature is a relational principle that acts between the sociosphere and the biosphere. That is, it is a general principle of law of pre-legal nature that should guide the relations between humans and non-human beings to establish the *ethos* of inter-species trust, and thus circumvent the anthropogenic crisis that compromises the main human right: the right to life.

Thus, it is a principle that is not even within the sphere of *jus cogens*, in which derogation is logically possible but prohibited by agreed fundamental values; the normativity of the legal principle of harmony with nature is similar to that of the principle of good faith; therefore, it is a binding and non-derogable principle.

The principle of harmony with nature is a general principle of law that arises from the natural laws of the Earth system and from the very ancestral legal consciousness of humanity, so this study considers it as an autonomous source of international law covered by Article 38 of the Statute of the International Court of Justice from 1920, and therefore binding.

5.6 The Normative Core of the Legal Principle of Harmony with Nature

As already demonstrated in previous topics, the principle of harmony with nature emerges autonomously as a general principle of international environmental law, endowed with pre-legal imperativeness and, therefore, dispensable from any express provision in legal texts. Its normative nature and substantive value do

[245] Kant (2008).

not derive from statements provided for in treaties but from the nature of things, that is, from the natural laws of physics, thermodynamics, biology, ecology, chemistry, and, above all, from the ethical principle of universal coherence proposed by Cirne-Lima,[246] which should guide human relations with non-human living beings and holistic organic entities.

This work adopts the method used by Bosselmann in arguing for the normativity of the principle of sustainability[247] to demonstrate the normative core of the principle of harmony with nature.

The investigation into the normative core of the principle of harmony with nature—that is, the fundamental value and central meaning on which human harmony with nature rests—should be made through the observation of the ancestral cultures of peoples.

By scrutinizing the oriental culture of *Tao*, the philosophy of Heraclitus, and the Andean philosophy, it can be inferred that these three currents of thought, although arising in such different times and cultures, have in common the search for harmony, which emerges as the synthesis of the confrontation of antagonistic forces. The core of this harmony, which emerges as a synthesis of opposing forces, is the balance of these forces—the balance of conflicting interests. This balance permeates all interactions and relations in the natural world, in the biosphere; it is the optimal point between the percentages of entropy and negentropy in biological and thermodynamic systems. The relationship and interaction of the human being with the natural world do not escape the reality of this need for balance. Human presence on Earth, more than ever, has affected the equation of this delicate balance.

Thus, it can be understood that the legal principle of harmony of the human being with nature has, as its fundamental core, the balance between human interests concerning the symbolic world created by language and the interests inherent to the health of the biosphere. Like the pointer that marks the balance between antagonistic weights, the principle of harmony with nature is the fulcrum of a large systemic scale, on whose plates are, on one side, the social well-being resulting from the dignity of the human person and, on the other side, the principle of sustainability, from which derives the *grundnorm* of ecological integrity.[248]

In this order of ideas, in the deontic core of the principle of harmony with nature lies the balance, which is the synthesis of social well-being-and ecological integrity, pointed out by Bosselmann as the normative core of the principle of sustainability. For the preservation of the dignity of the human person and the human rights already achieved, there is a need for distributive justice of natural resources; however, this distribution of natural resources must be done sustainably, respecting the integrity of living beings and ecosystems. The balance, which is the synthesis

[246] Cirne-Lima (1999).

[247] Bosselmann (2017), p. 93–96.

[248] Bosselmann (2017), p. 95–96.

of this dialectic, is the normative core of the principle of harmony of the human being with nature.

The language of harmony with nature is prescriptive; it is deontic, it is a duty-to-be rooted in the laws of thermodynamics, ecology, and in the ethics of universal coherence. This normative precept can thus be proposed: *one should always act coherently to find the balance between the social well-being of human beings and ecological integrity.*

The duty-to-be of harmony with nature is not abstract or empty, given that it is filled by the universal coherence found in the morality of various peoples at all times, so it presents aptitude and normative quality to be understood as a legal principle, as it imposes an action that reverberates not only in the biological sphere but also in the social sphere. This "duty-to-be" has as recipients the legislators, the administrators, and all moral agents who, when making their choices and taking their decisions, must observe the balance between human well-being and the integrity of the Earth's ecological systems.

Bosselmann, in defending the normativity of the principle of sustainability, identifies its normative core in integrity and then supports its character as a *grundnorm* (basic norm). He points out that when he argues that the principle of ecological integrity has the character of a fundamental norm, he does so not based on Kelsen's *grundnorm* theory,[249] for whom the basic norm is only an epistemological premise of unity and closure of the system. He proposes ecological integrity as a *grundnorm*, in the sense adopted by Kant and Robert Alexy, that is, a *grundnorm* filled with moral value, as he considers that ecological integrity, as the normative core of sustainability, is a natural consequence of the dictates of reason. He argues, based on John Finnis' natural law theory, that integrity is also a natural law resulting from life and practical reasonableness.

Bosselmann identifies, in the normative core of the principle of sustainability, the ecological integrity as a *grundnorm* for international environmental law:

> The commitment to safeguard the integrity of life support systems on Earth should be promoted as a basic norm of international law, as the current system of multilateral environmental agreements lacks a unifying and clearly agreed objective, for which international regulatory regimes and organizations are legally obligated to contribute. This means that if a treaty does not contain, expressly or implicitly, a fundamental duty around ecological sustainability, then the default position is state sovereignty, with its traditional right to exploit and use natural resources.[250]

As can be seen, Bosselmann argues for the existence of a basic norm implicit in international environmental law. He presents sufficiently convincing legal grounds, in the sense that the principle of sustainability is a principle of international environmental law, even if implicit. This work adheres to Bosselmann's thesis, adding, however, an instrumental condition, a logical antecedent for sustainability

[249] Kelsen (1999), p. 136.

[250] Bosselmann (2017), p. 96–97.

and for ecological integrity itself; this condition is the relational principle of harmony with nature, whose *ethos* is inspired by the need for universal coherence.

Indeed, to effectuate the principle of sustainability, it is necessary, first of all, to recognize nature as a subject in a perennial relationship with the human being—a relationship founded on the ethics of universal coherence—with the purpose of achieving a balance between human well-being, resulting from human dignity, and ecological integrity, which is at the core of sustainability. This is the tone of the legal principle of harmony with nature.

Ecological integrity, as the core of the principle of sustainability, cannot be thought of separately from human well-being, as a consequence of the principle of human dignity in its ecological perspective. It is not possible to think of the principle of ecological integrity in isolation without taking into consideration the economic and cultural needs of humanity, so that the principle of harmony with nature, founded on the ethics of universal coherence, emerges as a tool for this consideration, given that, at the normative core of the principle of harmony with nature, is balance, which is the synthesis of antagonistic interests.

The balance between the social well-being of the human being, resulting from human dignity, and ecological integrity, which resides at the core of the principle of sustainability, results from the harmonious relationship between these apparently antinomic principles. As stated, it is an apparent antinomy only, given that human well-being also depends on ecological integrity, due to the biological dimension of the human being.

Bosselmann emphasizes that, although the Earth Charter does not have the *status* of law within the structures of international *hard law* and *soft law*, one cannot:

> [...] discard it as a nullity. If considered within an ecological law paradigm, the Earth Charter can be seen as a central articulation of an ecological **grundnorm** [...]. Conceptually, a **grundnorm** exists independent of a legal system, but should be seen as a basic norm to bind and guide governmental power.[251]

Then, by adopting the premise proposed by Bosselmann, in the sense that the principle of integrity is a *grundnorm* in international environmental law, "as the core of the next generation of international environmental legislation, which could be called 'Earth system law'," the principle of harmony with nature, whose powers of binding and non-derogability are pre-legal, as already explained previously, has among its functions the hermeneutic role, similar to the relational principle of objective good faith, of establishing a bond of trust and coherence between the human being and nature, with the aim of ensuring balance, ultimately, between the *grundnorm* of ecological integrity[252] and the dignity of the human being.

Just like the principle of good faith, the principle of harmony with nature not only has an interpretative function but also an integrative one; that is, it serves as a source of norms for the relations between humans and nature.

---

[251] Bosselmann (2017), p. 98.

[252] Bosselmann (2017), p. 98.

At this point, it is worth recalling the lesson of Domenico Farias, quoted by Bonavides, who believes that principles are norms that, in addition to being characterized by a high degree of abstraction, also present the trait of *fecundity*. He derives from the idea of *fecundity* that the principles are the soul and the foundation of other norms and that they present two essential functions: interpretative and integrative:

> The most defined legal form through which the fecundity of principles is presented is, first and foremost, the interpretative and integrative function. The recourse to principles is imposed on the jurist to guide the interpretation of obscure laws, or to supplement their silence. Even before the Constitutional Charters, or rather, before, under the influence of Enlightenment natural law, very generic legal maxims spread in codifications, the recourse to principles was already a necessity to interpret and integrate laws.[253]

In this line, the principle of harmony with nature serves as an interpretative guide within the scope of international environmental law and domestic law. In addition, it has the function of filling the gaps in legal systems regarding the regulation of human relations with nature in various branches of law.

The principle of harmony with nature, at the core of which is ecological balance, as already demonstrated, is a principle endowed with binding force as a natural unfolding of the laws that govern the very emergence of life and universal coherence, to act as an interpretative guide in favor of ecological integrity. When the interpreter weighs principles involving ecological values, at the foundation of which is the basic norm of ecological integrity, the principle of harmony with nature serves as a hermeneutic criterion for the correct interpretation of international and national environmental law in order to safeguard the basic norm of ecological integrity.

The principle of harmony with nature, at the core of which is ecological balance, also serves the function of weighing and balancing two magnitudes: social well-being, resulting from the principle of human dignity, when in conflict with the principle of sustainability.

Unlike reasonableness and proportionality, whose rooting and measure are human reason itself, the foundation and measure of the principle of harmony with nature, as a hermeneutic criterion for weighing conflicting interests to achieve balance, is the law of universal coherence.

Coherence in the interconnection of the symbolic world of language with the natural world facilitates the achievement of ecological balance, proposed in this work as the normative core of the principle of harmony with nature, presented as a hermeneutic instrument to ensure the *grundnorm* of ecological integrity. As can be seen, the principle of harmony with nature expands the scope of the social contract and the discourse wheel to include all beings—humans, non-humans, and holistic organic entities—in the circle of moral and legal consideration.

In the sphere of interests, which are characteristic of the institutions forged by human beings in their symbolic universe, the realization of good and justice—that

[253] Bonavides (2001), p. 246.

is, coherence—is operationalized by principles of practical reason, such as reasonableness, proportionality, and objective good faith. Already at the interface of this human symbolic universe with the natural world, the biosphere, the realization of good and justice, as an expression of coherence in human relations with nature, resides in ecological balance. This balance is the very normative core of the principle of harmony with nature, which emerges as a general principle of international environmental law, operating at the interface of political and legal institutions with the natural world to consider the relevance of the laws of nature in formulating policies and legal norms that regulate human relations with the biosphere.

Thus, every human project must be coherent with the natural world. The coherent decision is the one that ensures the ecological balance that is at the normative core of the principle of harmony with nature, which, in addition to operating as a hermeneutic and instrumental principle of the *grundnorm* of ecological integrity proposed by Bosselmann, has significant substantive value in the ethical and legal system, as will be demonstrated later.

When the principle of harmony with nature prescribes to the human being, as a strong evaluator, to assess the coherence of acts that are characteristic of human language—ethics, esthetics, economics, politics, and legal norms—with natural laws, it imposes on him, above all, the moral and legal duty to dialog with non-human beings and with nature itself.

The ethical imposition of examining the coherence of human action with natural laws is not a subjective process based on human emotions and interests; rather, it is an objective process, to the extent that the human being, as a strong moral agent and evaluator, is the recipient of the duty to seek harmony with nature, based on the understanding of the language of the natural world itself. As can be seen, this coherence examination is constantly in dialog.

In this way, the principle of harmony with nature, at the core of which is ecological balance—measured by the universal coherence proposed by Cirne-Lima—presents two substantive effects: (i) It imposes on the human being, as a moral agent, the recognition of intrinsic value and subjectivity of non-human living beings and holistic organic entities; and (ii) it prescribes to the human being the duty to open space, in the wheel of political and legal discourse, for non-human living beings and holistic organic entities, since the balance between the interests of ecological integrity and development, apparently antagonistic, can only be achieved by understanding and respecting the needs of the other, through empathy.

When the legal principle of harmony with nature establishes for the human being a direct and immediate duty-to-be, in the sense of examining the coherence of his acts in relation to non-human living beings and holistic organic entities, with the observance of natural laws, it prescribes for the human being, as a moral agent, also the duty to dialog with all non-human living beings in the wheel of legal discourse of environmental law, at the base of which is the *grundnorm* of ecological integrity proposed by Bosselmann.

In this line, considering that the guarantee of expression of a being presupposes the recognition of its moral consideration and intrinsic value, it is inferred that one of the immediate and inexorable effects of the principle of harmony with nature is the recognition of moral consideration, intrinsic value, and the *status* of legal personhood for non-human living beings and holistic organic entities.

The eventual objection that the inclusion of non-human living beings and ecosystems in the wheel of discourse would be hindered by linguistic limitations is easily circumvented when one is aware that one is at a third level of coherence assessment—a hybrid space, an interface between the symbolic world forged by human language and the natural world, which includes a diversity of languages, the most prominent being the language of the very laws that govern natural processes.

5.7 The Principle of Harmony with Nature in the Brazilian Constitution of 1988

Ingo Wolfgang Sarlet and Tiago Fensterseifer emphasize that, just as the theory of constitutions and constitutional law was committed to the affirmation of liberal and social values, today it turns to the protection and promotion of the environment, raising it to the level of a constitutionally protected value. They cite the apt expression of Pereira da Silva, who named the "greening" of the theory of the constitution and constitutional law as this movement toward environmental protection as a value of constitutional *status*. They point to the existence of the construction of an "ecological constitutional theory" and cite the lesson of Gomes Canotilho, from the analysis of the Portuguese Constitution, in the sense that this Charter brings a *legal-constitutional program that embodies a true "Environmental Constitution."*[254]

Sarlet and Fensterseifer list the acceptance of the so-called Environmental Constitution in the following legal systems: the Brazilian Constitution of 1988, the Portuguese Constitution of 1976, the Spanish Constitution of 1978, the German Basic Law of 1949, the Colombian Constitution of 1991, the South African Constitution of 1996, the Swiss Constitution of 2000, and the French Constitution of 1958, which incorporated the Environmental Charter in 2004, as well as the Ecuadorian Constitution of 2008 and the Bolivian Constitution of 2009. They emphasize that, despite the singularities of each of these legal systems, all these political charters have in common the elevation of environmental protection as a constitutional value—a protection that is a task of the state.[255]

They highlight that in the constitutions of Portugal, South Africa, and Brazil, this duty of the state, in the sense of protecting the environment as a value, was elevated to the *status* of a fundamental right and fundamental duty; the Constitution of Ecuador went further and recognized the rights of nature.[256] In the same sense,

[254] Sarlet and Fensterseifer (2014), p. 31–32.

[255] Sarlet and Fensterseifer (2014), p. 32.

[256] Sarlet and Fensterseifer (2014), p. 32.

Boyd observes that the Bolivian Constitution also expressly protects the Rights of Mother Earth and emphasizes that this constitutional protection of the rights of nature was driven by the worldview of indigenous peoples.[257]

For Sarlet and Fensterseifer, the Brazilian Constitution of 1988 included the protection of the environment "among the permanent and fundamental values of the Brazilian Republic."[258] The authors argue for the consecration, by the Constitution of the Republic of 1988, of a "Socio-environmental State of Law,"[259] whose primary basis is the dignity of the human person, but they note that this basis is not exclusive, considering that it also rests on a series of other rights of a defensive, provisionary nature and the so-called fundamental duties.

When discussing fundamental duties, they mention the constitutional duty of solidarity as a development of the social and community dimension of human dignity, emphasizing "the relational perspective of the human person in relation to the social body it integrates, as well as the legal (and not just moral) commitment of the State and individuals in composing a social framework of dignity for (and with) everyone."[260]

Sarlet and Fensterseifer further delve into the topic to explore an ecological dimension of human dignity:

> [...] the legal concept of human dignity will be adopted formulated by the first author as an open conceptual-normative framework to a partial reformulation, especially, for the purpose of emphasizing the inclusion of an ecological dimension and, in such a way, make the concept more responsive to the new and old existential challenges imposed by environmental degradation, but also in view of cultural evolution and the new socio-environmental values legitimized in the community context. Similarly, the reflection aims to point out the need for recognition of a dignity of life in general, therefore not only of human life, as well as to suggest the need not only for attribution and recognition of a dignity to future generations, but, beyond that, the existence of legal-constitutional duties of protection of this non-human dignity and of future human generations.[261]

The authors propose an expansion of the conceptual framework of human dignity, built from the Kantian–anthropocentric matrix, to encompass "the new cultural and ethical values that sediment socio-environmental relations within the framework of the **risk society**."[262] They explain that the dignity of the human person should be interpreted from a multidimensional point of view, taking into account the historical evolution of humanity. Just as in other times, the dignity of the human person received a substantial meaning from liberal and social rights, it currently receives the influence of solidarity rights, among which is the right to live in a healthy, balanced environment, in which not only the dignity of human life is important, but also the dignity of the life of non-human beings.

[257] Boyd (2017), p. 196.

[258] Sarlet and Fensterseifer (2014), p. 75.

[259] Sarlet and Fensterseifer (2014), p. 78.

[260] Sarlet and Fensterseifer (2014), p. 80.

[261] Sarlet and Fensterseifer (2014), p. 81.

[262] Sarlet and Fensterseifer (2014), p. 82.

In their defense of the ecological dimension of human dignity, Sarlet and Fensterseifer present it as the axiological matrix of the socio-environmental state and expressly postulate the recognition of intrinsic value also for non-human beings, such as animals, plants, and ecosystems.[263] It is, therefore, verified that in their thesis on the ecological dimension of human dignity, the authors adhere to an ecocentric interpretation of the 1988 Constitution, considering that they recognize intrinsic value not only for living beings but also for ecosystems and, therefore, go beyond the animal liberation movement and biocentrism, adhering to a broader view, which also includes ecosystems in the circle of ethical consideration.[264]

In the same vein, the understanding of Antônio Herman Benjamin is noted, for whom the constitutional norm of paragraph 1, inc. I, of Article 225 of the CR/1988, in protecting the essential processes for the survival of the planet, surpassed the anthropocentric paradigm to adopt a biocentric, or even ecocentric, view.[265] He also observes that the CR/1988, in Article 225, § 1°, inc. VII, when explicitly prohibiting practices that may cause the extinction of species and, also, those that subject animals to cruelty, signaled the recognition of value not only instrumental for other forms of life, which corroborates the defense of his thesis of the adoption by the 1988 Constitution of an ecological human dignity that surpasses the anthropocentric model.

The recognition of this ecological dimension of human dignity, proposed by Sarlet and Fensterseifer, dialogs with the principle of harmony with nature in the 1988 Constitution.

As will be demonstrated, the principle of harmony with nature is implicitly provided for in the text of Article 225, *caput*, of the CR/1988. Despite the said prescriptive statement not making explicit mention of the word harmony in its text, it refers expressly to the ecological balance, protecting it as a fundamental right.

Indeed, the first part of the statement of Article 225, *caput*, of the CR/1988 states: "Everyone has the right to an **ecologically balanced** environment, a common good of the people and essential to a healthy quality of life [. . .]"[266] (emphasis ours).

In an anthropocentric, reductionist, and restrictive interpretation, the sign "everyone" would cover only human beings as the recipients of the norm. However, in light of the ontological and ethical paradigm shift, extensively examined in previous chapters, which recognizes intrinsic value in non-human living beings and holistic organic entities, the indefinite pronoun in the plural "everyone" takes on a new meaning. "Everyone" should include not only present human beings, but also future generations, as well as other species of non-human living

263 Sarlet and Fensterseifer (2014), p. 88.

264 Sarlet and Fensterseifer (2014), p. 95.

265 Benjamin (2007), p. 90.

266 Available at: http://www.planalto.gov.br/ccivil_03/constituicao/constituicao.htm. Accessed on: May 22, 2021.

beings and holistic organic entities: ecosystems, species, rivers, mountains, seas, oceans, and the biosphere itself.

This expansion of the subjectivity of the recipients of the protective norm of Article 225, *caput,* of the CR/1988 is primarily a consequence of the principle of harmony with nature implicitly contained in the Constitution of 1988, as will be seen below.

Indeed, the normative core of the principle of harmony with nature is ecological balance, as it represents the balance of a large systemic scale, on whose plates are, on one side, social well-being as a corollary of human dignity, and, on the other side, the principle of sustainability, at the core of which is the *grundnorm* of ecological integrity.

At the deontic core of the principle of harmony with nature lies ecological balance, as the synthesis of two seemingly conflicting interests: the social well-being of humanity and ecological integrity, the latter considered by Bosselmann as the normative core of the principle of sustainability.[267] Harmony, in its deepest conception, is dialectical, as can be seen in the fragments of Heraclitus' work, who explained its dialectical nature as follows: "They do not understand how the diverse agrees with itself, harmony of the antagonist as in the bow and the lyre."[268]

It can be inferred from fragment 51 of Heraclitus' work, the oldest account of harmony in Western culture, that its quintessence is the concord of antagonistic interests, which is only achieved by the balance of forces in tension. Thus, the normative core of the principle of harmony with nature is ecological balance, which synthesizes antagonistic interests embodied in the social well-being and progress of humanity, in the face of ecological integrity, which resides in the normative core of the principle of sustainability, according to Bosselmann.[269]

The principle of harmony with nature, as previously explained, is based on the laws of thermodynamics, ecology, and, above all, on the ethics of universal coherence. This normative precept can thus be proposed: *One should always act coherently to find the balance between the social well-being of human beings and the ecological integrity of the biosphere, with all living beings.*

It is therefore evident that the principle of harmony with nature is not an abstract or empty formula constructed by human rationality, as it is filled with the value of ecological balance, the content of which is provided by the sciences of the Earth system and by the ethical principle of universal coherence of Cirne-Lima.[270] The "ought-to-be" established in the principle of harmony with nature has as its recipients the legislators, administrators, and all citizens, individually or collectively, who, in making their choices and decisions, must observe the balance between human well-being and the integrity of the Earth's ecological systems. This is what is derived from the text of Article 225, *caput*, of the CR/1988, which

---

[267] Bosselmann (2017), p. 93.

[268] Ferrater Mora (2004), p. 1323.

[269] Bosselmann (2017), p. 93.

[270] Cirne-Lima (2017).

provides that: "Everyone has the right to an **ecologically balanced environment**, a common good of the people and essential to a healthy quality of life [...]" (emphasis ours).

When the original constituent power used the expression "ecologically balanced environment," it brought the value of balance to the constitutional text and thus implicitly positivized in Brazilian law the principle of harmony with nature, considering that ecological balance is the normative core of harmony itself. Indeed, harmony, in its dialectical root, as a synthesis of opposing forces, can only be achieved by the balance of these forces in tension.

In this line of thought, ecological integrity, as the core of the principle of sustainability, cannot be understood in isolation from human well-being and also in its intellectual and spiritual dimensions, as a consequence of the principle of human dignity itself. Thus, the principle of harmony with nature, based on the universal coherence ethos proposed by Cirne-Lima,[271] and in whose normative core lies ecological balance, emerges in the preamble of Article 225 of the 1988 Constitution as an instrumental principle for the weighing of these seemingly antagonistic interests.

In the 1988 Constitution, the antagonism between ecological integrity and social well-being is only apparent, much like that mentioned in Heraclitus' fragment 51. These two diverse and opposing interests, when weighed by ecological balance—which constitutes the normative core of the principle of harmony with nature—agree with each other and rise to the great synthesis in the socio-environmental state: the principle of human dignity in its ecological, multidimensional, and ecocentric dimension, as proposed by Sarlet and Fensterseifer.[272]

Human dignity in this ecological dimension is enhanced by two ethical principles that elevate the human being to the highest level of consciousness as a moral agent: the principle of universal coherence of Cirne-Lima[273] and the principle of responsibility of Hans Jonas.[274] Ultimately, the balance of tensions between ecological integrity and human social well-being benefits not only non-human living beings and holistic organic entities but also the human being who, like other living beings, has an inalienable biological dimension, which relies on the ecological integrity of the biosphere as a *hólon*[275] in the complex terrestrial biotic system, which points to an open becoming for the imponderable.

The "ecologically balanced environment" guaranteed as a fundamental right in the 1988 Constitution harbors the normative core of the principle of harmony with nature, that is, ecological balance. Just as the principle of due process, in its substantive conception, is implicit in Section LIV of Article 5 of the CR/1988, without making any mention of the words reasonableness or proportionality, the

[271] Cirne-Lima (1999), p. 962.

[272] Sarlet and Fensterseifer (2014), p. 88.

[273] Cirne-Lima (1999).

[274] Jonas (2006), p. 229.

[275] Koestler (1969), p. 68.

principle of harmony with nature is implicitly inscribed in the preamble of Article 225 of the CR/1988.

The principle of harmony with nature, as an implicit norm in the preamble of Article 225 of the CR/1988, emerges as a guiding principle, which can act as a "connecting vessel," in the expression used by Sadeleer to refer to the principles of prevention, precaution, and polluter-pays. Sadeleer explains that guiding principles are open and, thus, have the ability to link environmental law to other branches of law and also to other disciplines outside the legal scope, such as sciences and economics. Therefore, they are key to solving the interdisciplinary problems that characterize environmental law.[276]

Indeed, the constitutional principle of harmony with nature bridges environmental law and Earth system sciences, as it offers a semantic opening for the normative texts of environmental law to dialog with the texts of biology, physics, and thermodynamics, thus bringing to the normative field the understanding of the reality of natural laws, such as the law of entropy, the ontic opening of ecosystems, and the holistic principle.[277]

In addition, the principle of harmony with nature, as a general principle of international environmental law, allows courts to expand their hermeneutic horizons to consider the experiences of other legal systems that have implemented the principle of harmony with nature by recognizing the intrinsic value and subjectivity of non-human living beings and holistic organic entities, such as rivers and forests.

The principle of harmony with nature, implicitly provided for in the preamble of Article 225 of the CR/1988, is also intended to guide the legislator, who must adopt infraconstitutional norms that give it effectiveness and, in addition, act as a delimitation of the discretionary power of the public administrator.

The constitutional principle of harmony with nature emerges through the interpretative function of the current environmental legislation, to provide the significance that best suits the balance between human interest in social well-being and ecological integrity, which lies at the normative core of the principle of sustainability.

As previously mentioned, this work proposes an equivalence between the principle of objective good faith and the principle of harmony with nature. If the principle of objective good faith is the substrate, in international and domestic law, of human contractual relations to safeguard coherence and trust, the principle of harmony with nature emerges as the basis of relations between humans and non-human beings and holistic organic entities, serving as a guiding principle of the natural contract, in the expression of Michel Serres,[278] to guarantee the *ethos* of Cirne-Lima's universal coherence in interspecies relations.

---

[276] Sadeleer (2020), p. 411.

[277] Koestler (1969), p. 68.

[278] "Therefore, the return to nature! This implies adding to the exclusively social contract a celebration of a natural contract of symbiosis and reciprocity where our relationship with things would allow dominion and possession through admiring listening, reciprocity, contemplation, and

Just as the principle of objective good faith has the corrective function of addressing the abuse of rights in contractual relations between humans, as provided for in Article 187 of the Civil Code, the constitutional principle of harmony with nature, whose objective is to regulate relations between human beings and non-human living beings as well as holistic organic entities, also serves the corrective function of addressing the abuse of rights by humans in their interactions with the environment. For this purpose, all relations that disrespect the ecological balance, which constitutes the normative core of the constitutional principle of harmony with nature as provided for in Article 225, *caput*, of the CR/1988, are understood to be abusive.

Thus, as the doctrine of objective good faith offers, within the scope of contractual civil law, the so-called partial figures to correct possible abuses of rights in contracts, especially those resulting from contradictory behavior inhibited by the *venire contra factum proprium,* the constitutional principle of harmony with nature, inscribed in the *caput* of Article 225 of the CR/1988, in its corrective function of abuses perpetrated by humans in their relations with nature, unfolds in the principles of precaution, prevention, *in dubio pro natura,* and the polluter-pays principle.

As Sadeleer points out: "The principles of the polluter-pays, prevention and precaution form the meeting point of tremendous tensions: between supranational and national legal orders, between the global and the local, between law and science, and between modernity and post-modernity."[279] Thus, at the intersection of these tensions, these three principles, along with the *in dubio pro natura,* emerged as an unfolding of the principle of harmony with nature itself, in its corrective function of addressing abuses of environmental rights, to minimize the risks of irreversible ecological damage.

The constitutional principle of harmony with nature also has an integrative function, providing the law enforcer with the contents of Earth system science to fill the gaps in environmental law in the judgment of concrete cases, always with the purpose of achieving ecological balance.

From the integrative function of the principle of harmony with nature derives the recognition of intrinsic value and subjectivity of non-human living beings and holistic organic entities, as will be seen below. From the integrative function of the principle of harmony with nature, as a source of rights for non-human living beings and holistic organic entities, this work proposes, as will be seen later, the

respect, where knowledge would no longer imply ownership, nor action dominion, nor these their results or stercoraceous conditions. A contract of armistice in the objective war, a contract of symbiosis: the symbiont acknowledges the right of the host, while the parasite—our current status—condemns to death the one who inhabits without being aware that, in the long run, it condemns itself to disappearance. The parasite grabs everything and gives nothing, the host gives everything and grabs nothing. The right of domination and property is reduced to parasitism. On the contrary, the right of symbiosis is defined by reciprocity: what nature gives to man is what he owes to her, made a subject of law." Serres (1990), p. 65–66.

[279] Sadeleer (2020), p. 11.

recognition of biological dignity for living beings and of biological legal personality, on which the concept of biological legal person is based, which manifests itself in three dimensions: (i) plant biological person; (ii) animal biological person; and (iii) systemic biological person.

Finally, to understand the greatest impact of the constitutional principle of harmony with nature in the text of Article 225, *caput*, of the CR/1988, it is necessary to investigate the semantic dimension of the signs "ecological balance," first in its etymological root and, in a second moment, in the historical, social, and scientific reality of today.

The etymology of the sign "balance" intrinsically brings to its semantic content the relational value. The word "balance" originates from the Latin *aequilibrium*, composed of the adjectives *aequus* (equal) and *libra* (balance).[280]

The word "balance" is also used in fundamental concepts in other sciences, such as physics and physico-chemistry. Previously, the definition of thermodynamic equilibrium, a concept of physics, applied to ecology and was embodied in the law of entropy, which should be minimized and which, therefore, should not be confused with ecological balance or dynamic balance—these being, indeed, desirable and necessary for life on Earth and, therefore, explicitly provided for in Article 225, *caput*, of the CR/1988.

The notion of balance presupposes an equitable relationship between equals, a harmonious and coherent proportion. Intrinsic to the meaning of balance is the idea of a clash between antagonistic interests of equals. Balance can only be conceived between ontological categories of equals: (i) balance between the interests of subjects in opposing positions; and (ii) balance between the weight or force of objects in antagonistic positions. It is not possible to establish a balance between subject and thing, considering that the relationship between subject and thing is not guided by morality or equity, but only by the convenience of the subject.

At this point, it is worth remembering Leopold's lesson:

> When the divine Odysseus returned from the wars in Troy, he suspected that his slaves had misbehaved during his absence, so he hanged a dozen slaves from his house. This hanging of twelve women was considered only as a matter of property. Already at that time the disposition of property was, as it is today, a matter of convenience, not of right or wrong.[281]

Leopold explains that the concept of right and wrong already existed in the Greece of Odysseus and cites, as an example, the ethical protection of wives by husbands, who witnessed their fidelity before embarking on their journeys. However, the women enslaved by Odysseus were not covered by the ethical circle that protected the wives. The enslaved women were not considered subjects, as the wives were, but rather movable human goods, and thus were outside the reach of the circle of ethical consideration. Their hanging did not undergo an evaluation of justice criteria but was determined solely by the convenience judgment of the owner, within his power of disposition over the "thing."

---

[280] Houaiss (2001), p. 1184.

[281] Leopold (1949), p. 179.

According to Leopold, the evolution of the extension of ethics, commonly studied by philosophers, reveals "a process of ecological evolution." First, there was the ethics that deal with the relationship between individuals, and he cites as an example the Mosaic Decalogue; then came the ethics of relations between individuals and society, which reached its peak with democracy. However, an ethics that deals with the relationship of the human being with the Earth, animals, and plants concludes:

> The Earth, like Odysseus' slaves, is still property. The relationship with the Earth is strictly economic, implying privileges, but not obligations. The extension of ethics to this third element in the human environment is, if I read the evidence correctly, an evolutionary possibility and an ecological necessity. It is the third stage of a sequence.[282]

As long as non-human living beings and ecosystems are not included in the circle of ethical consideration, with the recognition of their intrinsic value and their subjectivity as rights holders, they will be like Odysseus' enslaved women. The establishment of an ethical relationship with the Earth, with non-human living beings and ecosystems, is a condition to achieve ecological balance.

Thus, there is no concrete possibility of achieving ecological balance while the human being does not have obligations or duties toward non-human living beings and holistic organic entities. In a relationship between unequals, where one species has the privilege of disposing of the members of other species as a simple legal category of "thing," there is no ethics, no judgment of right or wrong. This preponderance of one species over the others, in itself, is already an ecological imbalance and, therefore, does not comply with Article 225, *caput*, of the CR/1988.

Indeed, turning to the concept of ecological balance, Milaré defines it as follows:

> (1) Stable population size in which mortality and emigration rates are offset by birth and immigration rates. (2) Population in which gene frequencies are in balance. (3) Ecological balance is a requirement for maintaining the quality and essential characteristics of the ecosystem or a certain environment. It should not be understood as a static situation, but as a dynamic state in the broad context of the relations between various beings that make up the environment, such as trophic relations, the transport of matter and energy. Ecological balance presupposes mechanisms of self-regulation and feedback of ecosystems.[283]

As can be seen, the very definition of ecological balance brings values of a relational and equitable nature. However, as has already been demonstrated in this work, the human species, in its position of prevalence over the other species that make up the community of living beings on Earth, has become overpopulated and impacts, with its lifestyle, not only the existence of other species but also the very geological structure of the planet. This position of dominance and privilege of the human being over other living beings in the Earth system, in itself, denotes a serious ecological imbalance.

---

[282] Leopold (1949), p. 179.

[283] Milaré (2015), p. 338.

In this line, the right to ecological balance can only be respected if we consider, among the recipients of this right, within the scope of the term "all" in the *caput* of Article 225 of the CR/1988, non-human living beings and holistic organic entities.

The anthropocentric view, which restricts the recipients of the norm of Article 225, *caput*, of the CR/1988 only to human beings, by itself undermines the concept of ecological balance, considering that there is no possibility of balance in an interpretation where nature itself—animals, plants, and ecosystems—are not considered as holders of intrinsic value and subjects of rights.

As already demonstrated, ecological balance is the very normative core of the principle of harmony with nature, and the meaning of the word "harmony" adopted in this work, as already mentioned earlier, harks back to Heraclitean dialectics. The sign in the Greek language for harmony is *ἁρμονία*, whose meaning in Greek is "junction." Heidegger, in his interpretation of fragment 123 of Heraclitus, understood *ἁρμονία* as the "junction," the interconnection of two entities in interaction. Hence arises the so-called doctrine of the harmony of opposites, whose metaphor is the junction of the bow and the lyre as opposing forces—thesis and antithesis—from which the synthesis is musicality. From the unity of opposites, in dialectical synthesis, unfolds becoming, the movement.

According to Capra, similar to Heraclitus' doctrine, Taoism is based on the harmony of opposites. Furthermore, the Inca concept of *yanantin*, as already explained earlier, also carries the meaning of the synthesis of opposites, *yána* and *yánan*, where the suffix *tin* is the element of junction that seeks cosmic balance and harmony.[284]

It is therefore observed that the meaning of the word "harmony" in the constitutional principle of harmony with nature carries, as semantic content, the relational value and the balance between opposing interests of equals, as the final synthesis of a permanent dialectical movement. Thus, when the Constitution of Brazil states in Article 225, *caput*, that "Everyone has the right to an ecologically balanced environment [. . .]," it should first be understood that "everyone" also includes non-human living beings and holistic organic entities. The time has come to understand that the aforementioned legal provision has removed non-human living beings, plants, animals, and ecosystems from the position of mere things or even goods, to recognize them as subjects of rights.

The constitutional principle of harmony with nature, inscribed in Article 225, *caput*, of the CR/1988, in its integrative function, has as its main effect the expansion of the circle of ethical consideration of the social contract to include non-human living beings and holistic organic entities, recognizing them not only for their intrinsic value but also for their subjectivity and *status* as recipients of the right to ecological balance and a healthy quality of life, along with human beings, as members of a single biotic and ethical community and parts of a natural

[284] Calderón Galliani and Fernando (2015), p. 128.

contract,[285] whose foundations should be the universal coherence of Cirne-Lima, relationality,[286] reciprocity,[287] complementarity,[288] and asymmetric and unilateral responsibility[289] for the exacerbated risk in the Anthropocene.

References

Acosta A (2016) O bem viver: uma oportunidade para imaginar outros mundos. Tradução de Tadeu Breda. Autonomia literária. Elefante, São Paulo

Alexy R (2008) Teoria dos direitos fundamentais. Tradução: virgílio Afonso da Silva. Malheiros, São Paulo

Benjamin AH (2007) Constitucionalização do ambiente e ecologização da constituição brasileira. In: Canotilho JJG, Leite JRM (Org) Direito constitucional ambiental brasileiro. Saraiva, São Paulo

Beyerlin U, Marauhn T (2011) International environmental law. Hart Publishing. Oxford, UK, E-book

Bonavides P (2001) Curso de direito constitucional, 11 edn. rev., atual. e ampl. Malheiros, São Paulo

Bosselmann K (2017) The principle of sustainability: transforming law and governance, 2nd edn. Routledge, New York, NY

Boyd DR (2017) The rights of nature: a legal revolution that could save the world. ECW Press, Toronto, Canada

Calderón Galliani S, Fernando O (2015) Entre Eros y Wiracocha: un encuentro dialogico entre la filosofia griega y el pensamiento andino, p 148. Tesis (Licenciado en Filosofía)—Facultad de Letras y Ciencias Humanas. Universidad Nacional Mayor de San Marcos, Lima, Perú, 2015. Available: http://cybertesis.unmsm.edu.pe/bitstream/handle/20.500.12672/4395/Salazar_go.pdf?sequence=1. Accessed 04 Feb 2025

Capra F (2012) O ponto de mutação: a ciência, a sociedade e cultura emergente, 30 edn. Cultrix, São Paulo

Castro EVd (1996) Os pronomes cosmológicos e o perspectivismo ameríndio. Mana, Rio de Janeiro 2(2):115–144, out. Available: https://www.scielo.br/scielo.php?script=sci_arttext&pid=S0104-93131996000200005. Accessed 20 Apr 2025.

Chardin TD (1997) O lugar do homem na natureza: estrutura e direcções evolutivas. Tradução de Armando Pereira da Silva. Instituto Piaget, Lisboa

Cirne-Lima CRV (1999) Ética de coerência dialética. Veritas: revista de Filosofia da PUCRS, Porto Alegre 44(4), dez. Available: https://revistaseletronicas.pucrs.br/ojs/index.php/veritas/artcile/view/35248/18499. Accessed 20 Apr 2025.

Cirne-Lima CRV (2001) Platão: o uno e o múltiplo. In: Feltes HPDM, Zilles U (org) Filosofia: diálogo de hori-zontes: festschrift em homenagem a Jayme Paviani. Caxias do Sul, EDUCS; EDIPUCRS. Porto Ale-gre

Cirne-Lima CRV (2017) Dialética para principiantes. Escritos, Porto Alegre

Council of Europe (1979) Convention on the Conservation of European Wildlife and Natural Habitats. Bern, 19 Sept. Preâmbulo. Available: https://rm.coe.int/1680078aff. Accessed 21 Apr 2025

[285] Serres (1990), p. 65–66.

[286] Estermann (2006), p. 107.

[287] Estermann (2006), p. 145.

[288] Estermann (2006), p. 139.

[289] Jonas (2006), p. 229.

Dworkin R (2013) Taking rights seriously. Bloomsbury Academic, London, New York
Esser J (1961) Principio y norma en la elaboración jurisprudencial del derecho privado. Traducción del alemán por Eduardo Valentí Fiol. Bosch, Barcelona
Esser J (2019) Principio y norma en la elaboración jurisprudencial del derecho privado. Traducción del alemán por Eduardo Valentí Fiol. Olejnik, Santiago-Chile
Estermann J (2006) Filosofia andina: sabiduría indígena para un undo nuevo. 2 edn. Paz L, Instituto Superior Ecuménico Andino de Teología (ISEAT), Bolivia. (Teología y Filosoía Andinas, 1)
Ferrater Mora José (2004) Dicionário de filosofia, vol 2, 2 edn. Loyola, São Paulo
Filho G, da Silva M, Penha-Silva N (2005) Uma abordagem termodinâmica da vida. Ciência Hoje 37(221):34–39, nov. Available: http://www.leb.esalq.usp.br/leb/aulas/lce5702/termodinamica vida.pdf. Accessed 30 Apr 2025
Francisco P (2015) Carta Encíclica Laudato Si': sobre o cuidado com a casa comum. Roma, 24 maio. Available: http://www.vatican.va/content/francesco/pt/encyclicals/documents/papa-francesco _20150524_enciclica-laudato-si.html. Accessed 04 Feb 2025
Galuppo MC (1999) A contribuição de Esser para a reconstrução do conceito de princípios jurídicos. Revista de Direito Comparado, Belo Horizonte. Faculdade de Direito da UFMG, n. 3, maio
Globo Natureza (2013) Aposentado cria planta em garrafão fechado há mais de 40 anos. 25/03/ 2013. Available: http://g1.globo.com/natureza/noticia/2013/01/aposentado-cria-planta-em-garrafao-fechado-ha-mais-de-40-anos.html. Accessed 30 Apr 2025
Gudynas E (2019) Direitos da Natureza: ética biocêntrica e política ambientais. Tradução Igor Ojeda. Elefante, São Paulo
Houaiss A (2001) Dicionário Houaiss da língua portuguesa. Objetiva, Rio de Janeiro
Jonas H (2006) O princípio responsabilidade: ensaio de uma ética para uma civilização tecnológica. Tradução de Marijane Lisboa e Luiz Barros Montez. Contraponto; PUC Rio, Rio de Janeiro
Jørgensen SE, et al. (2019) A new ecology: systems perspective. Elsevier Science, Amsterdam
Jørgensen SE, Svirezhev YM (2004) Towards a thermodynamic theory for ecological systems. Elsevier, Amsterdam
Kant I (2008) A paz perpétua e outros opúsculos. Tradução de Artur Morão. Edições, 70, Lisboa
Kelsen H (1999) Teoria pura do direito. Tradução de João Baptista Machado, 6 edn. WMF Martins Fontes, São Paulo
Khoiyangban RS, Gupta N (eds) (2012) Introduction to environmental sciences. TERI. New Delhi, Ebook
Kiss A, Shelton D (2004) International environmental law, 3rd edn. Transnational Publications, Ardseley, NY
Koestler A (1969) O fantasma da máquina. Tradução de Christiano Monteiro Oiticica e Hesiodo de Queiroz Facó. Zahar, Rio de Janeiro
Kolb R (2000) Partie I. Les principes généraux: la place des principes généraux dans l'ordre juridique. In: Kolb R (ed) La bonne foi en droit international public: contribution à l'étude des principes généraux de droit. Graduate Institute Publications, Genève. Available: http://books.openedition.org/iheid/2263. Accessed 05 May 2025
Leopold A (1949) A Sand County almanac: with other essays on conservation from Round River. Oxford University Press, New York
Losano MG (2010) Sistema e estrutura no Direito, vol 2: tradução Lucas Lamberti. Editora WMF Martins Fontes, São Paulo
Milare É (2015) Dicionário de direito ambiental. Revista dos Tribunais, São Paulo
Müller F (2013) O novo paradigma do direito: introdução à teoria e metódica estruturantes, 3 edn. Ver.atual. e ampli. Editora Revista dos Tribunais, São Paulo
Nações Unidas. Resolución aprobada por la Asamblea General el 20 de diciembre de 2013 [sobre la base del informe de la Segunda Comisión (A/68/438/Add.8)] 68/216. Armonía con la

Naturaleza. Available: https://www.un.org/en/ga/search/view_doc.asp?symbol=A/RES/68/216. Accessed 28 Apr 2025
Nações Unidas. Asamblea General. A/RES/64/196. Available: http://undocs.org/A/RES/64/196. Accessed 24 Apr 2025
Nações Unidas. Asamblea General. A/67/317. Available: http://undocs.org/A/67/317. Accessed 26 Apr 2025
Nações Unidas. Asamblea General. A/68/325. Available: http://undocs.org/A/68/325. Accessed 26 Apr 2025
Nações Unidas. Asamblea General. A/69/322. Available: http://undocs.org/A/69/322. Accessed 26 Apr 2025
Nações Unidas. Asamblea General. A/70/268. Available: http://undocs.org/A/70/268. Accessed 28 Apr 2025
Nações Unidas. Asamblea General. A/71/266. Available: https://docs.un.org/A/71/266. Accessed 28 Apr 2025
Nações Unidas. Asamblea General. A/RES/65/164. Available: http://undocs.org/A/RES/65/164. Accessed 30 Apr 2025
Nações Unidas. Asamblea General. A/RES/66/204. Available: http://undocs.org/A/RES/66/204. Accessed 30 Apr 2025
Nações Unidas. Asamblea General. A/RES/67/214. Available: http://undocs.org/A/RES/67/214. Accessed 05 May 2025
Nações Unidas. Asamblea General. Grupo de Trabalho da sociedade civil para a Agenda 2030 do desenvolvimetno sustentável. Available: https://gtagenda2030.org.br/agenda-pos-2015/. Accessed 28 Apr 2025
Nações Unidas. Aseablea General. A/RES/64/196. Available: http://undocs.org/A/RES/64/196. Accessed 29 Apr 2025
Nações Unidas. Asemblea General. A/RES/63/278. Available: http://undocs.org/A/RES/63/278. Accessed 24 Apr 2025
OEA. Declaración Americana sobre los derechos de los Pueblos Indígenas. https://www.oas.org/es/sadye/documentos/DADPI.pdf. Accessed 04 Feb 2025
Oliveira Ad (2011) O equilíbrio é mesmo necessário? Ciência Hoje, de 18 fev. Available: https://cienciahoje.org.br/coluna/o-equilibrio-e-mesmo-necessario/. Accessed 04 Feb 2025
ONU Sobre o Programa das Nações Unidas para o Meio Ambiente (PNUMA). Available: https://www.unenvironment.org/pt-br/sobre-onu-meio-ambiente. Accessed 04 Feb 2025
Picazo LD (1983) Los Princípios Generales del Derecho em el pensamento de F. de Castro, in Anuario de Derecho Civil, t.XXXVI, Faz. 3°., Outubro-dezembro
Sadeleer Nd (2020) Environmental principles: from political slogans to legal rules, 2nd edn. Oxford University Press, New York
Sarlet IW, Fensterseifer T (2014) Direito constitucional ambiental: constituição, direitos fundamentais e proteção do ambiente, 4 edn. rev. e atual, Revista dos Tribunais, São Paulo
Serres M (1990) O contrato natural. Tradução de Serafim Ferreira. Instituto Piaget, Lisboa
Silveira VOd, Rocasolano MM (2010) Direitos humanos: conceitos, significados e funções. Saraiva, São Paulo
Tribunal Superior de Justiça. RECURSO ESPECIAL N° 1.713.167 - SP (2017/0239804-9). Available: https://animaiscomdireitos.ufpr.br/wp-content/uploads/2019/06/stj-guarda-de-animal-de-estimacao-1.pdf Accessed 20 Feb 2025
Trindade AAC (2017) Princípios do direito internacional contemporâneo, 2 edn. rev. e atual. Fundação Alexandre de Gusmão, Brasília
United Nations (1982) General assembly. World charter for nature. New York, 28 Oct, Preâmbulo. Available: https://www.dh-cii.eu/0_content/investigao/files_CRDTLA/convencoes_tratados_etc/carta_mundial_da_natureza_de_28_de_outubro_de_1982.pdf. Accessed 21 Apr 2025
United Nations (1992) Convention on Biological Diversity. Rio de Janeiro, 05 June. Preâmbulo. Available: https://www.cbd.int/doc/legal/cbd-en.pdf. Accessed 21 Apr 2025

United Nations. Harmony with Nature. Available: http://harmonywithnatureun.org/unDocs/. Accessed 04 Feb 2025

Vattel Ed (1758) Le droit des gens. Liv. II, Chap. XV, § 218. Available: https://archive.org/details/LEDROITDESGENS/LE-DROIT-DES-GENS/page/n383/mode/2up. Accessed 26 May 2025

Wieacker F (2010) História do direito privado moderno, 4 edn. Fundação Calouste Gulbenkian, Lisboa

Wohlleben P (2017) A vida secreta das árvores. Tradução de Petê Rissati. Sextante, Rio de Janeiro

Chapter 6
The Recognition of Legal Personality for Non-Human Beings and Holistic Organic Entities as a Consequence of the Principle of Harmony with Nature

From the theories of consciousness of living beings and organic entities, and Henri Bergson's creative evolution, it is possible to glimpse a dignity common to all living beings and organic entities, which denotes that subjectivity can also be recognized outside the province of human rationality.

Bergson, when dealing with evolution, instinct, and intelligence, points out that:

> [...] no precise character distinguishes the plant from the animal. Attempts to rigorously define the two kingdoms have always failed. There is not a single property of plant life that has not been found, to a greater or lesser degree, in certain animals, there is no characteristic trait of the animal that has not been observed in certain species or certain moments, in the plant kingdom. [...] There is no manifestation of life that does not contain, in a rudimentary, latent or virtual state, the essential characteristics of most other manifestations. The difference lies in the proportions.[1]

Bergson draws a parallel between the consciousness of animals and plants, based on the form of feeding, which was influenced during a long evolutionary flow by the accentuation of different traits that are found in animals and plants. While the plant has the extraordinary ability to extract nutrients directly from carbon and nitrogen, the animal does not have the same aptitude to directly assimilate these mineral elements for its nutrition. Therefore, it needs to feed on organic substances, that is, plants or other animals, and, consequently, in animals, the attribute of motility improved over the evolutionary course.

In other words, the fact that the plant takes the necessary nutrients directly from the air, water, and Earth deepened the difference between this and the animal. That is, for the plant, there is no need for mobility for nutrition, so the tendency toward fixity was consolidating. However, this is only an accentuated tendency, not a strict rule, as there are exceptions, such as the case of *droseras*, dioneas, and insectivorous plants in general that, in addition to feeding through the root and their green

[1] Bergson (2010), p. 123.

R. D. d. Amaral, *The Principle of Harmony with Nature as a Legal Foundation*,
https://doi.org/10.1007/978-3-032-05475-3_6

parts, as occurs in all plants, have also developed the ability to feed on the insects they capture. Bergson explains that this ability of insectivorous plants arose late in the course of evolution as an exceptionally developed tendency by plants that needed to supplement their nutrition in very poor soils that did not provide them with all the nutrients.[2]

The existence of movement in plants, although it is not a rule, exceptionally occurs; as an example, Bergson cites the case of dormideiras and climbers. In addition to motility, some plants also have the ability to mimic; in this sense, contemporary research by Stefano Mancuso refers, for example, to the mimetic attribute of the *Boquila trifoliata*, a climber native to the forests of Chile and Argentina. On each tree where the *Boquila* grows, it imitates the shape of the leaves and flowers of its host; its mimetic ability is so developed that, if a single *Boquila* hosts on more than one tree, it is capable of imitating the leaves and flowers of all the trees. Thus, in the same *Boquila,* various shapes of leaves and flowers can be found. This mimetic ability aims to statistically reduce the probability of attacks by herbivorous insects.[3]

Bergson warns that it would be an illusion to distinguish an animal from a plant based solely on the concepts of fixity or mobility, as these are attributes that coexist in both the animal and plant world. Fixity and mobility are thus only shallow signs of deeper tendencies. He emphasizes that there is a relationship between mobility and consciousness, so that the more a nervous system develops, the more precise and varied the movements of the being and the sharper its consciousness, enabling it to choose movements according to need. However, he asserts that consciousness and mobility, and even this ability to choose, do not necessarily require the existence of a nervous system, and further explains:

> [...] this (nervous system) only channels in certain directions, bringing it to the highest degree of intensity, a rudimentary and vague activity, diffused in the mass of organized substance. The further down the animal scale, the more the nervous centers simplify and also separate from each other; finally, there are no longer nervous elements, submerged in the whole of a less differentiated organism. But the same happens with all other apparatuses, with all anatomical elements; and it would be as absurd to deny consciousness to an animal, because it does not have a brain, as to declare it incapable of feeding because it does not have a stomach.[4] (our emphasis)

Antonio Damasio today also understands that "a nervous system does not form a mind on its own but in cooperation with the rest of its organism. This deviates from the traditional notion that the brain is the only source of the mind."[5]

For Bergson, the plant and the animal descend from a common ancestor, which combined, in a nascent state, the tendencies of both. However, due to the form of nutrition, animals, which need to seek their food, had to develop more motility and

---

[2] Bergson (2010), p. 123.

[3] Mancuso (2019), p. 42–48.

[4] Bergson (2010), p. 128.

[5] Damásio (2018), p. 21.

sensitivity: "The same impulse by which the animal gave itself nerves and nervous centers must have led, in the plant, to the chlorophyll function."[6]

Considering that plants and animals descend from a common ancestor, which held in its genesis the same tendency, which developed in different directions only to meet their nutritional abilities, there is a convergence of these two kingdoms in the sense of understanding that between them there is a relationship of complementarity and not hierarchy, as proposed by Aristotle in the chain of being and Lovejoy,[7] which completely changes the reflections on the intrinsic value of the organism and its subjectivity.

If motility in the animal organism denotes an evolutionary sophistication, the ability to photosynthesize also presents itself as admirably complex, especially because it is at the base of the entire planetary life system. In this order of ideas, it is a mistake to underestimate the cognitive processes of plants simply because they did not develop the tendency for motility in their respective nervous systems, as happened in animals. This tendency was not developed as a primary skill of plants simply because they are capable of nutrition by capturing carbon and nitrogen directly from their leaves and roots. Thus, if, as a rule, they do not move, it is only because they do not need mobility for their nutrition.

This different direction in the tendencies between the plant and the animal cannot be considered a hierarchical step; given the nutritional interdependence between the two kingdoms, it is just a division of tasks. Therefore, the relationship between plants and animals should be seen from the perspective of complementarity and cooperation in the workforce in favor of life as a whole.

After consciousness, driven by the form of nutrition of the organism, bifurcated its organization into complementary parts—plant and animal—there was again the dismemberment of a double direction within the animal kingdom, considering that instinct and intelligence developed, the latter related to the human being, the former to animals. To recognize the existence of a biological dignity shared by human and non-human animals, it is necessary to understand the common point between instinct and intelligence in their origins and analyze the directions to which they tended and accentuated, as well as their imbrications, points of intersection, and to what extent they oppose and complement each other.

Initially, Bergson clarifies that there is no superiority of intelligence over instinct, considering that they are not activities of the same order, they do not succeed each other, and there is also no difference in degrees between them. In their origins, intelligence and instinct interpenetrate, and even when they tend to different directions throughout evolution, "they conserve something from their common origin. Neither one nor the other ever find themselves in a pure state. [...] There is no intelligence in which traces of instinct are not discovered and, above all, there is no instinct that is not surrounded by a fringe of intelligence."[8]

[6] Bergson (2010), p. 132.

[7] Lovejoy (2009), p. 240.

[8] Bergson (2010), p. 153–154.

Bergson explains that it is precisely this fringe of intelligence that intersects with instinct that caused the various misconceptions which led many scientists to conclude that instinct and intelligence are of the same order, with varying degrees of complexity and perfection. However, instinct and intelligence are different things that complement each other. In this regard, Bergson points out that neither instinct nor intelligence allows for rigid definitions, as they are merely tendencies that have been accentuated in the direction of the organism's effort to obtain its nutrition and well-being from raw matter.

Humanity has considered the ability to manufacture things as the most primary indicator of intelligence. Bergson emphasizes that if humanity were to shed its pride and define its own species according to the characteristics that prehistory and history have attributed to the human being as an indicator of intelligence, the correct nomenclature to define the human species would be *Homo faber* and not *Homo sapiens*. In other words, "intelligence, considered in what appears to be its original activity, is the faculty of manufacturing artificial objects, especially tools that make tools, and of indefinitely varying their manufacture."[9]

However, it should not be forgotten that animals also have tools and machines, which are part of their own bodies. These instruments, naturally attached to the bodies of non-human animals, come with operations genetically programmed by instinct itself. Instinct emerges as an extension of the very organizing work of living matter. Bergson cites the instinct of insects as an example, which, with only the movement of their bodies, develops their spatial structure, organizing social life and work among the individuals that make up the group, imposing different instincts on the members to perform different tasks in the community. This is what happens in the polymorphism of ants, bees, and wasps.

When analyzing instinct and intelligence, advantages and disadvantages are observed.[10] Instinct governs the organic instrument attached to the organism, which is created by the very organizing work of life. This instrument, meticulously constructed as a work of nature itself, with structural complexity and functional simplicity, astonishes and challenges human intelligence to reproduce it. However, it has a disadvantage: its structure is unchangeable, so that change requires a genetic alteration in the species itself, which can take a long time to occur.

Intelligence, on the other hand, is focused on the manufacture of an instrument that did not naturally come attached to the human being. While the saber-toothed tiger was equipped with its powerful instrument—huge canines with which it tore the necks of its victims[11]—the human being had to manufacture its own fang: the flint daggers.[12] The intelligently manufactured instrument is imperfect, as it is made at the cost of effort and overcoming difficulties; however, because it is made of disorganized matter, it can take any form and be intended for various uses.

[9] Bergson (2010), p. 153–157.

[10] Bergson (2010), p. 158.

[11] Lopes (2004).

[12] Boaventura and Cardoso (2010/2011).

The initial flint dagger could be used by humans in the fight with non-human animals or to remove a tuber from the ground; however, over the course of evolution, it was perfected and gained new and varied functions, to the point that it is the ancestor of the modern medical scalpel. This is certainly one of the advantages compared to the organic instrument governed by instinct. However, the manufactured instrument is inferior to the natural instrument when it comes to meeting immediate needs. The more pressing the need, requiring a faster and more precise response, the natural instrument governed by instinct is more effective in response than the instrument manufactured by intelligence.

Several advantages and disadvantages of instinct and intelligence could be listed; however, for the purpose of this work, it is enough to demonstrate that there is no hierarchy of relevance between intelligence and instinct. Both are equally important and, on many occasions, they overlap. While instinct is "molded on the very form of life,"[13] "intelligence is characterized by a natural misunderstanding of life," because the human being has a stubborn tendency to treat the living as if it were inert matter, to think of reality mechanically, as if it were solid matter, when, in truth, reality is systemic, relational, and fluid.

It should not be forgotten that, even outside the province of intelligence, instinct has not evaded the district of the spirit and manifests itself in the phenomena of feelings, in unreflected, unrationalized sympathies and antipathies. Humans, Bergson points out, when they act instinctively, also experience sensations that pass through the consciousness of an insect.[14]

Among the characteristics that science attributes to intelligence are the ability to manufacture, action oriented by choice, language marked by the generality and mobility of signs, the prodigious creation of symbols, logic, and the ability to evoke a memory spontaneously without the need for a trigger from a current perception. Animals are endowed with organic instruments governed by instinct; they have a language with signs in a well-determined number and adherent to the thing signified, therefore without mobility.

Animals, despite having memory, can only awaken a memory when they are in front of a perception similar to the one that occurred in the past of the fact that is remembered; this perception is the impulse to awaken their memory. Among the characteristics of intelligence, one of the most important is the ability to form a value judgment to choose, which makes the human being a moral agent. Bergson emphasizes that "throughout the extent of the animal kingdom, consciousness reveals itself proportional to the power of choice allowed to the living being, illuminating the zone of virtuality that surrounds the act, measuring the distance between what is done and what could be done."[15]

Even animals with simpler organisms can exhibit a degree of consciousness proportional to the development of their nervous centers. The more developed the

[13] Bergson (2010), p. 185.
[14] Bergson (2010), p. 195.
[15] Bergson (2010), p. 199.

nervous system, the more the organism has the possibility of choosing its actions and the freedom to undertake them.

Bergson also emphasizes that:

> The capital error that, transmitted from Aristotle, vitiated most of the philosophy of nature was to see in vegetative life, in instinctive life and in rational life three successive degrees of the development of a single tendency, when they are three divergent directions of an activity that split with its growth. The difference between them is not a difference in intensity, nor, more generically, of degree - it is a difference in nature.[16]

What is observed, in the end, is that there is a vital impulse common to plants in their vegetative torpor, to non-human animals in their instinct, and to the human being with his intelligence. All seek flourishing, even though, in the course of their developments, they have followed different paths, which accentuated their necessary skills for nutrition. There is no hierarchy of importance among them. In vegetative torpor, in instinct, and in intelligence, living beings and organic entities share the longing for the freedom to flourish, perpetuate life, and exercise their natural abilities within a large, relational, and cooperative living system.

In this line, there is a vital value that is rooted in the origin of all living beings, whether considered individually or holistically. The tone of biological dignity lies in this vital value—a type of freedom common to all living beings, as explained by Paul Taylor:

> In addition to free will, autonomy and social freedom, there is a fourth sense in which human beings can be considered free (or not). This meaning of freedom, unlike the others, applies equally to non-human living beings. It is a concept of freedom of central importance to every creature that has a good of its own that it strives to achieve. For to be free, in this sense, is to be able to preserve one's own existence and promote the good, and not to be free, in this sense, is to be unable to do these things. The recognition of this type of freedom and its great value to all living beings is one of the main links between human and non-human beings.[17]

From Paul Taylor's perspective, the essence of this freedom, which is shared by all living beings, is the absence of restrictions. Thus, it is necessary to understand what the restrictions would be that could take away the freedom of these beings, considering that there will be a variation of situations according to the degree of cognition of each being. The curtailment of this fundamental freedom, which is rooted in a value common to all living beings and which this work extends to holistic organic entities, assumes different features in the plant, in the non-human animal guided by instinct, and in the human being endowed with rational intelligence; however, its root is common in all types of life, as it resides in homeostasis, that is, what Antônio Damásio defines as "fundamental set of operations at the core of life, from its earliest beginning—long ago disappeared in the beginnings of biochemistry—to the present. It is the powerful, unthought, tacit imperative, whose

[16] Bergson (2010), p. 153.
[17] Taylor (2011), p. 121.

fulfillment allows each living organism, small or large, nothing less than to endure and prevail."[18]

Antônio Damásio distinguishes, in the homeostasis of the organism, the aptitude to survive, which is necessary to prosper. He clarifies that this latter innate disposition is more subtle, considering that it ensures "that life is regulated not only within a range compatible with survival, but also conducive to prosperity, to a projection of life into the future of an organism or species."[19]

As can be seen, one of the aspects of homeostasis is the tendency toward full flourishing, and this is not restricted only to beings considered individually but also to species, ecosystems, and the biosphere itself. The author associates the concept of homeostasis with feelings, considering that they reveal the life condition of each organism, varying from positive to negative. If homeostasis is deficient, this indicates negative feelings, while positive feelings indicate adequate levels of homeostasis, opening up opportunities for the organism to flourish and prosper.

Damásio defines feelings in this context as "subjective experiences of the state of life, that is, homeostasis, in all creatures endowed with a mind and a conscious point of view. We can say that feelings are the mental representatives of homeostasis." Although Damásio emphasizes that not all living beings are endowed with feelings, he points out that all living beings are "equipped with the regulatory mechanisms that were the precursors of feelings."[20]

Damásio also points out that this innate force for thriving in living beings was scrutinized by Spinoza, who called it *conatus,* and that, currently, neuroscience understands it to be immanent on the microscopic scale of life in each cell and also on the macroscopic scale throughout nature. Indeed, Spinoza, in Proposition 6 of Part III of the *Ethics*, asserts: "Each thing strives, as far as it is in itself, to persevere in its being." In the explanation of the proposition, he clarifies:

> Indeed, singular things are modes by which God's attributes express themselves in a defined and determined manner (by the corollary of prop. 25 of P.1), that is (by prop. 34 of P.1), are things that express in a defined and determined manner the power of God, by which it exists and acts. And no thing has in itself something by which it can be destroyed, that is, that takes away its existence (by prop. 4); on the contrary, it opposes everything that can take away its existence (by the previous prop.). *And it strives, thus, as much as it can and is in itself, to persevere in its being.*[21] (our emphasis)

It is in Spinoza's concept of *conatus*, currently identified by Antonio Damásio's neuroscience as homeostasis, that a basic freedom shared by all living beings resides, which Paul Taylor identifies as a fourth freedom.[22] In this freedom, which emerges from the *conatus*, lies a vital value that this work identifies as the

[18] Damásio (2018), p. 19.

[19] Damásio (2018), p. 19.

[20] Damásio (2018), p. 19–22.

[21] Spinoza (2016), p. 108.

[22] Taylor (2011), p. 121.

root dignity—the one that is at the root of being, substantiated in the inexorable impulse for its flourishing.

Thus, it is proposed to bring the figure of Spinoza's *conatus* and Antonio Damásio's homeostasis to ethics and law as a self-value, experienced by all living beings and holistic organic entities[23]; it is a root dignity, in the sense that from it, living beings nourish themselves with the impulse for life. Everything that weakens vitality violates this dignity shared by all living beings. As it is a dignity that resides in the vital impulse of the organism as such, this work proposes a neologism to name it, in legal language, as *biodignity*.

The term *bio* has its etymology in the Greek *βίος*, whose most distant etymological roots point to the meaning of "vital energy" or "life."[24] Thus, it is shown to be suitable for composing the concept of *biodignity*, that is, this root dignity that emerges from the *conatus* or homeostasis as a value shared by all living beings and holistic organic entities for the full experience of life.

This root dignity, which is proposed to be named in the legal sphere as *biodignity*, radiates in three dimensions: (i) in the temporal dimension of life, as it concerns the experience of living the natural time of the vital cycle, which is peculiar to each living being and organic entity; (ii) in the substantial dimension, as it relates to the adequate conditions of nutrition for the flourishing of the organism; and (iii) in the sentimental dimension of the living being, insofar as "feelings are the mental representatives of homeostasis."[25]

The human person has its intrinsic self-value, its dignity, recognized based on rationality; this work proposes the concept of *biodignity* as the biological support on which the very dignity of the human person also rests. If the human being has a dignity that is inherent to his human condition, whether based on the *imago Dei* or based on rationality, this living being endowed with intelligence, self-awareness, privileged language, and moral agency is also the expression of a living organism, which shares with all other beings the same dignity on the biological level—that inexorable impulse for life, that is, the *conatus* or homeostasis. Thus, at the root of the dignity of the human person is biological dignity, the *biodignity* experienced by all living beings.

Not only rationality and language are the supports for dignity. As demonstrated by Bergson, in the beginning, the life of the plant, the animal, and the human being descends from the same trunk. Whether you call this initial, uncreated, driving force, endowed with *causa sui,*[26] "God" as did Augustine of Hippo, whether you name it *aítion heautoû*, as proposed by Plotinus, or simply a self-organized system, as Bertalanffy named it, or even universal coherence,[27] as Cirne-Lima did, the fact is that from it, as the ultimate and radical cause of all life on Earth, descends the

[23] Ecosystems.

[24] Rendich (2014), p. 343.

[25] Damásio (2018), p. 19–20.

[26] Of self-causation.

[27] Cirne-Lima (2012), p. 153–197.

dignity common to all beings—the notion of vital self-worth that is immanent in all forms of life.

It should be noted that between the dignity of the human person and *biodignity,* there is not a hierarchical step but an overlap, considering that the dignity of the human person, in its fullest sense, is based on and supported by biological dignity, on that vital value that drives all living and systemic organic beings toward flourishing. This reality reveals the beauty of the ecological dimension of the dignity of the human person, a unique living being that, among many others, unfolded from the one as an expression of individuality and the infinite multiplicity of nature, that is, biodiversity, and whose flourishing is interconnected with all other living beings.

The concept of *biodignity,* as a corollary of the principle of harmony with nature, in its integrative function, harbors the intrinsic value of life in the vegetative cognition of the plant that performs photosynthesis to nourish itself and also nourish all other living beings on the planet, in the instinct of the animal, and in the intelligence of the human being. All present *biodignity* in their different vital tendencies, which, although diverse, are viscerally interconnected in a large holistic and autopoietic system, driven by the same self-caused originating force.

As already mentioned, *biodignity* projects itself in three dimensions: (i) temporal; (ii) substantial; and (iii) sentimental. This means that the protection of the life of the organism, as a full experience, must cover the guarantee of fulfillment of the vital cycle from the perspective of time, which makes it morally reprehensible to prematurely interrupt the life of living beings to satisfy non-relevant human interests. It also covers the need for living beings to have their full nutrition guaranteed, with access to sunlight, drinking water, and other foods suitable for their organisms. Finally, one of the most relevant aspects of *biodignity* is respect for the feelings and affectivity of living beings and organic entities. As already highlighted by Antônio Damásio, this affects the level of vitality of the living organism.[28]

Thus, it is proposed to define *biodignity* as the intrinsic and radical value shared by all living beings and holistic organic entities, which is rooted in the core of the vital impulse and projects to ensure the right to the full experience of life by the organism in its temporal, substantial, and sentimental dimensions.

6.1 The Recognition of a Legal Personality Suitable for *Biodignity*

The recognition of *biodignity*, stemming from the principle of harmony with nature, brings as a consequence the need to redefine the concept of person and subject of law to include non-human living beings and holistic organic entities.

[28] Damásio (2018), p. 19–20.

The concept of person and subject of law rests on the notion of individuality. The concept of the individual developed in pre-modernity with Francisco Suarez, who "centers the metaphysical unity of the principle of individuation in the being."[29] However, the notion of individuals is preceded by the concept of person, as the human condition of that being capable of being inserted into a qualitatively legal relationship by Roman private law, especially in the laws that regulate the *dominium*, the *imperium*, and the *patrimonium*.

It should not be forgotten that, at this point in the evolutionary journey of human morality, there was the status of enslaved people in Roman private law. Some humans were considered by the legal system as mere *res* (things), therefore devoid of intrinsic value and only valued from an instrumental point of view. According to Gaius, these humans were called "human things" or "person-things." As can be seen, Western law itself, at its inception in the pre-Justinian period until the fifth century, reified the human being. Thus, many historians consider that, at this time, the concept of legal personality could not yet be spoken of.[30]

According to Michel Villey, the concepts of subject and subjective right will only be shaped during the transition from Roman language to modern language in the work "*Opus nonaginta*", by William of Ockham, which deals with the issue of poverty in the Franciscan order and, in whose context, Ockham developed the notion of subjective right.[31]

Franciscan philosophy greatly values the concept of individual freedom, understanding that this right is a basic condition for Christian life. While, in Aristotelian philosophy, the individual only has relevance as a member of the *polis*, Christian doctrine, as interpreted by the Franciscan nominalist current, values the person more in their individual aspect. Personalism is strengthened with the consolidation of Christianity. Thus, Ockham will transplant his way of thinking about freedom and individuality, cultivated in the spiritual field, to law. In this way, the concepts of person, individuality, individual power or subjective right, and freedom—purified through readings and interpretations of the Gospel in Franciscan cells—will migrate to the provinces of law, becoming the cornerstone of legal positivism in modernity.[32]

In this sense, Costas Douzinas clarifies that the individual, as a subject of law, first appears in the West in scholastic theology, based on the concept of *imago Dei*, through the philosophy of Duns Scotus and Guilherme of Ockham, who uphold the maximum expression of God's creation in the individuality of the human being as a person, considering that they rejected the collective concepts of city, community, and corporations, understanding that these were artificial creations.

Ockham argued that the power exercised by the individual over his own life was a form of *dominium*, that is, of property, rooted not in law but in a natural right, as

[29] Campos (2008), p. 13.
[30] Campos (2008), p. 14.
[31] Villey (2005), p. 265.
[32] Villey (2005), p. 294.

a basic fact of human life. This *dominium* of the human being over his life, this freedom, was a natural right granted by God himself to the human being, whom he created in his image and likeness.

The root of legal positivism lies precisely in the understanding of the nominalists, who deduced the law from the divine will as an absolute and binding will for all humans, because of the divine nature of the legislating authority, so it should be complied with regardless of criteria contained in the ideal of justice, in nature, and in reason. Douzinas notes that, at this point, the origin, the source of the law, and the method of its interpretation begin to change, migrating from reason to pure will, regardless of the nature of things.[33]

Nominalism plants the seed of the separation of God from nature and voluntarism, which will lead subsequent generations to legal positivism and the strengthening of the ontological dualism of modernity. At this moment, the transmutation of objective natural law into individual subjective law occurs, and the individual, the subject of law who will henceforth star in the legal canons, emerges: "A secularized deism replaced Christ with a God of Reason, and finally man became God."[34]

Man, as a divinized subject of law, did not delay in unfolding his personality to create another person—the legal person, the *persona moralis*. Franz Wieacker[35] points out that Justinian law was already rehearsing the creation of the *persona moralis*, which would later be constructed in a well-reflected manner by canon law and the conciliators.[36] Wieacker observes that the very constitution and organization of the church and, later, the modern state and mercantile societies were determining factors in the creation of the legal entity. Humans created the legal entity to act as an instrument in the service of commerce and the market economy.

Currently, the legal entity, recognized as a technical reality, has its legal personality consolidated, so it is supported by personality rights, which recognize, for example, its claim to compensation for moral damages due to the violation of objective honor. However, despite the legal entity having these rights and many others recognized, it is nothing more than a legal instrument, as Anderson Schreiber emphasizes:

> [...] the legal entity is an abstract entity, conceived by jurists so that humans can achieve certain practical results. The distinction is, therefore, radical: while humans are ends in themselves, legal entities consist of one of the many legal instruments put at the service of humans. Although this observation seems obvious, it often goes unnoticed in our doctrine and jurisprudence, which have ended up assimilating the two notions. Legal entities, as the name itself reveals, were built in the image and likeness of natural persons. Both are persons for the science of law, in the sense that they are endowed with legal personality in a subjective sense.[37]

---

[33] Douzinas (2009), p. 76.

[34] Douzinas (2009), p. 77.

[35] Wieacker (2010).

[36] Franz Wieacker uses the word "conciliares" spelled with an "s". Wieacker (2010), p. 270.

[37] Schreiber (2020), p. 98.

As it turns out, first the human being created itself as a person, endowed with an individualized personality, distinct and superior to all other living beings, justifying this exalted distinction in its likeness to God; then, as lord of the biosphere, he did not hesitate to create another artificial person, the legal entity, to serve him in the exploitation, reification, and enslavement of all living beings on Earth. He included in the list of enslaved even members of the human species itself, who were occasionally expelled from the sacred provinces of personality rights—sometimes for war and economic reasons, sometimes on religious grounds, and even based on racial criteria. Not content with building the concept of legal personality on the shameful foundation of speciesism, they did not hesitate to aggravate it also with racism.

Paradoxically, when it is proposed to the human being to recognize the intrinsic value and legal personality of non-human living beings, the prompt and obvious answer is that personality is the set of rights proper to the human person, who is deserving of protection for psychophysical integrity, honor, and dignity, so these rights could not be extended to animals and plants because they lack a soul, moral agency, and language. But, curiously, members of the human species not endowed with moral agency are considered persons and holders of rights, and, most curiously, there is the fact of attributing the protection of personality rights to a fiction or technical reality called a legal entity, which currently has objective honor recognized, while denying personality rights to great primates, rivers, birds, and millennial trees, for example.

There is no ontological basis that justifies the recognition of legal personality, with its consequences, to a technical reality created by human beings, and the denial of a similar right, for example, to rivers like the Paraguay, the Amazon, the Paraná, the São Francisco, or to the millennial samaúmas, to the felines, dogs, cats, bees, and to vital ecosystems like the Pantanal.

There is no ontological or ethical impediment to the recognition of legal personality for non-human living beings and organic entities; what exists is voluntarism and arbitrariness, which have been the true foundations of the legal anthropocentrism that still prevails in humanity, even in the face of the serious anthropogenic crisis that compromises the perpetuation of all life on Earth.

Now, if the human being personified the legal entity—an abstract entity devoid of life, a creation of human language—granting it subjective rights, what would be the ontological and legal difficulty in recognizing the intrinsic value and legal personality of non-human living beings? Perhaps the great difficulty is neither ontological nor legal, but economic—the same difficulty alleged for the maintenance of the enslavement of human beings, still in the recent eighteenth century.

However, in view of the principle of harmony with nature, on which the concept of biodignity is based, this work proposes the recognition of the existence of the biological person, endowed with a legal personality compatible with its own biodignity—that is, with its natural aptitudes and its homeostasis for vital flourishing.

If the legal entity is justified as a necessary institutional technical reality for the economic and social development of humanity, the biological person rests on the concept of biodignity, which derives from the integrative function of the principle of harmony with nature, to safeguard the vital dignity of all living beings, including the human being. Thus, it is fundamental for the preservation of human rights, as it safeguards ecological integrity as the normative core of the principle of sustainable development.

Just as the personality of the legal entity is not homogeneous, as it assumes different nuances according to its social objectives, the legal personality of biological persons should also be differentiated and adapted to the biodignity of different non-human living beings and holistic organic entities, with the purpose of protecting their basic freedom of flourishing and well-being.

The human being, as a moral agent endowed with self-awareness, has a denser and broader legal personality, as it harbors rights that are necessary for the dignity of the human person as an "inherent value that identifies the human being as such."[38] The human being, as a self-aware, creative, and complex being, presents needs and desires that are inherent to its own multidimensional condition; however, as already mentioned, like other living beings, it shares with the plant and animal kingdoms the same basic freedom, which pertains to biological flourishing and the nourishment of the physical body. Therefore, it is also a holder of *biodignity*.

For the protection of human dignity, legal systems ensure rights that are correlated to the various facets of human freedom, such as the right to life, the right to the body, the right to subjective and objective honors, the right to the name, the right to personal identity, the right to the image, the right to intimacy, and the right to privacy. The legal entity, in turn, as a technical reality, has a more restricted set of personality rights compatible with its instrumental objectives. In this line, this work proposes the recognition of the personality rights of the biological person according to their *biodignity*, based on the Spinozian concept of *conatus,* Antonio Damasio's homeostasis, and Henri Bergson's theory of creative evolution.

Personality, in a subjective sense, is considered to be the generic aptitude to be a holder of rights and obligations—that is, to be a subject of law. The concept of personality is tied to the notion of symmetry between rights and obligations. This idea has its roots in Kantian contractualism and has served as an obstacle to the recognition of personality rights for non-human living beings, under the pretext that they could not be subjects of law, given that they are not moral agents and, therefore, could not assume duties and obligations. Nevertheless, it proposes the concept of biological legal personality for plants, animals, and ecosystems in an asymmetric and unilateral way. This means that, although animals, plants, and ecosystems are not moral agents, by being possessors of *biodignity*, they have the right to recognition of their legal personality as moral subjects, with all the consequences resulting from it.

---

[38] Sarlet (2001), p. 38–39.

At this point, this work adopts Paul Taylor's expression "moral subject[39]"to designate non-human living beings and also holistic organic entities,[40] which, despite not having rationality and, therefore, not being moral agents, should be respected as moral subjects, that is, as recipients of respect and moral consideration, since they are also holders of the same *biodignity* experienced by human beings.

Biological entities, whether plant, animal, or systemic, enjoy a differentiated legal personality that conforms to their *biodignity*. The birth or hatching of life marks the initial term of the biological legal entity, which also ends with death or thermodynamic equilibrium in the case of the systemic entity. However, during the course of their lives, even if brief, plant, animal, and systemic biological entities should enjoy the rights derived from *biodignity* in its triple dimension.

In the anthropocentric legal paradigm, the concept of personality is linked to the ability to contract rights and obligations, so that, in this view, the fact that biological entities do not have the ability to establish obligations in the legal world—constructed by human language and in which obligatory links are established—would prevent them from being considered persons endowed with personality. Nevertheless, these plant, animal, and systemic biological entities perform other very important functions in the biosphere of the planet and contribute to the emergence and flourishing of life, contributing even more to humans than humans do to them.

The fact that they are not endowed with human language, necessary for them to be able to establish bilateral contractual obligations in the language proper to the legal system, does not mean that they do not fulfill functions governed by the natural principle of reciprocity, which guides the systemic relations of the biosphere to benefit all living beings, including humans.

Indeed, in the systemic natural contract, which regulates planetary life, plants, animals, and ecosystems perform functions that are governed by the natural principle of reciprocity. It is enough to remember that the plant biological entity produces, through photosynthesis, the oxygen necessary to sustain life on the entire planet. In addition, they generate thousands of fruits, tubers, seeds, and fibers that support the human economy. Similarly, the animal biological entity contributes to the sustenance of human beings, with the immeasurable work of providing, through its own vital energy, skins, wool, fat, meat, eggs, milk, and honey. Likewise, systemic organic entities carry out their continuous work to enable the emergence of life in the biosphere.

Thus, there is indeed bilaterality and reciprocity; if, at this very moment, human beings breathe, quench their thirst, and feed, it is due to the uninterrupted work of plant, animal, and systemic biological entities in the continuous execution of the

[39] Taylor (2011), p. 28.

[40] It is noted that this work diverges from Paul Taylor in two points: i) It did not adopt the expression inherent value used by Taylor, as equivalent to intrinsic value; ii) it recognizes the intrinsic value and also the subjectivity of holistic organic entities, while Taylor restricts the recognition of inherent value (equivalent to intrinsic value) only to living beings.

great natural contract of life, governed by the cosmic principle of reciprocity, which humans imitated in legal language with the names of commutativity and contractual bilaterality.

Moreover, just as the law recognizes the dignity and legal personality of humans without moral agency, such as newborns or human beings with severe cognitive limitations, it should likewise recognize the legal personality of non-human living beings, based on the concept of homeostasis, upon which rests the "biodignity." In this vein, this work proposes to establish the rights of the personality of the biological person in a differentiated way, based on the evolutionary trends presented by Bergson, establishing the scope of biological dignity to protect the evolutionary trends of non-human living beings and holistic organic entities according to the direction of homeostasis, which manifests differently in plants and animals.

The nature of the personality rights already recognized for the human being, as Carlos Alberto Bittar teaches, "is inherent rights in the person, due to their own physical, mental, and moral structuring."[41] Bittar further explains that, for the naturalistic conception of personality to which he adheres, he considers personality rights to be innate rights:

> We understand that personality rights constitute innate rights - as most writers now attest - it is up to the State only to recognize them and sanction them on one or another plane of positive law - at the constitutional level or at the level of ordinary legislation - endowing them with their own protection, according to the type of relationship they turn to, namely, against the arbitrariness of public power or the incursions of individuals.[42]

Just as the personality rights of the human person are natural rights, which unfold from their own dignity, and it is up to the state only to recognize them, the personality rights of plant, animal, and systemic biological persons are also innate, given that they derive from "biodignity," which is based on that natural impulse for life that Spinoza called "conatus," or homeostasis, for Antônio Damásio.

This is a right that already exists, that is immanent to all living beings; it is not derived or acquired, because it simply emerges from life itself, as an impulse, as a result of the vital self-value that lies in the "biodignity" of all living and organic beings. It must, therefore, be recognized by legal systems as an original right, respected by the state and by all, given that it is a right "erga omnes."

Thus, a proposal is presented for the recognition of the biological person endowed with a legal personality compatible with their original homeostatic abilities, from birth with life, structuring it into three aspects: (1) plant biological person; (2) animal biological person endowed with instinct; and (3) holistic organic biological person endowed with systemic cognition.

In addition to its immanent aspect, as an originating attribute resulting from "biodignity," the legal personality of the biological person, like that of the human person, projects itself into the social world, considering the necessary relations

---

[41] Bittar (2015), p. 35.

[42] Bittar (2015), p. 39.

waged by the biological person with human beings in intersection zones of the biosphere with social institutions, such as scientific research and property rights—this considered a natural right of humans. Thus, the rights of biological personality inevitably interfere in human legal relations in these intersection zones, from where conflicts of interest emerge between human beings and plant, animal, and systemic biological persons, whose resolution criteria will be addressed in the chapter that deals with the reaffirmation of human rights by the principle of harmony with nature.

As already mentioned, the legal personality of the biological person, like that of the human person, projects itself into the social world with "erga omnes" effects that oblige human beings and public and private law legal entities to respect the rights of plant, animal, and systemic biological persons. This is a duty guided by two ethical principles that underpin the principle of harmony with nature: the principle of responsibility proposed by Hans Jonas and the principle of universal coherence of Cirne-Lima.

Thus, the human person, endowed with moral agency and rationality, has the duty to respect and ensure the rights of the personality of biological persons, who are moral subjects without moral agency. This duty imposes an asymmetric and heightened responsibility, similar to the duty of respect and responsibility of parents toward their children, as proposed by Hans Jonas when addressing the principle of responsibility. In addition, it is a matter of cosmic coherence—that is, of choices that promote harmonious relationships between human beings and nature. Thus, in the following section, an individualized analysis of the rights derived from the biological personality for each type of biological person will be conducted, according to their "biodignity."

6.1.1 The Plant Biological Entity

The plant biological entity encompasses all beings of the plant kingdom. This work proposes including fungi in this group despite their unique characteristics, considering that they are not classified as either animals or plants.[43] The personality of the plant biological entity should be based on its *biodignity*, which includes its basic freedom to flourish and prosper. Plant homeostasis encompasses, in very basic terms, the need to remain in their natural territories, exposure to sunlight, access to water and minerals, and symbiosis with their pollinators and fungi, to fully flourish in their cognitive processes.

Anthony Trewavas, when discussing plant intelligence, notes that dictionaries define intelligence as self-recognition or understanding—definitions that are

[43] "Fungi are amazing beings. In the standard classification of living beings, they do not fit as animals or plants. Plants, by definition, produce their nutrients from inorganic matter, that is, they survive completely independently of other forms of life" (Wohlleben (2017), p. 51.

perfect for an anthropocentric view. However, he warns that for biologists who research the intelligence of other non-human organisms, these definitions lack substance.

Trewavas observes that one of the major problems in research on intelligence in other organisms is the subjective bias inherent in the concept of intelligence, specifically the comparisons made between other living beings and humans to establish the criteria for the characteristics that denote intelligence. This is an anthropocentric and partial view of what intelligence is, which is currently rejected by various branches of science, such as cybernetics, which considers the presence of aspects that allow one species to predominate, in biological terms, over another species as a fundamental criterion for defining intelligence.

Thus, the dominance that plants exert over other species on the planet, by being at the base of all vital processes, is, in itself, indicative of a type of intelligence that cannot be underestimated. Another common and erroneous assumption about what intelligence is relates to the common sense that associates intelligence with the brain, leading to the belief that only organisms with a developed brain, such as primates, cetaceans, crows, and elephants, for example, could be considered intelligent; however, science has long since overcome this view of "brain chauvinism."[44]

Trewavas points out that, just like animals move when provoked, plants also react, changing their phenotype. In this sense, green plants react to various environmental biotic factors, such as mechanical stimuli related to nutrition, humidity, soil formation, temperature, and gases; all these factors influence the plant, in its own way, affecting the strength, the direction of its development, and its own phenotypic plasticity. This information is integrated, processed, and absorbed at the cellular and tissue levels, triggering changes in plant shape.

Trewavas cites Darwin, who stated that "the tip of the roots of plants acts like the brain of one of the lower animals," and points out that green plants are composed of millions of cells, each individual cell being intelligent. He further explains that plants have developed a coordinated intelligence system based on their hormones. Plants, in their nutritional process, actively seek food resources that allow them to change their architecture, physiology, and phenotype. This system implies decision-making and choice, considering that when they locate nutrient-rich fragments through their roots, they trigger a proliferation of root branches to increase the absorption of these energy minerals and water, thus guiding the growth of roots, shoots, and leaves in the ideal direction to obtain nutrients—that is, toward areas where they detect the existence of energy minerals and water.

Trewavas also highlights that:

> Plants are territorial, they minimize competition from their own roots and prefer unoccupied soils. [...] Other convincing studies indicate that root systems are self-sensitive, an important aspect of intelligent behavior. When clones of the same plant are separated,

[44] Trewavas (2006), p. 2.

> within a few weeks the root systems recognize each other as strangers and proliferate accordingly. Plants assess and respond to local opportunities that, in the future, will benefit the whole plant.[45]

Witzany, in the same direction, clarifies that the development of plants does not happen automatically but through signs. Like all living beings, plants evaluate the reality of their surroundings to estimate the amount of energy they need to achieve their goals; they also control environmental resources, distinguish between self and non-self, and thus have the ability to protect their territories against invasions of harmful parasites. In the region of their roots, more than 20 different groups of molecules with communicative functions and up to 100,000 different substances, called secondary metabolites, have been identified. These substances are mobilized in the interactive processes carried out by the roots with microbes, insects, fungi, and roots of other plants for cooperation.[46]

In the same vein, Peter Wohlleben reports that in the partnership between trees and fungi, a symbiotic relationship is formed when the former find a type of fungus with a mycelium compatible with their roots, which open up to allow the fungal filaments to penetrate the soft root tissue, establishing a fruitful partnership for both parties. The tree expands its network into the surrounding soil, increasing the root's area of operation, which grows toward the roots of other trees, creating a network for nutrient and information exchange. This allows the trees, for example, to defend themselves promptly against attacks from hostile insects. Thus, the partnership between trees and fungi creates an intelligent data exchange network among the forest trees, benefiting them. The fungi, in turn, benefit from the nutrients, as they are compensated with sugars and carbohydrates. However, not content with this, the fungi offer an additional service of filtering heavy metals to obtain extra quantities of sugars.[47]

Plants, in addition to establishing mutualistic partnerships, have the ability, in their complex and sophisticated cognitive processes, to store representative information from experience for their learning through the process of comparing and evaluating recent experiences.[48]

František Baluška et al.,[49] when discussing plant neurobiology, point out the following similarities between plants and animals: (1) All major metabolic pathways are conserved in animal and plant cells; (2) plants use sexual reproduction processes identical to those in animals, that is, based on the fusion of cells, sperm, and oocytes; (3) when a plant is attacked by pathogens, it develops immunity, the processes of which are similar to those in animals;

---

[45] Trewavas (2006), p. 9.
[46] Witzany (2018), p. 9–11.
[47] Wohlleben (2017), p. 52–56.
[48] Witzany (2018), p. 9–11.
[49] Baluška et al. (2006), p. 20.

and (4) plants and animals use the same molecules and pathways to produce their circadian rhythms.[50]

They further clarify that the word "neuron," although used by animal neurologists, curiously has its etymology in Greek and means "plant fiber." They attribute the reason for the word being brought into the realm of animal neurology to the similarity between the tips of plant roots and animal neurons, given that root apices, in addition to being specialized in nutrition, also use a process similar to synapse for cell-to-cell communication.

Thus, the novel science of plant neurobiology considers plants as organisms with a peculiar type of intelligence, possessing the ability to learn and make decisions concerning their environmental situation. They are active organisms with the ability to identify herbivorous animals and recruit the enemies of their predators. In this context, researchers cite the example of corn roots which, when attacked by the Diabrotica beetle larva, emit volatile compounds to recruit entomopathogenic nematodes, the natural predators of the Diabrotica beetle larva, commonly known as the rootworm.

Regarding motility, they observe that although plants cannot physically move, their roots grow actively and are oriented toward the most nutritious soil niches. Thus, roots, in addition to having the function of nutrient absorption, also propel forward movement, which characterizes an attribute of the "anterior poles of multicellular organisms."[51]

Thus, for František Baluška et al., "recent new views on consciousness and self-awareness, when considered as inseparable biological phenomena from the processes of adaptation and learning, are compatible with the new neurobiologically oriented view of plants."[52]

This work took care to research, albeit briefly, the latest advances in the study of plant cognition by the novel science called plant neurobiology, to demonstrate the complexity and sophistication of the plant being in its biodignity, from which unfolds the legal personality of the biological plant person.

In this way, the rights of the legal personality of the biological plant person should encompass the basic rights that ensure the homeostasis of the plant. The following rights can be listed as rights of the biological plant personality, based on the biodignity of these living beings: (1) right to life; (2) right to natural territories; (3) right to sunlight; (4) right to water; (5) right to symbiosis with their natural pollinators and fungi; (6) right to the integrity of their bodies; (7) right to health; (8) right to rescue in cases of catastrophes and environmental disasters; (9) right to restoration of their territories, respecting the principle of biodiversity; (10) right to

---

[50] "*Circadian rhythm or circadian cycle (from Latin* ***circa*** *about+****diem*** *day) refers to the biological cycle of almost all living beings, which is based on a period of approximately 24 hours, being mainly influenced by variations in light, temperature, tides, and winds between day and night*" (Available at: https://pt.wikipedia.org/wiki/Ritmo_circadiano#:~:text=Ritmo%20circadiano%20ou%20ciclo%20circadiano,o%20dia%20e%20a%20noite. Accessed on: May 30, 2021).

[51] Baluška et al. (2006), p. 22.

[52] Baluška et al. (2006), p. 21.

biodiversity protection; (11) right to the prevalence of their basic interests, when in conflict with non-basic human interests; (12) right to protection against exotic invaders; and (13) right to action for the defense of their rights arising from plant biological personality.

6.1.2 The Animal Biological Person

The concept of *biodignity* proposed in this work is based on the vital impulse for life—*conatus* or homeostasis—which is shared by all living beings and systemic, holistic, organic entities, with the presence of homeostasis being enough for the recognition of intrinsic value and *biodignity*. However, in the formation of the animal biological person, one cannot ignore the specific aspects of animal cognition, which shape their personality and should be considered in the rights arising from this animal biological personality.

In this sense, one cannot ignore the fact that several species of animals exhibit feelings and emotions, such as empathy and joy, as a given part of their personality. For cognitive ethologist Marc Bekoff, these emotions are a strong link between humans and animals: "We can share our emotions, we can understand the language of feelings, and that's why we form deep and lasting social bonds with many other beings. Emotions are the glue that binds them. They catalyze and regulate social interactions in animals and humans."[53]

Bekoff explains that cognitive ethology is dedicated to the comparative, evolutionary, and ecological study of animal minds to understand what animals think and feel, their emotions, beliefs, reasoning, information processing, consciousness, and self-awareness. He highlights that Charles Darwin is considered the first scientist to dedicate himself to the in-depth study of animal emotions, having observed in mammals the experiences, with varying degrees, of anxiety, sadness, discouragement, despair, joy, love, tender feelings, devotion, bad mood, determination, hatred, anger, disdain, contempt, disgust, guilt, pride, patience, surprise, astonishment, fear, horror, shame, shyness, and modesty.[54]

For Bekoff, emotions in animals are more apparent, given that they do not hide or filter them. They communicate their raw emotions through their own bodies, such as tail and ear movements, exuding odors, specific facial expressions, differentiated looks, winks denoting gratitude, and oral manifestations, such as howling, chirping, and hissing. These emotions are present in wild animals like wolves and elephants, in cetaceans, in pets like dogs and cats, as well as in animals destined for food, like pigs, cows, and chickens.

Thus, in the formation of the legal personality of the animal biological person, these emotions should be taken into account, especially the capacity for affective

---

[53] Bekoff (2007), p. 15.

[54] Bekoff (2007), p. 31–32.

expression, which is quite complex and even includes the love manifested in mating. Bekoff emphasizes in this regard that romantic love is not a privilege of humans, given that many animal species spend time getting to know their partners and establishing intimacy, and, for this, there are mating rituals.

He reports that functional studies of magnetic resonance images show that many canids, that is, coyotes, wolves, foxes, jackals, and dingoes, make a careful evaluation of partners for mating and maintain the same partnerships for long periods, preserving a certain emotional bond, even after they change partners. Meanwhile, 90% of bird species are monogamous and maintain the mating partnership for life. In this sense, it is worth noting the monogamous relationship of the rufous hornero (*Furnarius rufus*); together, male and female collect the raw material—wet clay, straw, and dung—which they knead with their feet and beaks, forming clay balls. Then, in hundreds of trips, they transport all the material in their beaks. The couple, in partnership, builds the nest with walls up to 5 cm thick. The structure is divided into two rooms, with the entrance door located in the opposite direction of the rain and wind, to protect the future offspring during nesting, which occurs in the second chamber of the nest, safe from predators. The couple's investment in parental care is assumed equally by the male and the female.[55]

Another relevant aspect of animal affection relates to maternal love. In most species, females will fight to the death to protect their offspring. Even some invertebrate animals protect their offspring, and it has been found in this regard that Australian leeches protect their newborns, carrying and nourishing them for up to six weeks after birth.[56]

Bekoff observes that, even when attributing these family affections—love romantic, love for offspring—to the category of mere genetically programmed instincts for the perpetuation of the species, there is still such a complex range of affections in animals that goes beyond mere biological instinct, considering that many animals demonstrate devotion and care to such a high degree that they sometimes do so to the detriment of their own biological interests. In this sense, the story of two terrier dogs is worthy of being reported at this point, as it denotes an admirable ability to express care, affection, and loyalty:

> [...] they were found, filthy and terrified, huddled on the main street of a small town. The dogs were friends, not companions. One was bleeding from both eyes; the other was on guard, barking and attacking anyone who approached. They were taken to a veterinarian, who diagnosed that one of the dogs had been stabbed in both eyes, thus had his eyes removed and his eyelids sewn. Two days after the surgery, Ben, as the little dog whose eyes had been removed was named, was reunited with Bill at the local animal shelter. From that moment on, Bill spontaneously became Ben's guide dog; with Ben holding his neck, Bill walked with him around the yard until Ben knew the layout of the land. After the fact was reported on television, the dogs were adopted by an elderly couple.[57]

---

[55] Sabino (2015).

[56] Bekoff (2007), p. 73.

[57] Bekoff (2007), p. 49–50.

This ability to establish an emotional bond, as denoted by animals, should be recognized in the formation of their personality and should be reflected in the rights that unfold from the legal personality of the biological animal person.

In structuring the rights of the personality of the biological animal person endowed with instinct, emotions, and affectivity, there is a need to distinguish four categories of animals: (i) wild animals; (ii) companion and domesticated animals; (iii) animals used in entertainment and involved in research; and (iv) animals intended for human consumption.

This distinction is not established by considering the characteristics of the animals as organisms, but by considering their position as beings in the world, which requires differentiated rights for the protection of their biodignity. The life of wild animals requires a type of protection different from that which should be given to companion animals, to animals intended for food, or even to those involved in research. Each of these animals needs a bundle of specific rights that, in addition to ensuring their biological dignity in their ways of living, creates specific duties of respect for human beings within the ecological and social contexts of these different groups of animals.

6.1.2.1 The Personality Rights of Wild Animals

Wild animals are those that live free from human domination, governed by natural laws and not by human customs. Mammals, cetaceans, invertebrates, reptiles, amphibians, birds, insects, marsupials, fish, cephalopods, and others that live freely in nature are considered in these categories. Therefore, when thinking about the personality rights of the biological legal person of the wild animal, it should be borne in mind that the first right of this biological person is free life in intact ecosystems, protected from human impact. Thus, among their rights, the following can be listed: (a) wild life; (b) ecological integrity of natural territories; (c) right to unrestricted mobility within their territories; (d) protection of their territories from pollution, the presence of diseases triggered by humans, and invasive species; (e) protection against risks of being run over on roads near their habitats; (f) protection of their relationships with members of the same species and natural interactions with other species; (g) protection of their symbiotic relationships with other animals and plants; (h) right to full health and specialized veterinary care; (i) prohibition of sport hunting and fishing; (j) containment of invasive exotic species; (k) prohibition of the trade of live or dead wild animals, as well as parts of their bodies, such as feathers, skins, teeth, and others; (l) protection against extinction; (m) affirmative actions for the protection of species at risk; (n) provision of aid in cases of catastrophes and environmental disasters, with guaranteed nutrition; (o) guarantee of experiential well-being (absence of pain, anguish, suffering, exhaustion, stress, and other unpleasant experiences); (p) right to protection of biodiversity; (q) respect for their emotional bonds; (r) respect for effective relationships resulting from motherhood; (s) right of action for the defense of their rights arising from animal biological personality; (t) free access to justice; (u) place of speech, through their legal representatives, in political debates involving their interests and rights individually or diffusely; (v) right to be represented by indigenous peoples, the Public Prosecutor's Office, and protector associations in the defense of their individual and diffuse interests and rights; and (w) right to the prevalence of their basic interests when in conflict with non-basic human interests.

6.1.2.2 The Personality Rights of Domesticated Companion and Entertainment Animals

Considering that companion and domesticated animals are under human control, which interferes with their behaviors and abilities, humans who are in the position of guardians of these animals must directly assume a series of duties arising from guardianship to ensure the rights to life, nutrition, health, well-being, and affection of these animals.

Thus, the rights of the legal personality of the biological animal, when it comes to domesticated, companion, and pet animals, can be bundled as follows: (a) right to life; (b) right to nutrition; (c) right to mobility; (d) right to health, including preventive measures against zoonoses, such as vaccination; (e) right to preserve their emotional bonds with their guardians and other animals, particularly respect for the emotional bond of motherhood; (f) right to physical and emotional integrity; (g) right to protection against abandonment by their guardians; (h) right to clean and adequate shelter; (i) right to assistance in case of accidents or environmental disasters; (j) right to the opportunity for typical functioning of the species; (l) right to sufficient rest for the maintenance of physical and mental health; m) guarantee of experiential well-being (absence of pain, distress, suffering, exhaustion, stress, and other unpleasant experiences); (n) prohibition of the commercialization of adult and puppy companion animals; (o) right to be represented by their guardians, the Public Ministry, and protective associations in the defense of their interests and rights arising from animal legal personality; (p) right to action for the defense of their rights arising from the biological animal legal personality; (q) free access to justice; (r) place of speech, through their legal representatives, in political debates involving their interests and rights individually or diffusely; (s) right to the prevalence of their basic interests when in conflict with non-basic human interests; and (t) right to the continuity of life, provided their well-being and palliative care are guaranteed when diagnosed with incurable diseases.

The rights of the personality of the biological animal, arising from biodignity, are incompatible with the use of animals by humans for entertainment, considering that these animals are trained to entertain humans in macabre shows, in which they are induced to act, fight, and even kill. In this category are animals displayed in circuses, movies, races, and fighting pits. The use of animals for entertainment conflicts with the concept of *biodignity* and should be prohibited by legal systems, considering that these animals are removed from their natural *habitats*, from their biotic communities, and trained through painful and cruel conditioning to develop skills that are foreign to their natural instincts. Thus, this nefarious human cultural practice violates the principles of harmony with nature and *biodignity* and, therefore, viscerally conflicts with the rights of the personality of the biological animal.

Similarly, it violates the rights arising from the *biodignity* of the biological person—the enslavement of animals in work and economic production by human beings, using them to pull carts, transport goods, luggage, and humans. These activities are not compatible with the principle of harmony with nature and should be prohibited.

6.1.2.3 The Rights of the Personality of Animals Involved in Scientific Research

We must also not forget the situation of animals that are subjected to scientific experiments and research in the fields of cosmetology, the personal hygiene product industry, and the pharmaceutical industry itself. Waldau points out that many species are used for experiments in scientific research. Rats and mice make up 90% of the animals used in research in the United States. In 2008, the Hadwen Trust and the British Union Against Vivisection published in the journal *Alternatives to Laboratory Animal* a study suggesting that approximately 115 million animals are involved annually worldwide in laboratory experiments, with about 140,000 dogs, 35,000 cats, 90,000 primates, and over a million rabbits used per year.[58]

This work proposes the application of the six general principles of Beauchamp and DeGrazia to reconcile scientific research involving animals with the principle of harmony with nature and its main corollary, *biodignity*. These authors warn that such research causes harm to the animals involved, who cannot be seen only as objects but as participating subjects of the research, and thus must receive protection of their dignity during the procedures. These harms can occur throughout the course of the experiment, starting with stressful housing, handling, and transportation.

Another nefarious aspect of this reality is the fact that animals do not have the capacity to consent to the involvement of their bodies in research. In addition, non-therapeutic research with animals does not offer them any prospect of medical or veterinary benefits, either for the animal individually or even for their species.[59]

As can be seen, the current use of animals in research starts from a point of view of objectification of the living being, which is demonstrated to be incompatible with the *biodignity* of the biological animal person. Beauchamp and DeGrazia present six general ethical principles as criteria to justify this type of research:

1. The principle of non-existence of an alternative method: to justify the participation of an animal in research, researchers must demonstrate in the research protocol that there is no other alternative method; this means that animals should

[58] Waldau (2011), p. 44–45.

[59] Beauchamp and Degrazia (2020), p. 5.

not suffer harm to their integrity if there are other suitable and available alternative models to achieve the same ends.
2. The principle of expected net benefit: the prospect of social gains from research must outweigh its costs and risks to humans.
3. The principle of sufficient value to justify harm: the prospect of net benefits to human society from research must be sufficiently valuable to justify the expected harm to the animals involved.
4. The principle of no unnecessary harm: animals should not suffer harm to their integrity; harming an animal is only justified if it is necessary and morally justified for scientific purposes.
5. The principle of basic needs: during the conduct of studies, the basic needs of animals must be met. Any failure to attend to specific basic needs is only admitted if it is necessary and morally justified for scientific purposes.
6. The principle of upper limits for harm: animals cannot be subjected to severe suffering for a long period. This would only be admissible in very exceptional and necessary cases for research, which is morally justified, for social and scientific purposes of high relevance.[60]

Beauchamp and DeGrazia, when dealing with the contours of scientific necessity as a justification for harm, point out that the objectives of research must be justified by scientific standards and morally legitimized by moral standards. They also note:

> [...] that the main justification for the use of animals in research has been the scientific necessity to use animals to achieve desirable research results, such as medical benefits for humans. However, many of these studies do not meet the moral meaning of the term "scientific necessity". The existence of a scientific need for the use of animals is morally necessary, but not a morally sufficient condition for the justified use of animals. The fact that the use of animals is scientifically necessary to achieve a valuable scientific result does not make the research morally justified, because other conditions, besides scientific necessity, must be met - that is, the conditions required by all six principles of this framework.[61]

This work considers that the involvement of the biological animal person in research is only justified and compatible with biodignity if it simultaneously meets the six principles proposed by Beauchamp and DeGrazia, so it proposes the incorporation of these principles into the bundle of rights that protect the personality of the biological animal person involved in scientific research by humans.

Thus, the rights arising from the biological and legal personality of animals involved in scientific research are as follows:

(a) Compliance with the six principles proposed by Beauchamp and DeGrazia: (a.1) principle of non-existence of an alternative method; (a.2) principle of expected net benefit; (a.3) principle of sufficient value to justify harm; (a.4)

[60] Beauchamp and Degrazia (2020), p. 6–15.

[61] Beauchamp and Degrazia (2020), p. 20–21.

principle of no unnecessary harm; (a.5) principle of basic needs; and (a.6) principle of upper limits for harm.

(b) Assignment to the Public Prosecutor's Office and protective associations of the function of legal representatives of the biological animal person involved in scientific research.
(c) Informed consent by the Public Prosecutor's Office, as the representative of the interests and rights of the biological animal person involved in scientific research, as part of the scientific research protocols.
(d) Right to care, throughout the entire procedural iteration of the research (before, during, and after), for the basic needs of the animals, understood as: nutritious food; clean water; safe shelter; adequate stimulation; exercise; opportunity for the typical functioning of the species; sufficient rest for the maintenance of physical and mental health; and veterinary care. In the case of social species, access to members of the same species or compatible social groups must be guaranteed; security against significant experimental harm, such as pain, distress, and suffering; security against diseases, injuries, and disabilities; freedom of movement with adequate space; protection against premature death; and experiential well-being (absence of pain, distress, suffering, exhaustion, stress, and other unpleasant experiences).
(e) Right of action to guarantee their rights arising from the biological animal personality.
(f) Right to free access to justice.
(g) Right to the prevalence of their basic interests when in conflict with the non-basic interests of humans.

6.1.2.4 The Personality Rights of Animals Destined for Human Consumption

As paradoxical as it may seem to defend the personality rights of animals destined for food, it cannot be forgotten that, from an organic point of view, these animals do not differ from wild animals, as they are endowed with instinct, a nervous system, motility, sentience, and emotions; therefore, they experience life in its fullness, and they possess the homeostasis on which their *biodignity* rests. On the other hand, there is no consensus that veganism is an indispensable condition for respecting the life and dignity of animals. In this regard, it is worth mentioning the understanding of Temple Grandin, which this work considers as a possibility of reconciling the principle of harmony with nature and *biodignity* with the raising of animals for food. Grandin synthesizes her theory in the following statement: "We owe animals a decent life and a painless death."[62] (our emphasis).

Indeed, even though the lifespan of these animals is short, as they are born destined for slaughter, it is possible to guarantee them *biodignity*, ensuring the exercise of their instincts, their mobility, their experiential well-being (absence of

[62] Grandin (2017), p. 253.

pain, anguish, suffering, exhaustion, stress, and other unpleasant experiences) during their brief lives, and that their development is natural, without acceleration by genetic manipulation, use of antibiotics, or hormones.

Thus, even though they live for a short period of time, during their existence, they have the right to live in the world according to their natural abilities. However, this is not what has been happening. Waldau cites a 2008 document, jointly published by Pew Charitable Trusts and Johns Hopkins School of Public Health, reporting that the confined animal production systems currently in use are far below acceptable ethical and social standards.[63]

These are animals destined for human consumption: chickens, pigs, cattle, fish, ducks, turkeys, goats, sheep, rabbits, shellfish, and others. However, the most serious violations are found in the raising and slaughter of cattle, pigs, and chickens. This is mainly due to the large number of these animals that are raised and slaughtered for food. According to Waldau, the numbers are between 50 and 100 billion animals slaughtered every year for food, with the vast majority being chickens, pigs, and cattle.

These animals are raised in conditions that completely violate their instincts and their homeostasis, primarily because their right to motility is completely disregarded, as they are confined for fattening and subjected to high doses of antibiotics and hormones to artificially accelerate their growth and fattening. This way of raising animals for human consumption, in addition to violating their *biodignity*, also causes serious damage to humans and ecosystems.

Waldau cites data from the United Nations Food and Agriculture Organization (FAO), published in a 2006 report titled "Livestock's long shadow," which attributes confined cattle breeding facilities as the largest source of water pollution and eutrophication of coastal areas, along with the degradation of coral reefs. In addition, the report points out that this cattle breeding system causes problems for human health, as it creates resistance to antibiotics in the human body. All this occurs due to pollution from waste contaminated with antibiotics, hormones, tannery chemicals, fertilizers, and pesticides used in feed crops and pasture sediments.

The way of raising animals for food in industrial livestock farming, in addition to seriously violating the *biodignity* of the biological animal person, also puts at risk the health of humans and ecosystems as a whole, thus indirectly also offending the dignity of the human person.

Respect for the *biodignity* of animals destined for food is absolutely incompatible with their industrial breeding on farms, with the complete deprivation of motility and contact with the natural world, including sunlight, soil, and vegetation. In addition to mobility restriction, another serious violation of the *biodignity* of these animals is their genetic manipulation and the acceleration of fattening through antibiotics and hormones.

---

[63] Waldau (2011), p. 52.

Temple Grandin[64] warns that pig breeders in the United States may be pushing these animals beyond their biological limits. She denounces that pig breeders are making the same mistakes as broiler chicken breeders. Pigs have their growth induced quickly, so their bones are very weak, and their muscles are large but so fragile that insurers do not sell transport insurance to producers to cover the risk during the transport of these animals.

In the debate about veganism as a condition for respecting animal rights, Steven L. Davis[65] raises an objection to the ethical vegan proposal defended by Tom Regan. Davis argues that a vegan diet would not reduce animal deaths, considering that, although animals destined for food would benefit, the increase in agricultural activity resulting from the rise in grain and tuber planting to replace direct consumption of animal protein would increase the death of wild animals that inhabit the fields. Thus, even a vegan diet, indirectly, also causes the unintentional death of wildlife, which live on lands where crops are cultivated in a mechanized and intensive manner. The only difference is that these deaths of field animals would not be intentional but a side effect of industrial agriculture, while the death of cattle, pigs, and chickens in industrial livestock farming is intentional. He concludes, therefore, that a vegan diet is not free from animal blood, considering that thousands of small wild animals are collaterally killed in the preparation of the land for agriculture that also feeds vegans.

Davis's argument is partially true; however, it omits a relevant detail, as a large part of the beef cattle herds are already raised in confinement, just like pigs and chickens, and thus are fed with soy-based feed. This grain is widely grown in tropical countries, such as Brazil, in areas opened with the burning of large equatorial forests, which causes the mass death of thousands of species. Soy farming practiced in tropical countries causes an incalculable loss of plant and animal biodiversity, in addition to destroying entire ecosystems, creating a risk of droughts and desertification.

Thus, the cost to maintain industrial livestock farming continues to be more burdensome, as there is an extremely harmful intersection for the environment between large-scale agriculture and industrial livestock farming to sustain the animals fattened in confinement and, thus, supply the insatiable and growing market for animal protein in developed countries and those with emerging economies.

Achieving an ethical standard by humans in their relationship with animals intended for food is not possible through the radical imposition of a vegan diet, considering that such an imposition would conflict with the democratic principle and the very principle of harmony with nature, which presupposes the freedom for humans to make their choices according to universal coherence.

---

[64] Grandin (2017), p. 253.

[65] Davis (2017), p. 271.

Therefore, this work proposes, based on the principle of harmony with nature, another way to restore human coherence in its relationship with animals intended for food. This path involves recognizing the intrinsic value of these animals and respecting their *biodignity* during breeding and slaughter. This means abolishing the industrial method of meat production and returning to extensive and organic farming in harmony with nature, respecting the natural life cycle of the involved animal species.

Extensive livestock farming on natural pastures, with organic fattening of cattle, pigs, and chickens, is a way to harmonize human consumption of animal protein with the *biodignity* of slaughter animals and, also, with the conservation of ecosystems.

Organic extensive livestock farming can be practiced in harmony with the biotic conservation of territories in order to preserve the life of small wild animals and natural vegetation in these areas. It is possible to ensure, with extensive organic farming in already-exploited areas, the *biodignity* of slaughter animals, which, during their lives, will be able to exercise their natural abilities of mobility, nutrition, access to running water, and sunlight, without the stress caused by artificial confinement environments. In addition, the quality of the meat will be superior, as it is produced without the use of additives to promote artificial growth, such as hormones and non-protein nitrogen sources.[66]

In the same vein, dairy cattle should be treated with breeding and milking practices compatible with *biodignity*, completely abolishing the use of cruel techniques such as the opening of fistulas[67] for monitoring the animal's digestive process, in order to increase the longevity of the milking period. The *biodignity* of dairy cows also prohibits any other management that militates against their natural abilities, their maternal instinct, and their experiential well-being, such as early separation from the offspring, solitary confinement of the offspring, and painful mutilations (branding, dehorning, tail cutting, and the creation of fistulas).

Even though it is argued that extensive organic farming of cattle, pigs, chickens, and other animals intended for human consumption is economically unfeasible because it would increase the price of animal protein, it must be remembered that an attitude of universal coherence and harmony with nature implies the necessary reduction of meat consumption, so that quality should be prioritized over quantity. In this vein, it is necessary to restructure meat production organically and with respect for life, also guaranteeing humans a diet free of hormones, antibiotics, and, above all, free from animal pain. This is a legitimate way for humans to nourish themselves and will contribute not only to the health of their bodies but, above all, to their moral elevation and, thus, to sustainable and harmonious development with all living beings.

---

[66] Moraes (2010).

[67] "Fistulation involves surgically opening a channel between an organ and the outside by removing a piece of the abdomen of these animals to expose their stomachs and then equipping them with a plastic ring to keep the hole open." Pietra (2016).

Therefore, this work proposes the recognition of biological legal personality also for animals intended for food, with the recognition of the following rights for this biological animal person: (a) right to life with *biodignity*, in all its aspects, and especially in the temporal dimension, to ensure respect for the natural development cycle of each species, with the prohibition of early slaughter, as occurs, for example, with veal; (b) right to nutrition and natural lighting; (c) right to freedom of movement in a space suitable for satisfying the vital impulse of mobility of the species; (d) right to health, including preventive measures against zoonoses; (e) right to preserve their bonds of affection in relation to their offspring; (f) right to physical and emotional integrity; (g) right to protection against abandonment by their breeders; (h) right to clean and adequate shelter; (i) right to assistance in case of accidents or environmental disasters; (j) right to the opportunity for the typical functioning of the species; (k) right to sufficient rest for the maintenance of physical and mental health; (l) guarantee of experiential well-being (absence of pain, distress, suffering, exhaustion, stress, and other unpleasant experiences) during life and at the time of slaughter; (m) right to be represented as a biological animal person without moral agency by the Public Ministry and protective associations, for the defense of their individual and diffuse interests and rights; (n) guarantee of the right of action for the protection of their rights arising from the biological animal personality; (o) right to free access to justice; and (p) right to the prevalence of their basic interests when in conflict with non-basic human interests.

6.1.3 The Systemic Biological Person

Currently, the Earth's biosphere, with its biodiversity, species, and all ecosystems, is considered a living and complex organic entity endowed with homeostasis, governed by the principle of relationality and the principle of holism. Nevertheless, the biocentric movement still does not recognize the intrinsic value and rights of holistic organic entities. So the question arises: Which fundamental characteristic of living systems does this work consider as its *biodignity*? What legitimizes considering an ecosystem as a person?

For Maturana and Varela,[68] the fundamental characteristic of life is its self-reproduction or *autopoiesis*, which corresponds to something like creating oneself: this is the central point for defining that something is alive. In this sense, it is worth remembering the lesson of Jørgensen et al. when they cite the teaching of Prigogine, clarifying that there are few hypotheses in which an external event can radically alter the direction and constitution of a living system. In this line, the direction of a living system is always toward life and is formulated internally in its own constitution, as an act of choice. Ecosystems thus have a holistic memory, and for this reason, they

[68] Maturana and Varela (1991), p. 121.

communicate, interact, and direct themselves away from thermodynamic equilibrium, based on information recorded by their own experiences.[69]

Thus, when this work understands ecosystems as living, holistic, organic entities, it is because they are systems that continuously construct themselves; therefore, they are endowed with a direction toward flourishing, and in this lies their homeostasis, in which rests the *biodignity* resulting from the principle of harmony with nature.

In this order of ideas, all ecosystems—freshwater, maritime, coastal, and terrestrial biomes—are biological persons endowed with legal personality, from which the following basic rights derive: (a) right to genetic diversity of species, of *habitat*, and to the functional processes on which their complexities rest; (b) right to sunlight; (c) right to water; (d) right to soil nutrients; (e) right to ecological integrity; (f) right to non-interruption of energy and matter flows; (g) protection against invasion of exotic species; (h) protection against human interferences that cause any type of entropic acceleration; (i) protection against war experiences, nuclear tests and other harmful artifacts to ecological integrity; (j) right to full life and biodiversity; (k) right to the territories necessary for the full systemic functioning of biomes; (l) protection of watersheds against pollution and eutrophication by chemical and organic agents; (m) protection of rivers against silting, eutrophication, and course diversion; (n) protection against desertification; (o) protection against fires and any type of deforestation; (p) place of expression, through their legal representatives, in political debates involving their individual or diffuse interests and rights; (q) right to be represented by indigenous peoples, by the Public Ministry and by protector associations in the defense of their individual and diffuse interests and rights; (r) guarantee of the right of action for the protection of their rights arising from the systemic biological personality; (s) right to free access to justice; and (t) right to the prevalence of their basic interests, when in conflict with non-basic human interests.

6.2 The Legal Incapacity of the Biological Person, Their Representation, and Guardianship

As already demonstrated in previous topics, biological persons—plant, animal, and systemic—despite not being moral agents, are moral subjects and, therefore, have their legal personality based on the concept of *biodignity*, which grants them the quality of subjects of law in the sense of having their rights correlated to biological dignity, which is based on homeostasis and respected by the human being.

Just like members of the human community without moral agency, due to cognitive deficiencies or immaturity, are considered moral subjects—that is, their dignity and legal personality are recognized—biological entities such as plants,

[69] Jørgensen et al. (2019), p. 118.

animals, and systems are also subjects of law without moral agency. Therefore, they should not only have their rights arising from biological personality respected but should also be able to exercise these rights through the institution of legal representation, by their natural guardians and by the Public Prosecutor's Office.

For biological entities such as plants, animals, and systems to exercise their rights arising from biological personality, based on *biodignity*, it is necessary to recognize their legal capacity for enjoyment and fact. The latter is mitigated, as is the capacity of human beings without moral agency or those absolutely incapable of performing acts of civil life.

The right or enjoyment capacity of biological entities, such as plants, animals, and systems, is differentiated, considering that it coincides with the biological legal personality, which is based on *biodignity* and refers to the ability to acquire and exercise, through others who represent them, the rights circumscribed to this differentiated legal personality, already listed previously in a non-exhaustive list.

The factual capacity for the exercise of these rights by biological entities such as plants, animals, and systems is mitigated, similar to the factual capacity of human beings without moral agency. Biological entities such as plants, animals, and systems are absolutely incapable of exercising their rights before the human legal system, considering that they do not master human language. Thus, they should be represented by their natural and affective guardians, when available, and by institutionally established guardians in legal orders, such as the Public Prosecutor's Office, animal protection associations, and non-governmental organizations dedicated to the ecological cause.

6.2.1 The Natural and Institutional Guardianship of the Biological Entity

This work proposes the original peoples of the planet as the natural guardians of biological entities, such as plants, animals (wild), and systems.

Indeed, as previously mentioned, the original peoples relate to the Earth and living beings, both plant and animal, from a non-dichotomous, egalitarian, spiritual, and respectful perspective. In this sense, we refer to the thought of Philippe Descola, who reports on the Achuar cosmogony, in which all beings share the same soul, which makes them human.[70] From Sztutman's reading, it is inferred that this animistic communion between animals, plants, and human beings was established in a mythological time when all living beings shared the human form. However, even after speciation, despite the bodily multiplicity, the soul remained the same, and thus all living beings, human and non-human, still communicate through enchantments called *anents.*[71]

[70] Descola (2013).

[71] Sztutman (2020), p. 5–7.

In a similar direction, Viveiros de Castro reports on the Amerindian perspectivism of the original Amazonian peoples, for whom animals are people or see themselves as people.[72]

In addition to this egalitarian relationship with animals, from the soul, they also relate umbilically to the Earth. In this sense, Aguilera Urquiza and Nascimento report that, for the Guarani people (Kaiowá and Ñandeva), *tekoha* "means space, place (*ha*), possible for the way of living (*teko*). Thus, *tekoha* is not only linked to the territory; it also establishes a relationship with the social and political structure of the Kaiowá and Guarani people."[73] Adilson Crepaldi, when studying the meaning of the sign *tekoha* in the Kaiowá worldview, highlights that the Earth is seen as the mother who makes the bodies of human beings with her own matter; the Earth is sacralized, and the rivers are considered the veins through which the sap of the Earth, the water, flows. The *tekoha* is the link between the sky, the human being, and the Earth. In this visceral relationship lies the source of existence, identity, and balance, and its rupture leads to *ñmyrõ* (state of death), that is, thermodynamic imbalance.[74]

The original peoples are the bearers, among humans, of a relational and loving ethical reserve in relation to biological entities such as plants, animals (wild), and systems, which legitimizes them as their original guardians, considering that they understand and share life with all living beings in a single cosmic community.

The original peoples are the living memory of the principle of harmony with nature in its fullest conception, considering that it brings ethical harmony with nature in its cosmogony, in its ontology, and in the rules that govern its way of life, that is, in its customary law.

In this sense, one cannot forget what is stated in Principle 22 of the Rio Declaration:

Indigenous peoples and their communities, as well as other local communities, play a vital role in environmental management and development, due to their knowledge and traditional practices. States should recognize and adequately support their identity, culture, and interests, and provide conditions for their effective participation in achieving sustainable development.[75]

Thus, indigenous peoples are naturally entrusted with the original guardianship of the biological entities of plants, animals (wildlife), and systems in their regions, and can represent them before social, legal, and political institutions. The concept of guardianship adopted in this work does not refer to the strictest sense of guardianship provided for in the civil code, as a substitute for parental power. The guardianship by the original peoples of the biological entities of plants,

---

72 Castro (1996), p. 117.

73 Aguilera Urquiza and Nascimento (2013), p. 65.

74 Crepalde (2014).

75 Rio Declaration on Environment and Development. Rio de Janeiro, June 1992. Available at https://cetesb.sp.gov.br/proclima/wp-content/uploads/sites/36/2013/12/declaracao_rio_ma.pdf. Accessed on: May 5, 2021.

animals (wildlife), and systems stems from a deep and spiritual bond that unites the original peoples with the biosphere of planet Earth.

As the original natural guardians of the biological entities of plants, animals (wildlife), and systems, indigenous peoples have the ability to represent them, compensating for their lack of actual capacity to exercise rights before public legal entities, private legal entities, natural persons, and, above all, before social, political, and legal institutions.

As can be seen, this natural guardianship of the biological entity by the original peoples does not have the legal nature of a legal duty, but rather a faculty that naturally arises from the spiritual and affective relationship of these peoples with nature.

It is also up to the original peoples to represent the biological entities of plants, animals (wildlife), and systems in the wheel of democratic political discourse, ensuring their place of speech in political and social debates that directly or indirectly involve their interests and rights.

As for the biological entity of the animal, only the guardianship of wild animals naturally belongs to the original peoples. However, animals that are inserted into the social context of non-indigenous peoples, such as companion animals, those involved in research, and those intended for food, should have a specific guardianship regime that is outside the circle of life of the original peoples.

In addition to the natural guardianship of biological entities by the original peoples, it is necessary to establish an institutional and mandatory guardianship of these biological entities by the state itself. This guardianship is the responsibility of the agencies and institutions of each country in charge of the legal guardianship of the environment. In Brazil, this institutional and mandatory guardianship of the biological entities of plants, animals (wild, companion, research, and food), and systems constitutionally belongs to the Public Prosecutor's Office, by virtue of the provisions of Art. 129, inc. III, of the CR/1988, which will be responsible for representing them legally for the exercise of rights arising from their biological personality based on the concept of *biodignity*, in the civil, administrative, and criminal spheres, as well as for the purposes of Art. 225, § 3°, of the CR/1988.

As for the biological entity of the companion or pet animal, its legal representation belongs to its natural guardians—those who adopted it and with whom it maintains a relationship of family affection. The natural and affective guardians are directly responsible for fulfilling the duties related to the rights of the biological entity of the companion animal resulting from *biodignity*. In this vein, their natural and affective guardians, in addition to representing them legally before institutions and politically in the community, are, above all, the direct recipients of the duty to ensure all their rights arising from the biological animal personality listed in the previous topic.

The legal nature of the duty to safeguard the rights arising from the *biodignity* of the biological entity of the companion animal is based on the principle of affection and has a legal nature similar to the family duty of parents toward their children, as provided for in civil legislation. However, without prejudice to this natural and affective guardianship, the biological entity of the companion animal must also be represented by the Public Prosecutor's Office as its institutional legal guardian, which is also responsible for defending its interests and rights, especially when there are conflicts between the interests of the biological entity of the companion animal and its natural and affective guardians.

The guardianship and representation of the biological entity of the animal involved in research and intended for human consumption must be institutionally and mandatorily entrusted to the Public Prosecutor's Office, which will represent them in the exercise and defense of their rights arising from *biodignity* before social and political institutions and, optionally, may have their interests represented in court and in the realm of political discourse by institutions whose objective is the defense of animal rights.

This work proposes, based on the principle of harmony with nature—from which the concept of *biodignity* is derived, and on which the biological legal personality is based—the creation of a statute for the biological legal entities of plants, animals (wild, companion, research, and food), and systems, with the legal provision of all rights arising from *biodignity,* as well as the civil, administrative, and penal regulation of relations involving biological entities, both plant and animal, and systemic entities with natural and legal human persons.

Within the scope of civil law, Schreiber reports a change in the civil legislation of some countries that have already removed animals from the position of goods or things, as exemplified by the civil codes of the Czech Republic, France, and Portugal.[76]

Currently under consideration in the National Congress, with approval in the Senate, is the Chamber of Deputies Bill No. 27 of 2018, initiated by federal deputy Ricardo Izar, which adds a provision to Law 9.605/1998, providing for the legal nature of non-human animals in the sense that "non-human animals have a legal nature **sui generis** and are subjects of non-personal rights, which they should enjoy and obtain judicial protection in case of violation, their treatment as things being prohibited."

Despite representing a small advance, the project is still quite timid, as it does not consider the possibility of recognizing a dignity inherent in animals and a personality suitable for this dignity. The project refers to animals generically, even though we know that animals, according to their position in the world, require differentiated protection. In addition, it does not cover plants and holistic systemic entities.

The principle of harmony with nature, as a general principle of law, which in Brazil is implicitly enshrined in Art. 225, *caput*, of the CR/1988, imposes the recognition of the concept of *biodignity*, from which unfold the biological legal personality and, consequently, the ethical and legal imperative of recognizing the existence of the biological person, with the respective adaptation of infraconstitutional legislation through the hermeneutic filter of the principle of harmony with nature. Thus, it is urgent to harmonize the interest of the human person in socio-economic development with the interest of the biological person in fulfilling the

---

[76] Schreiber (2020), p. 186.

principle of ecological integrity, which is the core of the principle of sustainability, a principle that is beneficial to all living beings, including human beings, who share with biological persons the *biodignity* on which the principle of human dignity rests.

As will be demonstrated in the next chapter, the rights of the biological person arising from the principle of harmony with nature, from which *biodignity* unfolds, are not incompatible with the rights won by human beings; rather, they strengthen them even more, as they elevate the human being to the position of a free moral agent for making decisions that enhance their intergenerational and interspecies responsibility on planet Earth.

References

Baluška F et al. (2006) Neurobiological view of plants and their body plan. In: Baluška F, Mancuso S, Volkmann D (eds) Communication in plants: neuronal aspects of plant life, Springer Verlag, Berlin, Heidelberg

Beauchamp TL, Degrazia D (2020) Principles of animal research ethics. Oxford University Press, New York

Bekoff M (2007) The emotional lives of animals: a leading scientist explores animal joy, sorrow, and empathy: and why they matter. New World Library, Novato, CA

Bergson H (2010) A evolução criadora. Tradução de Adolfo Casais Monteiro. Editora UNESP, São Paulo

Bittar CA (2015) Os direitos da personalidade. 8 edn rev. aum. e modificada por Eduardo C. B. Bittar. Saraiva, São Paulo

Boaventura R, Cardoso JL (2010/2011) Revendo os artefactos lascados da Anta de Pedras da Granja (Sintra). Estudos Arqueológicos de Oeiras, Oeiras, Portugal, Câmara Municipal 18:175–199. Available https://repositorio.ul.pt/bitstream/10451/10616/1/Boaventura_e_JLC_anta_de_Pedras_da_Granja_EAO_18.pdf. Accessed 23 May 2025

Campos AdS (2008) O indivíduo em Spinoza: absorção da personalidade. Polymathea: Revista Filosófica, Fortaleza, Universidade Estadual do Ceará (UECE) 4(5). Available on http://seer.uece.br/?journal=PRF&page=article&op=view&path%5B%5D=475. Accessed 09 May 2025

Castro EVd (1996) Os pronomes cosmológicos e o perspectivismo ameríndio. Mana, Rio de Janeiro 2(2): 115–144. Available on https://www.scielo.br/scielo.php?script=sci_arttext&pid=S0104-93131996000200005. Accessed 20 April 2025

Cirne-Lima CRV (2012) Causalidade e auto-organização. In: Luft E, Cirne-Lima CRV (eds) Ideia e movimento. Civilização Brasileira, Rio de Janeiro

Crepalde A (2014) A construção do significado de *Tekoha* pelos *Kaiowá* do Mato Grosso do Sul. Tese (Doutorado). – Faculdade de Letras da Universidade Federal do Rio Grande do Sul. Porto Alegre, 2014. p. 266. https://www.lume.ufrgs.br/handle/10183/115758.

Damásio A (2018) A estranha ordem das coisas: as origens biológicas dos sentimentos e da cultura. Companhia das Letras, São Paulo

Davis SL (2017) The least harm principle may require that humans consume a diet containing large herbivores, not a vegan diet. In: Armstrong SJ, Botzler RG (eds) The animal ethic readers, 3 edn. Routledge, New York, Ebook

Descola P (2013) Beyond nature and culture. Tradução de Janet Lloyd, The University of Chicago Press, Chicago

Douzinas C (2009) O fim dos direitos humanos. Tradução de Luzia Araújo. Unisinos, São Leopoldo, RS

Douzinas C (2009) O fim dos direitos humanos. Tradução de Luzia Araújo. Unisinos, São Leopoldo, RS

Grandin T (2017) Thinking like animal. In: Armstrong SJ, Botzler RG (eds) The animal ethic readers, 3 edn. Routledge, New York, E-book
Jørgensen SE et al. (2019) A new ecology: systems perspective. Elsevier Science, Amsterdam
Lopes RJ (2004) Tigre-de-dente-de-sabre viveu com humano. Folha de S. Paulo, São Paulo, p. A16–A17, 23 fev. Available on https://www1.folha.uol.com.br/fsp/ciencia/fe2302200401.htm. Accessed 25 May 2025
Lovejoy AO (2009) The great chain of being: a study of the history of an idea. Transaction Publishers, London
Mancuso S (2019) Revolução das plantas: um novo modelo para o futuro. Tradução de Regina Silva. Ubu Editora, São Paulo
Maturana HR, Varela FJ (1991) Autopoiesis and cognition: the realization of the living. Kluwer, Boston, Ebook
Moraes ASd (2010) Pecuária orgânica no Pantanal: alternativa rentável e sustentável. Embrapa Pantanal, Corumbá. Available on https://www.infoteca.cnptia.embrapa.br/infoteca/bitstream/doc/868950/1/ADM143.pdf. Accessed 10 May 2025
Pietra R (2016) Fistulação: como a indústria mutila e tortura vacas para garantir a qualidade do leite e da carne. Agência de Notícias de Direitos Animais (ANDA). Available on https://www.anda.jor.br/2016/12/16/fistulacao-como-a-industria-mutila-e-tortura-vacas-para-garantir-a-qualidade-do-leite-e-da-carne/. Accessed 10 May 2025
Rendich F (2014) Comparative etymological dictionary of classical indo-european languages: indo-european - sanskrit - greek - latin. Createspace Independent Publishing Platform, 2 edn. North Caroline, SC
Sabino U (2015) Área de vida e comportamento de cuidado parental do Furnarius rufus (joão-de-barro). Dissertação (Mestrado) – Programa de Pós-Graduação em Ecologia e Conservação da Biodiversidade do Instituto de Biociências da Universidade Federal de Mato Grosso, Cuiabá, 2015. Available on https://ri.ufmt.br/bitstream/1/1725/1/DISS_2015_Ursola%20Sabino.pdf. Accessed 13 June 2025
Sarlet IW (2001) Dignidade da pessoa humana e os direitos fundamentais na Constituição Federal de 1988. Livraria do Advogado, Porto Alegre
Schreiber A (2020) Manual de direito civil contemporâneo. 3 edn. rev. e ampl. Saraiva, São Paulo
Spinoza B (2016) Ética: edição monolíngue. Tradução de Tomaz Tadeu. 2 edn, 5. reimpr. Autêntica, Belo Horizonte
Sztutman R (2009) Natureza e cultura, versão americanista: um sobrevoo. Ponto Urbe: Revista do Núcleo de Antropologia Urbana da USP, São Paulo 3(4). Available on https://journals.openedition.org/pontourbe/1468?lang=en Accessed 10 Jan 2025
Taylor PW (2011) Respect for nature: a theory of environmental ethics, 25th anniversary edn. Princeton University Press, Princeton
Trewavas A (2006) The green plants as an intelligent organism. In: Baluška F, Mancuso S, Volkmann D (eds) Communication in plants: neuronal aspects of plant life. Springer Verlag, Berlin; Heidelberg
Urquiza A, Hilário A, Nascimento AC (2013) Povos indígenas e as questões da territorialidade. Urquiza A, Hilário A Org Culturas e história dos povos indígenas em Mato Grosso do Sul, Editora da UFMS, Campo Grande, MS
Villey M (2005) A formação do pensamento jurídico moderno. Martins Fontes, São Paulo
Waldau P (2011) Animal rights: what everyone needs to know. Oxford University Press, New York
Wieacker F (2010) História do direito privado moderno, 4 edn. Fundação Calouste Gulbenkian, Lisboa
Witzany G (2018) Memory and learning as key competences of living organisms. In: Baluška F, Gagliano M, Witzany G (eds) Memory and learning in plants. Springer International Publishing, Berlin
Wohlleben P (2017) A vida secreta das árvores. Tradução de Petê Rissati. Sextante, Rio de Janeiro

Chapter 7
The Reaffirmation of Human Rights Through the Principle of Harmony with Nature

The recognition of the principle of harmony with nature in this century of climate crisis reaffirms human rights because it recognizes the rooting of human dignity in a dimension deeper and broader than language and reason.

The principle of harmony with nature shares its ontological root with the principle of human dignity, revealing the ecological dimension of human dignity.[1] This work adopts Sarlet and Fensterseifer's proposal on the existence of an ecological dimension of human dignity and aims to demonstrate the foundation of this ecological aspect of human dignity in the principle of harmony with nature, from whose integrative function unfolds the concept of *biodignity*—a biological dignity that is shared by all living beings.

Understanding this proposal is only possible through ontology and ethics, as Hans Jonas[2] observes. When dealing with the principle of responsibility, before the doctrine of action—that is, ethics and law—one must investigate the doctrine of existence, ontology, since it precedes them.

In this sense, this work establishes itself as a starting point for understanding the origin of the ontological relationship between the principle of harmony with nature and human dignity, Henri Bergson's vitalist philosophy,[3] and Hans Jonas's theory of the biological foundations of individuality.[4]

[1] Sarlet and Fensterseifer (2014), p. 75.

[2] Jonas (2006), p. 42.

[3] Bergson (2010).

[4] Jonas (2017).

R. D. d. Amaral, *The Principle of Harmony with Nature as a Legal Foundation*,
https://doi.org/10.1007/978-3-032-05475-3_7

7.1 The Principle of Harmony with Nature and the Ecological Dimension of Human Dignity

As already examined in the previous chapter, for Bergson's theory of creative evolution,[5] all living beings, in their origin, descend from a common ancestor, with the same original tendency toward life that, due to the skills developed for nutrition, separated and followed different evolutionary directions, leading to the accentuation of certain characteristics in plants and other characteristics in animals. These, during the evolutionary journey, bifurcated once again into two paths, distinguished by the prevalence of instinct or reason.

In human animals, reason and language developed more than instinct, as they needed to construct the necessary tools for their nutrition and were thus driven by nutritional necessity to become *Homo sapiens/Homo faber*. However, *sapiens* are also endowed with instinct. As will be discussed later through the analysis of Winnicott's psychoanalytic theory, the instinct in the human baby is the driving force of psyche integration.

Non-human animals, on the other hand, come equipped with their tools constituted in their own organisms and, in this way, tend toward the accentuation of instinct, which functions as a powerful "software" that automates and optimizes the use of the "tools" attached to their bodies, such as fangs, claws, and wings.[6]

Just like humans, non-human animals also have a language—less complex but sufficient to allow them communication and affectivity—considering that instinct is not alien to the realm of emotions and allows the manifestation of emotional and affective experiences.

In this line, for Bergson, there is no hierarchy of successive degrees in a single tendency of development in plant life, animal life, and rational life; what is observed are different directions that split at the origin as a necessity for survival and flourishing.[7] Nevertheless, living beings hold in their existential root the same impulse for life, and they need a basic freedom, which is shared by all species, to survive and flourish. According to the direction of their evolution, their flourishing needs will be simpler or more complex, involving sentience, affectivity, emotions, self-awareness, political sociability, and spirituality. However, all living beings share a basic degree of freedom necessary to live, flourish, and evolve. This work proposes respect for this basic freedom as an imperative of biological dignity, that is, of *biodignity*.

As already discussed, humans, as living organisms, also possess biological dignity, but due to self-awareness, which provides them with a range of other needs, there is an expansion of their need for freedom in dimensions that may not yet be experienced by other living beings.

---

[5] Bergson (2010).

[6] Bergson (2010).

[7] Bergson (2010).

For the full satisfaction of human flourishing from this *biodignity*, rooted in the organismic vital impulse, other dimensions of dignity emerge for them, no less important than biological dignity, though more complex, considering that they adapt to the complexity of human self-awareness and rationality, as a creative, political, and spiritual animal.

To say that the human being is more complex is not to consider him superior or to legitimize hateful privileges based on speciesism,[8] but to recognize that his life is multidimensional,[9] considering that, while being a biological being with the basic vital needs of the soma (living body), the human being also lives in a symbolic dimension, which was forged by his own language. In this symbolic dimension, spirituality, social experience, political action, artistic creation, literature, science, philosophy, and law are projected.

Thus, the dignity of the human person must be understood from the multidimensionality of the human being and not just within the province of intellect and reason. The dignity of the human person encompasses all dimensions of the human being: the biological dimension, the psychic dimension, the affective dimension, the political dimension, the social dimension, the intellectual dimension, the spiritual dimension, and others that we will still experience during the evolutionary journey.

The first dimension of the human person is based on the person's body, the living and metabolizing organism, guided by a teleological impulse toward organic individuality and driven by a *telos* of self-constitution, self-preservation, and flourishing, in a continuous evolutionary movement beyond.[10]

Hans Jonas, in explaining the biological foundations of individuality and identity formation in the organism, brings us ontological elements that allow for the understanding of this first dimension of the dignity of the human person. Jonas supports the existence of an identity in the living organism, even when it is still a metabolic phenomenon, which mobilizes the most elementary level of life to provide energy to the most diverse superior functions of life, such as motility, sentience, perception, and desire.[11]

In this organismic base of life, there is already an introduction of individuality, the "I," as internal identity, and the perception of the "not-I," as otherness. The establishment of this polarity ("I" and "not-I," "being" and "not being") makes the organism distinguish itself from the environment through the limits set by its internal identity. This is the condition for the vital impulse of the organism in its evolutionary course beyond.[12]

---

[8] "[...] was defined, with a neologism that alludes to parallel intra-human prejudices, the view that grants members of our own species a privileged status in relation to all other creatures—are internally inconsistent. For speciesism and racism are twin doctrines." Cavalieri (2017), p. 27.

[9] Morin (2002), p. 42.

[10] Jonas (2017).

[11] Jonas (2017).

[12] Jonas (2017).

Although the organism identifies itself as an individual, an "I," which struggles every moment in its environment to maintain its identity (substance, form, and *telos*) and continue in its evolutionary purpose, it needs the other, the "not-I," the world, and everything that is beyond its individuality.[13] Enclosed in its singularity, it would cease to exist; therefore, the relationality so well understood by the ontology of the Andean indigenous peoples[14] is a condition of the existence of the living being, even as a metabolizing organism.

Even at the base of the organism, as a metabolic phenomenon, there is already the polarity of "I" and "not-I," "being" and "non-being," which drives the most elementary organism toward relationality. The organism continually confronts this polarity, but its *telos*, its intrinsic goal, is to continue its existence through regenerative activity, which Jonas calls "interest," with the organism's minimum interest being to continue to "be." For this, it establishes a constant existential relationship with the other, which is the "not-I," even on the metabolic plane.[15]

Spinoza named this phenomenon *conatus*, that is, the vital impulse of the organism to remain in existence. However, Jonas notes that Spinoza, in his time, did not have the epistemological resources to understand that the organism is not guided by a *telos* of only remaining in life, but also by a *telos* of continuous movement beyond the state of things, or, in other words, of evolutionary flourishing. This evolutionary tendency, highlighted by Jonas, is currently confirmed and deepened by the neuroscience of Antonio Damasio in his concept of homeostasis.[16]

The driving force of continuation in life is more than the preservation of a static "being" in a current state; it is to become the "being" always beyond, in an eternal evolutionary becoming.[17]

What provides this movement, this *telos* evolutionary, is the fact that the organism, in its individuality, perceives a persistent "lack," a deficiency, an incompleteness of something that is outside the limits of its individuality. This teleological need drives it in its relations with the "not-I," that is, the other and beyond. There lies the driving force of its evolutionary impulse of survival and flourishing.[18] This is quite similar to the principle of complementarity present in the Inca worldview, as a corollary of the principle of relationality between living and cosmic beings as a condition of possibility of the being itself.[19]

In the search for the satisfaction of this "lack," this need, the organism needs freedom—a freedom that is at the base of life, in the metabolic function of all living organisms; therefore, a freedom needed and shared by all living beings.

[13] Jonas (2017).

[14] Estermann (2006).

[15] Jonas (2017).

[16] Damásio (2018).

[17] Damásio (2018).

[18] Damásio (2018).

[19] Estermann (2006).

Jonas explains that this ontology of the individuality of the living being will fully materialize in the so-called "centralization of animal individuality"[20] to manifest functions such as motility, perception, and sentience. As can be seen, at the base of all biological manifestations of the living being, from a simple nuclear organization to the human body, there is a needed freedom that is fundamental for the survival and flourishing of each living being.

In this basic freedom is rooted the concept of *biodignity*; that is, the biological aspect of the human being constitutes the first dimension of the dignity of the human person: the *biodignity*.

In this sense, it cannot be ignored that even the complex psychic dimension of the human being is forged in its condition as a biological organism, with the decisive contribution of instinct.

The creative nature that allowed the *sapiens* to build the symbolic sphere of language and culture is preceded and established by an experience on the biological plane, that is, the integration of psyche and soma. Winnicott[21] explains that the human being, after its birth, lives in a situation of absolute dependence on the environment, which, at this moment, is represented by its mother. At the beginning of the life of a human baby, there is not yet a formed "I," but only an innate tendency toward integration that is given to the human being. However, this integration, which is necessary for the formation of the psyche, is still only a possibility and not a certainty.[22]

At this stage, the baby develops the inventive and abstract human capacity that manifests in adult life. This human creative potential, developed by the baby, is called by Winnicott the *illusion of omnipotence.*[23] This occurs in the baby's contact with its mother's physical body, especially the maternal breast.

Winnicott emphasizes that, during breastfeeding, the baby will experience the warmth of its mother's body as the first experience of feeling the world. Throughout the breastfeeding process, the baby, driven by the oral instinct, which regulates its feeding function, is able to hallucinate (imagine) the mother's nipple. When she offers the nipple to the offspring, the newborn human being experiences an illusion of being the creator of this external object, which it has a visceral need for.[24]

From this primary creative experience of relating to a subjectively created object, human creative capacity is triggered.[25] This experience, driven by the nutritional instinct, forms the basis of integration into a unitary SELF and the primary development of creativity. It is perceived that the instinct is at the beginning of the formation of the *self* and the *psyche* of the human being and, therefore,

---

[20] Jonas (2017), p. 313.

[21] Winnicott (2024a, b).

[22] Winnicott (2024a, b).

[23] Winnicott (2024a, b), p. 153.

[24] Winnicott (2024a, b), p. 153.

[25] Winnicott (2024a, b), p. 55.

contributes to the constitution of reason and language, which will enable the human being to grasp culture, thus constituting the psychosocial principle of the human condition.[26]

In this biological and affective experience provided by maternal care, the baby develops the *self*, creativity, and trust, which make up the human condition. Driven by the driving force of instinct, which regulates feeding function, the newborn human being experiences the inaugural encounter with the biological world—the interaction with its mother's physical body.[27]

In the first days of life, the human baby creates its world, realizes the insertion of the psyche into the soma, manifests personalization—that is, understands itself as an individual—and makes its first movement toward the other, thus experiencing the condition of being a human person.[28]
For this to occur successfully, Winnicott observes that:

> What the mother needs is the chance to be natural and to find her way with the baby, just as other mothers have found their own ways since the dawn of human history, and even before human evolution from mammals.[29]

It is perceived that the relationship between the psyche and the body is not something given to the human being; it is an achievement that occurs in the primitive development of the human person during its first months of life through the relationship between the baby and its mother.[30] The mother, in this inaugural experience of the human being, is the very representation of the biosphere—that is, of Mother Earth—activating the relationality of the human person in the world in its biological and psychic dimensions.

As can be seen, the soma (living body) and the instinct precede the psyche of the human being and are the very basis of its formation. The psyche is constituted from the biological dimension of the human individual, as an imaginative elaboration of the somatic function guided by instinct. This shows us that self-awareness, rationality, and creative nature, which Kantian ethics elected as the *locus* of intrinsic value of the human person, are rooted in the very soma (living body) activated by instinct, being, therefore, an unfolding of the biological realization of life.

Hence, the reason for this work is to postulate the reconnection of the human being with nature, also in the ethical and legal spheres, as an imperative for the realization of the dignity of the human person in its full sense—that is, in its ecological dimension.

Edgar Morin, when dealing with the human condition, argues that the importance of understanding hominization is fundamental to the education of the human

[26] Morin (2002), p. 42.
[27] Winnicott (2024a, b), p. 55.
[28] Winnicott (2024a, b), p. 55.
[29] Winnicott (2024a, b), p. 152.
[30] Winnicott (2024a, b), p. 152.

condition "because it shows us how animality and humanity together constitute our human condition."[31]

For Morin, the human being is simultaneously a fully biological and fully cultural being. Indeed, as already demonstrated by Winnicott's text, the soma (living body) plays a relevant role in the integration of the psyche. From this integration of the psyche with the physical body, which is organized by the mind, the human being develops self-awareness, the ability to relate, language, and the necessary condition to grasp culture.

Morin also makes a striking warning: "without culture the human being would be a primate of the lowest level." Culture always exists in the plurality of cultures, being acquired and constituted by sets of knowledge, norms, beliefs, prohibitions, strategies, values, and myths that are transmitted from generation to generation.[32]

Through culture, *Homo sapiens* forged human language and reason, thus being able to narrate their stories, construct their tools, and architect a complex symbolic world where they reproduced their experiences and developed their social and legal institutions. However, it must not be forgotten that the condition for the apprehension of culture is the constitution of the *self* and the psyche—phenomena that occur in the biological dimension of the human being, as demonstrated by Winnicott.[33]

Thus, the greatest mistake of the human species was to separate nature from culture, considering that, in the natural and biological dimension of human life, the conditions of possibility for rationality, language, and culture are created. The separation of nature and culture allowed the instrumentalization of human reason[34] in the service of the utilitarianism of capital and forged the *Homo demens* spoken of by Edgar Morin. The *Homo demens* is a delirious animal who denied its biological dimension, objectified and enslaved the Earth, and triggered the climate crisis on the planet.

Morin emphasizes that the human being is complex because it carries within itself a constant tension of antagonistic characters: *sapiens* and *demens* (rational and delirious); *faber* and *ludens* (worker and player); *empiricus* and *imaginarius* (empirical and imaginary); *economicus* and *consumans* (economist and consumer); and *prosaicus* and *poeticus* (prosaic and poetic). He proposes, as a harmonizing synthesis of these opposites, a rationality that considers the complexity of the human condition in this era, which he calls the planetary era, in which the human being needs to act as a citizen of the Earth, imbued with an earthly identity.[35]

This earthly identity and consciousness are indispensable for ecological consciousness, that is, "the consciousness of inhabiting, with all mortal beings, the same living sphere (biosphere); recognizing our substantial connection with the

[31] Morin (2002), p. 55.

[32] Morin (2002), p. 55.

[33] Winnicott (2024a, b).

[34] Horkheimer (2002).

[35] Morin (2002), p. 81.

biosphere leads us to abandon the Promethean dream of dominating the universe to nourish the aspiration to conviviality with the earth."[36]

This ecological consciousness that Morin speaks of dialogs with the ecological dimension of human dignity, mentioned by Sarlet and Fensterseifer, as one of the foundations of the socio-environmental state.[37]

The recognition that we live in a continuous relationship with nature and the desire for respectful conviviality can emerge from the consciousness that we share, with non-human living beings, common freedoms, and, thus, partake of the same dignity, which is based on a more radical level than the plane of language and human reason. The *locus* of this dignity is the impulse for life, present in all living beings and in holistic organic entities. The impulse to live and flourish equals and unites us as members of an earthly community.

To illuminate this interconnection of human dignity with the biological dignity of other living beings, this work presents a report about the coexistence of the maned wolf, the human being, the plant known as lobeira, and the biome of the Brazilian Cerrado.

Think, dear reader, of a human person who, after a long walk, delights in the fresh and crystalline water of a spring with the same pleasure as a thirsty maned wolf; however, this person is also capable of feeling intense satisfaction in listening to music, perhaps writing a poem, or saying a prayer. This does not make them more important than the maned wolf, but rather different and more complex, and therefore in need of guarantees and freedoms that, for the maned wolf, are unnecessary.

The human being and the maned wolf share common experiences, such as thirst, hunger, the need to breathe, move, and affection; thus, they share the same dignity at the biological level, in the vital impulse.

The human person, being complex and multidimensional, experiences aspects of a dignity that is unique to them. This dignity of the human person, despite being rooted in *biodignity*, which it shares with the maned wolf and all living and systemic beings, projects itself to broader dimensions than the biological dignity of the maned wolf, but both are equally important, as they are connected in the web of life to a common root.

Full flourishing for the maned wolf means living and moving freely through its territories in the Brazilian savannah, nourishing itself with drinking water, sunlight, the meat of its small prey, and the fruits of the wolf apple (*Solanum lycocarpum*) and the custard apple tree, interacting with members of its species in mating rituals, bonding, reproducing, and ensuring the perpetuation of its species, which is currently at serious risk of extinction.

For humans, flourishing means, in addition to nourishing their own body and having freedom of movement and procreation, also having freedom of thought, belief, sexual orientation, and political expression, among many others. The

[36] Morin (2002), p. 81.

[37] Sarlet and Fensterseifer (2014), p. 75.

guarantee of the biological dignity of the maned wolf does not detract from human dignity. The same water that quenches the wolf quenches the human; the custard apple tree, which nourishes the wolf, can nourish the human being.

Humans need the Cerrado biome, just like the maned wolf, because within the vegetation of these savannas lie the remedies for many diseases of their bodies, as well as the cure for the diseases of the maned wolf.[38] Their interests are not incompatible; on the contrary, they complement and interconnect.

When the maned wolf roams its territories and defecates the seeds of the wolf apple and custard apple fruits, it is strengthening the dignity of humans, at whose root lies the basic need to breathe oxygen, which is photosynthesized by the leaves of the wolf apple trees and custard apple trees. These plants also need the Cerrado to continue their evolutionary journey in the biosphere.

Just as humans and the maned wolf should have their dignities respected and protected, the wolf apple, the custard apple tree, and the Cerrado itself, as the biome that shelters and sustains them, also need respect, given that they continuously engender their lives and have a relevant function in the biosphere.

The wolf apple, the custard apple, and the Cerrado cannot be considered less important than the maned wolf, nor less relevant than humans. They all live in communion, in a relationship of complementarity and reciprocity. The wolf apple is capable of growing in arid, acidic, and nutrient-poor lands, and even degraded ones, and it has been considered a positive element in the recovery of the Cerrado soil.[39] In addition, it produces oxygen and nutrient-rich fruits, which are raw materials for the synthesis of antibiotics and anti-inflammatories.[40]

Between the wolf apple, the maned wolf, humans, and the Cerrado, there is a relationship of cooperation, complementarity, and reciprocity, which begins with the work of this brave shrub that resists and bears fruit even in anthropized areas, cooperates in soil recovery, and offers its therapeutic fruits to the maned wolf[41] and to humans themselves. This partnership continues with the maned wolf, which is cured of kidney worms by the fruit of the wolf apple and carries its seeds to places

---

[38] "The fruit of the lobeira acts as a natural vermifuge against the giant kidney worm, Dioctophyme renale, which causes serious kidney complications in this wolf, as well as in other canids and mustelids (martens, otters, coatis, among others.) On the other hand, by defecating, the maned wolf promotes the dispersion of the seeds. Therefore, to preserve this species, it is also necessary to preserve the lobeira and the region where it is found: the cerrado." (Delecave (n.d.), online).

[39] Rosa et al. (2014), p. 51.

[40] Gellen et al. (2019).

[41] "The common name of this small tree already gives a clue about one of its main functions: it is indispensable for the survival of the maned wolf, since 50% of its diet comes from this plant, not to mention the therapeutic action it exerts on its health (it has the power to eliminate the giant kidney worm, which is frequent and usually fatal to the wolf). The local population of the Cerrado knows and applies the properties of this tree for the same purpose. The fruits are used for sweets and jellies. It is also used against spasms, as a diuretic and sedative. In addition, the starch of its fruits is used against diabetes and the juice, for external use, serves to eliminate warts. Even the tea of its flowers is indicated against hemorrhoids." G1 (2014), online.

where the plant cannot go, thus becoming its sower. This work, in the end, also contributes to the prosperity and health of humans, as it recovers degraded land areas.

Between the Cerrado, the wolf apple, the maned wolf, and humans, there is a continuous relationship of reciprocity, which reveals the deepest sense of the principle of harmony with nature: the reaffirmation of human dignity and the human rights already achieved by recognizing human dignity also in its ecological dimension, which is realized in the respectful relationship of humans with nature.

The principle of harmony with nature, by exacerbating the responsibility of humans toward the lives of other species, does not weaken human rights; on the contrary, it strengthens their position as a moral agent and strong evaluator[42] and reaffirms their self-worth, impelling them toward ethical and legal evolution as a global citizen.[43] Furthermore, the principle of human dignity dialogs with the principle of harmony with nature. As already demonstrated, *biodignity*, the ethical and legal expression of the phenomena of *conatus*[44] *and* homeostasis,[45] is a consequence of the integrative function of the principle of harmony with nature as a source of nature's rights.

Thus, considering that *biodignity* is the most basic dimension of human dignity, it can be considered that there is an interweaving between the principle of harmony with nature and the principle of human dignity, which reveals the ecological dimension of human dignity.

This reality shows that the human being, as a living being singularly endowed with intelligence and self-reflection, is related, in the biological sphere where life pulsates, to all other living beings, sharing the biological dimension of human dignity, which this work refers to as *biodignity.*

The violation of this root biological dignity, at the base of all planetary life, affects all living beings and organic entities, and also puts at risk the historical achievement of human dignity, whose rationality and spirituality are expressions of the creative evolution of life itself.

In the emergence of life is founded the *biodignity*, as a primordial value shared by all living beings and holistic organic entities in their common ancestry—the one—from which unfolded the multiplicity of life, revealed in biodiversity.

In this so biodiverse terrestrial community, the human being is a singular and complex expression, considering its rational and abstract consciousness that created language. However, it cannot be forgotten that the symbolic world created by the *logos,* which Teilhard de Chardin called the noosphere (thinking sphere), is nourished and sustained by the biosphere.

---

42 Taylor (1989), p. 72.

43 Morin (2002), p. 81.

44 Spinoza (2014).

45 Damásio (2018).

Thus, *biodignity*, as a corollary of the principle of harmony with nature, in its integrative function, is a primary and root dimension of human dignity, without which the other dimensions of human dignity would not subsist.

In this line, the *biodignity*, as a consequence of the integrative function of the principle of harmony with nature, while glorifying the human being as a moral agent, strong evaluator,[46] and subject of a cognitive ethics of universal coherence,[47] equates it, in its biological condition, to all other living beings with whom it coexists in the terrestrial community,[48] revealing, in this way, the ecological dimension of the principle of human dignity.

As will be demonstrated in the following topics, the practical agreement between the principle of harmony with nature and human dignity radiates concrete effects on human rights, reaffirming them in this era of severe climate crisis, which the scientific community tends to call the Anthropocene.

7.2 The Principle of Harmony with Nature and the Resolution of Conflicts of Interest Between Human Beings and Non-Human Beings

The first effect of the principle of harmony with nature is the establishment of criteria for the resolution of potential conflicts between the interests of human beings and non-human beings. For this, this work proposes the adoption of Paul Taylor's priority principles.

For the resolution of potential conflicts of interest between the human person and the biological person, whether plant, animal, or systemic, this work adopts Paul Taylor's priority principles: (1) principle of self-defense; (2) principle of proportionality; (3) principle of minimal error; (4) principle of distributive justice; and (5) principle of restorative justice.

The principle of self-defense assures human beings, as moral agents, the right to protect themselves from the actions of dangerous or harmful organisms, based on the same normative parameters as the institution of legitimate defense in criminal law. The principle of self-defense authorizes actions:

> [...] that are absolutely necessary to maintain the very existence of moral agents and to enable them to exercise the capacities of moral agency. It does not allow actions that involve the destruction of organisms when these simply promote the interests or values that moral agents may have as people.[49]

[46] Taylor (1989).

[47] Cirne-Lima (1999), p. 941–964.

[48] Berry (1988).

[49] Taylor (2011), p. 279–280.

However, when faced with a conflict of interest between humans and non-humans, which are not harmful—that is, a situation that is outside the area of incidence of the principle of self-defense—Taylor proposes the application of four other principles: (i) principle of proportionality; (ii) principle of minimal error; (iii) principle of distributive justice; and (iv) principle of restorative justice.

In the face of conflict between the basic interests of plants or animals and the non-basic interests of humans, he suggests the application of the principles of proportionality and minimal error.

Interest, for Taylor, is any object or event useful for preserving and protecting, to some degree, the good of a living being. In this context, the interests are classified into basic interests and non-basic interests. A basic interest is one whose violation causes severe harm to an organism. The basic interests of humans are related to their own rationality and autonomy for biological maintenance, that is, to ensure their primary goods.[50]

Besides these universal values or primary goods, there are other interests, which are non-basic and related to particular ends; hence, their valuation depends on the person's cultural references. The primary goods that justify basic interests are common to all humans, while "non-basic" interests are variable and individual, as they change according to the cultural and historical context.

For Taylor, the principles of reasonableness and minimal error are based on the distinction between basic and non-basic interests. These principles are used to resolve conflicts between competing claims, that is, hypotheses where the basic interests of animals or plants collide with non-basic human interests.[51]

He distinguishes two types of non-basic human interests: (a) non-basic human interests that are intrinsically incompatible with the basic interests of plants, animals, and a respectful attitude toward nature; (b) non-basic human interests, which do not "exemplify in themselves an exploitative attitude towards nature, but in many practical circumstances, the means used to satisfy these interests produce effects in the natural world that, in the eyes of those who respect nature, should be avoided whenever possible."[52] These latter interests are not intrinsically incompatible with the basic interests of nature; however, their satisfaction has harmful collateral consequences for nature and, therefore, should be avoided.

The satisfaction of non-basic human interests that are intrinsically incompatible with the basic interests of other living beings demonstrates a serious disregard for the biodignity of living organisms, as it reinforces the idea of the instrumentality of nature. He cites examples of non-basic human interests, intrinsically incompatible with a respectful attitude toward nature: the slaughter of elephants so that the ivory of their tusks can be used in the manufacture of souvenirs; the killing of rhinoceroses to extract their horns and use them in the making of daggers; recreational hunting and fishing; and bullfighting.[53]

[50] Taylor (2011), p. 284–286.

[51] Taylor (2011), p. 288.

[52] Taylor (2011), p. 291.

I would also add to Taylor's examples the "vaquejada," a typical non-basic interest of humans in some places in Brazil, which is intrinsically incompatible with the basic interest of the cow in having its physical integrity respected.

The second type of non-basic human interests, that is, those that are not intrinsically incompatible with the basic interests of nature but whose satisfaction has harmful collateral consequences for plants and animals, are those that do not imply, in themselves, a harmful attitude toward plants, animals, and the environment. However, the concrete circumstances and the means employed to satisfy them generate collateral damage. These concrete effects, which affect the balance of the environment, the life, the physical and mental integrity of animals, and the health of plants, should be avoided whenever possible.[54] Examples include the construction of a road in a biome that has not yet been interfered with by humans, which will put the fauna of the region at risk, or the construction of a dam on a river.

Taylor proposes the principle of proportionality to resolve conflicts between non-basic human interests (intrinsically incompatible with a respectful attitude toward nature) and the basic interests of animals and plants. In these situations, greater weight should always be given to the basic interest, regardless of the species. The interpreter should take into account the essentiality of the conflicting interests, regardless of the species holding the interest in collision, be it human or non-human; the relevant thing is to always privilege the basic interest when it is in conflict with a non-basic interest.

Taylor presents, as conditions for the application of the principle of proportionality, the competition and collision between non-basic human interests that are intrinsically incompatible with a respectful attitude toward nature and the basic interests of other living beings in a harmless situation for the human being. This is considering that, in a situation of serious risk to the physical integrity, health, and life of the human being, the applicable principle is the principle of self-defense.[55]

The principle of minimal error should be applied when there is a conflict between the basic interests of plants, animals, and the non-basic interests of human beings, which, although not intrinsically incompatible with respect for nature, can generate collateral damage to the basic interests of nature in its achievement.

In this case, the non-basic human interests involved, as a rule, represent a civilizational and social ideal shared by the human community, and for this reason, are considered relevant, even by enlightened people who have respect for nature. Even though they are aware of the risks of negative effects on the environment and are concerned about this, they prefer to take the risk rather than dispose of values they consider dear to civilization, such as social development, technology, culture, and lifestyle.

---

[53] Taylor (2011), p. 288.

[54] Taylor (2011), p. 291.

[55] Taylor (2011), p. 293.

For these cases, Taylor proposes the application of the principle of minimal error; that is, the choice of a solution that causes the fewest number of violations of the rule of non-maleficence in the ethical system of respect for nature. In this way, non-basic human interests should only be met if there is no alternative to achieve the desired social good that is less harmful to nature. The ethical permission for the realization of these non-basic human interests is conditioned on the possibility of minimizing errors that may violate the basic interests of nature.[56]

For Taylor, the principle of distributive justice should be applied to the demands of competing interests of humans and non-humans when the interests that give rise to the claims are of the same degree of relevance. Distributive justice establishes criteria for an equitable distribution of the satisfaction of interests among all parties involved in a conflict when these colliding interests are all basic, therefore of equal relevance and moral weight. In such situations, each party should be apportioned equally.[57]

Taylor emphasizes that, given the insufficiency of distributive justice in apportioning humans and non-humans equally, it should be supplemented by the application of another priority principle—the so-called principle of restorative justice—that is, if perfect justice cannot be achieved, there should be reparation or compensation.

Taylor exemplifies that the preservation of unexplored ecosystems is, at the same time, an application of the principle of distributive justice and the principle of restorative justice, considering that the preservation of wildlife is a matter of justice for wild animals and plants in two aspects: (a) The preservation of a desert, for example, is a sharing of nature's grace with other beings, who equally have the right to enjoy it and, therefore, is a form of distributing justice; (b) The impartial judgment that inspires humans to preserve a desert or jungle is a form of reparation and restitution for the immeasurable harms that humanity has already caused to nature. In this way, it is also a form of restorative justice.[58]

Taylor, finally, proposes the following criteria for formulating judgments of appropriate reparation and compensation: (a) The greater the damage caused, the greater the reward; (b) all reparation should be made with a focus on the health of interior ecosystems and their biotic communities, and not solely considering isolated individuals.[59]

Although Taylor's theory does not recognize the intrinsic value and subjectivity of holistic organic entities—that is, ecosystems—this work adopts his priority criteria for resolving conflicts between the interests of human persons and those of non-human biological persons, also including the holistic organic biological person endowed with systemic cognition—that is, ecosystems and the biosphere itself.

---

[56] Taylor (2011), p. 295.

[57] Taylor (2011), p. 306.

[58] Taylor (2011), p. 317–319.

[59] Taylor (2011), p. 321.

7.3 The Principle of Harmony with Nature as the Foundation of the Person/Place Relationship

As already mentioned, the legal personality of the biological person, as well as that of the human person, projects itself into the social world with effects *erga omnes* that oblige human persons and legal entities of public and private law to respect the rights of plant, animal, and systemic biological persons. This is a duty based on two ethical principles that underpin the principle of harmony with nature: the principle of responsibility proposed by Hans Jonas and the principle of universal coherence of Cirne-Lima.

Thus, the human person, endowed with moral agency and rationality, has the duty to respect and ensure the rights of the personality of biological persons, who are moral subjects but without moral agency.

This duty imposes on the human being an asymmetric and exacerbated responsibility, similar to the duty of respect and responsibility of parents toward their children, as proposed by Hans Jonas when dealing with the principle of responsibility. Moreover, it is a matter of cosmic coherence, that is, of choices that promote harmonious relationships between the human being and nature.

Another consequence of the practical agreement of the principle of harmony with nature and the principle of human dignity, in its ecological dimension, is the redefinition of the relationship between the human being and the Earth to recover the sense of the person/place relationship, which was deconstructed by the right of property.

The evolution of the right of property, from feudalism to modernity, deconstructed the link between the human person and the landscape—their place in the world.[60] in a world where there are no people and places, there came to exist only things. Thus, Karl Marx,[61] in analyzing the fetishism of commodities, considered that the relationship of property rights became a thing–thing relationship—not in the physical sense, but "thing" as commodity.

This deconstruction of the human being's relationship with place is a factor in human rights vulnerability because it created favorable conditions for the enclosure laws of common goods in England between the sixteenth and nineteenth centuries, as well as for the invasions of the lands of the indigenous peoples in the Americas, Africa, Oceania, and Asia.

Graham explains that the process of dephysicalization of the right of property was the apex of the anthropocentric division of the world into nature and culture. This division is at the base of the modern idea of property, and its first consequence was to disregard the existing link between the person and the place as an expression of the natural world—a bond, in many cases, ancestral and affective.[62]

---

[60] Graham (2011).

[61] Marx (2002).

[62] Graham (2011).

According to Graham, the idea of property as possession, initially in the feudal period under Norman influence, was characterized more as a political interest than an economic one, given that land possession symbolized power and *status* for the nobles. After the seventeenth century, land possession began to be understood as capital; the land ceased to represent power and began to be considered the object of property.[63]

For the subject of law in the property rights relationship, the land began to have a merely instrumental value. In this seventeenth-century view, the land ceased to be seen as a provider of power, as it was in the feudal period, and became, itself, the object of power. The link of the person with their place was converted into an economic and legal relationship between person and thing (land).[64]

Later, Bentham perfected the modern concept of land ownership, distinguishing the land as a thing from the right itself. He reduced the land to the mere function of capital, that is, a non-qualitative object susceptible to alienation.[65]

Graham, in discussing the impact of the theoretical and material structure that converted the person/place relationship into person/thing, emphasizes the importance of understanding this process through the phenomenon of alienation. He refers to the etymological root of the word alienation in Latin, *alius* (other) and *alienus* (belonging to another person or another place), to explain that, until the fourteenth century, in English, the word alienation was used with a negative connotation—that is, to indicate the breaking of the individual's relations with God or with the community to which they belonged.[66]

After the fifteenth century, the word "alienation" began to suggest the transfer of rights, property, and money. In this phase, at first, the word was used to indicate a non-voluntary transfer of goods. From the seventeenth century, the word "alienation" began to be used positively with the advent of the consolidation of the right of absolute private property.[67]

Graham explains that the word "alienation" came to name a founding principle of modern property law, but without the correct interpretation of its meaning—that is, that alienation is a dynamic principle that refers not only to one entity (person) but necessarily to two entities (person and thing). The act of alienating affects both; both the person and the entity (thing) are alienated. This bilateral aspect of alienation was erased from modern property law theory, in which the person became the active subject of alienation—that is, the alienator—and the land was reduced to an object or thing, merely the alienated entity of the land market.[68]

For Graham, the alienation conceived in modern property law brought impacts on the land, the person, and the people: (i) the alienation of the land, making it

[63] Graham (2011).

[64] Graham (2011).

[65] Graham (2011).

[66] Graham (2011).

[67] Graham (2011).

[68] Graham (2011), p. 105.

a mere object of property with the same fluidity as capital; (ii) the alienation of people, given that they began to be uprooted and deprived of their ancestral places by the enclosure laws, by the appropriation of lands of the indigenous peoples in the colonies, and by emigration; and (iii) the alienation of people from the people with the urbanization and triumph of individualism. He also points out that private property caused the greatest physical alienation of people from place in the history of English land law with the enclosures.[69]

As Graham asserts, Locke's justification[70] for private property, published in the seventeenth century, continues to resonate in contemporary legal and political orders, given that it served to underpin colonial invasions and also supported the physical separation of people from their places.

Locke's theory reduced the Earth to the category of an amorphous and powerless entity and created the legal conditions for the perpetration of serious human rights violations, that is, the removal of the commoners from their common goods in Europe and the appropriation of the lands and bodies of the original peoples in the colonies.

Although Locke invoked labor to justify private property as a natural right, he failed because he established a concept of labor different from what was practiced by people who had ancestral ties to the land.[71] The concept of labor proposed by Locke, as a justification for the natural right of property, was intentionally designed to serve capitalism.[72]

Indeed, in Locke's conception, the labor justifying the natural right of property was qualified by the cultivation of the land, by large-scale agricultural activity requiring wage labor and even the enslavement of bodies, and was always oriented toward profit. He did not consider as labor the shepherding, the extractivism, the subsistence planting of the commoners on the common goods before the enclosures occurred, or the collection of fruits and roots practiced by the original peoples. His conception of labor delegitimized the ancestral way of life of peoples around the world and privileged only the nobility that aspired to the private titling of common lands in Europe and the emerging bourgeoisie that enriched themselves with the invasion of the lands of the original peoples on other continents.[73]

In fact, for Locke, the custom of possession of traditional and original peoples, linked identitarily to the land, did not serve as a justification for the natural right of property, simply because "Property law was thus, from the outset, the key technology of the entire colonial Project."[74]

---

[69] Graham (2011), p. 105.

[70] Locke (1998).

[71] Graham (2011).

[72] Graham (2011).

[73] Graham (2011).

[74] Graham (2011), p. 217. Our translation: "The right of property was, therefore, from the beginning, the key technology of the entire colonial project."

In the nineteenth and twentieth centuries, the model of property-right person/thing, conceived by Locke, was rearticulated by Bentham into a person–person model. In this phase, Graham identifies the reaffirmation of the so-called dephysicalization of the right of property, that is, the removal of land as a physical and natural entity from the property relationship and its replacement by the concept of "thing" as an abstract right.[75]

Graham explains that, according to Bentham, the concept of the right of property came to be understood as a legal and abstract category rather than a physical thing in itself. In the legal relationship model proposed by Bentham, the right of property ceases to be a person–thing relationship, as proposed by Locke, and instead becomes a person–person relationship. This is because, in the passive pole of this relationship, the thing is no longer present; rather, it is all other people who now have the legal duty to respect the right of property of the active subject of the property, making it a right opposable against all, *erga omnes.*[76]

Definitely, the place, as part of the Earth and the natural world, is extracted from the property relationship, which henceforth will become an abstract relationship between people. Graham highlights that Bentham's theory will face criticism from Karl Marx, for whom property relations are not about people–people, but about thing–thing, with the thing, in this context, being transmuted into a commodity. For Marx, the person does not integrate into the property relationship because it also became objectified and commodified by capitalism.[77]

Indeed, capitalism, supported by the tool of the theory of property rights, subtracted from the world the people and the places in their deepest ontological meanings.

As can be seen in this very brief historical analysis of the right of property, it brought deleterious consequences not only for the natural world, which was reduced to the legal category of a thing with mere instrumental value, but also weakened human rights.

Even though the liberal revolutionary movements have bequeathed to humanity the Declarations of Rights of the eighteenth century, these were not enough to contain the disruptors of humanist reason, who brutally broke with the dignity of the human person in the first quadrant of the twentieth century, in conflicts motivated by territorial expansionism taken to the extreme by the logic of capitalism.

The two world wars violated the principle of human dignity with a refinement of cruelty unimaginable until then, in addition to seriously wounding the natural world with the harmful experience of atomic bombs.

Under the weight of the rubble of totalitarian regimes, suffocated by the gloomy smoke of Auschwitz-Birkenau chimneys, still sleepwalking under the deadly impact of the bombs on Hiroshima and Nagasaki, humanity renewed its faith in

[75] Graham (2011), p. 217.

[76] Graham (2011).

[77] Marx (2002).

the dignity of the human person in the Universal Declaration of Human Rights of 1948.

The most concrete fruit of this redemption was the fruitful constitutionalist movement, which consolidated the normative force of human dignity with all its consequences, especially in the spheres of social justice and the rights of nations.

Nevertheless, humanity continued to evade what would be the only effective remedy to prevent a new ethical, legal, and social collapse: the rescue of genuine rationality, in its Kantian conception, considering that reason remained captured by the dehumanizing logic of capitalism, which had deformed it into instrumental and utilitarian reason.[78]

In this context, unfortunately, after 77 years, the Universal Declaration of Human Rights of 1948, the result of arduous multilateral work, does not prove strong enough to contain a new vertigo of human reason, now in the twenty-first century.

Precisely at the moment I write this chapter, humanity is horrified by the news that the President of the United States of America has announced to the world his deliberate intention to build a complex of luxury resorts on the rubble and mortal remains of the Palestinian people in the Gaza Strip,[79] completely ignoring the significance of this place for people who are living days of profound collective mourning.

This sounds absurd, but under the aegis of Article 2 of the Universal Declaration of Human Rights, adopted and proclaimed by the United Nations General Assembly (Resolution 217 A III) on December 10, 1948, it provides:

> Article 2.
>
> 1. Everyone is entitled to all the rights and freedoms set forth in this Declaration, without distinction of any kind, such as race, color, sex, language, religion, political or other opinion, national or social origin, property, birth, or other status.
> 2. Furthermore, no distinction shall be made on the basis of the political, jurisdictional or international status of the country or territory to which a person belongs, whether it be independent, trust, non-self-governing or under any other limitation of sovereignty.

Despite the normative text of the Universal Declaration of Human Rights transcribed above, the President of the United States of America, Donald Trump, with a certain tranquility that is disturbing to humanity, made an open threat of "ethnic cleansing" to the Palestinian people, blatantly violating their rights, and he did so as the head of state of a nation signatory to the declaration.

This is quite disturbing but predictable, considering that the attitude of the current US President, Donald Trump, is symptomatic of an ontological, ethical, and legal paradigm that engendered the alienation of the human being and the Earth and normalized the instrumentalization of the Earth and the human person in the

[78] Horkheimer (2002).

[79] The Guardian (2025), online.

process of constructing property rights as an abstract right, which completely detached the person from the place and transformed both into commodities.

Donald Trump's intention to expel the Palestinians from their ancestral place in the Gaza Strip to build a luxury development, although bizarre, is a ghostly manifestation of the same legal paradigm which instituted the alienation of the land and the human being to legitimize traumatic historical situations, such as the enclosure of common goods and the expulsion of the plebeians from their ancestral place in England between the fifteenth and seventeenth centuries; the invasion of the lands of indigenous peoples in the Americas and Oceania; and the criminal appropriation of the bodies of enslaved Africans.

This alienating legal paradigm has no limits; the threat of ethnic cleansing in Gaza is not yet at its peak, and if not recalibrated, it will lead the Earth and the human being, as a multidimensional being, to a sad twilight of absolute dehumanization and entropic death.

The practical agreement of the principle of human dignity with the principle of harmony with nature allows a semantic opening for the redefinition of the human being's relationship with the Earth and with its place, this understood not as the abstract thing of property rights but as an aspect of the human being's own identity.

The original and traditional peoples of various places on the planet were not affected by the capitalist colonial process of reification of the Earth and alienation of the place, so they maintain an ancestral and affective bond with the Earth, which integrates their own identity as a person. Even among westernized peoples, there are individuals who relate to their place through the dimension of affectivity. In all these situations, the principle of harmony with nature relocates the place from the legal category of a thing to the category of personality rights as a dimension of human identity.

This repositioning of the person/place bond to personality rights, as an aspect of the human person's identity, allows a concrete intervention of the principle of harmony with nature in strengthening human rights.

By considering that the human person's relationship with the place of their existence can constitute their own identity and, therefore, constitute a personality right, a legal prohibition is instituted against dehumanizing projects of removing people and peoples from their ancestral territories, from their traditional and affective communities.

This ethical and legal understanding of the place as an aspect of the human person's own identity removes the place, the landscape, from the legal category of mere property governed by the concept of alienation proposed by Bentham, elevating it to the *status* of the rights of personality of indigenous and traditional peoples, and of individuals or communities that establish an emotional bond with their place of coexistence.

Thus, the principle of harmony with nature, in addition to establishing, through its integrative function, the recognition of the intrinsic value and dignity of non-human beings—that is, *biodignity*—also strengthens and reaffirms human rights by redefining the relationship of the human being with the natural world as an aspect of their identity and, therefore, encompassed by the rights of personality that, despite having economic implications, are inalienable and imprescriptible.

References

Bergson H (2010) A evolução criadora. Tradução de Adolfo Casais Monteiro. Editora UNESP, São Paulo

Berry T (1988) The dream of the earth. Sierra Club Books, San Francisco, CA

Cavalieri P (2017) Are human rights human? In: Armstrong SJ, Botzler RG (eds) The animal ethic readers, 3rd edn. Routledge, New York, Ebook

Cirne-Lima CRV (1999) Ética de coerência dialética. Veritas: Revista de Filosofia da PUCRS, Porto Alegre 44(4): 941–964, dez. Available on https://revistaseletronicas.pucrs.br/ojs/index.php/veritas/article/view/35248/18499. Accessed 20 April 2025

Damásio A (2018) A estranha ordem das coisas: as origens biológicas dos sentimentos e da cultura. Companhia das Letras, São Paulo

Delecave B. Lobo-guará, um solitário no cerrado. Available on http://www.invivo.fiocruz.br/cgi/cgilua.exe/sys/start.htm?infoid=1081&sid=2. Accessed 15 May 2021

G1 (s.d.) Lobeira (*Solanum lycocarpum*). G1, Terra da gente, Flora. Available on http://g1.globo.com/sp/campinas-regiao/terra-da-gente/flora/noticia/2014/12/lobeira.html. Accessed 15 May 2025

Gellen LFA et al (2019) Viabilidade de extratos etanólicos de folhas de lobeira (*Solanum lycocarpum* St. Hil.) no controle de bactérias de interesse médico. *Biota Amazônia*, Macapá, AP 9(3): 24–29. Available on https://periodicos.unifap.br/index.php/biota/article/viewFile/3603/v9n3p24-29.pdf. Accessed 15 May 2025

Graham N (2011) Lawscape: property, environment, law. Routledge, New York

Horkheimer M (2002) Eclipse da razão; tradução de Sebastião Uchoa Leite. Centauro, São Paulo

Jonas H (2006) O princípio responsabilidade: ensaio de uma ética para uma civilização tecnológica. Tradução de Marijane Lisboa e Luiz Barros Montez. Contraponto; PUC Rio, Rio de Janeiro

Jonas H (2017) Ensaios Filosóficos: da crença antiga ao homem tecnológico. Tradução: wendell Evangelista Soares Lopes. Paulus, São Paulo

Locke J (1998) Dois Tratados sobre o governo. [S.l.], Martins Fontes

Marx K (2022) Manuscritos econômico-filosóficos. Martin Claret, São Paulo

Morin E (2002) Os Sete Saberes para a Educação do Futuro. Tradução: Ana Paula de Viveiros. Ed. Instituto Piaget, Lisboa-PT

Rosa PAL, et al (2014) Recuperação de um solo de cerrado após 19 anos: ocorrência espontânea de espécies arbóreas. *Revista de Agricultura Neotropical*, Cassilândia, MS, 1(1) p. 51 jul./set. Available on https://periodicosonline.uems.br/index.php/agrineo/article/view/221. Accessed 31 May 2025

Sarlet IW, Fensterseifer T (2014) Direito constitucional ambiental: constituição, direitos fundamentais e proteção do ambiente, 4th edn. rev. e atual. Revista dos Tribunais, São Paulo

Spinoza B (2014) Spinoza: obra completa I: (breve) tratado e outros escritos. In: Guinsburg J, Cunha N, Romano R (Org) Perspectiva, São Paulo

Taylor C (1989) Sources of the self: the making of the modern identity. Harvard University Press, Cambridge, MA

The Guardian (2025) Who is Trump to decide our fate?': takeover threat adds to uncertainty in Gaza. Available on https://www.theguardian.com/world/2025/feb/14/trump-decide-fate-takeover-threat-uncertainty-gaza. Accessed 16 Feb 2025

Winnicott DW (2024a) Natureza Humana.Tradução: Davy Litman Bogomo-letz. Ubu Editora/WMF Martins Fontes, São Paulo

Winnicott DW (2024b) Família e Desenvolvimento Individual.Tradução: Davy Litman Bogomoletz. Ubu Editora/WMF Martins Fontes, São Paulo

MIX
Papier aus verantwortungsvollen Quellen
Paper from responsible sources
FSC® C105338

If you have any concerns about our products,
you can contact us on
ProductSafety@springernature.com

In case Publisher is established outside the EU,
the EU authorized representative is:
Springer Nature Customer Service Center GmbH
Europaplatz 3, 69115 Heidelberg, Germany

Printed by Libri Plureos GmbH
in Hamburg, Germany